UNITED STATES POLICY
TOWARD CHINA

Mei-kuo Tui Hua Cheng-ts'e
Po-nien-lai Yao-chien Hsüan-tu
Hu Shih T'i

UNITED STATES POLICY TOWARD CHINA

DIPLOMATIC
AND
PUBLIC DOCUMENTS
1839-1939

Selected and Arranged by

PAUL HIBBERT CLYDE

NEW YORK

RUSSELL & RUSSELL · INC

1964

DEDICATED

to

His Excellency Dr. Hu Shih

FATHER OF THE MODERN CHINESE WRITTEN LANGUAGE
EDUCATIONAL LEADER AND REFORMER
HISTORIAN ESSAYIST POET AND DIPLOMAT

PREFACE

Although nearly one hundred years have elapsed since the United States signed its first treaty with China, it is only within the past two decades that American universities and colleges have recognized the need for courses covering the relations of this country with the Far East. Even as late as 1898, when through acquisition of the Philippines the United States became an Asiatic power, there were few Americans who desired even a superficial acquaintance with the empire of the Manchus.

More recent years have altered in some degree this picture. The Pacific Ocean has now assumed the importance in American affairs that William H. Seward prophesied for it. The result has been a slow but steady increase in the number of university and college courses devoted in whole or in part to the study of eastern Asia and its relations with the United States.

A proper increase in such courses, particularly in the liberal arts colleges, has been hampered not only by lack of competently trained teachers but also by the inability of college libraries to secure adequate funds for the purchase of collateral reading with which students might supplement a textbook. It is the purpose of this volume to fill in some degree this need.

While it may be admitted readily that there is no satisfactory substitute for wide reading in any field of history, the fact remains that many liberal arts colleges are not in a position to provide their students with these admittedly desirable facilities. In such cases a volume of selected documents may serve in some degree as a substitute.

The vast store of materials from which the compiler of a volume of this character may make selections renders the problem of choice an extremely difficult and hazardous one. From the outset in the present case the compiler has been held to specific limitations of space. He has in fact, from his original selections, been forced to discard enough material to fill several volumes of this size.

The documents presented here are not presumed to give a complete picture of American relations with China. They are designed rather to give the student ready access to important treaty texts and exchanges of notes; to provide him with textual examples of Instructions sent to United States ministers in China, and likewise to provide him with some significant examples of Despatches from the ministers to the State Department touching significant phases of policy and the conditions in which policy was to be applied.

The organization adopted is essentially chronological. In a few instances where for obvious reasons it seemed desirable documents have been grouped topically.

Editorial paragraphs have been limited to a mere placing of the document. For the factual narrative of the story and for its interpretation the instructor and student are referred to the following textbook surveys: Paul H. Clyde, *A History of the Modern and Contemporary Far East* (New York: Prentice-Hall, Inc., 1937); H. B. Morse and M. F. MacNair, *Far Eastern International Relations* (Boston: Houghton Mifflin Co., 1931); Payson J. Treat, *The Far East* (Revised Edition; New York: Harper and Brothers, 1935); and Harold M. Vinacke, *A History of the Far East in Modern Times* (Second Revised Edition; New York: F. S. Crofts and Co., 1937).

If therefore this volume serves the practical end of providing teachers and students with the means of ready reference to the texts of some of the more obvious official records on the policy of the United States in China it will have served its purpose.

The editor acknowledges his indebtedness to the Research Council of Duke University and to the Duke University Press.

PAUL H. CLYDE

Durham, North Carolina

TABLE OF DOCUMENTS

A MEMORIAL FROM THE AMERICAN MERCHANTS
AT CANTON, 1839

THE FIRST WAR between Great Britain and China, sometimes referred to as the Opium War (1840-42), affected the interests of all foreign traders at Canton. A number of American merchants there memorialized the Congress of the United States (May 25, 1839), setting forth their need for protection, commenting on the nature of their commercial activities, and suggesting lines of policy, some of which were later adopted by their government.

MEMORIAL OF R. B. FORBES AND OTHERS TO THE CONGRESS OF THE U. S. AMERICAN CITIZENS, MERCHANTS IN CANTON, CHINA, FOR A COMMERCIAL AGENT TO BE SENT OUT TO CHINA TO NEGOTIATE, IF POSSIBLE, A COMMERCIAL TREATY, WITH A NAVAL FORCE FOR THE PROTECTION OF THE PERSONS RESIDENT THERE, AND PROPERLY BELONGING TO CITIZENS OF THE UNITED STATES[1]

The undersigned, native citizens of the United States, resident at the port of Canton, in China, beg leave to present this our memorial:

That, upon the twenty-second day of March last, we were, in common with the resident foreigners of all nations, made prisoners in our factories, and surrounded by armed men and boats; deprived of our servants, and cut off from all communication with our ships at Whampoa, Lintin, and Macao; by which means, together with the threatened forfeiture of life if his arbitrary exactions were not complied with, a commissioner from the Imperial Government at Peking has succeeded in wresting from residents here upwards of twenty thousand chests of British owned opium, which may be valued at more than ten millions of dollars. We have, also, been threatened with severe but undefined penalties for refusing to sign a bond by which all concerned in a vessel that may hereafter be found bringing opium to China are required to be given up to the authorities for punishment by death.

The occasion for these acts of violence and aggression on the part of the Chinese Government is an extensive opium trade, of the rise and progress of which we propose to submit a brief review.

Opium had been for many years imported into China at an established rate of duty, until about the year 1800, at which time the then reigning Emperor prohibited its introduction; it was, however, subsequently openly delivered from vessels stationed at Whampoa, until about the year 1821, when the opium-receiving vessels were expelled from the river and took their stations at Lintin, where the trade has since been carried on with the knowledge and

---

[1] U. S. House Document, No. 40, 26th Congress, 1st Session, Serial Number 364. Hereinafter Congressional documents are cited in the following form: H. Doc. 40: 26-1 (364).

consent of the chief local authorities, and with little interruption, rapidly increasing in amount and value, as shown by the following statement:

In the year 1816-'7 were sold	3,210 chests, for $	3,657,000
1822-'3 "	5,822 "	7,988,930
1827-'8 "	9,535 "	10,425,075
1832-'3 "	23,670 "	15,332,759

In 1833-'34, the opium trade in foreign vessels (chiefly British) along the whole coast of China, eastward of Canton, began to assume an importance which has greatly increased until the present crisis.

In 1836 it was announced to the foreign residents that the imperial councils at Peking proposed to admit opium at a fixed rate of duty, as was done prior to the year 1800; the high officers of this, as well as of several other provinces, memorialized the Emperor, recommending the adoption of the proposed measure; and so little doubt was entertained, either by the resident foreigners, or by the best informed of the native merchants, that it would speedily take effect, that arrangements were made for an increased production of the drug in India, to an extent that, had the trade been suffered to continue without interruption, the amount of opium that would have found purchasers in China during the present season of 1839-'40, would not have fallen short of about forty thousand chests.

Edicts and proclamations have from time to time been promulgated, prohibiting the opium trade; but notwithstanding these, the highest officers in the province have not only connived at the smuggling or introduction of the drug by the Chinese, receiving a fee or duty varying from twenty to seventy dollars per chest, but they have been active participators therein; and it is a well-known fact, that a large amount of the opium delivered at Lintin has been delivered to boats belonging to, and bearing the flags of the Governor, the Hoppo, or collector of customs, and other high officers of the province. The increase of this trade since 1817 is of itself sufficient evidence that it has been favored by the fostering care as well as by the connivance of the officers of Government; and the circumstances that during the past six months the sale of opium to the Chinese has almost ceased, shows clearly that whenever it pleases this Government to abolish the trade, they possess ample power over their own people to do it effectually.

We have no wish to see a revival of the opium trade; on the contrary, before the adoption of the violent measures that have given occasion for the present memorial, we had, most of us, signed a voluntary pledge that, believing in the sincerity of this Government in their efforts to destroy the trade, we would in future abstain from dealing in the drug. We are alive to the fact, that during the last five years Great Britain and her Indian possessions have drawn from this empire thirty to thirty-five million dollars in gold and silver, and forty to forty-five millions of dollars in teas, raw silk, etc., in exchange for a drug which has been productive of much evil and of scarcely a single good to the Chinese; a drug, the introduction of which, we have reason to fear, has degraded the foreign character in the estimation of the better portion of the Chinese. And whether we view the subject in a moral and philanthropic light, or merely as a commercial question, we are extremely desirous to see the importation and consumption of opium in China entirely at an end.

We cannot, however, perceive the slightest ground for justification of the robbery committed upon British subjects here, nor for the detention of the persons, ships, and property of those who are entirely disconnected from the obnoxious trade. The measures of the Imperial Government should have been directed first against its own officers, who have been engaged and most active in the trade; but, taking advantage of the unprotected state of the foreign community of Canton, the commissioner has proceeded in his high-handed measures, regardless alike of the respect due to the representatives of foreign powers resident in Canton, and of the laws or customs and usages that have heretofore been observed and considered the chief guaranties for the safety of the foreign trade.

If, as it is confidently believed, the British Government should determine to demand explanation and satisfaction for the outrages committed upon Her Majesty's officers and subjects resident here, her naval force may find it necessary to resort to a blockade of the chief ports and rivers upon the coast, and to interrupt an immense coasting trade in grain, salt, and other merchandise, which is transported from the southern provinces of the empire, Formosa, etc., to the more northern ports, for the supply of the less productive vicinity of Peking. A perseverance in these measures, it is believed, would, in a very few months, reduce the Chinese Government to a willingness to listen to all the just and reasonable demands of the foreign power; while the consequence of suffering the present attack to pass without remonstrance or redress, we cannot doubt, will be such an aggravation of existing evils as would lead to constant interruptions of the trade, if not eventually to the total expulsion of foreign commerce from the empire.

We would, therefore, with all deference and respect, express our opinions that the United States Government should take immediate measures; and, if deemed advisable, to act in concert with the Governments of Great Britain, France, and Holland, or either of them, in their endeavors to establish commercial relations with this empire upon a safe and honorable footing, such as exists between all friendly powers; and by direct appeal to the Imperial Government at Peking, to obtain a compliance with the following among other important demands:

1st. Permission for foreign envoys to reside near the court at Peking, on the terms and with all the privileges accorded at other courts, through whom appeal may be made to the Imperial Government in cases of difficulty with the local authorities in the prosecution of our commercial pursuits.

2nd. The promulgation of a fixed tariff of duties on articles, both of import and export, from which no deviation shall be allowed under any pretext whatever.

3d. A system of bonding warehouses, or some regulations permitting the transhipment of such goods as it may be desirable to re-export for want of a market in China. (See note *a*.)

4th. The liberty of trading at other port or ports in China than that of Canton. (See note *b*.)

5th. Compensation for the losses caused by the stoppage of the whole legal trade of the port, and the consequent detention of vessels and property; with a guaranty against the recurrence of similar arbitrary acts, and security for the free egress from Canton, and other ports, of all persons not guilty of crimes or civil offences, at any and at all times.

6th. That until the Chinese laws are distinctly made known and recognised, the punishment for wrongs committed by foreigners upon the Chinese, or others, shall not be greater than is applicable to the like offence by the laws of the United States or England; nor shall any punishment be inflicted by the Chinese authorities upon any foreigner, until the guilt of the party shall have been fairly and clearly proved.

Should our Government determine to abstain from any interposition in the affairs of its citizens in China, the undersigned beg leave to represent the necessity which will exist for the appointment of an agent or commissioner qualified by his commercial and general information, with a sufficient naval force to protect our commerce (see note *c*) and our persons from being held responsible for the acts of lawless traders and the hostile operations of a British or other foreign fleet; or at least to prevent any paper blockade from interfering with our commerce, as well as to secure a participation in any privileges which this Government may hereafter be induced to concede to other powers.

In conclusion, we have but to express our candid conviction that the appearance of a naval force from the United States, England, and France, upon the coast of China, would, without bloodshed, obtain from this Government such acknowledgments and treaties as would not only place our commerce upon a secure footing, but would be mutually beneficial, and greatly increase the extent and importance of our relations with this empire.

NOTES

(a.) The demands urged in the first, second, and third articles, are rendered necessary by the rapacity of the local officers, who farm their offices from the Imperial Government, paying therefore large sums of money in addition to the revenues raised upon the trade and productions of the province; and when it is known that a frequent change of officers is practised, and that each incumbent accumulates great wealth, the extent of fraud and extortion may perhaps be imagined.

(b.) We have but now experienced the unhappy consequences of residing at a distance of near ten miles from the foreign shipping, which is anchored at a distance of thirty miles from the sea, and escape prevented by sufficient fortification at the mouth of the river.

(c.) A comparison of the American trade to China, with that upon the coast of South America, will show the very great importance of the former, and improve its claims upon Government for protection.

RUSSELL STURGIALL,
W. DELANO, JR.,
GIDEON NYE, JR.,
R. B. FORBES,
A. A. LOW,
EDWARD KING,
S. B. RAWLE,
JAS. RYAN,
of Russell H.

Canton, *May* 25, 1839.

COMMODORE KEARNY AND THE MOST-FAVORED-NATION PRINCIPLE, 1842

In 1842, two years before the most-favored-nation principle was embodied in the first treaty between the United States and China, the commander of the American naval squadron in the Far East, Commodore Lawrence Kearny, requested the Governor of Canton to accord the principle to American commerce. This the Chinese readily consented to do.

COMMODORE KEARNY'S MOST-FAVORED-NATION POLICY. KEARNY TO THE GOVERNOR OF CANTON, MACAO ROADS, OCTOBER 8, 1842[1]

The address of Commodore Kearny, commander-in-chief of a squadron of United States ships, respectfully represents that he learns with deep interest the high Imperial commissioners deputed to arrange commercial affairs with the British are expected in a short time to arrive at Canton, and that a commercial treaty is to be negotitated to operate in favor of "British merchants" exclusively.

The undersigned is desirous that the attention of the Imperial government might be called with respect to the commercial interests of the United States, and he hopes the importance of their trade will receive consideration, and their citizens, in that matter, be placed upon the same footing as the merchants of the nation most favored.

The undersigned does not press this matter at present, but, trusting to the good and friendly understanding which exists, he submits the case, and has the honor to be

Your Excellency's most obedient
servant.

CHINA'S REPLY. THE GOVERNOR OF CANTON TO COMMODORE KEARNY, CANTON, OCTOBER 15, 1842[2]

Ke, guardian of the young prince, member of the Board of War, member of the Imperial cabinet, and Governor of the two Kwang Provinces, states, in reply . . . that I have received your polite communication relating to the English commerce. I, the governor, have ever hitherto treated the merchants of every nation with the same kindness. Moreover, the Americans who have come to Canton have had free commerce, month after month, and year after year. These merchants have been better satisfied with their trade than any other nation; and that they have been respectfully observant of the laws, is what the august Emperor has clearly recognised, and I, the governor, also well know. How, then, should I not rather, on the cessation of difficulties

[1] S. Doc. 139: 29-1, p. 21.   [2] Ibid., pp. 21-22.

with the English, wish to show favor to them? Now, I have ordered the Hong merchants, with the said English nation's merchants, to devise beforehand, and to wait the arrival, in Canton, of the Imperial commissioners, great ministers of state. When I shall have received the newly devised regulations concerning the free trade of the English, then I, the governor, together with the lieutenant governor and Tartar General, will immediately deliberate upon the proper adjustment of the regulations, and will make a representation to the Emperor that he may hear and direct what shall be done.

Decidedly it shall not be permitted that the American merchants shall come to have merely a dry stick, (that is, their interests shall be attended to). I, the governor, will not be otherwise disposed than to look up to the heart of the great Emperor in his compassionate regard towards men from afar, that Chinese and foreigners with faith and justice may be mutually united, and forever enjoy reciprocal tranquillity, and that it be granted to each of the resident merchants to obtain profit, and to the people to enjoy life and peace, and universally to participate [in] the blessings of great prosperity, striving to have the same mind.

SECRETARY WEBSTER'S INSTRUCTIONS TO
CALEB CUSHING, 1843

THE INSTRUCTIONS of Secretary of State Webster, dated May 8, 1843, to Caleb Cushing for his guidance in the negotiation of the first United States treaty with China, constitute the first comprehensive statement of American policy toward The Middle Kingdom.

INSTRUCTIONS OF SECRETARY WEBSTER TO CALEB CUSHING, WASHINGTON, MAY 8, 1843[1]

It now remains for this department to say something of the political objects of the mission, and the manner in which it is hoped those objects may be accomplished. It is less necessary than it might otherwise be to enter into a detailed statement of the considerations which have led to the institution of the mission, not only as you will be furnished with a copy of the President's communication to Congress, recommending provision to be made for the measure, but also as your connexion with Congress has necessarily brought those considerations to your notice and contemplation.

Occurrences happening in China within the last two years have resulted in events which are likely to be of much importance, as well to the United States as to the rest of the civilized world. Of their still more important consequences to China herself, it is not necessary here to speak. The hostilities which have been carried on between that Empire and England have resulted, among other consequences, in opening four important ports to English commerce, viz: Amoy, Ning-po, Shang-hai, and Fu-chow.

These ports belong to some of the richest, most productive, and most populous provinces of the Empire, and are likely to become very important marts of commerce. A leading object of the mission in which you are now to be engaged is, to secure the entry of American ships and cargoes into these ports on terms as favorable as those which are enjoyed by English merchants. It is not necessary to dwell here on the great and well-known amount of imports of the productions of China into the United States. These imports, especially in the great article of tea, are not likely to be diminished. Heretofore they have been paid for in the precious metals, or, more recently, by bills drawn on London. At one time, indeed, American paper, of certain descriptions, was found to be an available remittance. Latterly, a considerable trade has sprung up in the export of certain American manufactures to China. To augment these exports, by obtaining the most favorable commercial facilities, and cultivating, to the greatest extent practicable, friendly commercial intercourse with China, in all its accessible ports, is matter of moment to the commercial and manufacturing as well as the agricultural and mining interest of

[1] S. Doc. 138: 28-2 (457). See also Hunter Miller (ed.), *Treaties and Other International Acts of the United States of America*, IV, 638-641.

the United States. It cannot be foreseen how rapidly or how slowly a people of such peculiar habits as the Chinese, and apparently so tenaciously attached to their habits, may adopt the sentiments, ideas, and customs, of other nations. But if prejudiced, and strongly wedded to their own usages, the Chinese are still understood to be ingenious, acute, and inquisitive. Experience, thus far, if it does not strongly animate and encourage efforts to introduce some of the arts and the products of other countries into China, is not, nevertheless, of a character such as should entirely repress those efforts. You will be furnished with accounts, as accurate as can be obtained, of the history and present state of the export trade of the United States to China.

As your mission has in view only friendly and commercial objects—objects, it is supposed, equally useful to both countries—the natural jealousy of the Chinese, and their repulsive feeling toward foreigners, it is hoped, may be in some degree removed or mitigated by prudence and address on your part. Your constant aim must be to produce a full conviction on the minds of the Government and the people, that your mission is entirely pacific; that you come with no purposes of hostility or annoyance; that you are a messenger of peace, sent from the greatest Power in America to the greatest Empire in Asia, to offer respect and good will, and to establish the means of friendly intercourse. It will be expedient, on all occasions, to cultivate the friendly dispositions of the Government and people, by manifesting a proper respect for their institutions and manners, and avoiding, as far as possible, the giving of offence either to their pride or their prejudices. You will use the earliest and all succeeding occasions to signify that the Government which sends you has no disposition to encourage, and will not encourage, any violation of the commercial regulations of China, by citizens of the United States. You will state in the fullest manner the acknowledgment of this Government, that the commercial regulations of the empire, having become fairly and fully known, ought to be respected by all ships and all persons visiting its ports; and if citizens of the United States, under these circumstances, are found violating well-known laws of trade, their Government will not interfere to protect them from the consequences of their own illegal conduct. You will at the same time assert and maintain, on all occasions, the equality and independence of your own country. The Chinese are apt to speak of persons coming into the empire from other nations as tribute bearers to the Emperor. This idea has been fostered, perhaps, by the costly parade of embassies of England. All ideas of this kind respecting your mission must, should they arise, be immediately met by a declaration, not made ostentatiously, or in a manner reproachful towards others, that you are no tribute bearer; that your Government pays tribute to none, and expects tribute from none; and that, even as to presents, your Government neither makes nor accepts presents. You will signify to all Chinese authorities and others, that it is deemed to be quite below the dignity of the Emperor of China and the President of the United States of America to be concerning themselves with such unimportant matters as presents from one to the other; that the intercourse between the heads of two such Governments should be made to embrace only great political questions, the tender of mutual regard, and the establishment of useful relations.

It is of course desirable that you should be able to reach Peking, and the Court and person of the Emperor, if practicable. You will accordingly at all times signify this as being your purpose and the object of your mission; and perhaps it may be well to advance as near to the capital as shall be found practicable, without waiting to announce your arrival in the country. The purpose of seeing the Emperor in person must be persisted in as long as may be becoming and proper. You will inform the officers of the Government that you have a letter of friendship from the President of the United States to the Emperor, signed by the President's own hand, which you cannot deliver except to the Emperor himself, or some high officer of the Court in his presence. You will say, also, that you have a commission conferring on you the highest rank among representatives of your Government; and that this, also, can be exhibited to the Emperor or his chief officer. You may expect to encounter, of course, if you get to Peking, the old question of the *Kotou*. In regard to the mode of managing this matter, much must be left to your discretion, as circumstances may occur. All pains should be taken to avoid the giving of offence, or the wounding of the national pride; but, at the same time, you will be careful to do nothing which may seem, even to the Chinese themselves, to imply any inferiority on the part of your Government, or any thing else less than perfect independence of all nations. You will say that the Government of the United States is always controlled by a sense of religion and of honor; that nations differ in their religious opinions and observances; that you cannot do any thing which the religion of your own country or its sentiments of honor forbid; that you have the most profound respect for His Majesty the Emperor; that you are ready to make to him all manifestations of homage which are consistent with your own sense; and that you are sure His Majesty is too just to desire you to violate your own duty; that you should deem yourself quite unworthy to appear before His Majesty, as peace bearer from a great and powerful nation, if you should do anything against religion or against honor, as understood by the Government and people in the country you come from. Taking care thus in no way to allow the Government or people of China to consider you as tribute bearer from your Government, or as acknowledging its inferiority, in any respect, to that of China, or any other nation, you will bear in mind, at the same time, what is due to your own personal dignity and the character which you bear. You will represent to the Chinese authorities, nevertheless, that you are directed to pay to His Majesty the Emperor the same marks of respect and homage as are paid by your Government to His Majesty the Emperor of Russia, or any other of the great Powers of the world.

A letter, signed by the President as above intimated, and addressed to the Emperor, will be placed in your hands. As has been already stated, you will say that this letter can only be delivered to the Emperor, or to some one of the great officers of State, in his presence. Nevertheless, if this cannot be done, and the Emperor should still manifest a desire to receive the letter, you may consider the propriety of sending it to him, upon an assurance that a friendly answer to it shall be sent, signed by the hand of the Emperor himself.

It will be no part of your duty to enter into controversies which may exist between China and any European State; nor will you, in your communications, fail to abstain altogether from any sentiment, or any expression which might give to other Governments just cause of offence. It will be quite proper, however, that you should, in a proper manner, always keep before the eyes of the Chinese the high character, importance, and power, of the United States. You may speak of the extent of their territory, their great commerce spread over all seas, their powerful navy every where giving protection to that commerce, and the numerous schools and institutions established in them, to teach men knowledge and wisdom. It cannot be wrong for you to make known, where not known, that the United States, once a country subject to England, threw off that subjection years ago, asserted its independence, sword in hand, established that independence after a seven years' war, and now meets England upon equal terms upon the ocean and upon the land. The remoteness of the United States from China, and still more the fact that they have no colonial possessions in her neighborhood, will naturally lead to the indulgence of a less suspicious and more friendly feeling than may have been entertained towards England, even before the late war between England and China. It cannot be doubted that the immense power of England in India must be regarded by the Chinese Government with dissatisfaction, if not with some degree of alarm. You will take care to show strongly how free the Chinese Government may well be from all jealousy arising from such causes towards the United States. Finally, you will signify, in decided terms and a positive manner, that the Government of the United States would find it impossible to remain on terms of friendship and regard with the Emperor, if greater privileges or commercial facilities should be allowed to the subjects of any other government than should be granted to citizens of the United States.

It is hoped and trusted that you will succeed in making a treaty such as has been concluded between England and China; and if one containing fuller and more regular stipulations could be entered into, it would be conducting Chinese intercourse one step further towards the principles which regulate the public relations of the European and American States.

THE FIRST AMERICAN TREATY WITH CHINA, 1844

THE FIRST TREATY between the United States and China (Treaty of Wang Hiya), July 3, 1844, contains (Article II) the basic most-favored-nation clause, fundamental to American policy in China from that day to the present; and likewise a clearer definition of criminal extraterritoriality than was contained in the British-China treaties of Nanking (1842) and The Bogue (1843). The principle was likewise extended to civil cases.

TREATY BETWEEN THE UNITED STATES AND CHINA. TREATY OF WANG HIYA, JULY 3, 1844[1]

.   .   .   .

ARTICLE I.

There shall be a perfect, permanent, universal peace, and a sincere and cordial amity, between the United States of America on the one part, and the Ta Tsing Empire on the other part, and between their people respectively, without exception of persons or places.

ARTICLE II.

Citizens of the United States resorting to China for the purposes of commerce will pay the duties of import and export prescribed in the Tariff, which is fixed by and made a part of this Treaty. They shall, in no case, be subject to other or higher duties than are or shall be required of the people of any other nation whatever. Fees and charges of every sort are wholly abolished, and officers of the revenue, who may be guilty of exaction, shall be punished according to the laws of China. If the Chinese Government desire to modify. in any respect, the said Tariff, such modifications shall be made only in con-sultation with consuls or other functionaries thereto duly authorized in behalf of the United States, and with consent thereof. And if additional advantages or privileges, of whatever description, be conceded hereafter by China to any other nation, the United States, and the citizens thereof, shall be entitled thereupon, to a complete, equal, and impartial participation in the same.

ARTICLE III.

The citizens of the United States are permitted to frequent the five ports of Kwangchow, Amoy, Fuchow, Ningpo and Shanghai, and to reside with their families and trade there, and to proceed at pleasure with their vessels and merchandize to and from any foreign port and either of the said five ports, and from either of the said five ports to any other of them. But said vessels shall not unlawfully enter the other ports of China, nor carry on a

---

[1] Miller (ed.), *op. cit.*, IV, 559-570.

clandestine and fraudulent trade along the coasts thereof. And any vessel belonging to a citizen of the United States, which violates this provision, shall, with her cargo, be subject to confiscation to the Chinese government.

ARTICLE IV.

For the superintendence and regulation of the concerns of the citizens of the United States doing business at the said five ports, the government of the United States may appoint Consuls, or other officers, at the same, who shall be duly recognized as such by the officers of the Chinese government, and shall hold official intercourse and correspondence with the latter, either personal or in writing, as occasions may require, on terms of equality and reciprocal respect. If disrespectfully treated or aggrieved in any way by the local authorities, said officers on the one hand shall have the right to make representation of the same to the superior officers of the Chinese Government, who will see that full inquiry and strict justice be had in the premises; and on the other hand, the said Consuls will carefully avoid all acts of unnecessary offence to, or collision with, the officers and people of China.

ARTICLE V.

At each of the said five ports, citizens of the United States lawfully engaged in commerce, shall be permitted to import from their own or any other ports into China, and sell there, and purchase therein, and export to their own or any other ports, all manner of merchandize, of which the importation or exportation is not prohibited by this Treaty, paying the duties which are prescribed by the Tariff hereinbefore established, and no other charges whatsoever.

ARTICLE VI.

Whenever any merchant-vessel belonging to the United States shall enter either of the said five ports for trade, her papers shall be lodged with the Consul, or person charged with affairs, who will report the same to the commissioner of customs; and tonnage duty shall be paid on said vessel at the rate of five mace per ton, if she be over one hundred and fifty tons burden; and one mace per ton if she be of the burden of one hundred and fifty tons or under, according to the amount of her tonnage as specified in the register; said payment to be in full of the former charges of measurement and other fees, which are wholly abolished. And if any vessel, which having anchored at one of the said ports, and there paid tonnage duty, shall have occasion to go to any others of the said ports to complete the disposal of her cargo, the Consul, or person charged with affairs, will report the same to the commissioner of customs, who, on the departure of the said vessel will note in the port-clearance that the tonnage duties have been paid, and report the same to the other custom-houses; in which case on entering another port the said vessel will only pay duty there on her cargo; but shall not be subject to the payment of tonnage duty a second time.

ARTICLE VII.

No tonnage duty shall be required on boats belonging to citizens of the United States, employed in the conveyance of passengers, baggage, letters, and articles of provision, or others not subject to duty to or from any of the five ports. All cargo-boats, however, conveying merchandize subject to duty shall pay the regular tonnage duty of one mace per ton, provided they belong to citizens of the United States, but not if hired by them from subjects of China.

ARTICLE VIII.

Citizens of the United States for their vessels bound in shall be allowed to engage pilots, who will report said vessels at the passes and take them into ports; and when the lawful duties have all been paid they may engage pilots to leave port. It shall also be lawful for them to hire at pleasure, servants, compradors, linguists, and writers, and passage or cargo boats, and to employ laborers, seamen, and persons for whatever necessary service for a reasonable compensation to be agreed on by the parties, or settled by application to the consular officer of their government, without interference on the part of the local officers of the Chinese government.

ARTICLE IX.

Whenever merchant vessels belonging to the United States shall have entered port, the Superintendent of Customs, will, if he see fit, appoint custom-house officers to guard said vessels, who may live on board the ship or their own boats, at their convenience; but provision for the subsistence of said officers shall be made by the superintendent of customs, and they shall not be entitled to any allowance from the vessel or owner thereof; and they shall be subject to suitable punishment for any exaction practiced by them in violation of this regulation.

ARTICLE X.

Whenever a merchant-vessel belonging to the United States shall cast anchor in either of said ports, the supercargo, master, or consignee, will, within forty-eight hours deposit the ship's papers in the hands of the Consul, or person charged with the affairs of the United States; who will cause to be communicated to the superintendent of customs, a true report of the name and tonnage of such vessel, the names of her men, and of the cargo on board; which being done, the superintendent will give a permit for the discharge of her cargo.

And the master, supercargo, or consignee, if he proceed to discharge the cargo without such permit, shall incur a fine of five hundred dollars; and the goods so discharged without permit shall be subject to forfeiture to the Chinese government. But if the master of any vessel in port desire to discharge a part only of the cargo, it shall be lawful for him to do so, paying duties on such part only, and to proceed with the remainder to any other ports.

Or, if the master so desire, he may, within forty-eight hours after the arrival of the vessel, but not later, decide to depart without breaking bulk; in which case he will not be subject to pay tonnage or other duties or charges, until on his arrival at another port he shall proceed to discharge cargo, when he will pay the duties on vessel and cargo according to law. And the tonnage-duties shall be held to be due after the expiration of said forty-eight hours.

ARTICLE XI.

The Superintendent of Customs, in order to the collection of the proper duties, will, on application made to him through the Consul, appoint suitable officers, who shall proceed, in the presence of the captain, supercargo, or consignee, to make a just and fair examination of all goods in the act of being discharged for importation, or laden for exportation, on board any merchant vessel of the United States. And if dispute occur in regard to the value of goods subject to an ad valorem duty, or in regard to the amount of tare, and the same cannot be satisfactorily arranged by the parties, the question may, within twenty-four hours, and not afterwards, be referred to the said Consul to adjust with the Superintendent of Customs.

ARTICLE XII.

Sets of standard balances, and also weights and measures, duly prepared, stamped, and sealed, according to the standard of the custom-house at Canton, shall be delivered by the Superintendents of Customs to the consuls at each of the five ports, to secure uniformity, and prevent confusion in measures and weights of merchandize.

ARTICLE XIII.

The tonnage duty on vessels belonging to citizens of the United States shall be paid on their being admitted to entry. Duties of import shall be paid on the discharge of the goods, and duties of export on the lading of the same. When all such duties shall have been paid, and not before, the Superintendent of Customs shall give a port-clearance, and the Consul shall return the ship's papers, so that she may depart on her voyage. The duties shall be paid to the shroffs authorized by the Chinese government to receive the same in its behalf. Duties payable by merchants of the United States shall be received, either in sycee silver or in foreign money, at the rate of exchange as ascertained by the regulations now in force. And imported goods, on their resale or transit in any part of the empire, shall be subject to the imposition of no other duty than they are accustomed to pay at the date of this Treaty.

ARTICLE XIV.

No goods on board any merchant vessel of the United States in port are to be transhipped to another vessel, unless there be particular occasion therefor; in which case the occasion shall be certified by the Consul to the Superintendent of Customs, who may appoint officers to examine into the facts, and permit the transhipment. And if any goods be transhipped without such application, inquiry and permit, they shall be subject to be forfeited to the Chinese Government.

ARTICLE XV.

The former limitation of the trade of foreign nations to certain persons appointed at Canton by the government, and commonly called hong-merchants, having been abolished, citizens of the United States engaged in the purchase or sale of goods of import or export, are admitted to trade with any and all subjects of China without distinction; they shall not be subject to any new limitations, nor impeded in their business by monopolies or other injurious restrictions.

ARTICLE XVI.

The Chinese Government will not hold itself responsible for any debts which may happen to be due from subjects of China to citizens of the United States, or for frauds committed by them: but citizens of the United States may seek redress in law; and on suitable representation being made to the Chinese local authorities through the Consul, they will cause due examination in the premises, and take all proper steps to compel satisfaction. But in case the debtor be dead, or without property, or have absconded, the creditor cannot be indemnified according to the old system of the co-hong so called. And if citizens of the United States be indebted to subjects of China, the latter may seek redress in the same way through the Consul, but without any responsibility for the debt on the part of the United States.

ARTICLE XVII.

Citizens of the United States residing or sojourning at any of the ports open to foreign commerce, shall enjoy all proper accommodation in obtaining houses and places of business, or in hiring sites from the inhabitants on which to construct houses and places of business, and also hospitals, churches and cemeteries. The local authorities of the two Governments shall select in concert the sites for the foregoing objects, having due regard to the feelings of the people in the location thereof; and the parties interested will fix the rent by mutual agreement, the proprietors on the one hand not demanding any exorbitant price, nor the merchants on the other unreasonably insisting on particular spots, but each conducting with justice and moderation. And any desecration of said cemeteries by subjects of China shall be severely punished according to law.

At the places of anchorage of the vessels of the United States, the citizens of the United States, merchants, seamen, or others sojourning there, may pass and repass in the immediate neighborhood; but they shall not at their pleasure make excursions into the country among the villages at large, nor shall they repair to public marts for the purpose of disposing of goods unlawfully and in fraud of the revenue.

And, in order to the preservation of the public peace, the local officers of government at each of the five ports, shall, in concert with the Consuls, define the limits beyond which it shall not be lawful for citizens of the United States to go.

ARTICLE XVIII.

It shall be lawful for the officers or citizens of the United States to employ scholars and people of any part of China without distinction of persons, to teach any of the languages of the Empire, and to assist in literary labors; and the persons so employed shall not, for that cause, be subject to any injury on the part either of the government or of individuals; and it shall in like manner be lawful for citizens of the United States to purchase all manner of books in China.

ARTICLE XIX.

All citizens of the United States in China, peaceably attending to their affairs, being placed on a common footing of amity and goodwill with subjects of China, shall receive and enjoy, for themselves and everything appertaining to them, the special protection of the local authorities of Government, who shall defend them from all insult or injury of any sort on the part of the Chinese. If their dwellings or property be threatened or attacked by mobs, incendiaries, or other violent or lawless persons, the local officers, on requisition of the Consul, will immediately dispatch a military force to disperse the rioters, and will apprehend the guilty individuals, and punish them with the utmost rigor of the law.

ARTICLE XX.

Citizens of the United States who may have imported merchandize into any of the free ports of China, and paid the duty thereon, if they desire to re-export the same, in part or in whole, to any other of the said ports, shall be entitled to make application, through their Consul, to the Superintendent of Customs, who, in order to prevent frauds on the revenue, shall cause examination to be made by suitable officers to see that the duties paid on such goods, as entered on the custom-house books, correspond with the representation made, and that the goods remain with their original marks unchanged, and shall then make a memorandum in the port-clearance, of the goods, and the amount of duties paid on the same, and deliver the same to the merchant; and shall also certify the facts to the officers of customs of the other ports. All which being done, on the arrival in port of the vessel in which the goods are laden, and everything being found on examination there to correspond, she shall be permitted to break bulk and land the said goods, without being subject to the payment of any additional duty thereon. But if, on such examination, the superintendent of customs shall detect any fraud on the revenue in the case, then the goods shall be subject to forfeiture and confiscation to the Chinese Government.

ARTICLE XXI.

Subjects of China who may be guilty of any criminal act towards citizens of the United States, shall be arrested and punished by the Chinese authorities according to the laws of China; and citizens of the United States, who may commit any crime in China, shall be subject to be tried and punished only by the Consul, or other public functionary of the United States, thereto authorized according to the laws of the United States. And in order to the prevention of all controversy and disaffection, justice shall be equitably and impartially administered on both sides.

ARTICLE XXII.

Relations of peace and amity between the United States and China being established by this Treaty, and the vessels of the United States being admitted to trade freely to and from the five ports of China open to foreign commerce, it is further agreed that in case at any time thereafter, China should be at war with any foreign nation whatever, and for that cause should exclude such nation from entering her ports, still the vessels of the United States shall not the less continue to pursue their commerce in freedom and security, and to transport goods to and from the ports of the belligerent parties, full respect being paid to the neutrality of the flag of the United States: Provided that the said flag shall not protect vessels engaged in the transportation of officers or soldiers in the enemy's service; nor shall said flag be fraudulently used to enable the enemy's ships with their cargoes to enter the ports of China; but all such vessels so offending shall be subject to forfeiture and confiscation to the Chinese Government.

ARTICLE XXIII.

The Consuls of the United States at each of the five ports open to foreign trade, shall make annually to the respective Governors-general thereof, a detailed report of the number of vessels belonging to the United States which have entered and left said ports during the year, and of the amount and value of goods imported or exported in said vessels, for transmission to and inspection of the Board of Revenue.

ARTICLE XXIV.

If citizens of the United States have special occasion to address any communication to the Chinese local officers of government, they shall submit the same to their consul, or other officer, to determine if the language be proper and respectful, and the matter just and right; in which event he shall transmit the same to the appropriate authorities for their consideration and action in the premises. In like manner, if subjects of China have special occasion to address the consul of the United States, they shall submit the communication to the local authorities of their own Government, to determine if the language be respectful and proper and the matter just and right; in which case the said authorities will transmit the same to the Consul or other officer for his consideration and action in the premises. And if controversies arise between citizens of the United States and subjects of China, which cannot be amicably settled otherwise, the same shall be examined and decided conformably to justice and equity by the public officers of the two nations acting in conjunction.

ARTICLE XXV.

All questions in regard to rights, whether of property or person, arising between citizens of the United States in China shall be subject to the jurisdiction, and regulated by the authorities of their own Government. And all controversies occurring in China between citizens of the United States and the subjects of any other government, shall be regulated by the treaties existing between the United States and such governments respectively, without interference on the part of China.

ARTICLE XXVI.

Merchant vessels of the United States lying in the waters of the five ports of China open to foreign commerce, will be under the jurisdiction of the officers of their own government, who, with the masters and owners thereof, will manage the same without control on the part of China. For injuries done to the citizens or the commerce of the United States by any foreign power, the Chinese Government will not hold itself bound to make reparation. But if the merchant-vessels of the United States, while within the waters over which the Chinese Government exercises jurisdiction, be plundered by robbers or pirates, then the Chinese local authorities, civil and military, on receiving information thereof, will arrest the said robbers or pirates, and punish them according to law, and will cause all the property which can be recovered, to be placed in the hands of the nearest Consul, or other officer of the United States, to be by him restored to the true owner. But if, by reason of the extent of territory and numerous population of China, it should, in any case, happen that the robbers cannot be apprehended, or the property only in part recovered, then the law will take its course in regard to the local authorities, but the Chinese Government will not make indemnity for the goods lost.

ARTICLE XXVII.

If any vessel of the United States shall be wrecked or stranded on the coast of China, and be subjected to plunder or other damage, the proper officers of government on receiving information of the fact, will immediately adopt measures for their relief and security; and the persons on board shall receive friendly treatment, and be enabled at once to repair to the most convenient of the free ports, and shall enjoy all facilities for obtaining supplies of provisions and water. And if a vessel shall be forced in whatever way to take refuge in any port other than one of the free ports, then in like manner the persons on board shall receive friendly treatment, and the means of safety and security.

ARTICLE XXVIII.

Citizens of the United States, their vessels and property, shall not be subject to any embargo; nor shall they be seized or forcibly detained for any pretense of the public service; but they shall be suffered to prosecute their commerce in quiet, and without molestation or embarrassment.

ARTICLE XXIX.

The local authorities of the Chinese Government will cause to be apprehended all mutineers or deserters from on board the vessels of the United States in China, and will deliver them up to the consuls or other officers for punishment. And if criminals, subjects of China, take refuge in the houses or on board the vessels of citizens of the United States, they shall not be harbored or concealed, but shall be delivered up to justice, on due requisition by the Chinese local officers addressed to those of the United States.

The merchants, seamen, and other citizens of the United States, shall be under the superintendence of the appropriate officers of their government. If individuals of either nation commit acts of violence and disorder, use arms to the injury of others, or create disturbances endangering life, the officers of the two governments will exert themselves to enforce order, and to maintain the public peace by doing impartial justice in the premises.

ARTICLE XXX.

The superior authorities of the United States and of China, in corresponding together, shall do so in terms of equality, and in the form of mutual communication *(chau hwui)*. The Consuls, and the local officers civil and military, in corresponding together, shall likewise employ the style and form of mutual communication *(chau hwui)*. When inferior officers of the one government address superior officers of the other, they shall do so in the style and form of memorial *(shin chin)*. Private individuals, in addressing superior officers, shall employ the style of petition *(pin ching)*. In no case shall any terms or style be suffered which shall be offensive or disrespectful to either party. And it is agreed that no presents, under any pretext or form whatever, shall ever be demanded of the United States by China, or of China by the United States.

ARTICLE XXXI.

Communications from the government of the United States to the court of China shall be transmitted through the medium of the Imperial Commissioner charged with the superintendence of the concerns of foreign nations with China, or through the Governor-general of the Liang Kwang, that of Min and Cheh, or that of the Liang Kiang.

ARTICLE XXXII.

Whenever ships of war of the United States, in cruizing for the protection of the commerce of their country, shall arrive at any of the ports of China, the commanders of said ships and the superior local authorities of Government, shall hold intercourse together in terms of equality and courtesy, in token of the friendly relations of their respective nations. And the said ships of war shall enjoy all suitable facilities on the part of the Chinese Government in the purchase of provisions, procuring water, and making repairs if occasion require.

ARTICLE XXXIII.

Citizens of the United States, who shall attempt to trade clandestinely with such of the ports of China as are not open to foreign commerce, or who shall trade in opium or any other contraband article of merchandize, shall be subject to be dealt with by the Chinese Government, without being entitled to any countenance, or protection from that of the United States; and the United States will take measures to prevent their flag from being abused by the subjects of other nations, as a cover for the violation of the laws of the Empire.

ARTICLE XXXIV.

When the present convention shall have been definitively concluded, it shall be obligatory on both Powers, and its provisions shall not be altered without grave cause; but, inasmuch as the circumstances of the several ports of China open to foreign commerce are different, experience may show that inconsiderable modifications are requisite in those parts which relate to commerce and navigation: in which case, the two Governments will, at the expiration of twelve years from the date of said convention, treat amicably concerning the same, by the means of suitable persons appointed to conduct such negotiation.

And when ratified, this Treaty shall be faithfully observed in all its parts by the United States and China, and by every citizen and subject of each. And no individual State of the United States can appoint or send a minister to China to call in question the provisions of the same.

The present Treaty of peace, amity, and commerce, shall be ratified and approved by the President of the United States, by and with the advice and consent of the Senate thereof, and by the August Sovereign of the Ta Tsing Empire, and the ratifications shall be exchanged, within eighteen months from the date of the signature thereof, or sooner if possible.

.   .   .   .

VIEWS AND POLICIES OF HUMPHREY MARSHALL, 1853-1854

THE TENURE of Humphrey Marshall, of Kentucky, as American commissioner in China, though extending for little more than a year, is possessed of both interest and importance. Marshall wrote with clarity on the conditions he observed at the principal treaty ports, especially Canton and Shanghai. He analyzed the conflict between the Imperial forces and the Taiping rebels in dispatches in which he enunciated the principle "that the highest interests of the United States are involved in sustaining China." His dispatches likewise contain the most concise account of the manner in which the United States opposed successfully the creation of an exclusive British concession at Shanghai.

SHANGHAI AND CANTON IN 1853. HUMPHREY MARSHALL TO THE SECRETARY OF STATE, SHANGHAI, APRIL 28, 1853[1]

. . . .

The rapid growth of the American trade at Shanghai will arrest attention, though it yet remains at a figure far inferior to the British trade to the same port. Every year, however, diminishes the difference. In the brief space of nine years this city has become the principal depôt in China for American manufactures, and the chief exporting point for the green teas of commerce. The monopoly of foreign trade, so long enjoyed by Canton, attracted to the vicinity of that city the manufacturers of silk, and time will be required to transfer the market for silks to Shanghai. As this is the natural outlet from the silk-growing district of China, no doubt is entertained that, so soon as the manufacturers of Hangchow and Suchan find the advantages of this market they will concentrate the trade here.

Shanghai is a healthy city. The means of living are abundant. All of the vegetables grown in the United States with which I am acquainted are successfully cultivated here, besides others which are peculiar to China. The market furnishes plentifully beef, mutton, fish, pork, poultry, and wild game of the finest qualities. I have not seen at home, in any city, evidence of greater abundance in the supplies of the table than are met with here, and nowhere have I seen tables more bounteously or elegantly provided than among the "foreign residencies" in Shanghai. I mention these small items because in the United States a gross error prevails among all classes as to the means and style of living in China. Observation and experience teach me that the rules of economy must be strictly observed to enable the Commissioner of the

[1] H. Ex. Doc. 123: 33-1 (734), pp. 99-102.

United States to maintain a respectable style here, and that his salary may be easily expended without ostentation in an attempt to emulate the greater part even of the limited foreign population among whom he resides.

The city of Shanghai contains about three hundred thousand Chinese inhabitants. Like most of the cities in China, it is enclosed by a strong high wall, and is built upon streets about twelve feet wide. These are usually *very filthy*. Indeed, the habits of the Chinese people are not examples of cleanliness in *any* particular. The Chinese live in houses which are not commodious; and though the country is fertile, and produces abundantly, the condition of the people is far less comfortable than that of the people of either the United States, England, or France, or even of Italy. Very few foreigners reside in the city of Shanghai—perhaps none but the Christian missionaries. Outside of the city walls, a tract of land, containing several hundred acres, has been set apart for settlement by "foreigners." This fronts on the Hoangpo river, and there has arisen here since the treaty a town of exceeding beauty and great prosperity. I have not seen elsewhere a town of the same size that surpasses Shanghai in the architectural style of the buildings, the comfort of its residences, or the means of living agreeably. Every residence has attached to it a pleasant yard and garden, and these are beginning to display the taste of the "foreigners," and their enterprise in transplanting hither the trees, shrubs, and flowers, not merely of China, but of the East. It is curious to see the Chinese lingering around the yards and gardens of Shanghai to behold the improvements which adorn and beautify the homes of the "barbarians." In this part of Shanghai the streets are wide enough to admit the passage of carriages and exercise on horseback—a convenience which is liberally used for that purpose by the people from Europe and America.

The residences of the foreigners in Shanghai have been erected by merchants, for themselves and their employés; so that it is extremely difficult to find a residence for rent, and then only at enormous rates. I have inquired minutely into this branch, and find that such a house as would command $400 per year at Washington would rent here for $1,200, and they range from that to $3,500 per annum.

The British government has built for its consuls, both at Canton and Shanghai, very excellent residences connected with the public offices; and it seems to me that when the government of the United States shall have ascertained the place for the residence of the commissioner, the observance of true economy will suggest an imitation of this example. No comparison can be instituted between China and any other country to which a minister is accredited. Effect, arising from appearances, *must* be regarded here. It is the spirit of this people which dictates it. The government that is represented in China by officers who occupy steadily the public building *belonging to the government* will be regarded as entitled to precedence and as possessing superiority.

The demeanor of the Chinese at Shanghai towards foreigners contrasts very strongly with that of the Chinese at Canton. There the gates of the city proper remain closed against foreigners, and such is the aversion of the people to intercourse with the Europeans and Americans, that triumphal arches were erected, and are yet standing, in Canton to celebrate the refusal of Commissioner Su to open the city gates in 1848 to the British, in accordance with the treaty. There it is unsafe to walk a mile from the foreign factories in any direction.

Repeated instances might be cited of the personal maltreatment and even the murder of foreigners, who were peaceably walking for amusement within two miles of the factories. It is not safe to venture alone more than a few squares from the foreign mercantile houses. The whole foreign community at Canton is crowded into the houses which were built for trading establishments, and the only place of resort for exercise and amusement is a garden or park, which is enclosed within the square of foreign mercantile houses, and which measures some two hundred yards long by one hundred wide. I have heretofore remarked that I could not even obtain a suite of two rooms at Canton for my accommodation at any price, though I had friends who were inquiring for them more than a month. I would be understood, however, as remarking that several houses were open to me *as a guest* so long as I chose to remain, but there were none to rent.

Here every part of the city is free of access. I have walked alone through all sections of it. A lady might do so with perfect impunity, and as safe from insult as she would be in New York. Gentlemen ride into the country, twenty, thirty, and forty miles, as securely as they would travel the same distance from Washington City. All concur in representing the people of the country as kind and hospitable, and well inclined to cultivate the most friendly relations with foreigners. In the city of Shanghai Christian churches are erected, and the truth of the gospel is proclaimed from their pulpits every Sabbath, as also in other public places, without the slightest hindrance or molestation of the missionaries by the Chinese. In a word, one feels as in a prison at Canton, but here he realizes that he is free.

Should the Chinese government fail to agree to the residence of the Commissioner of the United States at Pekin, and it should agree to appoint an imperial commissioner to confer with a commissioner resident at Shanghai, there is no doubt in my mind that this is the most proper as well as the best place to establish the legation of the United States permanently. It is eight hundred miles nearer than Canton to Pekin.

.   .   .   .

The armies of the Emperor and his [Taiping] rebels are centered yet around Nanking. Rumors of engagements constantly arrive, but none of decisive battles; and so little are Chinese reports to be depended upon, that I have ceased to credit them, much less to repeat them, unless sustained by testimony *aliunde*. I think I may safely say, however, that from all I can learn the government of China is fully employed by the rebels, and that any day may bring forth the fruits of successful revolution in the utter overthrow of the existing dynasty.

The Taiping Rebellion and the Policy of "Sustaining" China. Marshall to Secretary William L. Marcy, Shanghai, July 10, 1853[2]

.   .   .   .

The imperial government is impotent, ignorant, conceited; all its ministerial and subordinate officers are superlatively corrupt. The rebels have no idea of the true functions of government. They struggle merely for *power,* and were they to succeed in acquiring it would neither change the substantial exercise of power as it is now wielded, nor essentially the forms of etiquette and ceremony now practiced at court. The leading chief of the rebels is already *invisible;* the chiefs are generally men of low degree, and the mass

[2] *Ibid.*, pp. 203-205.

is ready for the worst excesses. They are superior to the imperialists in energy and courage, but both armies are only burlesques on the military.

The people of China are indifferent as to the success or defeat of either faction, and may be regarded as so far paralyzed, by the long despotism under which they have lived, as to be insensible to popular rights, and incapable of declaring or maintaining them. The only question for them is, "who will be our masters?"

Terrified by the progress of the rebellion, and constantly warned by defeats of the insufficiency of his generals, as well as of their mendacity, the Emperor of China looked abroad for assistance. Clinging from conceit or from ignorance to his pretended superiority, he thought it would be sufficient to ask aid or to offer to *hire* aid, for the western nations to enter upon the task with alacrity of suppressing the rebellion, and neither his Majesty nor his cabinet saw anything amiss in the style of the application. You have already among my despatches my reply to that application. It substantially waived the question until his Imperial Majesty should propound it by his express authority in due and proper form, that it might be *considered* without derogation from the dignity of the United States.

The British minister, I have reason to believe, addressed the court at Pekin, but the nature of his communication has not transpired.

Report declares that the Czar of Russia has promised to render the assistance requested. Some suppose that this implies his marching troops from St. Petersburg, or at least from Siberia, but not so. Russia maintains a considerable body of troops along the border between the Russian and Chinese empires, who could be thrown into China with great ease. A Russian fleet, now at Hong Kong, watches the Japan expedition of the United States, and may be put into action, without difficulty, in behalf of the Emperor.

The Emperor has no navy. A few miserable schooners, purchased at this port since my arrival, and manned by English and American deserters from merchant ships, together with some sixteen lorchas manned by Portuguese desperadoes, constitute his naval force.

Russia already enjoys, substantially, a monopoly of Chinese western trade through the passes; Kiachta in the northwest, and Muzdaban on the west. Her assistance would probably end in passing China under a Russian protectorate, and in the extension of Russian limits to the Hoangho, or the mouth of Yangtsze; or, it may be, when circumstances and policy shall favor the scheme, in the partition of China between Great Britain and Russia. The interference of the Czar would readily suppress the rebellion, by driving the rebels from the great highways of commerce, and from the occupation of the towns on the seaboard. Whatever might be the ultimate compensation demanded by Russia for this timely service, China could not resist its collection; and Russia might avail herself of the conjuncture to add Chinese territory *ad libitum* to her already enormous geographical boundaries, and by commanding the Hoangho, the Sagalien, and the Yangtsze, acquire a power on the Pacific which would not only nullify the projects of the United States for the future, but materially annoy us in the present, by disturbing the fisheries, which are now opening their treasures to our hardy mariners in the North Pacific. I think, then, that almost any sacrifice should be made by the United States to keep Russia from spreading her Pacific boundary, and to avoid her coming directly to an interference in Chinese domestic affairs; for China is like a lamb before the shearers, as easy a conquest as were the provinces of

India. Whenever the avarice or the ambition of Russia or Great Britain shall tempt them to make the prizes, the fate of Asia will be sealed, and the future Chinese relations of the United States of America may be considered as closed for ages, unless *now* the United States shall foil the untoward result by adopting a sound policy. It is my opinion that the highest interests of the United States are involved in sustaining China—maintaining order here, and gradually engrafting on this worn-out stock the healthy principles which give life and health to governments, rather than to see China become the theatre of a widespread anarchy, and ultimately the prey of European ambition.

An interference by the United States to quiet and tranquilize China would be a mission of humanity and charity. It would be essentially a work of peace, unlike the ruthless conquest of India, made upon the sordid calculations of a cruel avarice; or the late subjugation of Pegu, by means of which the British crown has completed its mastery over all the natural outlets for the produce of southwestern Asia, and has commenced in every part that debasement of the people to a condition far worse than that of the African slave, which in other parts she has effectually accomplished already. An interference by the United States in Chinese affairs would have no object but to preserve the nationality of China; to revivify her, to elevate her people, and to stimulate them to win augmented happiness by a proper and peaceful, but scientific, employment of their natural energies. There are conditions which I would make precedent to any interference, however, and these will be now exhibited.

When the Emperor of China shall proclaim an amnesty for past political offences to all the rebels who shall at once return to their homes and avocations; freedom of religious opinion, and religious worship throughout the realm; freedom to citizens of nations having treaties of amity and commerce with China to pass and repass through his dominion at will, without distinction of place; when the Emperor shall install a department of foreign affairs, which can meet the ambassadors of foreign countries; when, in fine, the Emperor shall open the Yangtsze and its affluents to steam navigation, and shall devise some just mode of regulating the same by registry or license; and, finally, when *he shall become a subscriber to the laws of nations*—then, and not till then, would I suggest any interference whatever.

You will be pleased to bear in mind that this basis presupposes the voluntary creation of rights to the citizens of the United States in China, by the supposed proclamations and treaty stipulations, which would justify the interference of the United States to protect those rights whenever they shall be assailed. It guards and preserves that well-known policy of neutrality in the disputes of other countries, which thus far has been the guide of the national councils of the United States. It would only be intervention in vindication of the rights of the American citizen—an intervention promised in the President's inaugural address—wherever the citizen might of right be when the power is invoked.

.   .   .   .

ORIGINS OF THE SHANGHAI INTERNATIONAL SETTLEMENT. MARSHALL TO SECRETARY MARCY, SHANGHAI, JULY 26, 1853[3]

.   .   .   .

After the treaty of Nankin was ratified, (August, 1842,) it seems a memorial was presented to the Emperor; in reply to which, he directed the local

[3] *Ibid.*, pp. 210-213.

authority at Shanghai to consult with the consuls, and to allow "merchants and others *of all nations* to bring their families to the five ports, and to reside there," in accordance with the treaty stipulations; for the Emperor always regarded his treaty with Great Britain as inuring to the benefit of all nations, and was not induced to that liberality by the advice of Sir Henry Pottinger, as has been sometimes alleged. Under this direction from the Emperor, the intendant of this circuit entered into an arrangement with Mr. Balfour, the British consul, whereby a large tract of ground outside of the city walls, between the Yang King Pang and Lekea Chang, (two creeks,) were set apart for settlement. In the language of the intendant's proclamation, it was arranged "that the ground north of the Yang King Pang and south of the Lekea Chang should be rented *to English merchants* for erecting their buildings and residing upon." The authority from the Emperor, as you will see, was to grant for the use of all nations; but the action of the intendant confined it to the *use of English merchants.* However, before any proclamation was made by the intendant and Captain Balfour, (which bears date in November, 1845,) Mr. Cushing had secured the treaty of Wanghya, whereby the citizens of the United States acquired a common right to reside and trade at Shanghai, and there to rent and hold real estate, (17th article.) In November, 1845, the intendant and the British consul issued a proclamation, and certain land regulations applicable to the district between the creeks aforesaid, of which I send you herewith a printed copy which I have secured. By reference to the 14th and 21st regulations you will perceive that this ground was considered as *dedicated* for *an English settlement or quarter,* and was to be held as a district within which none but a British subject could settle except by consent of her Majesty's consul, and within which the British subject was to have the right of pre-emption. It happened that this concession included more land than her Majesty's subjects could occupy within any reasonable time, and almost all that is very convenient for trade. The most convenient anchorage fronts this concession.

Mr. Woolcot was the only American citizen at Shanghai at the time these things were done. He lived inside of this concession, and happened to be appointed to act as consul for the United States. When he raised the American flag the British authorities interfered, and denied the right to fly the consular flag of any other nation inside of the *British settlement,* and Mr. Woolcot pulled down the American flag. Mr. J. Alsop Griswold was shortly afterwards appointed consul for the United States, and came to Shanghai to reside. He raised the flag in front of his consulate, and inside of *the concession* to the English merchants, as it was called. The British consul again interposed, but Mr. Griswold determined to float the national ensign in front of the consulate of the United States. This act was duly noted by the British consul. The French consul then acquired another *concession* of land, which took the ground from the city wall to the Yang King Pang, (between the British concession and the city walls.) The American consul protested against this concession, which was at the time duly noted; and then the right of the local authorities and consuls to dedicate land in this way, in advance of the wants of the people of different nations, so as to create pre-emptive rights in the subjects of certain powers to the exclusion of others, and in abridgment of the right of American citizens to agree upon terms of sale or leasing with the Chinese landholders, arose and became matter for discussion between the imperial commissioner, Sen, and my predecessor, Mr. Davis, of Indiana. The honorable commissioner at first, like a fair jurist, discountenanced the right to make any such concession by the local authority of this circuit; but, as the discussion proceeded, his views were tempered by notions of expediency; and as the American Commissioner remained unmoved, Sen at length intimated that he saw no good reason to repudiate the condition in which affairs had been placed by grants to the English and French, and hoped the Americans would be content to have a distinct quarter set apart for them elsewhere. Should you choose to read, in the volume of the archives of this mission, Mr. Davis's despatches, and Governor Sen's replications, you will perceive that the Chinese commissioner never conceded the principle that the local authority of Shanghai *could* create an exclusive right in the English merchants to a district of unoccupied land by such a machinery as the so-called "concession;" but he desired to waive all difficulty, and to place the citizens of the United States on a similar footing by making them parties to a similar arrangement. His excellency Mr. Davis despaired of bringing the Chinese commissioner to assert the proper principle, and concluded to post-pone the discussion until some case should arise to bring the rights of parties to a practical test.

The American consul himself soon presented an opportunity to have the case reviewed. He purchased ground inside of the British concession, and settled the terms with the owners of the land, and presented his conveyance for the seal of the intendant, and for registration at the consulate of the United States, without in any way recognising the right of the British consul to interfere in the transaction. His deed was examined, sealed, and registered accordingly, *apparently* without question; and the matter of the "concession" to the use of English merchants exclusively *seemed* to have received a practical solution, consistent with the rights and claims of citizens of the United States, under the treaty between the United States and China.

But *without the knowledge of the United States consul* the intendant *had submitted the deeds to Mr. Griswold to the British consul for his approval;* so that the only point *really* decided was the registration of the conveyance at the consulate of the United States instead of that of her Britannic Majesty. In the spring of 1852, however, Mr. Roundy, an American citizen, purchased land within the British concession, and Mr. Cunningham, the vice-consul of the United States, sent in the conveyance to be examined and sealed by the intendant, and returned for registration at the consulate of the United States. The intendant informed the vice consul that the conveyance must be submitted to her Britannic Majesty's consul, and *must be registered in his office.* This the vice-consul promptly but firmly refused to do; and thereupon gave the intendant forty-eight hours within which to perform his duty, according to the interpretation of it adopted by the authorities of the United States, or to close the communication between the authorities of the United States and China at this port.

The intendant yielded, and returned the conveyance duly sealed and ready for registration. The British consul then addressed a remonstrance; whereupon, the vice-consul issued a proclamation to the citizens of the United States declaratory of the course to be pursued by them in obtaining lands, and this paper distinctly *repudiated* the validity or binding force of the British concession. This proclamation was officially protested by the British consul. and referred, with the papers, to her Majesty's plenipotentiary, and by him to the Foreign Office at London. The instructions referred to by the letter of the consul, now submitted, is the reply from the home government; and, whatever may be their exact tenor, it is palpable that Great Britain does not intend to insist on an exclusive right to the dedication to possible future uses for her subjects, which the "concession" originally attempted to effect, and which would have amounted virtually to an abridgement of rights, under the treaty, of citizens of the United States to purchase or rent lands from Chinese proprietors at Shanghai. The foregoing brief history of a matter which has been in dispute for several years, in a sort of tripartite war, (upon paper,) between Great Britain, China, and the United States, is necessary, to save you the trouble of looking through a large volume of documents to obtain a correct understanding of the subject. . . .

VI

ORIGINS OF THE FOREIGN INSPECTORATE OF THE CHINESE MARITIME CUSTOMS, 1854

ROBERT M. McLANE, who served as American commissioner to China in 1854, was responsible for a notable settlement affecting the Chinese customs service at Shanghai, a service which had collapsed as a result of the conflict in and about the city between the Imperial troops and the Taiping rebels. When the Chinese proposed to meet the situation by establishing customhouses in the interior, McLane protested that this would violate the American treaty. Meanwhile, however, Shanghai had reverted to the status of a free port, the Imperial government being deprived of all customs revenue. In these circumstances Commissioner McLane proposed a plan designed to re-establish the Chinese customs service on a permanent and efficient basis. McLane's proposal called for re-establishment of the Shanghai customhouse under the direction of a board of foreign inspectors. The Chinese had already confessed their inability to secure efficient Chinese customs officials, and they therefore suggested that suitable foreigners be appointed by the taotai (superintendent of trade) to act as his agents in the collection of the customs. It was in this manner that the foreign-officered inspectorate of Chinese customs came into being.

COLLAPSE OF THE CUSTOMS ADMINISTRATION AT SHANGHAI. COMMISSIONER McLANE TO SECRETARY MARCY, SHANGHAI, JULY 27, 1854[1]

Meanwhile measures have been matured, under the immediate supervision of the British minister and myself, for the efficient administration of the customs at Shanghai, and for the protection and defence of the foreign settlement, with the sanction of the imperial authorities, and without infringing upon the belligerent rights of those within the walls of the city.

This has been happily effected in a manner promising greater permanency and a more efficient administration than could have been expected in the present state of China. By the treaties already existing the consuls and the superintendent of customs are associated in ascertaining and levying the duties, and upon them, respectively, is conferred the necessary power and jurisdiction over all engaged in commerce at the Five Ports. So, too, in the selection of

[1] S. Ex. Doc. 22: 35-2 (982), pp. 122-123.

sites for warehouses and residences, and for the municipal government of such settlement. Since the 7th September, 1853, these functions of the local authorities of China have been generally suspended, and the consuls themselves, being no longer in the presence of a civil authority that could act in behalf of the imperial government when it was proper to recognize it, practically surrendered to the naval authorities of the three treaty powers the defence of the foreign settlement. Such a state of things was well calculated to aggravate the evils caused by civil war and political disorganization, and induce acts of violence and wrong on the part of the foreign population as unjustifiable as those against which they had sought military protection.

.   .   .   .

MINUTES OF A CONFERENCE HELD AT SHANGHAI, JUNE 29, 1854[2]

Present: His excellency Woo, Taoutae, and chief superintendent of customs.
Rutherford Alcock, her Britannic Majesty's consul.
R. C. Murphy, consul for the United States of America.
Monsieur Edan, his Imperial Majesty's consul *ad interim*.

The consular representatives of Great Britain, France, and the United States of America have met together to receive his excellency Woo, Taoutae, who has expressed a wish to consult with them as to the best mode of reorganizing the Chinese custom-house with a view to its greater efficiency in the collection of foreign maritime duties, and a desire to receive from them any suggestions in their power to offer regarding the practical means of insuring the better observance and execution of treaties in the levy of duties at this port.

The undersigned taoutae and consuls, having maturely considered and discussed the best means of giving efficiency to the administration of customs and carrying out the treaty provisions for the collection of duties, agree upon and have adopted the following articles as embracing all the most essential conditions of an improved organization and the ground work of a more satisfactory system of administration than has heretofore been attainable. The taoutae, on his part, is prepared, in the interest of the Chinese revenue, and for the protection of the honest merchant, at once to give effect to the principles so sanctioned and adopted.

1. The chief difficulty hitherto experiènced by the superintendent of customs having consisted in the impossibility of obtaining custom-house officials with the necessary qualifications as to probity, vigilance, and knowledge of foreign languages, required for the enforcement of a close observance of treaty and custom-house regulations, the only adequate remedy appears to be in the introduction of a foreign element into the custom-house establishment, in the persons of foreigners carefully selected *and appointed by the taoutae,* who shall supply the deficiency complained of, and give to his excellency efficient and trustworthy instruments wherewith to work.

2. The mode in which this may best be effected, it is considered will be by the appointment on the part of the taoutae, of one or more foreigners of undoubted probity, to act under his orders as *inspectors of customs,* with a mixed establishment of Chinese and foreign subordinates, to consist of linguists, writers, and tide-waiters, together with a revenue cutter well manned by foreign sailors, and under the command of a trustworthy and intelligent

[2] *Ibid.,* pp. 153-157.

master, the whole expense of such establishment to be paid out of the proceeds of the revenue, and at such liberal rate as shall suffice to secure the highest qualification of character and capacity in the persons selected for the different offices; the said salaries to be paid monthly by the chief superintendent of customs.

3. In the appointment of the head inspectors, and the organization of the whole auxiliary department, it has been agreed as the best mode of guarding against any future difficulties and sources of complaint, and at the same time ensuring, by the better knowledge of persons, a proper selection, that the consular representative of each treaty power shall select and nominate, for appointment by the taoutae, one inspector, so soon as fit persons can be found, and these three to form a board of inspectors, with a single and united action, to whom will be intrusted the selection of the various subordinates, foreign and Chinese, receiving in such duty of selection all facility and assistance from his excellency the taoutae, in regard to the natives to be chosen. The taoutae will confer the several appointments on the presentation of the inspectors, their rate of remuneration, in accordance with the principle established in art. 2, having previously been fixed.

In the event of three proper and competent persons for the office of inspectors not being procurable in the first instance, as the nominee of each consul, it is agreed that either one of the three consular representatives may exercise his faculty of nomination at once, and the party so selected, upon receiving his appointment from his excellency the taoutae, shall be recognized by the consuls of the three treaty powers as representing the whole board of inspectors, and consequently charged with the collective functions of the office, without prejudice to the power distinctly reserved on the part of the other consuls of nominating at any time the remaining two of the number required, to complete the establishment on the footing now contemplated. The scale of remuneration, numbers, and office of the persons to be employed will shortly after the signature of this minute be determined upon by his excellency the taoutae, and communicated to the consuls collectively in an official note.

4. In reference to such inspectors of customs, the consuls will undertake to try and adjudicate upon any case of exaction, corruption, or neglect of duty made out against them, and charges for misconduct may be made by foreign residents direct to their respective consuls, who will take action upon them after due notice to the Chinese authorities and other treaty consuls; and provided such charges are reasonably supported by the circumstances of the case, an investigation shall take place in the presence of the taoutae and consuls of the three treaty powers, and the finding of such mixed court shall, by previous contract on the part of the said inspectors on their nomination, be binding equally upon the party accused and the chief superintendent of customs from whom they will hold these appointments, the same to be taken by votes, the taoutae having two. The inspectors not to be liable to dismissal or removal, by any other process, unless a total change of system, with the concurrence of the consuls, should render their services no longer needful or advantageous; in which case they will be held entitled to a three months notice, or equivalent salary. All subordinates under the inspectors to hold office during good behavior, and subject only to dismissal on the recommendation of the inspector, if single, or a majority of them if there be three, but upon such

recommendation the taoutae will undertake to give effect to the dismissal without delay.

5. The functions and duties of the auxiliary department of inspectors to be considered as those especially of *surveillance* as to the due observance of the custom-house regulations and provisions of treaties in regard to shipping and duties. There will be a single and united action among the heads, and full authority with all necessary means shall be given to enable them to scrutinize reports of shipping, manifests of cargo, landing and shipping off chops, payment of duties, and port clearances, for the detection of all errors, irregularities, or frauds, whencesoever proceeding. They will, each and severally, on appointment, be sworn truly and honestly to administer the duties of their office, and to abstain from all personal interest in trade, and to hold themselves equally accountable for the faithful observance of these engagements to the taoutae appointing, and to the consuls of the three treaty powers, these authorities together constituting the members of a mixed court, to which they are, by their own consent, to be made legally accountable. It will be their duty to expose all frauds or irregularities, whenever discovered, to the chief superintendent of customs, and the consuls of the three treaty powers collectively; to obtain the necessary evidence for conviction to be had in the court of legal proceedings being necessary; and to take all proper steps under the authority of the said superintendent of customs for the prosecution of the several parties engaged in any irregularity or attempt to defraud the revenue. And the taoutae, on his part, undertakes rigorously to enforce the penalties, whether of fine or confiscation, in all cases without exception or distinction, whenever an act of fraud or irregularity can be brought home to the offending parties, and he will further make public declaration of this, his intention. The superintendent of customs, in any case of confiscation, upon information, will make over to the party or parties instrumental in discovering the fraud or irregularity, a percentage on the value of the goods confiscated, as an additional motive for vigilance, according to a scale hereafter to be specified. The inspector or inspectors will have location for an office within the building occupied as a custom-house, with free access to the Chineses custom-house, books, and documents. They will be responsible for keeping with perspicuity and accuracy a complete set of custom-house books, in English and Chinese, showing in detail the whole course of administration in reference to the shipping and levy of duties. These books, from time to time, or at set periods, as may be hereafter determined, to be carefully compared under the eye of the taoutae and consuls of the three treaty powers, with the books and records kept by the Chinese department, when, if any discrepancy be discovered, it shall be the subject of rigorous investigation; such collective and official examination at any time to be obligatory on the requisition either of the taoutae or one of the consuls. In order the better to regularize and give identity of action to the whole custom-house service, the chief superintendent of customs undertakes that no landing or shipping off chops, duty receipts, port clearances, or any other official document shall be issued from the more exclusively Chinese departments of the custom-house for any foreign vessel or shipper, or be permitted to take effect without the counter signature and seal of the inspector or inspectors, and of all such documents a careful record shall be kept by these for reference. It is further agreed to be of essential importance that no foreign ship, under any circumstances shall be permitted to report except through a foreign consul, duly recognized, or to remain in port, or load or

discharge cargo, without conformity to this regulation. The inspectors will at all times be prepared to afford to the chief superintendent of customs, information and advice on every point connected with foreign customs and laws, and the administration of the same under treaties in China; they will equally afford to the said superintendent, and to each of the three consuls of treaty powers, upon official demand, all the information in their power as to the shipping and levy of duties, together with free access to their books; but the inspectors will not be authorized to give access to these to any other parties.

6. In the event of the inspector or inspectors appointed not possessing competent knowledge of the Chinese language, it is agreed that it will, in that case be necessary to appoint a foreign interpreter at an adequate salary to supply the deficiency.

7. An armed revenue cutter well found and manned under the command of a foreign master, small enough to work quickly in the river, and overtake vessels leaving the port without due authority, and large enough to go with safety to Gutzlaff, if required, is deemed indispensable. And in order the more faithfully to secure their utmost vigilance, it is further agreed that the informer of any violations or intention to violate the revenue laws, in the event of confiscation, shall receive five per cent. of the gross amount so confiscated, and the captain of said cutter for capturing a vessel or vessels attempting to violate the revenue laws to receive five per cent. of the gross amount of property thus confiscated; the first officer three per cent., and the crew two per cent., to be divided equally among all on board below the captain and the first officer.

8. A careful revision of the custom-house regulations of August, 1851, is considered necessary with a view to any modification that may be found desirable, and their conformity with treaty regulations, after which they should be reissued with the greatest publicity in Chinese and English.

9. Upon these bases unanimously concurred in and adopted at this conference, his excellency the taoutae desires and undertakes to reorganize the custom-house establishment, and to forward within ten days an official communication to the undersigned consuls, giving the details of such organization and establishment, and inviting their concurrence and active support, (in so far as by treaty they can legitimately afford the same,) and the consuls on their part declare their desire to contribute by all the means in their power to the organization of an honest and efficient custom-house administration, and their readiness on the receipt of such communication to announce at a day fixed, the resumption by the chief superintendent of customs of all the duties of his office, and the obligations of consignees and masters of ships under their respective flags scrupulously to observe the custom-house and port regulations, under penalty of fine or confiscation as by treaty provided.

VII

PROPOSALS FOR TREATY REVISION AND OCCUPATION OF FORMOSA, 1856-1857

DR. PETER PARKER, who had served long as a medical missionary in China, and who occupied the post of United States Commissioner from 1855 to 1857, was a vigorous, though by no means always an effective, spokesman of American interests in eastern Asia. He was ambitious to be the instrumentality through whom the United States would secure the revision of its treaty (1844). Learning that this privilege was to be denied him, Parker advocated the occupation of Formosa to force the Chinese to observe the treaty, to prevent some European power from taking it, and to provide the United States with coaling stations. His proposals were disavowed in Washington.

IDEAS ON TREATY REVISION. PETER PARKER TO SECRETARY W. L. MARCY, MACAO, DECEMBER 12, 1856[1]

SIR: As intimated in despatch No. 28, which I had the honor to address you on the 1st November, I now beg to resume the subject of the revision of the treaty.

The causes that have operated to prevent the revision from now being a fact accomplished, instead of an object looming up in the future, are familiar to you. That those causes have been unforeseen and beyond the control of human agencies, will not be questioned when the events of the past year are reviewed; and I may be permitted to claim that, *with the means at my command, I have done all that was possible in the premises, and that I have not been to Peking, and thence transmitted a revised treaty to Washington, have been no choice of mine, neither have I pretermitted any opportunity or means of accomplishing ends so important.*

The disposition has not been wanting on the part of England, France, or America to have improved the present year for the adjustment of their relations with China, but extraordinary and providential circumstances, one after another, have occurred to postpone the attainment of an object so desirable, directly affecting so large a portion of the world, socially, commercially, and politically. The paramount interests affecting their relations to each other and to nations nearer home have necessarily demanded and received their first attention to the exclusion of those of China. It may yet appear, however, in the progress of events, that this has been wisely ordered, and that there is no just occasion for dissatisfaction or complaint. But it is to be assumed that another year may be more propitious, and that a deliberate and determined

[1] S. Ex. Doc. 22: 35-2 (983), pp. 1081-1083.

purpose exists on the part of the three powers to reach Peking and to revise existing treaties within a twelvemonth. I am advised by his excellency Sir John Bowring that an efficient naval force will be at his disposal in the Chinese waters the coming year, and the recent events at Canton will doubt-less increase rather than diminish the number of vessels expected before their occurrence.

The relations of the French government to that of China have become serious, and the "judicial murder" in July last of a French subject in Kwang-Si will probably not long remain unavenged. Count De Courcy, the French chargé d'affaires, has obligingly furnished me an extract from a despatch he addressed his excellency Count Walewski on the 25th August last, conveying his views of the measures to be adopted in the revision of the treaty, which I beg to enclose, (exhibit A) [not printed].

The absolute expediency of negotiating at Peking, or as near as possible to the capital, I regard as a settled point, and that the early season, May or June, is the one to be chosen for the occasion admits not a doubt. I am unwilling to allow another mail to depart without conveying to the depart-ment a renewed expression of my settled conviction of the importance of these two facts, and again most respectfully and earnestly suggesting the indis-pensable necessity of *increasing our naval force in China.* The number of vessels specified in my despatch to the Secretary of the Navy, under date of October 28, 1855, (every sentiment of which I now confirm, and to which I respectfully invite attention,) is the least that could be chosen, and it is de-sirable the commissioner and commodore have the authority to supply any providential deficiency by *temporarily* chartering a small steamer or steamers in China. From all I have learned from my intercourse with Chinese officials the past year, and my knowledge of the present condition of the empire, I am sanguine of the success of well directed negotiations in 1857. The present order of things in China cannot continue in *statu quo.* Firm, friendly, and determined policy must be adopted; [and I here venture *confidentially* to sug-gest for the consideration of the President and his cabinet, the propriety of *each* of the plenipotentiaries being authorized by their respective governments to adopt, *as a last resort,* any of those measures authorized by the laws of nations—"when a State refuses to fulfil a perfect obligation which it has con-tracted, or to permit another nation to enjoy a right which it claims."— (Wheaton's *Elements of International Law,* p. 362.) Were the three repre-sentatives of England, France, and America, on presenting themselves at the Peiho, in case of their not being welcomed to Peking, to say the French flag will be hoisted in Corea, the English again at Chushan, and the United States in *Formosa,* and there remain till satisfaction for the past and a right under-standing for the future are granted; but, being granted, these possessions shall *instantly* be restored, negotiation would no longer be obstructed, and the most advantageous and desirable results to *all* concerned secured. Nothing could be more alarming to this government, and justly so, than the apprehension of the possession of any of its territory by foreigners. This will be a legitimate, effectual, and *humane* policy, far preferable to the destruction of forts, the bombardment of cities, and the destruction of life and property. It is only the extreme state of foreign relations with China to which we have arrived that authorizes the suggestion of such a startling policy. Treaty obligations have been violated, just claims are treated with contempt, the lives of for-eigners are wantonly sacrificed, the supreme authorities of western nations, as well as their representatives in China, have been treated with contempt by the imperial authorities, commerce has been impeded, and hostile and deadly collisions have been brought about, so that some decisive measures on the part of western governments have become inevitable. It is as a *last resort,* not to be adopted till friendly application has been made at Peking, that the above suggestion is made, and with a strong probability it will not be necessary; that a mere intimation to the authorities at the north will suffice; that, if by them compelled, the measure will be adopted, the intimation being made in a way that they shall understand the foreign ministers are empowered and ready to carry it into effect if need be. If, unfortunately, driven a step beyond the threat to its execution, the presumption is still stronger that *that* will certainly prevail, and the *last* resort of injured nations will thus be avoided, which, unless superseded by the success of these intermediate measures which are short of actual hostilities, may be the deplorable issue.]

.   .   .   .

FORMOSA AS AN AMERICAN OUTPOST. PETER PARKER TO SECRETARY W. L. MARCY, MACAO, MARCH 10, 1857[2]

SIR: Reference has been made to Formosa in my despatch No. 34 of the 12th of December, and No. 5 of the 12th of February last. I have now the honor herewith to transmit to the department an important communication (exhibit 3,) [not printed] bearing upon the same subject, from W. M. Robinet, esq., a Peruvian by birth, and formerly holding a commission in the Peruvian navy, which he has resigned, notifying that government that he has become a naturalized citizen of the United States. His certificate of naturalization, he informs me, was obtained in San Francisco. Mr. Robinet has been an enterprising merchant in China for a number of years, and appears to be imbued with views truly American. His paper contains very authentic information respecting this beautiful island [Formosa], such as few men could furnish. It is a most valuable one for its great mineral and agricultural wealth. From the table appended, it appears that the exports of the last year amounted to $1,654,000, and, under proper management, they may be doubled and quadrupled in a few years. The coal mines seem to be inexhaustible, and are very accessible and of good quality, which, in this age of steam navigation, is a circumstance of special interest.

The position of the island is also one that renders it very desirable in a commercial and political point of view, especially as respects the United States. In the event of the establishment of a line of steamers between California, Japan, and China, this source of supply of coal will be most advantageous. That the island may not long remain a portion of the empire of China is possible; and in the event of its being severed from the empire politically, as it is geographically, that the United States should possess it is obvious, particularly as respects the great principle of balance of power. Great Britain has her St. Helena in the Atlantic, her Gibraltar and Malta in the Mediterranean, her Aden in the Red sea, Mauritius, Ceylon, Penang, and Singapore in the Indian ocean, and Hong Kong in the China seas. If the United States is so disposed, and can *arrange* for the possession of Formosa, England certainly cannot object.

If there ever was a State which has laid herself open to just reprisals it is China, "which has refused to fulfil a perfect obligation which she has con-

[2] *Ibid.,* pp. 1208-1210.

tracted" with the United States, "and does not permit them to enjoy rights which they claim" under the solemn stipulations of treaty; and in the event of her persisting in this course, it seems clear that, by the acknowledged principles of international law, the United States have the right, if they have the inclination, to take Formosa by way of reprisal, "until a satisfactory reparation should be made for the injuries they have sustained."—(See Wheaton, *International Law,* page 362.)

The governor of Hong Kong and the British admiral on this station have both betrayed their interest in Formosa. The former observed to Mr. Robinet: "In the event of your being *disturbed* in your business there, *I have no doubt Admiral Seymour would send a man-of-war* up there to look after affairs," &c. I am, however, under less apprehension of the immediate action of the English authorities in this matter than at the date of my note to Commodore Armstrong, on the 24th ultimo. My hope is that the British authorities, in China, being sufficiently occupied for the present, will not find it convenient to take any steps in regard to Formosa; and that, in a couple of months at latest, the instructions of the department in relation to the views I had the honor to submit in my despatch of the 12th of December will have been received.

The propositions, first of G. Nye, jr., esq., (despatch No. 5, exhibit G,) and now those of Mr. Robinet, are made in ignorance on their part of any views having been submitted by me in relation to Formosa, and look to its becoming an independent colony, or "an independent and weak government," under the protection, at least, of the United States.

According to the plan suggested for the three powers to adopt "in respect to Formosa, Chusan, and Corea," (despatch No. 34,) the opening of the former, to free and unrestricted commercial intercourse, will follow under any satisfactory solutio of the difficulties, and those will profit most who were first in the field.

Explanatory of my views expressed in the memoranda of interview with Commodore Armstrong on the 27th ultimo, (enclosure 2,) [not printed] I wish to state that I am aware that, under the laws of nations, ordinarily in making reprisals, the State "delivers (special) commissions to its officers and subjects," (see Wheaton, page 362;) and had our naval force been adequate, and I had resolved to act at once, it had been under a somewhat forced construction of my "full powers" to revise the treaty and adjust all claims and grievances; and the act would have been conditioned *pending reference to the government at Washington* for confirmation, or to be ignored if it should suit the pleasure of government to do so, relying upon the disinterestedness, patriotism, and justice of my motive for the vindication of my course to my own conscience.

I believe Formosa and the world will be better for the former coming under a civilized power. Cannibalism and savage massacres of the unfortunate shipwrecked citizens and subjects of Christian nations will then be terminated, and the whole island become what its name implies, in more senses than one, *beautiful,* physically and morally.

Right or wrong, what I have done and all I have proposed in relation to Formosa, I faithfully record and transmit to the department, and beg respectfully to submit the same for the consideration of the President and the decision of the government, requesting thereon early and specific instructions.

VIII

THE UNITED STATES AND THE TREATY OF TIENTSIN, 1857-1858

As EARLY as 1854 Great Britain was seeking co-operation on the part of the United States in her efforts to secure revision of the China treaties. In 1857 the British were asking for not only political but also military and naval co-operation in the policies they sought, together with their French allies, as a result of the Arrow War then in progress. The British objectives in China were set forth fully in a memorandum to Secretary Cass (March 30, 1857). The British overture was essentially a proposal for an alliance, which naturally was not acceptable in Washington. Nevertheless, in anticipation of the new treaty settlement which it was assumed would result from the war, the American government appointed, in May, 1857, William B. Reed as envoy extraordinary and minister plenipotentiary to China in order that the United States might be in a position to press China for all those commercial and diplomatic gains won by the force of British and French arms. The American policy is characterized in the Instructions of Secretary Cass to Reed. The nature of China's policy at the time is suggested by the letter found in the yamen of the unfortunate Viceroy Yeh at Canton. The advantages of the American Treaty of Tientsin are explained by Reed.

INSTRUCTIONS OF SECRETARY LEWIS CASS TO WILLIAM B. REED. WASHINGTON, MAY 30, 1857[1]

. . . .

The objects which it is understood the allies seek to accomplish by treaty stipulations are:

1. To procure from the Chinese government a recognition of the right of other powers to have accredited ministers at the court of Pekin, to be received by the emperor, and to be in communication with the authorities charged with the foreign affairs of the empire.

2. An extension of commercial intercourse with China, which is now restricted to five ports enumerated in the treaty.

3. A reduction of the tariff of duties levied upon domestic produce in its transit from the interior to the coast, as the amount now imposed is said to be a violation of the treaty.

[1] S. Ex. Doc. 30: 36-1 (1032), pp. 7-10.

On this subject you will be able to ascertain the true state of the alleged grievance when you reach China, and to act accordingly.

4. A stipulation for religious freedom to all foreigners in China.

5. An arrangement for the suppression of piracy.

6. Provision for extending the benefits of the proposed treaty to all the other civilized powers of the earth.

These objects are recognized by the President as just and expedient, and so far as you can do so by peaceful coöperation, he expects that you will aid in their accomplishment. In conformity with this policy, you will communicate frankly with the British and French ministers upon all the points of common interest, so that it may be distinctly understood that the three nations are equally influenced by a determination to obtain justice, and by a desire to procure treaty arrangements for the extension and more adequate protection of their commercial intercourse with China. But on your side these efforts must be confined to firm representations, appealing to the justice and policy of the Chinese authorities, and leaving to your own government to determine upon the course to be adopted, should your representations be fruitless.

.   .   .   .

This country, you will constantly bear in mind, is not at war with the government of China, nor does it seek to enter that empire for any other purposes than those of lawful commerce, and for the protection of the lives and property of its citizens. The whole nature and policy of our government must necessarily confine our action within these limits, and deprive us of all motives either for territorial aggrandizement or the acquisition of political power in that distant region. During the hostilities which now exist in China, we may be able to avail ourself of this fortunate position, not only for the benefit of our countrymen who reside there, or who have extensive interests there of a commercial character, but in order to facilitate also the general objects sought to be accomplished by a revision of the existing treaties. It is possible even that it may be employed with advantage as a means of communication between the belligerent parties, and tend in this way to the termination of the war. You will therefore not fail to let it be known to the Chinese authorities that we are no party to the existing hostilities, and have no intention to interfere in their political concerns, or to gain a foothold in their country. We go there to engage in trade, but under suitable guarantees for its protection. The extension of our commercial intercourse must be the work of individual enterprise, and to this element of our national character we may safely leave it. With the domestic institutions of China we have no political concern, and to attempt a forcible interference with them would not only be unjust in itself, but might defeat the very object desired. Fortunately, however, commerce itself is one of the most powerful means of civilization and national improvement. By coming into peaceful contact with men of other regions and other races, with different habits and greater knowledge, the jealous system of seclusion which has so long separated China from the rest of the world will gradually give way, and with increased intercourse will come those meliorations in the moral and physical condition of its people which the Christian and the philanthropist have so long and so ardently desired.

In connection with these views, there is one subject to which, from its relation to the internal policy of China, as well as its important bearing upon the intercourse of foreigners with that empire, I desire to call your particular attention. The effort of the Chinese government to prevent the importation and the consumption of opium was a praiseworthy measure, rendered necessary by the prevalent use and the terrible effects of that deleterious drug. All accounts agree as to the magnitude of the evil, and the wide-spread desolation caused by it.

Upon proper occasions, you will make known to the Chinese officers with whom you have communication that the government of the United States does not seek for their citizens the legal establishment of the opium trade, nor will it uphold them in any attempt to violate the laws of China by the introduction of that article into the country. While desirous that the blessings of Christianity and the benefits of a more advanced civilization should be extended over the empire, and while convinced that free commercial intercourse will become a powerful agent in the accomplishment of these great results, it would be a subject of deep regret and mortification to the American people should these hopes be disappointed by the illegal cupidity of their countrymen.

There are other matters of importance which will engage your attention, and which ought to make part of the proposed modification of the treaty. Among these is the absurd regulation which reduces the true standard of our coin much below its actual value, and does serious injury to our trade. A legal currency ought to be established at its true standard.

Some of the stipulations of the existing treaty have been neglected or violated, and our merchants have suffered by this bad faith. Among these is the provision that American citizens "shall enjoy all proper accommodations in obtaining homes and places of business, or in hiring sites from the inhabitants on which to construct houses and places of business." This engagement has been rendered nugatory, not by the indisposition of the holders of property to dispose of it, but by the interference of the local authorities, who have prohibited the making of such an engagement, and in some instances have actually imprisoned and tortured their unfortunate countrymen who have ventured to violate the prohibition.

The treaty also provides that the government shall examine the complaints of American citizens against Chinese subjects for frauds or debts, and "take the proper measures to compel satisfaction." This stipulation has been rendered useless by the neglect of the authorities to enforce it.

Entire security of persons and property is among the guarantees which this same treaty expressly holds out to our citizens. Practically the engagement is a barren one, for the prompt and efficient interposition of the authorities to protect foreigners from the injuries to which they are exposed is a rare event in the annals of Chinese justice.

In relation to these and other subjects of a similar character, you will be able in China to obtain more exact information than can be furnished here, and you will govern your conduct accordingly. With respect to all your official action, much of course must be left to your discretion.

The empire to which you are accredited is so remote, and its condition so extraordinary, that it is difficult to decide with confidence upon the particular measures which events may, from time to time, render necessary.

These instructions will indicate to you the general wishes of the President, but as to the best mode of carrying them into effect you may often be obliged to exercise your own judgment; and I am gratified to believe that this authority is vested where it will be safely employed.

The internal dissensions of the Chinese empire will not fail to engage your earliest attention, connected as they may be, in their varying phases, with both the rights and interests of the United States, and with the course you may find it necessary to adopt. It is difficult, with the scarcity of information which reaches this country, to form any definite opinion of the causes and objects of the insurrection [the Taiping Rebellion], or any probable conjecture as to its issue. We have no other concern as to its progress or result than to take care that our rights are preserved inviolate. We have no reason to believe that one of the contending parties is more favorably disposed towards foreigners than the other, or more ready to extend commercial intercourse with them, while both are bound by treaty stipulations to us and to other powers, and will be held to their faithful observance; but in all that relates to these internal disturbances you must be guided by your own discretion, applied to the circumstances in which you may find yourself placed.

.   .   .   .

CHINA'S POLICY IN FOREIGN RELATIONS, 1857. WILLIAM B. REED TO SECRETARY CASS, HONG KONG, FEBRUARY 4, 1858[2]

Sir: I hasten to communicate to you the copy of an important document, which has been sent to me from Canton, where it was found among the viceroy's archives.

It is, in form, a letter from the consul of state at Pekin to the imperial commissioner at Canton, and to the governors general of the two eastern provinces. It is, in fact, an imperial decree. It is most significant in its illustration of the views of the Emperor, or those who control him, and especially interesting, as it appears to refer particularly to the action of the United States.

I regret to say, and in this view, I have the concurrence of the secretary of legation, Mr. Williams, whose long experience entitled his opinion to great consideration, that it confirms the most discouraging judgment as to the relation of the viceroys to the imperial court, showing beyond question, that in all that Yeh said and did in relation to the treaty powers, he was a faithful exponent of the imperial will. In his refusal in the dispatches sent to me in November and December last, to listen to a revision of the treaty, he used almost the language, as he certainly expressed the leading idea of this decree, that nothing but "inconsiderable modifications" were to be permitted, though with all the craft of his peculiar diplomacy, he did not disclose an authority to negotiate, even as to minute alterations. He was ordered to refuse to treat on matters of substance, and he obeyed. There is in this rescript the usual dash of falsehood in the assertion that the allied plenipotentiaries in 1854, Mr. McLane and Sir John Bowring yielded the grounds of controversy. They did nothing of the kind. They were tantalized by vexatious ceremonial till they were obliged to retire in consequence of the severity of the season.

It will be seen that this decree seems to have been induced by Mr. Parker's avowed intention to go north in the spring of 1856, which as you are aware, he carried into effect later in the season, by visiting Shanghai, whence the letter of the President was forwarded. It was returned, as you know, with the seals broken, and unanswered.

The reply which Mr. Parker received on this visit, that the governors generals were not competent to enter on a discussion of foreign business, but that everything of the kind was intrusted to the commissioner at Canton, seems to have been honest.

The decree satisfies me that any attempt on my part during this winter to have opened negotiations at Shanghai, or elsewhere, would have been fruitless.

It shows further the extreme anxiety of the imperial court to prevent any access to Pekin, or its neighborhood, and strengthens the opinion which has always and strenuously been expressed by the Russian plenipotentiary, that an actual approach to that neighborhood with a decisive tone and available force, might produce a result, and that nothing short of this will.

Above all, it settles the question as to any distinction being taken among the nations of the West to our advantage. Steadfast neutrality and consistent friendship make no impression on the isolated obduracy of this empire. I never thought that there was, on the part of the officials, any such distinction. I am sure of it now. The only doubt that remains, and this the events of the next two months will solve, is whether the catastrophe at Canton [the Arrow War] is to produce any distant effect. On this, yet, there is nothing but the vaguest speculation to enlighten us.

It shows, too, that the imperial government at Pekin is far from ignorant of what occurs at distant points. The Emperor, or his council, have accurate knowledge, and give precise directions, which are implicitly obeyed. It shows that at Pekin the contents of the treaties are, according to the gloss the Chinese choose to put upon them, well understood. The real responsibility is with the central authority.

All the authenticated facts are now before the President. I ask for them his most considerate attention. My best judgment on the specific wrongs received by citizens of the United States was communicated in a dispatch written before this imperial decree was known to me. It does not in any way weaken that judgment. I am better satisfied than ever that decisive action is necessary with the officials who rule this people.

. . . .

Letter from the Great Council to Yeh, a Secretary of State, (or senior member of the inner cabinet,) and Governor General of the two Kwang; to Iliang, Governor General of the two Kiang; and to Keihonga, Governor of Kiang Su, entitled to wear the insignia of the first grade.

On the 18th day of the 2d moon of the 6th year of Hienfung, (March 24, 1856,) we had the honor to receive the following imperial decree:

Iliang and Keihonga represent that the Mei and Ying barbarians (Americans and English) are about to request some exchange in their treaty regulations. The American chief, Parker, writes to Kiang Su that he is waiting for a ship to proceed to Shanghai to reconsider the treaty, and the English chief, Si Tai Kwoh, (Mr. Lay,) also holds language to the effect that application will certainly be made by every State for a revision of its treaty; that the exclusiveness of the Kwang Tung (authorities) has reached such a point that none of their ministers will hold any further communication with them.

The idea (of the barbarians) is to use their intended visit to Shanghai as a means of pressure, while they make it their ground of complaint that they are so buffed and refused intercourse by the Kwang Tung (authorities). The thing is plain (now;) though the original treaties under which the five ports were opened, did contain a provision that they should be revised, nothing more was meant than that if, in the course of time, abuses came to exist, or points of difficulty or hindrance (were discovered,) as it was to be feared might be the case, there would be no objection to slight modifications. It was never (contemplated) that there could be any alteration in the substance of their conditions. The demands these barbarians made the year before last at Shanghai and Tientsen were so utterly inadmissable that Tsunghun and his colleagues, in their interview with them, rejected (their propositions) with rebuke; and the chiefs themselves, pereceiving their own unreasonableness, (the crookedness of their own reason, the badness of their cause,) did not renew the controversy. They are now going to Shanghai on the plea that the exclusiveness of the Kwang Tung [governor] is past bearing; but the governor general and governor in Kiang Su being in no respect competent to the chief superintendent of barbarian business, and of course unable to accede to what they require, and their refusal certain to bring the barbarians to Tientsin, to the yet greater violation of what is right and proper, let Yeh Ming Chin inform himself of the particulars of the case, and hold in the barbarian securely. If the changes they require be merely on points of small significance, there will be no harm in his considering these with them, and forwarding a representation to us; (which received) some slight modifications may be adopted. If they repeat the extravagant demands of the year before last, he will speak plainly, repel (their advances,) and break off [negotiations.] It is absolutely incumbent on him, by an equal employment of graciousness and awe, to put an end to this project of an expedition northward altogether. Let him not show himself utterly inaccessible, (lit., steep and lofty, refuse to see them,) lest his refusal to receive them be converted into matter of complaint. Let Iliang and Keihunga desire Lan-wei-wan to convey their commands to the different barbarian consuls (at Shanghai,) and inform them that all business concerning the trade of the five ports must be referred to Kwang Tung, (and that the authorities of) other provinces cannot overstep the bounds of their own jurisdiction; that if the barbarians do not choose to have intercourse with Kwang Tung, no other provincial government can properly take cognizance of their business in its stead; that they have in this instance reported the different subjects of [Dr. Parker's] communication to the throne, but that they cannot even now do more than request them to hand these over to the imperial commissioner in Kwang Tung for his disposal, and that as regards the proposed revision, they, the governor general and governor, are not competent to entertain applications regarding it. With gentle words, let them persuade them to sail to Kwang Tung, and to prevent anything else coming of it. This is most important. Let copies of the original papers of Iliang and his colleague be supplied to Yeh Ming Chin for his information, and let this decree be forwarded at the rate of 500 li a day, and communicated in confidence to the different authorities whom it concerns. Respect this. In obedience to his Majesty's decree, [the council] write this note.

[Translated] Thomas Wade.

REED'S COMMENTS ON THE AMERICAN TREATY OF TIENTSIN. WILLIAM B. REED TO SECRETARY CASS, TIENTSIN, JUNE 30, 1858[3]

.   .   .   .

The signature of the new treaty puts an end entirely to the pretension of the Chinese, as stated in Yeh's correspondence last December, that in con-

[3] *Ibid.*, pp. 352-357.

sequence of the peculiar phraseology of the treaty of Wanghia, it was in substance a compact forever, and could only be modified on matters of inconsiderable import. The imperial commissioners never whispered this objection here, but went to work earnestly, and apparently in good faith, to make a new and revised treaty, exactly as if no such difficulty had been suggested. I have thought it best, observing how these people reason, to omit any limitation as to time in the new treaty. This leaves us at liberty to negotiate a change when the necessity arises, and you may depend on it, whether there is an express limitation or not in the treaty, the Chinese, in the first instance, will always object to change. The object of a limitation as to time is only of advantage as a matter of mutual obligation. The Chinese will never, of their own accord, ask for a change, and will be very apt to object whenever we do; so that a limitation of time would really only be a restriction on us.

. . . .

The fourth article gives to the United States the right of direct correspondence under sealed envelopes, the sacredness of which is expressly guaranteed, with the privy council, *(Nui Koh,)* at the capital. This right, as you will easily infer, may be a most important one, for a retrospect of the correspondence of all my predecessors shows that not a word they ever wrote is known to have reached the immediate counsellors of the Emperor, except by reports from governors-general and local authorities; and so persistent have the Chinese been in this, that no one of the communications addressed by the western plenipotentiaries to Pekin have been directly acknowledged. My belief is that the suppression was rather apparent than real, and that more information reached the capital than was supposed. But my predecessors never had the satisfaction of knowing it. This article puts an end to all this, and its willing adoption, following so soon on the letter of the Emperor to the President, gives every reason to believe that it will be honestly observed. The privy council is the most powerful of the official boards, and as such is the fit organ of correspondence with the highest diplomatic representative of the United States. Its duties, according to the imperial statutes, are "to deliberate on the government of the empire, proclaim abroad the imperial pleasure, regulate the canons of state together with the whole administration" of what they call "the great balance of power." What in other countries is performed by a prime minister, is in China done by this council. It is not the "Board of Rites," but superior to it, nor the *Li-fan-yuen,* or colonial office, having control of intercourse with tributary nations. If the permanent legation of the United States shall be, as I hope it will be, established at Shanghai, communications may be made directly to the privy council at the capital and answered in twenty days.

The fifth article stipulates under certain limitations, for the annual visit and sojourn of an American minister at Pekin. These limitations may be somewhat modified by the provisions of the other treaties, but as they are, I see no difficulty in agreeing to them. The details as to the arrangements to be made for the journey and residence of the minister at the capital were cordially assented to, and I have no doubt that all facilities will be afforded by the Chinese authorities. The journey from Shanghai inland to the capital is, of course, an interesting one, though now much obstructed by the deflection of the Yellow river, and the want of water in the grand canal, but our recent experience in coming to this point, and the concurrent testimony of others show that any time from April to November, the capital is easily accessible by this route. I see no reason to anticipate, now that the treaty stipulation exists, any difficulty on the part of the Chinese. But I venture to express the hope there will be perfect good faith in the representative of the United States observing the limitations on this right of visit; I mean that it should only be made on important occasions, of which he must, of course, be the judge, and not be unnecessarily protracted.

.   .   .   .

The sixth article contains a stipulation providing for our having a permanent minister at Pekin, if one ever be allowed to any other nation. The Chinese plenipotentiaries most readily agreed to this. I thought it best beside a general "most favored" clause," to insert a special stipulation for a resident minister, so that should the fears of the Chinese, and the presence of the military array now here at the last moment, induce the concession of permanent ministers, there should be no pretense for refusal to us.

.   .   .   .

The 11th article combines the 19th and 21st articles of the treaty of Wanghia, with the additional stipulation that arrests, in order to trial, may be made either by American or Chinese officials.

I may make this article the subject of separate communication, but I cannot allow it to pass now without saying, in the most emphatic terms, that no greater wrong could be done to a weak nation, no clearer violation of the spirit or letter of a treaty, than claiming exemption from local law for our citizens who commit crime, and then failing to punish them ourselves. We extort from China "ex-territoriality," the amenability of guilty Americans to our law, and then we deny to our judicial officers the means of punishing them. There are consular courts in China to try American thieves and burglars and murderers, but there is not a single jail where the thief or burglar may be confined. Our consuls in this, as in many other particulars, have to appeal to English or French liberality, and it often happens that the penitentiary accommodations of England and France are inadequate to their own necessities, and the American culprit is discharged. Hence it follows that many claim the privilege of American citizenship, in order to have the benefit of this immunity, and every vagabond Englishman, or Irishman, or Scotchman, any one, who, speaking our language, can make out a *prima facie* claim to citizenship, commits crime according to his inclination, secure that if he is tried in the American courts there is no power of punishment. In the case of a murder, the provision of the act of Congress in 1848 is, that before the capital sentence can be carried into effect, the prisoner must be detained a year in custody. This, so long as the United States refuse or neglect to provide for the erection of prisons, gives to the worst crime the greatest privilege, and the wretch—and I regret to say there are many capable of this crime now haunting the coast—who commits a deliberate murder is sure of escape. I consider the exaction of "ex-territoriality" from the Chinese, so long as the United States refuse or neglect to provide the means of punishment, an opprobrium of the worst kind. It is as bad as the cooly or the opium trade. Were it not that I have strong confidence that when this matter is fully understood Congress will apply the remedy, I should be ashamed to put my name to a treaty which asserts this boasted privilege of "ex-territoriality."

.   .   .   .

The 12th article contains a most important modification of the treaty of Wanghia, and one to which my attention was particularly directed by my instructions. The former treaty (article 17) provided for the interposition of the local authorities before the site of any leasehold property could be determined. The effect of this was to create an unnecessary embarrassment; for the officials, knowing that their previous consent was necessary, were always ready to interpose, and forbid the selection of a site which they or any interested or ill-disposed person wished to prevent. No such previous consent is now needed, and perfect freedom of individual contract is secured, and the authorities are only permitted to interfere when there is a direct appeal to them. This change is considered here of great advantage. The concluding provision of the article of the former treaty, which required the local authorities, in concert with the consuls, to define the limits beyond which it would not be lawful for the citizens of the United States to go, is omitted. There is no express prohibition of a citizen of the United States going anywhere in the neighborhood of the open ports, provided he engages in no unlawful trade in fraud of the revenue.

In my instructions I was directed not to unite in any effort to legalize the opium trade, and by a fair inference I was led to conclude that it was the wish of the government that the trade should not be legalized in any treaty, but be left to the prohibitory statutes of the Chinese. In the treaty of Wanghia, (Article 33,) dealing in opium was in terms prohibited to American citizens. In the new treaty I have omitted the word "opium," and left the trade to be dealt with as with that of any other article declared by law to be contraband. My reasons for this were twofold. In the first place, the retention of the word made the open defiance of the treaty more scandalous; and when, at every port, I found Americans dealing in opium freely and unreservedly, and at least one American built, but British owned steamer, with the American flag, plying regularly up and down the coast as a quick carrier of the poison, I felt that it was worse than a mockery to retain the specific prohibition, and much better to class opium in the general list of contraband. Another motive, also, influenced me. In one of the few interviews I have had with Lord Elgin, he expressed a strong wish that the word "opium" should be omitted in the American and Russian treaties. He seemed to think, and I thought with some reason, that it was a reflection on England, who derived a large revenue from the trade, and he assured me that if I would accede to this he would not attempt to legalize the trade by treaty, as he was instructed to do. (Dispatch of the Earl of Clarendon to Lord Elgin, April 20, 1857.) I confess this was an inducement to me, for I could not but believe, from the great indifference the Chinese commissioners at Takoo expressed on the subject, they might be easily persuaded to legalize the trade if the English insisted on it, and I thought Lord Elgin's half-expressed reluctance to comply with his instructions was very creditable to him, believing as I do that he feels a strong repugnance to this infamous traffic, and the connection of his government with it. Not having yet seen the English treaty, I am unable to say whether it contains any reference to it.

.   .   .   .

THE UNITED STATES AND CHINA. THE TREATY OF TIENTSIN, JUNE 18, 1858[4]

ARTICLES.

  I. Declaration of amity.
  II. Deposit of treaty.
  III. Promulgation.

[4] U. S. Compilation of Treaties in Force (Washington, 1899), pp. 95-105.

IV. Diplomatic privileges.
V. Visit of minister to Capital.
VI. Residence of minister at the Capital.
VII. Correspondence.
VIII. Personal interviews.
IX. Naval vessels in Chinese waters.
X. Consuls authorized.
XI. United States citizens in China.
XII. Privileges in open ports.
XIII. Shipwrecks; pirates.
XIV. Open ports; clandestine trade prohibited.
XV. Commerce permitted; tariff.
XVI. Tonnage duties.
XVII. Pilots, etc.
XVIII. Control of ships, etc.
XIX. Ships' papers, etc.
XX. Customs examinations.
XXI. Re-exportation.
XXII. Payment of duties.
XXIII. Transhipment of goods.
XXIV. Collection of debts.
XXV. Chinese teachers, etc.
XXVI. Trade with China in case of war.
XXVII. Rights of United States citizens.
XXVIII. Communications with officers.
XXIX. Freedom of religion.
XXX. Most favored nation privileges to United States citizens; ratification.

The United States of America and the Ta Tsing Empire, desiring to maintain firm, lasting, and sincere friendship, have resolved to renew, in a manner clear and positive, by means of a Treaty or general convention of peace, amity and commerce, the rules which shall in future be mutually observed in the intercourse of their respective countries; for which most desirable object, the President of the United States and the August Sovereign of the Ta Tsing Empire have named for their Plenipotentiaries to wit: The President of the United States of America, William B. Reed, Envoy Extraordinary and Minister Plenipotentiary to China and His Majesty the Emperor of China, Kweiliang, a member of the Privy Council and Superintendent of the Board of Punishments; and Hwashana, President of the Board of Civil Office and Major General of the Bordered Blue Banner Division of the Chinese Bannermen, both of them being Imperial Commissioners and Plenipotentiaries: And the said Ministers, in virtue of the respective full powers they have received from their Governments, have agreed upon the following articles.

ARTICLE I.

There shall be, as there have always been, peace and friendship between the United States of America and the Ta Tsing Empire, and between their people respectively. They shall not insult or oppress each other for any trifling cause so as to produce an estrangement between them, and if any other nation should act unjustly or oppressively, the United States will exert their good offices, on being informed of the case, to bring about an amicable arrangement of the question, thus showing their friendly feelings.

ARTICLE II.

In order to perpetuate friendship, on the exchange of ratifications by the President, with the advice and consent of the Senate of the United States, and by His Majesty the Emperor of China, this treaty as ratified by the President of the United States, shall be deposited at Pekin, the capital of His Majesty the Emperor of China in charge of the Privy Council; and as ratified by His Majesty the Emperor of China, shall be deposited at Washington, the capital of the United States, in charge of the Secretary of State.

ARTICLE III.

In order that the people of the two countries may know and obey the provisions of this treaty, the United States of America agree immediately on the exchange of ratifications to proclaim the same and to publish it by proclamation in the gazettes where the laws of the United States of America are published by authority and His Majesty the Emperor of China, on the exchange of ratifications, agrees immediately to direct the publication of the same at the capital and by the Governors of all the Provinces.

ARTICLE IV.

In order further to perpetuate friendship, the Minister or Commissioner or the highest diplomatic representative of the United States of America in China, shall at all times have the right to correspond on terms of perfect equality and confidence with the Officers of the Privy Council at the capital, or with the Governors General of the Two Kwangs, the Provinces of Fuhkien and Chehkiang or of the Two Kiangs, and whenever he desires to have such correspondence with the Privy Council at the Capital he shall have the right to send it through either of the said Governors General or by the General Post, and all such communications shall be sent under seal which shall be most carefully respected. The Privy Council and Governors General, as the case may be, shall in all cases consider and acknowledge such communications promptly and respectfully.

ARTICLE V.

The Minister of the United States of America in China, whenever he has business, shall have the right to visit and sojourn at the capital of His Majesty the Emperor of China, and there confer with a member of the Privy Council, or any other high officer of equal rank deputed for that purpose, on matters of common interest and advantage. His visit shall not exceed one in each year, and he shall complete his business without unnecessary delay. He shall be allowed to go by land or come to the mouth of the Peiho, into which he shall not bring ships of war and he shall inform the authorities at that place in order that boats may be provided for him to go on his journey. He is not to take advantage of this stipulation to request visits to the capital on trivial occasions. Whenever he means to proceed to the capital he shall communicate in writing, his intention to the Board of Rites at the capital, and thereupon the said Board shall give the necessary directions to facilitate his journey and give him necessary protection and respect on his way. On his arrival at the capital, he shall be furnished with a suitable residence prepared for him and he shall defray his own expenses and his entire suite shall not exceed twenty persons, exclusive of his Chinese attendants, none of whom shall be engaged in trade.

ARTICLE VI.

If at any time His Majesty the Emperor of China shall by Treaty voluntarily made, or for any other reason, permit the Representative of any friendly nation to reside at his Capital for a long or short time, then without any further consultation or express permission, the Representative of the United States in China shall have the same privilege.

ARTICLE VII.

The superior authorities of the United States and of China in corresponding together, shall do so on terms of equality, and in form of mutual communication (chau hwui). The Consuls and the local officers, civil and military, in corresponding together, shall likewise employ the style and form of mutual communication (chau-hwui). When inferior officers of the one government address superior officers of the other, they shall do so in the style and form of memorial (shin-chin). Private individuals in addressing superior officers, shall employ the style of petition (pin ching). In no case shall any terms or style be used or suffered which shall be offensive or disrespectful to either party. And it is agreed that no presents, under any pretext or form whatever shall ever be demanded of the United States by China, or of China by the United States.

ARTICLE VIII.

In all future personal intercourse between the Representative of the United States of America and the Governors General or Governors the interviews shall be had at the official residence of the said officers or at their temporary residence or at the residence of the Representative of the United States of America, whichever may be agreed upon between them nor shall they make any pretext for declining these interviews. Current matters shall be discussed by correspondence so as not to give the trouble of a personal meeting.

ARTICLE IX.

Whenever national vessels of the United States of America in cruising along the coast and among the ports opened for trade, for the protection of the commerce of their country, or for the advancement of science, shall arrive at or near any of the ports of China, Commanders of said ships and the superior local authorities of Government shall, if it be necessary, hold intercourse on terms of equality and courtesy in token of the friendly relations of their respective nations, and the said vessels shall enjoy all suitable facilities on the part of the Chinese Government in procuring provisions or other supplies and making necessary repairs. And the United States of America agree that in case of the ship wreck of any American vessel and its being pillaged by pirates or in case any American vessel shall be pillaged or captured by pirates on the seas adjacent to the coast, without being shipwrecked, the national vessels of the United States shall pursue the said pirates, and if captured deliver them over for trial and punishment.

ARTICLE X.

The United States of America shall have the right to appoint Consuls and other commercial agents for the protection of trade to reside at such places in the dominions of China as shall be agreed to be opened, who shall hold official intercourse and correspondence with the local officers of the Chinese Government (a Consul or a Vice-Consul in charge taking rank with an intendant of circuit or a prefect) either personally or in writing as occasions may require, on terms of equality and reciprocal respect. And the Consuls and local officers shall employ the style of mutual communication. If the officers of either nation are disrespectfully treated or aggrieved in any way by the other authorities they have the right to make representation of the same to the Superior Officers of the respective Governments who shall see that full inquiry and strict justice shall be had in the premises; and the said Consuls and agents shall carefully avoid all acts of offense to the officers and people of China. On the arrival of a Consul duly accredited at any port in China, it shall be the duty of the Minister of the United States to notify the same to the Governor General of the province where such port is, who shall forthwith recognize the said Consul and grant him authority to act.

ARTICLE XI.

All citizens of the United States of America in China, peaceably attending to their affairs, being placed on a common footing of amity and good will with the subjects of China, shall receive and enjoy for themselves and everything appertaining to them the protection of the local authorities of government, who shall defend them from all insult or injury of any sort. If their dwellings or property be threatened or attacked by mobs, incendiaries, or other violent or lawless persons, the local officers, on requisition of the consul, shall immediately despatch a military force to disperse the rioters, apprehend the guilty individuals and punish them with the utmost rigor of the law. Subjects of China guilty of any criminal act towards citizens of the United States shall be punished by the Chinese authorities according to the laws of China. And citizens of the United States, either on shore or in any merchant vessel, who may insult, trouble or wound the persons or injure the property of Chinese or commit any other improper act in China, shall be punished only by the Consul or other public functionary thereto authorized according to the laws of the United States. Arrests in order to trial may be made by either the Chinese or the United States authorities.

ARTICLE XII.

Citizens of the United States residing or sojourning at any of the ports open to foreign commerce shall be permitted to rent houses and places of business or hire sites on which they can themselves build houses or hospitals, churches and cemeteries. The parties interested can fix the rent by mutual and equitable agreement, the proprietors shall not demand an exorbitant price, nor shall the local authorities interfere unless there be some objections offered on the part of the inhabitants respecting the place. The legal fees to the officers for applying their seal shall be paid. The citizens of the United States shall not unreasonably insist on particular spots but each party shall conduct with justice and moderation. Any desecration of the cemeteries by natives of China shall be severely punished according to law. At the places where the ships of the United States anchor or their citizens reside, the merchants seamen or others can freely pass and repass in the immediate neighborhood, but in order to the preservation of the public peace, they shall not go into the country to the villages and marts to sell their goods unlawfully in fraud of the revenue.

ARTICLE XIII.

If any vessel of the United States be wrecked or stranded on the coast of China, and be subjected to plunder or other damage, the proper officers of

Government, on receiving information of the fact, shall immediately adopt measures for its relief and security: the persons on board shall receive friendly treatment and be enabled to repair at once to the nearest port, and shall enjoy all facilities for obtaining supplies of provisions and water. If the merchant vessels of the United States, while within the waters over which the Chinese Government exercises jurisdiction, be plundered by robbers or pirates, then the Chinese local authorities civil and military, on receiving information thereof, shall arrest the said robbers or pirates, and punish them according to law, and shall cause all the property which can be recovered, to be restored to the owners or placed in the hands of the Consul. If by reason of the extent of territory and numerous population of China, it shall in any case happen that the robbers cannot be apprehended, and the property only in part recovered, the Chinese Government shall not make indemnity for the goods lost. But if it shall be proved that the local authorities have been in collusion with the robbers, the same shall be communicated to the superior authorities for memorializing the Throne, and these officers shall be severely punished and their property be confiscated to repay the losses.

ARTICLE XIV.

The citizens of the United States are permitted to frequent the ports and cities of Canton and Chau-chau or Swatau, in the Province of Kwang-tung: Amoy, Fuh-chau, and Tai-wan in Formosa, in the Province of Fuh-Kien: Ningpo in the Province of Cheh-Kiang and Shanghai in the Province of Kiang-su, and any other port or place hereafter by treaty with other powers or with the United States opened to commerce, and to reside with their families and trade there: and to proceed at pleasure with their vessels and merchandise from any of these ports to any other of them. But said vessels shall not carry on a clandestine and fraudulent trade at other ports of China not declared to be legal or along the coasts thereof; and any vessel under the American flag violating this provision shall, with her cargo, be subject to confiscation to the Chinese Government; and any citizen of the United States who shall trade in any contraband article of merchandise, shall be subject to be dealt with by the Chinese Government, without being entitled to any countenance or protection from that of the United States; and the United States will take measures to prevent their flag from being abused by the subjects of other nations as a cover for the violation of the laws of the Empire.

ARTICLE XV.

At each of the ports open to Commerce, citizens of the United States shall be permitted to import from abroad and sell, purchase, and export, all merchandise of which the importation or exportation is not prohibited by the laws of the Empire. The Tariff of duties to be paid by citizens of the United States on the export and import of goods from and into China shall be the same as was agreed upon at the treaty of Wanghia, except so far as it may be modified by treaties with other nations; it being expressly agreed that citizens of the United States shall never pay higher duties than those paid by the most favored nation.

ARTICLE XVI.

Tonnage duties shall be paid on every merchant vessel belonging to the United States entering either of the open ports at the rate of four mace per ton of forty cubic feet, if she be over one hundred and fifty tons burden:

and one mace per ton of forty cubic feet, if she be of the burden of one hundred and fifty tons or under, according to the tonnage specified in the register, which with her other papers, shall on her arrival, be lodged with the Consul, who shall report the same to the Commissioner of Customs. And if any vessel having paid tonnage duty at one port shall go to any other port to complete the disposal of her cargo, or being in ballast to purchase an entire or fill up an incomplete cargo, the Consul shall report the same to the Commissioner of Customs, who shall note on the port clearance that the tonnage duties have been paid and report the circumstances to the collectors at the other customhouses, in which case the said vessel shall only pay duty on her cargo, and not be charged with tonnage duty a second time. The collectors of customs at the open ports shall consult with the consuls about the erection of beacons or light houses, and where buoys, and light-ships should be placed.

ARTICLE XVII.

Citizens of the United States shall be allowed to engage pilots to take their vessels into port, and when the lawful duties have all been paid, take them out of port. It shall be lawful for them to hire at pleasure servants, compradores, linguists, writers, labourers, seamen and persons for whatever necessary service with passage or cargo boats for a reasonable compensation, to be agreed upon by the parties, or determined by the Consul.

ARTICLE XVIII.

Whenever merchant vessels of the United States shall enter a port, the collector of customs shall, if he see fit, appoint custom house officers to guard said vessels, who may live on board the ship or their own boats at their convenience. The local authorities of the Chinese Government shall cause to be apprehended all mutineers or deserters from on board the vessels of the United States in China on being informed by the Consul, and will deliver them up to the consuls or other officers for punishment. And if criminals, subjects of China, take refuge in the houses or on board the vessels of citizens of the United States, they shall not be harbored or concealed, but shall be delivered up to justice, on due requisition by the Chinese local officers, addressed to those of the United States. The merchants, seamen and other citizens of the United States, shall be under the superintendence of the appropriate officers of their Government. If individuals of either nation commit acts of violence or disorder, use arms to the injury of others, or create disturbances endangering life, the officers of the two governments will exert themselves to enforce order, and to maintain the public peace by doing impartial justice in the premises.

ARTICLE XIX.

Whenever a merchant vessel belonging to the United States shall cast anchor in either of the said ports, the supercargo, master or consignee, shall within forty-eight hours, deposit the ship's papers in the hands of the Consul, or person charged with his functions, who shall cause to be communicated to the superintendent of customs, a true report of the name and tonnage of such vessel, the number of her crew and the nature of her cargo, which being done, he shall give a permit for her discharge. And the master, supercargo or consignee, if he proceed to discharge the cargo without such permit, shall incur a fine of five hundred dollars, and the goods so discharged without permit shall be subject to forfeiture to the Chinese Government. But if a master of any vessel in port desire to discharge a part only of the cargo, it shall be lawful for him to do so, paying duty on such part only, and to proceed with the remainder to any other ports. Or if the master so desire, he may within forty-eight hours after the arrival of the vessel, but not later, decide to depart without breaking bulk; in which case he shall not be subject to pay tonnage or other duties or charges until, on his arrival at another port, he shall proceed to discharge cargo, when he shall pay the duties on vessel and cargo according to law. And the tonnage duties shall be held due after the expiration of the said forty-eight hours. In case of the absence of the Consul or person charged with his functions, the captain or supercargo of the vessel may have recourse to the Consul of a friendly power, or if he please, directly to the Superintendent of customs, who shall do all that is required to conduct the ship's business.

[On the seventeenth of July, 1867, it had been agreed between the Chinese Government and Mr. Burlingame, United States Minister at Pekin, that, subject to ratification by the Government of the United States, Article XIX should be modified as hereinafter stated. The proposed modification having been submitted to the Senate, that body, by its resolution of January 20, 1868, did "advise and consent to the modification of the treaty between the United States and China concluded at Tientsin on the 18th of June, 1858, so that the nineteenth article shall be understood to include hulks and storeships of every kind under the term merchant vessels: and so that it shall provide that if the supercargo, master, or consignee shall neglect, within forty-eight hours after a vessel casts anchor in either of the ports named in the treaty, to deposit the ship's papers in the hands of the consul, or person charged with his functions, who shall then comply with the requisitions of the nineteenth article of the treaty in question, he shall be liable to a fine of fifty taels for each day's delay, the total amount of penalty however shall not exceed two hundred taels."]

ARTICLE XX.

The Superintendent of customs in order to the collection of the proper duties, shall on application made to him through the consul, appoint suitable officers, who shall proceed in the presence of the captain, supercargo or consignee, to make a just and fair examination of all goods in the act of being discharged for importation, or laden for exportation, on board any merchant vessel of the United States. And if disputes occur in regard to the value of goods subject to ad valorem duty, or in regard to the amount of tare, and the same cannot be satisfactorily arranged by the parties, the question may within twenty-four hours, and not afterwards, be referred to the said consul to adjust with the superintendent of customs.

ARTICLE XXI.

Citizens of the United States who may have imported merchandise into any of the free ports of China, and paid the duty thereon, if they desire to reëxport the same in part or in whole to any other of the said ports, shall be entitled to make application, through their Consul, to the superintendent of customs, who in order to prevent fraud on the revenue, shall cause examination to be made by suitable officers to see that the duties paid on such goods as are entered on the customhouse books, correspond with the representation made, and that the goods remain with their original marks unchanged, and shall then make a memorandum in the port clearance, of the goods and the amount of duties paid on the same, and deliver the same to the merchant, and shall also certify the facts to the officers of customs of the other ports; all of which being done, on the arrival in port of the vessel in which the goods are laden, and everything being found on examination there to correspond, she shall be permitted to break bulk and land the said goods without being subject to the payment of any additional duty thereon. But if on such examination, the superintendent of customs shall detect any fraud on the revenue in the case, then the goods shall be subject to forfeiture and confiscation to the Chinese Government. Foreign grain or rice brought into any port of China in a ship of the United States, and not landed, may be re-exported without hindrance.

[On the seventh of April, 1863, it was agreed between Mr. Burlingame, United States Minister at Pekin, and the Government of China, that, subject to the ratification of the Government of the United States, the twenty-first article of the treaty of June 18, 1858, "shall be so modified as to permit duties to be paid, when goods are re-exported from any one of the free ports of China, at the port into which they are finally imported, and that drawbacks shall be substituted for exemption certificates at all the ports, which drawbacks shall be regarded as negotiable and transferable articles and be accepted by the Custom House from whatsoever merchant who may tender them either for import or export duty to be paid by him."

The Senate advised and consented to this modification by resolution of February 4, 1864; and it was accepted, ratified, and confirmed by the President, February 22, 1864.]

ARTICLE XXII.

The tonnage duty on vessels of the United States shall be paid on their being admitted to entry. Duties of import shall be paid on the discharge of goods, and duties of export on the lading of the same. When all such duties shall have been paid and not before, the collector of customs shall give a port clearance, and the Consul shall return the ship's papers. The duties shall be paid to the shroffs authorized by the Chinese Government to receive the same. Duties shall be paid and received either in sycee silver or in foreign money at the rate of the day. If the Consul permits a ship to leave the port before the duties and tonnage dues are paid, he shall be held responsible therefor.

ARTICLE XXIII.

When goods on board any merchant vessel of the United States in port require to be transshipped to another vessel, application shall be made to the consul, who shall certify what is the occasion therefor to the superintendent of customs, who may appoint officers to examine into the facts and permit the transshipment. And if any goods be transshipped without written permits, they shall be subject to be forfeited to the Chinese Government.

ARTICLE XXIV.

Where there are debts due by subjects of China to citizens of the United States, the latter may seek redress in law; and on suitable representations being made to the local authorities through the consul, they will cause due examination in the premises, and take proper steps to compel satisfaction. And if citizens of the United States be indebted to subjects of China, the latter may seek redress by representation through the consul, or by suit in the Consular Court. But neither Government will hold itself responsible for such debts.

ARTICLE XXV.

It shall be lawful for the officers or citizens of the United States to employ scholars and people of any part of China without distinction of persons to teach any of the languages of the Empire, and to assist in literary labors; and the persons so employed shall not for that cause be subject to any injury on the part either of the Government or of individuals; and it shall in like manner be lawful for citizens of the United States to purchase all manner of books in China.

ARTICLE XXVI.

Relations of peace and amity between the United States and China being established by this treaty, and the vessels of the United States being admitted to trade, freely to and from the ports of China open to foreign commerce, it is further agreed, that in case at any time hereafter China should be at war with any foreign nation whatever, and should for that cause exclude such nation from entering her ports, still the vessels of the United States shall not the less continue to pursue their commerce in freedom and security, and to transport goods to and from the ports of the belligerent powers, full respect being paid to the neutrality of the flag of the United States: provided that the said flag shall not protect vessels engaged in the transportation of officers or soldiers in the enemy's service, nor shall said flag be fraudulently used to enable the enemy's ships, with their cargoes to enter the ports of China: but all such vessels so offending shall be subject to forfeiture and confiscation to the Chinese Government.

ARTICLE XXVII.

All questions in regard to rights whether of property or person, arising between citizens of the United States in China shall be subject to the jurisdiction and regulated by the authorities of their own Government. And all controversies occurring in China between citizens of the United States and the subjects of any other Government, shall be regulated by the treaties existing between the United States and such Governments respectively without interference on the part of China.

ARTICLE XXVIII.

If citizens of the United States have special occasion to address any communication to the Chinese local officers of Government, they shall submit the same to their consul or other officer to determine if the language be proper and respectful, and the matter just and right, in which event he shall transmit the same to the appropriate authorities for their consideration and action in the premises. If subjects of China have occasion to address the Consul of the United States, they may address him directly at the same time they inform their own officers, representing the case for his consideration and action in the premises. And if controversies arise between citizens of the United States and subjects of China, which cannot be amicably settled otherwise, the same shall be examined and decided conformably to justice and equity by the public officers of the two nations acting in conjunction. The extortion of illegal fees is expressly prohibited. Any peaceable persons are allowed to enter the court in order to interpret, lest injustice be done.

ARTICLE XXIX.

The principles of the Christian religion as professed by the Protestant and Roman Catholic churches, are recognized as teaching men to do good, and to do to others as they would have others do to them. Hereafter, those who quietly profess and teach these doctrines shall not be harassed or persecuted on account of their faith. Any person, whether citizen of the United States or Chinese convert, who according to these tenets peaceably teach and practice the principles of Christianity, shall in no case be interfered with or molested.

ARTICLE XXX.

The contracting parties hereby agree that should at any time the Ta Tsing Empire, grant to any nation or the merchants or citizens of any nation, any right, privilege or favor, connected either with navigation, commerce, political or other intercourse which is not conferred by this treaty, such right, privilege, and favor shall at once freely enure to the benefit of the United States, its public officers, merchants and citizens.

The present treaty of peace, amity and commerce shall be ratified by the President of the United States, by and with the advice and consent of the Senate, within one year, or sooner, if possible, and by the August Sovereign of the Ta Tsing Empire forthwith: and the ratifications shall be exchanged within one year from the date of the signatures thereof.

In faith whereof, we the Respective Plenipotentiaries of the United States of America and of the Ta Tsing Empire, as aforesaid, have signed and sealed these presents.

Done at Tientsin, this eighteenth day of June, in the year of our Lord one thousand eight hundred and fifty eight, and the Independence of the United States of America the eighty second, and in the eighth year of Hien-fung, fifth month and eighth day.

WILLIAM B. REED.

[SEAL.]

KWEILIANG.

HWASHANA.

[SEAL.]

THE UNITED STATES AND CHINA. TREATY ESTABLISHING TRADE REGULATIONS AND TARIFF, NOVEMBER 8, 1858[5]

[Among the rules attached to the treaty and tariff schedule of November 8, 1858, (not printed) were the following:]

RULE V.

Regarding certain commodities heretofore contraband.

The restrictions affecting trade in opium, cash, grain, pulse, sulphur, brimstone, saltpetre and spelter, are relaxed under the following conditions:

1. Opium will henceforth pay thirty taels per pecul, import duty. The importer will sell it only at the port. It will be carried into the interior by Chinese only, and only as Chinese property; the foreign trader will not be allowed to accompany it. The provision of the Treaty of Tien-tsin, conferring privileges by virtue of the most favored clause, so far as respects citizens of the United States going into the interior to trade, or paying transit-duties, shall not extend to the article of opium, the transit-duties on which will be

arranged as the Chinese government see fit; nor in future revisions of the tariff is the same rule of revision to be applied to opium as to other goods.

. . . .

RULE VII.

It is agreed that the amount of transit dues legally levyable upon merchandise imported or exported shall be one-half the Tariff duties, except in the case of the duty-free goods liable to a transit duty of two and a half per cent. *ad valorem,* as provided in No. 2 of these Rules.

Merchandise shall be cleared of its transit dues under the following regulations:—

In the case of imports. Notice being given at the port of entry from which the imports are to be forwarded inland, of the nature and quantity of the goods, the ship from which they have been landed, and the place inland to which they are bound, with all other necessary particulars, the Collector of Customs shall, on due inspection made, and on receipt of the transit duty due, issue a Transit Duty Certificate. This must be produced at every barrier station and viséed.—No further duty will be levyable upon imports so certificated, no matter how distant the place of their destination.

In the case of exports. Produce purchased by a citizen of the United States in the interior, will be inspected and taken account of at the first barrier it passes on its way to the port of shipment. A memorandum, showing the amount of the produce, and the port at which it is to be shipped, will be deposited there by the person in charge of the produce. He will then receive a certificate, which must be exhibited and viséed at every Barrier on his way to the port of shipment. On the arrival of the produce at the barrier nearest the port, notice must be given to the customs at the port, and the transit dues due thereon being paid it will be passed. On exportation the produce will pay the tariff duty.

Any attempt to pass goods inwards or outwards otherwise than in compliance with the rule here laid down, will render them liable to confiscation. Unauthorized sale *in transitu* of goods that have been entered as above for a port, will render them liable to confiscation. Any attempt to pass goods in excess of the quantity specified in the certificate will render all the goods of the same denomination, named in the certificate liable to confiscation. Permission to export produce which cannot be proved to have paid its transit dues, will be refused by the customs until the transit dues shall have been paid.

RULE VIII.

Trade with the Capital.

It is agreed that no citizen of the United States shall have the privilege of entering the capital city of Peking for the purposes of trade.

IX

THE SO-CALLED CO-OPERATIVE POLICY, 1862-1863

FROM 1861 until 1867 the United States was represented in China by its first resident minister at Peking, Anson Burlingame. His appointment coincided with the opening of a new era in China's foreign relations. The Manchu court had been humbled in some degree by the victories of British and French arms in the Arrow War. The Treaties of Tientsin (1858) and the subsequent Conventions of Peking (1860) had opened more ports to foreign trade, and Peking to the residence of foreign ministers. Although the United States had not participated in the hostilities against China, she had demanded and received most-favored-nation treatment in the new privileges won by the British and the French.

At Peking in 1860-61 the extreme antiforeign party was overthrown. Foreign affairs were placed in the hands of Prince Kung, a brother of the emperor, who was disposed to meet the letter if not the spirit of the new treaties. His efforts were at times frustrated by intrigues of the reactionaries, by the jealousies and obstructionist views of local officials, and finally by weakening of the dynasty by the Taiping Rebellion.

To meet a numerous assortment of problems in relations between China and the United States, Burlingame, by reason of his liberal instructions, was able to apply with much success the so-called co-operative policy. This policy was based on the assumption that the interests of the treaty powers in China were identical. The purpose of the policy was by united diplomatic pressure to insure fulfillment of the treaties without the necessity of recourse to force.

Burlingame's views covered a wide range of American interests in China: the activities of Americans in the Taiping Rebellion, jurisdiction in the foreign concessions at the treaty ports, the coolie trade, and the inadequacy of the American diplomatic establishment in Peking.

As minister, Burlingame enjoyed the invaluable counsel of S. Wells Williams, who as interpreter, acting secretary of legation, and chargé d'affaires during Burlingame's leave of absence in 1865, contributed a knowledge of things Chinese possessed by no American minister during the latter nineteenth century.

THE CO-OPERATIVE POLICY. BURLINGAME TO SECRETARY OF STATE SEWARD, SHANGHAI, JUNE 17, 1862[1]

.   .   .   .

Your despatches Nos. eight and nine have been received and have given me great gratification. The former relieves me from arbitrary instructions and permits me to "consult and cooperate" with the western powers; the latter approves of my course at Ningpo and of the policy thus far pursued by me. It certainly is not our policy to acquire territory in China, nor do we desire to interfere in the political struggles of the Chinese further than to maintain our treaty rights. When these are endangered by Pirates and bandits (and the rebels [Taipings] are nothing else) and the English, French and Chinese are seeking to maintain treaty rights, to be neutral is to be indifferent, not only, to the rights of our citizens but to the interests of civilization. If at any future time the English & French, or either of them, should menace the integrity of the Chinese territory then the very fact that we had acted with them for law and order would give us greater weight against such a policy. There is great temptation for them to aggress. Here are over three hundred millions of people who are without arms—industrious, patient and wealthy and who, it is thought would be but too happy to submit to any power that would protect them. If the treaty powers could agree among themselves to guarantee the neutrality of China and together secure order in the treaty Ports and give their moral support, at least, to that party in the Empire which would most favor a stable government—the interests of humanity would be subserved. The Treaty powers are practically doing this now, but how long they may remain in agreement it is impossible to imagine. I will not however speculate too much with regard to the future of this singular people. As you well write "revolutions are apt to effect sudden and even great changes in very short periods of time." I shall endeavor, in a spirit of friendship for this people to meet the requirements of each hour as wisely as I can, seeking honestly to develop a higher civilization in their midst.

THE CO-OPERATIVE POLICY (Continued). BURLINGAME TO SECRETARY SEWARD, PEKING, JUNE 20, 1863[2]

SIR: In despatch No. 18, of June 2, 1862, I had the honor to write, "if the treaty powers could agree among themselves to the neutrality of China, and together secure order in the treaty ports, and give their moral support to that party in China, in favor of order, the interests of humanity would be subserved."

Upon my arrival at Peking, I at once elaborated my views, and found, upon comparing them with those held by the representatives of England and Russia, that they were in accord with theirs. After mature deliberation, we determined to consult and co-operate upon all questions. . . .

Since our agreement thus to act together, the French minister, Mr. Berthemy, has arrived, and enters most heartily into the policy of co-operation.

[1] U. S. Dept. of State, *China Despatches*, Vol. XX, No. 18. Hereinafter the Despatches and Instructions are cited as *China Despatches* and *China Instructions*.
[2] U. S. *Foreign Relations*, 1863, Pt. 2, No. 42, p. 859. Hereinafter cited as *Foreign Relations*.

Preliminary to entering into thorough co-operation, I held it to be my duty to ascertain the ulterior purposes of the treaty powers, having, by position and trade, a leading place in China.

I found Mr. Balluzeck, the Russian minister, prompt to answer, in the spirit of the Russian treaty, that his government did not desire to menace, at any time, the territorial integrity of China, but, on the contrary, wished to bring it more and more into the family of nations, subject, in its relation with foreign powers, to the obligations of international law. That he was but too happy to co-operate in a policy that would engraft western upon eastern civilization, without a disruption of the Chinese Empire.

With Sir Frederick Bruce, the British minister, my conversations were elaborate and exhaustive.

I said to him, frankly, that we represented the first trading powers here, and that our interests were identical, and I was ready, not only from individual desire, but because of the wishes of my government, to co-operate with him.

He met me in a large and generous spirit, and said that he had ever desired to co-operate with the other treaty powers, and pointed out in his despatches to his government the evidences of such desires, and expressed his delight that the representative of the United States should hold views so coincident with his own. I said to him, that while I paid full homage to the energy of his government in opening China, and for affording protection to the citizens of the United States, still I felt, looking to British antecedents, a little distrust about the future; that our trade by the way of California was increasing, and I felt anxious about its future condition.

I illustrated my views of distrust by reference to the controlling influence of the British in the custom-house, and in the pretensions set up by his countrymen in the treaty ports in favor of territorial concessions.

He agreed with me that the sensitiveness was natural, and replied that he would be pleased to remove every ground for it. He said that circumstances, more than design, had given the English the seeming control of affairs at the treaty ports; that, in the first place, the English trade was very large, and besides, from long connexion with the East, many of his countrymen had acquired knowledge of the Chinese language, and when persons were wanted it was natural that those most qualified in that respect should be selected. He pointed out that long ago he had recommended that the custom-house should be put upon a cosmopolitan footing, and that Mr. Lay, who was at the head of it, had endeavored to carry out his views. I must admit that in this he was right.

I was applied to by the Chinese, through their employé, Mr. Hart, then at the head of the customs, for Americans to fill places, but I could not find any who had studied Chinese.

One of the first places in the Chinese service was tendered to our consul, Mr. Seward, but he could not, he thought, with justice to his own government, accept it. If we had had a school for interpreters, our proper influence would have been far greater than it is now. Besides, the English have been compelled to defend the treaty ports without any assistance from us, and we have enjoyed the fruits of that protection. But, in the face of these obvious facts, Sir Frederick admitted that it was not in the interest of England to hold a position which gave her no special privileges, and subjected her needlessly to the criticisms of the other treaty powers, and therefore he was willing to have any arrangements made by which she would not be put in a false position.

He did not wish, as far as he was concerned, that English officers should lead against the Taipings.   He prefers that the Chinese should employ, for purposes of drill and discipline, men from the smaller states of Europe, and that I might rely upon it that he would do all he could to relieve England from the charge of being the "great bully" of the East; to relieve her "from the dilemma of being forced by local clamor to commit acts of violence, which, though in accordance with past usage, and perhaps justified by our (their) former situation, do not fail to jar unpleasantly on the conscience of England and of the civilized world."   The force policy was wrong, and he was certain that his government had had enough of wars brought about through hasty action of men in the East not under the sway of large ideas. He was for a change of policy.   To show me that he did not wish to have an English officer at the head of the Ward force, he showed me that he himself had urged the appointment of General Burgevine, an American—a fact I did not know when I wrote my despatch No. ——, or I should have given him the credit which was his due; and when Governor Li and Tackee conspired to put Burgevine out of the force, (of which I shall write fully,) I must say that the most determined man for his restoration was Sir Frederick, on the broad ground that it was not good policy to have an Englishman at the head of that force.   When I raised an objection to the so-called concessions, and presented my argument against them, he fully concurred with me, and scouted the whole doctrine as dangerous; and to stop all pretensions on the part of his people, he wrote those very able letters to his consul at Shanghai which I send in despatch No. ——.

In all our conversations he, with great force, urged the adoption of a cooperative policy in China, and, as a representative of the largest trading power here, said that he was willing to lead in a liberal direction.   Indeed, so striking were his views, (and so in accordance were they with the policy strongly urged by me before I came to Peking, and so in contrast to what had hitherto been the English policy,) that I expressed a warm desire that he would present them to his government, that they might become the basis of our future cooperation.   He accordingly wrote the powerful despatch marked A, which he communicated to me for my private use, and which, with his permission, I send to you confidentially, with the most positive request that it is not to appear until it is first published in England. [Not printed.]

Upon this frank avowal of the policy of England, it would be impossible to refuse co-operation.   The Russian minister and myself both concurred in the view that the position of Sir Frederick was just what we desired, and we hailed with delight its avowal.   The French minister, Mr. Berthemy, agrees with us. Being a broad and experienced statesman, he at once saw the advantage that would flow from the casting down of all jealousies, and by a co-operation on every material question in China.   Indeed he has realized largely the advantages of such action; the French chargé d'affaires, before him, acting upon the old-school policy of antagonizing everybody, thus causing the Chinese to believe that we were divided among ourselves, for one year failed to get justice from the Chinese government, where it was due, in a case in which we were all interested.

The case was briefly this: A French priest with a passport was put to death with circumstances of unusual cruelty, by a high Chinese official in the province of Kweichan.   Satisfaction was demanded, but no result obtained.

The moment Mr. Berthemy came he frankly communicated the facts to his colleagues, who made common cause with him, and in a few weeks this question, menacing war under other arrangements, was settled, to the credit of Mr. Berthemy, and in the interests of all the treaty powers.

The policy upon which we are agreed is briefly this: that while we claim our treaty right to buy and sell, and hire, in the treaty ports, subject, in respect to our rights of property and person, to the jurisdiction of our own governments, we will not ask for, nor take concessions of, territory in the treaty ports, or in any way interfere with the jurisdiction of the Chinese government over its own people, nor ever menace the territorial integrity of the Chinese empire. That we will not take part in the internal struggles in China, beyond what is necessary to maintain our treaty rights. That the latter we will unitedly sustain against all who may violate them. To this end we are now clear in the policy of defending the treaty ports against the Taipings, or rebels; but in such a way as not to make war upon that considerable body of the Chinese people, by following them into the interior of their country. In this connexion, while we feel desirous, from what we know of it, to have the rebellion put down, still we have come to question the policy of lending government officers to lead the Chinese in the field, for fear of complications among ourselves, growing out of the relative number to be employed, &c. That while we wish to give our moral support to the government, at the present time the power in the country, which seems disposed to maintain order and our treaty rights, we should prefer that it would organize its own people, as far as possible, for its own defense, taking only foreigners for instruction in the arts of peace and war, and these, as far as possible, from the smaller treaty powers.

To maintain the revenue laws of the government, to relieve the treaty powers from the burdens attending the suppression of piracy along the coast, the Chinese government has been persuaded to purchase several small war steamers, and to man them temporarily with foreigners. This fleet is coming out under the command of Thervard Osburne, and is manned chiefly by English sailors, with the understanding that it is a temporary arrangement; and that, too, is to become cosmopolitan; and on the idea that we are to co-operate upon all questions in China, no special objection is made to the force by the other treaty powers. I confess that I should be pleased, were it more cosmopolitan now, but it was arranged before I came out, and before the above policy was developed and agreed upon.

While Sir Frederick Bruce shall remain, or while the policy now agreed upon shall be maintained, no harm can come from it.

That the indemnity may be collected and accounted for, and that the Chinese government may have a fund to maintain a national force, organized upon European principles; that the local authorities may be checked in their corrupt practices, and a uniform system for the collection of the revenue maintained, it is agreed on all hands that the present foreign custom-house system is the best as yet devised, and, as it has been administered by Mr. Lay, entitled to our support. Indeed it is alone through such instrumentalities that we can hope to advance in the cause of civilization in China. As Sir Frederick states, there can be nothing more unmeaning than antagonism between the United States and Great Britain in China. I need not attempt to prove the advantages which must flow from co-operation; that we should do so, all must admit. By the favored-nation clause in the treaties, no nation can gain, by any sharp act of diplomacy, any privilege not secured to all.

The circumstances conspires to make this a fortunate movement in which to inaugurate the co-operative policy.

The treaty powers are represented here by men of modern ideas; by men who, in this land, where everything is to be done, do not choose to embarrass each other by sowing distrust in the Chinese mind, but who, with an open policy and common action, deepen each other's confidence and win the respect of the Chinese. That the too sanguine hopes in relation to China of our more advanced civilization may be fully realized by an action we may take, ought not to be expected. The peculiar people we are among must be remembered; how hoary is their civilization, and how proud they are, and how ignorant of us they have always been, and how little their knowledge of some of us, has tended to create in their minds a desire for a change. Their government is good in theory, but not now well administered. The people are free to license, and, as in our own country, we find a portion of them in rebellion, because they have felt too little the influence of the central government.

The trouble here now is, that we are dealing with a regency which, in a few years, must hand over its doings to the Emperor and those he may call around him. The regency dare not depart in the smallest particular from the old traditions, and yet these will not do for these times. They are distrustful of us, and are afraid of their censors and distant local authorities. Besides, there is a large anti-foreign party here. There are members of the foreign board who, if left to themselves, would at once place China in perfect international relations with us; but sitting with them are spies, who paralyze them in their action with us, to fall, as they frequently do, far short of their promises. In their weakness they resort to tergiversations to such an extent as to invite menace, and to cause us, in our passionate modes, almost to despair of holding, with dignity, any relations at all with them. Our only hope is in forbearance and perfect union among ourselves; if these are maintained, and our government sustains us in the policy we have adopted, I cannot but be hopeful of the future, and feel that a great step has been taken in the right direction in China.

X

ESTABLISHING THE UNITED STATES LEGATION AT PEKING, 1862

Not until the conclusion of the Treaties of Tientsin (1858) did the Chinese government concede to the treaty powers the right of resident ministers at Peking. Problems which confronted the United States in establishing its legation in the exclusive capital of China were set forth ably by S. Wells Williams, secretary of legation, at the request of Minister Burlingame.

DIPLOMACY AT PEKING IN 1862. WILLIAMS TO BURLINGAME, PEKING, SEPTEMBER 15, 1862[1]

During the two months that the Legation has been in this city, I have learned enough to convince myself that it is desirable to establish it here, and take measures for its permanent location, like the legations of the three other leading treaty Powers; and in compliance with your request I place before you the chief reasons for forming such a conclusion. The details of the interviews which you have had with Prince Kung and the members of the Great Council who specially manage foreign affairs, need not be referred to further than as indicating, in their cordial expressions of good will towards the United States, the entire willingness of the Chinese Government to have the American minister reside here; and I believe that these expressions were as sincere as these officials, in their imperfect knowledge of all foreign relations, could make. It is the duty, and I hope the privilege too, of all who belong to the legations here, who have influence and opportunity, to enlighten these high officers in every point likely to aid them to a better discharge of their duties.

One point connected with the establishment of this Legation at Peking is the desirableness of our Government possessing a house of its own, a building where the archives can be kept, and the business devolving on the minister performed. I suppose that such a proposition is not fortified by any precedent; but the circumstances attending the Legation to China are unlike those of any other country, and should be considered on their own merits. Our position in this city is different from that of the English and French ministers, who accompanied the allied army in October 1860, and after the exchange of ratifications, desired the Chinese authorities to select suitable places for their respective legations. At that moment, the officials could probably have obtained almost any buildings for this purpose; but beyond those appropriated to public purposes, temples, and literary halls, few available spots were found. After some inquiry, two establishments near the Russian Legation were selected, consisting of several large edifices inclosed within a wall, most of them unoccupied and all of them in a dilapidated state, which had been originally

[1] *China Despatches*, Vol. XX, Incl. A in Burlingame's No. 25.

built for junior members of the Emperor's Kanghi's family more than 150 years ago, whose descendants had fallen into poverty, and been obliged to give up their original state and influence. Engineers were employed to alter and repair them at the expense of the English and French governments of more than forty thousand dollars each—little besides the walls, inclosures and roofs then remaining of the original structures. Besides the apartments designed for the minister and his suite, there are rooms for a dozen students, a guard of soldiers, and for visitors. The Russians have from time to time spent about the same amount altogether as the English, but their legation has not so much accommodation.

These three legations are designedly located near each other, so as to afford mutual support and council in case of difficulty and danger; and the reasons which induced the two late-comers to select places near the Russians act with stronger force to lead the Americans to take up their quarters near the three. When this legation reached Peking two months ago, we had no knowledge of the intentions of the Chinese officials as to offering it a residence; whether they would carry out the stipulations of Art. V. of the Treaty, which only contemplated a visit to their capital, and merely ask it to occupy a residence for a few months; or whether they expected it to take up a permanent residence and were ready to grant facilities to accomplish that end. Though notice of your coming had been sent to Prince Kung six weeks before arrival, nothing was made ready beforehand; but when the question was brought to the notice of the Foreign Office on arrival, the utmost readiness to assist us to a certain extent was exhibited. The same suite of buildings occupied by Mr. Ward [John E. Ward, of Georgia, who exchanged the ratified copy of the American Treaty of Tientsin] in 1859 was first proposed; it is in rather worse condition than then, having been somewhat neglected and misused, and was objected to for its contracted accommodations. Another establishment was then pointed out as being at our service, larger and in better order, and fully adequate in respect of arrangements and space to satisfy all our requirements. There is therefore nothing to complain of; the Chinese have carried out the provision of the treaty and aided in locating the Legation as far as we could expect. To fit up either of these dwellings, and make them comfortable and healthy, would require an outlay of several thousand dollars, for like all native houses, the windows are of paper, the floors of tiles and the rooms without fireplaces.

In considering these spots as suitable for our purpose, their distance from the other legations is the first objection which suggests itself when we think of constant intercourse; for in Peking a separation of nearly three miles is nearly equivalent to non-intercourse after sunset. To visit them at any time will not be an easy matter, and in times of danger assistance could be obtained only with great delay if not difficulty. I am informed that when the location of the English Legation was under discussion, the northern parts of the city near these two houses, were regarded as the healthiest and most accessible, but those advantages were waived for the sake of being near to the Russians. Few people go out after dark, the city gates are shut at twilight, no lamps light the passenger along the forsaken streets, and riding is hazardous through their centre. Social intercourse would be much restricted; and as the only foreign physician here resides near the English, medical assistance might sometimes arrive when it is too late.

More important than these domestic reasons is the defenselessness of our

Legation. The others, being near each other, can concert plans of common defense in case of trouble; and it is in view of such an emergency that the Allies now maintain a force at Taku, and would bring up a detachment as soon as it was necessary. Our remote position would justify them in refusing to detach a portion to protect us, and if we removed temporarily to their quarters, all would be crowded and uncomfortable. The sources and chances of trouble in Peking itself are not many at present, and the popular feeling towards foreigners, as well as towards the rulers, is favorable; but in case of investment by rebels (not a remote contingency) foreigners must depend entirely on themselves to resist assault and violence. If such a condition of things should arise, or famishing multitudes throng us, our position at the other end of the city would be doubly hazardous; and as merchants are not allowed to settle in it, there is no prospect of a community gradually gathering there.

The Chinese authorities appreciated these considerations when they were adduced to explain why we declined these houses, and wished a place near the other embassies. In a few days they designated four spots, all of them within a long half-mile of the French Legation. Three of them, however, are little better than open lots of a few acres area, for the buildings on them are mere sheds and storerooms for iron coin, and two or three dwelling-rooms for the overseers of the mints formerly worked within the inclosures, and are wholly unavailable in their present condition. All must be rebuilt under our guidance. The other place is a small dwelling-house, offered to us as an apology for aught better in this part of the city; and, though it can accommodate only a part of the Legation, can be made comfortable with a small outlay.

This is all the authorities are at present inclined to do; it is quite as much as we could ask of them under the circumstances; it is more, perhaps, than we should have asked of another nation.

The reasons for establishing the United States Legation at Peking had better be considered on their own merits in relation to our own position, than in reference to what the other Treaty Powers have done. Hitherto, the U. S. Minister, when in China itself, has always been domiciled in the houses of his countrymen—a course rendered almost imperative by the absence of proper public hotels at the open ports, the uncertainty of his stay, and the exigencies of the service requiring him to go from one port to another. The dwellings inhabited by foreigners at the ports are less in number than their requirements, and are not commonly rented; and thus a minister whose family was not with him (as has been usually the case) had no motive to open a house of his own, much less to build one. This state of things has been attended with many serious inconveniences. The archives and books of the Legation have either been left in the south of China, or the few volumes which were indispensible for the transaction of business, have been lugged about on ship and shore from one port to another in boxes, trunks and escritoires, greatly to their damage and risk. Most of this property has been kept in my own house at Canton or Macao since 1855, while the legation itself has been moved from Canton to Peking, along a coast of nearly 2000 miles. If former ministers had had a *locum tenens* they would probably have remained longer in China, and become better acquainted with its institutions and position, and thereby the better able to conduct the affairs of their mission.

In all parts of Eastern Asia, foreigners build their own houses sooner or later, for native dwellings are constructed on vicious principles in respect of ventilation, warmth, and lighting; it is about the same expense to build anew as to rearrange their rooms. In China, the foreign settlements present a striking contrast to the native town, for the people nowhere imitate our domestic architecture, and few foreigners can safely live in their damp and exposed rooms for a long time. The preparation of ample and suitable quarters at Peking is an enterprise which is not likely to be undertaken by any minister; it would involve an outlay far beyond his salary, and with no certainty that his successor would take the establishment off his hands.

It surely is a matter for our government to consider, in an empire where it has taken upon itself the responsibilities and duties of establishing a government over its own citizens, how far it will place the functionaries of that government in a well understood position, and support their authority in a manner compatible with its own dignity and efficiency. Heretofore the machinery of this inchoate government has been inadequate to carry it out—either to protect our citizens against the Chinese rulers or lawless insurgents; or, what is more needed just now, to restrain some of them in their unlawful and dangerous conduct towards the natives. I do not so much refer to the present withdrawal of our naval force from these waters in the exigencies of national affairs, as to the general fact that the protection and restraint of our citizens in these waters demands more action on our part than has ever been the case. The obligations of the last Treaty involve the consolidation of a stronger control, for which the Act of 1860 furnishes the basis; and we cannot, as a nation, well avoid the duties therein assumed. Our national character has already suffered by neglecting these duties, much to the chagrin of those who are jealous of its purity.

By settling the Legation at Peking, the minister puts himself in direct and personal relation with the high authorities of the empire; he can suggest, explain, remonstrate or refuse, according to the circumstances of the case, and without the unsatisfactory delay of writing, expediting every part of the public business far more than elsewhere. This point needs no further argument. The advantages now enjoyed for acting on the Chinese government (advantages which we owe to the Allied Powers) are daily becoming more and more evident, and their influence must increase rather than diminish. The objects of the French in China differ from those of the English, and both more or less from those of the Russians; our's harmonize rather with the English in the protection and development of commerce; but all equally desire to see a strong and intelligent government established, if possible, and as far [as] one can now see are willing to cooperate to the promotion of that end. The efficient performance of his duties by our own minister at this capital would be much weakened by his living in the poor way he will for the present take up with; since the Chinese authorities would tardily attend the demands of a functionary who exhibited in his own house all the indicia of comparative poverty and weakness. Mere show of itself is not necessary, tho it goes for not a little, but the display of a certain extent of resources is desirable to impress upon the people and rulers that the United States is a nation able to take care of itself. The dispersion of the members of the Legation in two or three small dwellings entails inconveniences in the transaction of business which cannot be avoided; and as already hinted, times may come when marines and sailors may be necessary for their protection, and where can they be lodged?

All these considerations occur to me to strengthen the argument for a single establishment large enough to contain all and serve these requirements.

I would respectfully suggest, that what is needed is a grant of $25,000 to build or purchase a suitable Legation, to be owned by the Government of the United States, and regarded by the Minister as his appropriate residence. No Chinese will ever fit up such a place in expectation of its being rented from him; the minister cannot do more than keep it in repair and furnish it while he occupies it. So far as I can see, there is no other means of attaining this object than for the Government to make the initial outlay, and that seems now to be all that is required.

Furthermore it will soon become indispensible for our Government to take measures to provide interpreters for the consulates; and the students can best learn the language and character of the Chinese in their metropolis. I cannot forbear here to refer to the humiliating shifts our consuls are often put to for want of interpreters in their intercourse with the Chinese authorities. They cannot speak or write a word of the language themselves, and are obliged to ask favors at other consulates or of missionaries, or take up with the interpretation of a native whose proficiency in English is exhibited in such phraseology as, "You talkee my, my can so fashion talkee he." Three of the consulates have interpreters indeed, but if we are to have qualified scholars they must be educated for their functions; the present state of things is derogatory to our national character, and can be remedied only by the same means that other foreign nations adopt. There are fourteen students now in the three legations here, who will soon be qualified for consular assistants at the ports.

Let me also refer to the extent of our trade with China as a reason for placing the Legation on a suitable footing. Its amount is next to that of the English, and will probably increase more rapidly in proportion after the Pacific railroad is opened. Our countrymen in China think it discreditable that a nation carrying on a commerce amounting to many millions annually, should not place its public functionaries on a par with even a second class merchant at the ports. Hitherto, the minister has been accommodated in a makeshift manner among them, but the location of his embassy at Peking will require some outlay to make it worthy of the country. Merchants being forbidden to settle here, will yet desire to visit the city; naval officers and travelers will also come, and all will naturally look to be received under their country's flag.

The present may be an inopportune moment to apply to Congress for such a grant, when our beloved country is involved in a life struggle that demands all her resources; but it cannot be improper to represent this matter to the Government, and show the desirableness—yea, the necessity—of doing something to place its officers in Peking on a better footing. The Chinese are aware of the struggle going on in our midst; and tho they are too ignorant of its causes to feel sympathy for either party, they can appreciate the reasons furnished thereby for delay in building on the lot. A year or two would not be an overlong period within which to carry out the plans here suggested.

CONVERSATIONS BETWEEN BURLINGAME AND THE CHINESE FOREIGN OFFICE, 1865

DURING the early months of 1865, prior to his departure for the United States on leave of absence, Burlingame met on several occasions with Prince Kung and other members of the Chinese Foreign Office. These conversations, reported by Dr. W. A. P. Martin, an American missionary and educator already distinguished as the translator of the Chinese edition of Wheaton's *International Law,* suggest the character of Burlingame's relationship with the Chinese. Their effects on Secretary Seward's policy are also illustrated.

INTERVIEW BETWEEN PRINCE KUNG AND MR. BURLINGAME AT THE CHINESE FOREIGN OFFICE. PEKING, MARCH 3, 1865[1]

MR. BURLINGAME. In taking leave of your Highness, it is pleasant to recollect the kindness and the confidence with which I have been treated by your government since my residence among you.

PRINCE KUNG. It is not without sincere regret that we part with one whom we have found to be our true friend, and I cannot refrain from asking is it necessary that you should leave us? Are you recalled by the authority of your sovereign?

MR. BURLINGAME. I am going home on temporary leave.

PRINCE KUNG. O, then we may expect to see you back again. Your President has a second term, and you ought to have another; as the books say, we like to change our clothes, but not our friends.

MR. BURLINGAME. I certainly would return if I thought I could render your government any signal service.

PRINCE KUNG. But we will take no denial. We wish you to pledge yourself to return to us. If you are willing to resume your mission, you will join me in draining a glass in token of consent. (Mr. Burlingame, after a brief pause, takes the glass.) The covenant is ratified; friends are not allowed to forget a promise sealed by a glass of wine.

MR. BURLINGAME. Perhaps, in my absence, I may serve you as effectually as I could if I were here.

PRINCE KUNG. We have been indebted to you on many occasions, and especially with regard to the English flotilla.

CONVERSATION (BURLINGAME AND MEMBERS OF THE CHINESE FOREIGN OFFICE), UNITED STATES LEGATION. PEKING, MARCH 6, 1865[2]

The day being slightly overcast, Prince Kung supposed it would be unsuitable for taking a sun picture, and deferred his visit until the next day.

[1] *Foreign Relations,* 1865, Pt. 2, No. 112, p. 447.
[2] *Ibid.,* pp. 447-448.

At an early hour, however, Tung-Seun came in; somewhat late he was joined by Hangkee and Chunlun. Before the arrival of the two last Mr. Burlingame gave Tung Ta-jen a few hints for the benefit of his government.

In the event, he said, of difficulties arising between the Chinese government and any representative of a foreign power, there were two methods by which they might be prevented from issuing in serious consquences:

1. To make sure that they were in the right, and then to send copies of the whole correspondence to each of the other resident ministers, with a request that it might be published in their respective countries. The fear of public opinion would prove a wholesome safeguard against violent or unjustifiable proceedings.

2. To send a diplomatic mission to the west. Both of these Mr. Burlingame illustrated with considerable detail, and Tung Ta-jen appeared to appreciate their value.

In regard to the last, he remarked that his government is convinced of the necessity of sending envoys to western nations, and that some of the youth in the government school now receiving instruction from Tien Sien Hang (Dr. Martin) were expected to become qualified for serving as interpreters and secretaries to such embassies. Mr. Burlingame closed the conversation on this topic by wishing Tung the good fortune to be appointed chief of the first embassy to the western world. Certain it is that few among its great officials would represent the empire with more intelligence or dignity, or be more disposed to profit by what they might see in foreign lands.

Tung has taken a leading part in promoting the publication of Dr. Martin's translation of Wheaton's International Law, and gave its pages the benefit of his own finished scholarship. On this occasion, when three mandarins sat for their photographs, Tung held in his hand a volume of the Chinese Wheaton, apparently ambitious of having his name associated with this work.

TUNG TA-JEN. You will be able to speak a word in our behalf, and correct misapprehensions that may exist concerning us in the countries through which you pass.

WEUSIANG. An impression seems to have gone abroad that we treat the envoys of foreign powers with a want of consideration. You will be able to testify that we heap on them all the attention which it is possible for us to bestow on our most honored guests.

THE NONTECHNICAL POLICY OF SECRETARY SEWARD. SECRETARY SEWARD TO S. WELLS WILLIAMS, WASHINGTON, D. C., AUGUST 14, 1865[3]

SIR: Mr. Burlingame's despatch, No. 112, submitting an account of his interviews with Prince Kung and other members of the foreign board, has been received.

The President of the United States desires to make known his satisfaction with the very just, liberal, and friendly sentiments expressed by Prince Kung and his associates of the foreign board at these interviews.

The government of the United States is not disposed to be technical or exacting in its intercourse with the Chinese government, but will deal with it with entire frankness, cordiality, and friendship. The United States desire neither to interfere with the distinct and ancient habits and customs of the Chinese people, nor to embarrass the members of the foreign board in their difficult and responsible labors. While insisting always upon rights stipulated

[3] *Ibid.*, No. 151, p. 461.

in solemn treaties, the wish of this government is to promote that esteem which will conduce to the mutual advantage of both nations.

The President also desires to express his satisfaction with the attention and courtesies which were shown to Mr. Burlingame previous to his departure from Peking. They are regarded by the President as a just compliment to the services of our minister, and at the same time an evidence of good will to the nation he represents.

Seward Proposes a Chinese Minister to the United States. Seward to Burlingame, Washington, December 15, 1865[4]

Sir: The harmonious condition of the relations between the United States and China, and the importance of the commerce between them, would make it agreeable to this government to receive from the Emperor a diplomatic representative of a grade corresponding with your own. It is true that this would be a novel, if not an unprecedented step, on the part of that government. As treaties, however, have for many years been in force between China and Christian nations; and as the empire may now be disposed to respect the obligations of public law, it strikes us that the Emperor's government would be consulting their own interest, and would also be reciprocating that which, to a degree, at least, is a courtesy on our part, by having a diplomatic agent here, whose province it would be to see that our obligations toward China, under the treaties and law of nations, are fulfilled, and who might report to his government upon that and other interesting topics. China also may be said to have special reasons for the measure in respect to the United States, as her subjects are so numerous in this country, particularly in California. You will consequently bring this matter to the attention of that government, and may say that, if the suggestion should be adopted, it would be peculiarly gratifying to the President.

[4] *Foreign Relations,* 1866-67, Pt. 1, No. 156, p. 487.

XII

THE DILEMMA OF TREATY ENFORCEMENT, 1866

THE FULL enforcement of the treaties, particularly in the matter of the protection of foreign lives and property, was at times a problem beyond the control of the Chinese government, even in cases where that government recognized its obligations and wished to carry them into effect. The following dispatch from S. Wells Williams to Secretary Seward illustrates some of the problems involved. In this case the American vice-consul at Niuchwang (Newchwang) in southern Manchuria, a port open to foreign trade by the Treaties of Tientsin (1858), had requested that he be supplied by the legation with arms and ammunition with which the American community of the port might protect itself from armed ruffians. The request was referred to Washington and approved.

ATTACKS UPON AMERICANS IN MANCHURIA. WILLIAMS TO SECRETARY SEWARD, PEKING, MAY 21, 1866[1]

I have the honor to send you a correspondence with Mr. Knight at Niuchwang. . . .

The part of China where Niuchwang lies has long been infested with bands of mounted robbers, whose depredations have become so serious as to render nugatory all law, and cause the Imperial family and Manchu nobility some anxiety as to their sway over their paternal inheritance. The population has become more assimilated to other parts of Northern China by the immigration of Chinese during many years past, whose superior industry and thrift over the native Manchus give it much of its prosperity. Their influence is shown, too, in the fact that their language has almost supplanted the Manchu language as the common speech. The government of this wide region is still administered on a military basis, but the Chinese have little part in it and hold few offices. This would cause them little regret if they could be protected; but, on the contrary, life and property are both of light account, and many of the immigrants are almost forced to join the robbers.

The cabinet minister Wansiang went to the Capital Mukden last autumn to examine the state of affairs. Three or four thousand foreign drilled troops have been sent to aid him, and it is now reported that they have at last obtained a victory, killing 700 or more of the banditti. The swordracks are of the same class, and the plan referred to by Mr. Knight of employing such brigands to aid in keeping the peace, is a common device with craven officials all over China; and does much to exasperate, impoverish and demoralize their subjects, and egg them on to rebellion. The check on this policy is found

[1] *China Despatches*, Vol. XXIII, No. 33.

in the literati and landed gentry, whose united influence countenances and aids the industrious classes to join in plans to resist violence; but the evil is often beyond their powers, and anarchy over-rides the whole region, until stronger force can be brought from abroad, as in this instance, to suppress the lawless.

It is not surprising that foreigners should be sometimes involved in these internal troubles; and if we expect that the Chinese authorities at such times will always wish or dare to protect us, it is likely that we shall be disappointed. They readily assent that the treaties require them to afford us all the protection in their power, but as individuals, they may have their own opinion about the expediency or possibility of doing much for us against their countrymen; or, as at Niuchwang, sometimes may have no reliable or adequate force to help them.

During the past winter, the community in that port have drilled themselves under the guidance of the British consul, and the knowledge that they were preparing for an emergency has prevented, it is not unlikely, an attack. But the temptation of treasure and property of various kinds, guarded by only a few persons, may some day prove too strong, and the whole foreign settlement be swept away. The probability of such a catastrophe at present is not imminent; but the fact that the local authorities are not always able to protect our citizens, and our men-of-war may not be at hand at the time, forms my present argument for making the inquiry of the Department, whether drafts made upon it for arms and ammunition to defend them in such cases, would be honored. If the Legation has control of the outlay, it will not be excessive; and if the weapons afterwards should not be needed, they can be sold. Americans have heretofore been more indebted for their safety in China to the measures taken by the English for their defense, than is good policy.

It should be borne in mind, too, that while the treaties place us beyond the jurisdiction of Chinese laws, and we do nothing for the support of the government, their stipulations require that Government to afford us full protection against injury, both from seditious natives and unprincipled officials. The first treaties were extorted at the cannon's mouth, and may be distasteful not only to the officers who negotiated them; but—what is more important—so far beyond the ideas of the people at large, that their rulers become discouraged in trying to carry them out. The treaties thus become like great charters of civilization and Christianity, and we have need to exercise forbearance and patience while educating a pagan and ignorant people up to their requirements. Yet the principle of exterritoriality contained in them, like the egg of the ichneumon-fly in a caterpillar, is likely to destroy the autonomy of this Government, unless its development is sedulously watched. Meanwhile, the strongest party often interprets treaty stipulations in its own favor when a doubt arises; and natives are always too ready to side with the strongest when advantageous to themselves.

It is the earnest desire of all foreign powers, I do not doubt, and of their representatives in China, to strengthen the Emperor's government in its authority, and encourage the people to look to their own rulers for their safety; but the latter have had too long experience of wrong and oppression, or are too ready to cheat and oppose them, to look to their rulers if foreigners can help them. Neither can the inertness and ignorance of the rulers be removed until a new set arises, a new generation which shall have learned new ideas. It is well for the Chinese people, and indeed all Asiatics, that they have models before them in Western lands of the workings of free governments, and have not to work out the problems that Europeans have solved since 1500. However, if the workings of the treaties bring benefits with them, which on the whole is the case, the future of China is still one of promise; though the urgency of foreigners to hasten the adoption of railroads, telegraphs, and other improvements, before the people can appreciate their uses, or the rulers provide for the details, may over do the power of native institutions.

I have been led into these remarks in order to explain at length the position of Mr. Knight in asking for aid to defend himself and American interests at Niuchwang, as there is a propriety in it which will, I hope, appear to you; and the same exigency may at any time occur at Chifu, Taiwan, or elsewhere. I have reason for believing that the "Wachusett" is at Niuchwang (or Yingtsz, the port) by this time, so that there is no present danger.

XIII

THE CHINESE COOLIE TRADE, 1866-1867

THE CHINESE coolie trade, a traffic in human life and labor, conducted principally from South China to Cuba and Peru, was, during the middle decades of the nineteenth century, a hideous stigma on many of the foreigners who frequented the ports of China, and upon the Chinese agents who dealt in human flesh. At Hong Kong the worst features of the traffic were prevented through government regulation. In 1862 the United States forbade Americans to engage in the trade. These restrictive measures only served to concentrate and further brutalize the traffic at the Portuguese controlled port of Macao. Its barbarities are suggested in the following dispatches from S. Wells Williams and Burlingame at a time when the Chinese government was attempting to control the trade by regulation. The Portuguese government abolished finally the coolie trade at Macao in 1874.

THE CHARACTER OF THE COOLIE TRADE. WILLIAMS TO SECRETARY SEWARD, PEKING, APRIL 3, 1866[1]

I have the honor to transmit to you a dispatch from Prince Kung (Inc. A) [inclosures not printed] covering a copy of a set of Regulations (Inc. B.), which have been agreed upon between him and the representatives of Great Britain and France, to prescribe the mode of hiring Chinese laborers to go abroad. The English and French versions are both inclosed. In my reply (Inc. C.) I have mentioned the law of Feb. 19, 1862, which I am almost sure is the only ordinance on this subject in the statute book of any nation, as the reason for not notifying them to our countrymen. I may also add, that before they appeared, Baron Rehfues, the Prussian Minister to China, had refused to allow Prussian vessels to carry coolies pending a reference to Berlin.

The history of the coolie traffic, since 1849, when the Peruvians came to Canton to get laborers to dig guano on the Chinchas Is., is a sad result of the foreign intercourse which has been forced upon China and its people. In carrying it on, the most flagitious acts have been committed by the natives upon each other, under the stimulus of rewards offered by foreigners to bring them coolies; while the character of all foreigners has been covered with infamy among the inhabitants of Canton province, especially in the rural districts. The cruel treatment suffered by many of these deceived people in the barracoons to force them to sign contracts and embark, is too well

[1] *China Despatches*, Vol. XXIII, No. 27.

authenticated to be doubted; and especially has this evidence deepened the opprobrium which has fastened upon Macao as the place where the worst deeds were done. In 1859, the terror of kidnappers was so great among the natives in that city and neighborhood, that they durst not venture abroad by night; and I printed a small tract for circulation in that region, warning the people of the wiles practiced to entrap them "like pigs in a basket." Out of the cargoes which have left Macao during the last fifteen years, consisting mostly of men between the ages of 18 to 30 years, only a few scores have returned.

The records of this Legation contain so many statements going to prove these remarks, that I need not enlarge. Since 1861, less has been written to the Department, partly because our flag has not been used; and partly, because the trade itself dwindled to a few ships carrying the coolies to Peru, Trinidad, and Cuba, during the civil war in the United States. It has revived within the last fifteen months, especially to Cuba. In the year 1859, emigration offices were established by the provincial authorities in Kwangtung province to protect the lives and rights of their people emigrating as laborers; but a large majority of the coolies have gone from Macao, where the delay, expense and surveillance which attended their engagements in the emigration offices were greatly diminished or avoided, so that the laudable efforts of Chinese rulers were in a great measure neutralized. All those taken to English colonies, (chiefly to Trinidad) have, I believe been engaged in the emigration offices; but the enterprise of thus supplying labor there is said not to pay, though the emigrants and their families are reported to be satisfied with their lot.

The failure to effect the exchange of the ratifications of the treaty with Portugal in 1864, has apparently led the Macao authorities to put the settlement in a state of defense; but the Chinese have no wish to provoke hostilities. However, being unable to exercise any supervision over the emigration thence, they disallow it altogether in these Regulations; and I hope their people will soon learn that it is illegal, and that erelong the supply will be altogether cut off. No coolies have been shipped from Hongkong for several years; indeed, it is well understood in all that region, that emigrants go from Hongkong, and coolies from Macao.

I am somewhat skeptical how far these Regulations will prevent the evils now complained of, until a year or so of trial has proven whether the energy of those who make gain by the traffic will not overcome the remedial measures now to go into immediate operation. Even the most disinterested officials cannot at once remove the ignorance which is imposed upon by specious tales, or the poverty which is tempted by the bounty offered; and, after all, these two facts—poverty and ignorance—underlie the whole business, and are worked upon by crafty agents to fill their own pockets. Yet I think it altogether probable that the largest proportion of the coolies go willingly, though stupidly ignorant where they are going, and what they are to do.

My expectation is, however, that; though other flags can be obtained to carry on the trade from Macao, the Portuguese authorities will not persistently set themselves against these reasonable rules to protect every emigrant leaving his native land as a hired laborer.

I am indebted to the British Minister for a copy of his dispatch accompanying the Regulations (Inc. D.), which he furnished me at my request. Its perusal will repay you, especially the remarks on the appointment of consuls from China to countries with which she has treaties. Such a functionary would do much to reconcile the laborer to his new condition, by sending letters and funds home, interpreting for and counseling him in cases of accusation for crime, aiding him to return to his friends, &c. It seems to me to be quite plain that the Chinese Government has a reciprocal right to appoint consuls, but I respectfully request your instructions upon this point, as it is unlikely to come up after the return of Pin-tajin. Almost all the treaties stipulate for the reception of ministers from the Emperor of China, but none of them specially mention consuls; yet the lesser privilege is doubtless involved in the greater.

I regard these Regulations as an index of progress. They show some solicitude for the welfare of subjects who have gone abroad; and form the first recognition from the Emperor that his people emigrating to other lands are not expatriated or forgotten. If carried out honestly, the obloquy heretofore attendant upon the trade, and the bad reputation of the foreign name, will both soon cease.

If Congress sees proper to repeal the law of 1862, laborers could be taken to California, where railroads and other public works will demand thousands of hands to complete them; though, if high wages and good treatment were offered, as many free emigrants might go as were needed.

.   .   .   .

DIFFICULTIES IN SUPPRESSING THE COOLIE TRADE. BURLINGAME TO SECRETARY SEWARD, PEKING, MARCH 13, 1867[2]

It is found that the regulations (see Dr. Williams' despatch No. 27,) adopted on the 5th of March, 1866, by the British, French, and Chinese Governments in relation to the Coolie trade do not meet the just expectations of those who hoped to find in them a sufficient check to the rigors of that trade.

They were proposed by M. de Bellonet, French Chargé d'Affaires, and approved by Sir Rutherford Alcock, British Minister, and the Chinese Government, to prevent abuses and to render, if possible, the Coolie trade less infamous; but these intentions have been defeated by the anomalous position of Macao and the conduct of the Portuguese Officials. The sovereignty over Macao is claimed by the Chinese but held by the Portuguese, and it was a difference of opinion upon this subject which prevented the ratification of the treaty in 1864. The agents of the Coolie trade, driven by the stringency of the Regulations from the Chinese ports, have found protection at Macao, which has now become the centre of the business. I learn from a letter by Mr. de Mas, the Spanish Minister, now at Macao, that there are now at that place six agents from Peru and ten from Havana; that there are also thirty Barracoons and offices; and that during the last monsoon, from the first of October to the first of April there were sent to Cuba alone, mostly from Macao, 13,500 (thirteen thousand and five hundred) Coolies, in forty vessels, thirty of which were French at an expense of from $2,800,000 (two million eight hundred thousand dollars) to $3,000,000 (three million dollars). The Regulations have been rendered useless also by the action of the French Government, which, when M. de Bellonet forbade French agents and vessels from engaging in the Coolie trade from Macao, overruled him and caused a notice (Inclosure A.) to that effect to be issued by the French Consul at

[2] *Ibid.*, Vol. XXIV, No. 130.

Hongkong. Beyond the difficulty created at Macao it may be suggested that the Regulations themselves carry the seeds of slavery in the right given to agents to persuade the Chinese to sell his labor for five years. This contract amounts to a practical selling of the man himself, and if permitted or encouraged by the Governments cannot but result in a species of slavery. It is this contract, procured by unscrupulous agents pandering to the cupidity of planters in Cuba, and guano merchants in Peru, which distinguishes the Coolie trade from legitimate emigration. The Russian Government has refused to agree to the Regulations, in the following language: "the Imperial Government of Russia considers that the admission of Regulations, which will define the powers of emigration agents among the Chinese population, will not probably be able to secure the rights of those, who, being in a state of extreme poverty, decide to deliver themselves up entirely to Foreign speculators": and forbids entirely the Coolie trade. The Prussian Minister has written to his Government in the same sense. We stand on our noble law of 1862 (U. S. Statutes at large, Vol. 12, p. 340) which prohibits the Coolie trade while it permits legitimate emigration. The Chinese Government has a right to make these Regulations and as far as they are necessary in addition to our own laws for the protection of proper emigration we are wise in requiring our officials to conform to them. This is the sense of your instructions contained in despatch No. 170, and does in no wise make our Government a party to the Regulations. The Chinese Government desires very much to have the Treaty Powers exercise their moral influence upon Portugal, against the conduct of her officials at Macao, as well as to agree among themselves to forbid the Coolie trade. I had a long interview with the Chinese Officials at the Foreign Office a few days since in relation to these subjects. The Chinese Government does not wish to prevent emigration, but wishes to break up the Coolie trade, and I hope the Treaty Powers will unite for the same object. To strengthen our position, already strong, I would suggest the appointment of a commissioner of Chinese immigration at San Francisco, California, to whom all shippers of emigrants should be required to report, and whose duty it should be to protect the emigrants upon their arrival and facilitate their efforts to procure employment. I fear that now they are largely a prey to sharpers, particularly among their own countrymen.

This officer should be a man of the most elevated character. On the Atlantic side we are already provided with officers to look after the welfare of immigrants. I have reason to believe that the emigration from China to California will be large, and that it will be of a different character from that hitherto known. I have urged all with whom I have come in contact to treat the Chinese well. The agents of the Pacific Mail Steamship Company have responded warmly in favor of such treatment, and have informed me that no blow shall be struck against a Chinese on board of their Steamers.

THE STATUS OF AMERICAN-CHINESE RELATIONS, 1868

RELATIONS between the United States and China during 1867-68 were most cordial. Anson Burlingame had been selected by China to head China's diplomatic mission to the Western Powers. His oratory in New York pictured a China eager to enter fully into the Western family of nations. The Seward-Burlingame Treaty, signed at Washington in July, 1868, breathed an amity not frequently found in legal documents. In Article VIII the United States disclaimed "any intention or right to intervene in the domestic administration of China in regard to the construction of railroads, telegraphs, or other material internal improvements." It appeared therefore that the United States would refrain from pressing for those very "improvements" which the foreign commercial community in China hoped would result from the contemplated revision of the treaties. Later developments, however, were to indicate that the Seward-Burlingame Treaty was not to be interpreted as a renunciation of well-established American policy.

ENCOURAGEMENT TO IMMIGRANT LABORERS. SEWARD TO DIPLOMATIC AND CONSULAR OFFICERS, WASHINGTON, AUGUST 8, 1862[1]

At no former period of our history have our agricultural, manufacturing or mining interests been more prosperous than at this juncture. This fact may be deemed surprising in view of the enhanced price for labor, occasioned by the demand for the rank and file of the armies of the United States. It may, therefore, be confidently asserted that, even now, nowhere else can the industrious laboring man and artisan expect so liberal a recompense for his services as in the United States. You are authorized and directed to make these truths known in any quarter and in any way which may lend to the migration of such persons to this country. It is believed that a knowledge of them will alone suffice to cause them to be acted upon. The government has no legal authority to offer any pecuniary inducements to the advent of industrious foreigners.

[1] *China Instructions*, Vol. I, Cir. No. 19.

ADDRESS BY ANSON BURLINGAME. DELIVERED IN NEW YORK, JUNE 23, 1868[2]

You have given a broad and generous welcome to a movement made in the interests of all mankind. We are but the humble heralds of the movement. It originated beyond the boundaries of our own thoughts and has taken dimensions beyond the reach of our most ardent hopes. That East, which men have sought since the days of Alexander now itself seeks the West. China, emerging from the mists of time but yesterday suddenly entered your Western gates, and confronts you by its representatives here to-night. What have you to say to her? She comes with no menace on her lips. She comes with the great doctrine of Confucius, uttered two thousand three hundred years ago, "Do not unto others what you would not have others do unto you." Will you not respond with the more positive doctrine of Christianity, "We will do unto others what we would have others do unto us?" She comes with your own international law; she tells you that she is willing to come into relations according to it, that she is willing to abide by its provisions, that she is willing to take its obligations for its privileges. She asks you to forget your ancient prejudices, to abandon your assumptions of superiority, and to submit your questions with her, as she proposes to submit her questions with you—to the arbitrament of reason. She wishes no war; she asks of you not to interfere in her internal affairs. She asks of you not to send her lecturers who are incompetent men. She asks you that you will respect the neutrality of her waters and the integrity of her territory. She asks, in a word, to be left perfectly free to unfold herself precisely in that form of civilisation of which she is most capable. She asks you to give to those treaties which were made under the pressure of war a generous and Christian construction. Because you have done this, because the Western nations have reversed their old doctrine of force, she responds, and in proportion as you have expressed your goodwill, she has come forth to meet you; and I aver, that there is no spot on earth where there has been greater progress made within the past few years than in the Empire of China. She has expanded her trade, she has reformed her revenue system, she is changing her military and naval organisations, she has built or established a great school where modern science and the foreign languages are to be taught. She has done this under every adverse circumstance. She has done this after a great war lasting through thirteen years, a war out of which she comes with no national debt. You must remember how dense is her population. You must remember how difficult it is to introduce radical changes in such a country as that. The introduction of your own steamers threw out of employment a hundred thousand junkmen. The introduction of several hundred foreigners into the civil service embittered, of course, the ancient native employees. The establishment of a school was formidably resisted by a party led by one of the greatest men of the empire. Yet, in defiance of all these, the present enlightened Government of China has advanced steadily along the path of progress, sustained, it is true, by the enlightened representatives of the Western powers now at Peking, guided and directed largely by a modest and able man, Mr. Hart, the inspector-general of customs, at the head of the foreign employees in the Empire of China. . . . Yet, notwithstanding this manifest progress there are people who will tell you that China has made no progress, that her views are retrograde; and they tell you that it is the duty of the

[2] Quoted by F. W. Williams, *Anson Burlingame* (New York: Charles Scribner's Sons, 1912), pp. 134-139. Printed with the permission of the publishers.

Western treaty powers to combine for the purpose of coercing China into reforms which they may desire and which she may not desire—who undertake to say that this people have no rights which you are bound to respect. In their coarse language they say, "Take her by the throat." Using the tyrant's plea, they say they know better what China wants than China herself does. Not only do they desire to introduce now the reforms born of their own interests and their own caprices, but they tell you that the present dynasty must fall, and that the whole structure of Chinese civilisation must be overthrown. I know that these views are abhorred by the governments and the countries from which these people come; but they are far away from their countries, they are active, they are brave, they are unscrupulous, and if they happen to be officials, it is in their power to complicate affairs and to involve, ultimately, their distant countries in war. Now it is against the malign spirit of this tyrannical element that this Mission was sent forth to the Christian world. It was sent forth that China might have her difficulties stated. That I happened to be at the head of it was, perhaps, more an accident than any design. It was, perhaps, because I had been longer there than any of my colleagues, and because I was about to leave; and perhaps, more than all, because I was associated with the establishment of the co-operative policy which by the aid of abler men than myself was established not many years ago; and it is to sustain that policy—which has received the warm approval of all the great treaty powers, and which is cherished by China—that we are sent forth. It is in behalf of that generous policy, founded on principles of eternal justice, that I would rally the strongest thing on earth, the enlightened public opinion of the world. Missions and men may pass away, but the principles of eternal justice will stand. I desire that the autonomy of China may be preserved. I desire that her independence may be secured. I desire that she may have equality, that she may dispense equal privileges to all nations. If the opposite school is to prevail, if you are to use coercion against that great people, then who are to exercise the coercion, whose force are you to use, whose views are you to establish? You see the very attempt to carry out any such tyrannical policy would involve not only China, but would involve you in bloody wars with each other. There are men—men of that tyrannical school—who say that China is not fit to sit at the council board of the nations, who call her people barbarians, and attack them on all occasions with a bitter and unrelenting spirit. These things I utterly deny. I say, on the contrary, that that is a great, a noble people. It has all the elements of a splendid nationality. It is the most numerous people on the face of the globe; it is the most homogeneous people in the world; it has a language spoken by more human beings than any other in the world, and it is written in the rock. It is a country where there is greater unification of thought than any other country in the world. It is a country where the maxims of great sages, coming down memorised for centuries, have permeated the whole people, until their knowledge is rather an instinct than an acquirement; a people loyal while living, and whose last prayer, when dying, is to sleep on the sacred soil of their fathers. . . .

China, seeing another civilisation approaching on every side, has her eyes wide open. She sees Russia on the north, Europe on the west, America on the east. She sees a cloud of sail on her coast, she sees the mighty steamers coming from everywhere—bowon. She feels the spark from the electric telegraph falling hot upon her everywhere; she rouses herself, not in anger, but for argument. She finds that by not being in a position to compete with other nations for so long a time she has lost ground. She finds that she must come into relations with this civilisation that is pressing up around her, and feeling that, she does not wait but comes out to you and extends to you her hand. She tells you she is ready to take upon her ancient civilisation the graft of your civilisation. She tells you she is ready to take back her own inventions, with all their developments. She tells you that she is willing to trade with you, to buy of you, to sell to you, to help you strike off the shackles from trade. She invites your merchants, she invites your missionaries. She tells the latter to plant the shining cross on every hill and in every valley. For she is hospitable to fair argument. . . .

Let her alone; let her have her independence; let her develop herself in her own time and in her own way. She has no hostility to you. Let her do this, and she will initiate a movement which will be felt in every workshop of the civilised world. She says now: "Send us your wheat, your lumber, your coal, your silver, your goods from everywhere—we will take as many of them as we can. We will give you back our tea, our silk, free labour, which we have sent so largely out into the world." It has overflowed upon Siam, upon the British provinces, upon Singapore, upon Manila, upon Peru, Cuba, Australia, and California. All she asks is that you will be as kind to her nationals as she is to your nationals. She wishes simply that you will do justice. She is willing not only to exchange goods with you, but she is willing to exchange thoughts. She is willing to give you what she thinks is her intellectual civilisation in exchange for your material civilisation. Let her alone, and the caravans on the roads of the north, towards Russia, will swarm in larger numbers than ever before. Let her alone, and that silver which has been flowing for hundreds of years into China, losing itself like the lost rivers of the West, but which yet exists, will come out into the affairs of men. . . . The imagination kindles at the future which may be, and which will be, if you will be fair and just to China.

THE UNITED STATES AND CHINA. TREATY OF TRADE, CONSULS, AND EMIGRA-
TION, JULY 4, 1868[3]

ARTICLES.

I. Jurisdiction over land in China.
II. Regulation of commerce.
III. Chinese consuls.
IV. Religious freedom.
V. Voluntary emigration.
VI. Privileges of travel and residence.
VII. Education.
VIII. Internal improvements in China.

Whereas since the conclusion of the treaty between the United States of America and the Ta-Tsing Empire, (China) of the 18th of June, 1858, circumstances have arisen showing the necessity of additional articles thereto, the President of the United States and the August Sovereign of the Ta-Tsing Empire, have named for their Plenipotentiaries, to wit: The President of the United States of America, William H. Seward, Secretary of State, and His Majesty the Emperor of China, Anson Burlingame, accredited as his Envoy

[3] U. S. Compilation of Treaties in Force, pp. 115-118.

Extraordinary and Minister Plenipotentiary, and Chih-Kang and Sun Chia-Ku, of the second Chinese rank, associated High Envoys and Ministers of his said Majesty; and the said Plenipotentiaries, after having exchanged their full powers, found to be in due and proper form, have agreed upon the following Articles:

ARTICLE I.

His Majesty the Emperor of China, being of the opinion that, in making concessions to the citizens or subjects of foreign powers of the privilege of residing on certain tracts of land, or resorting to certain waters of that Empire for purposes of trade, he has by no means relinquished his right of eminent domain or dominion over the said land and waters, hereby agrees that no such concession or grant shall be construed to give to any power or party which may be at war with or hostile to the United States the right to attack the citizens of the United States or their propery within the said lands or waters. And the United States, for themselves, hereby agree to abstain from offensively attacking the citizens or subjects of any power or party or their property with which they may be at war on any such tract of land or waters of the said Empire. But nothing in this article shall be construed to prevent the United States from resisting an attack by any hostile power or party upon their citizens or their property.

It is further agreed that if any right or interest in any tract of land in China has been or shall hereafter be granted by the Government of China to the United States or their citizens for purposes of trade or commerce, that grant shall in no event be construed to divest the Chinese authorities of their right of jurisdiction over persons and property within said tract of land, except so far as that right may have been expressly relinquished by treaty.

ARTICLE II.

The United States of America and His Majesty the Emperor of China, believing that the safety and prosperity of commerce will thereby best be promoted, agree that any privilege or immunity in respect to trade or navigation within the Chinese dominions which may not have been stipulated for by treaty, shall be subject to the discretion of the Chinese Government and may be regulated by it accordingly, but not in a manner or spirit incompatible with the treaty stipulations of the parties.

ARTICLE III.

The Emperor of China shall have the right to appoint Consuls at ports of the United States, who shall enjoy the same privileges and immunities as those which are enjoyed by public law and treaty in the United States by the Consuls of Great Britain and Russia, or either of them.

ARTICLE IV.

The 29th Article of the treaty of the 18th of June, 1858, having stipulated for the exemption of Christian citizens of the United States and Chinese converts from persecution in China on account of their faith, it is further agreed that citizens of the United States in China of every religious persuasion, and Chinese subjects in the United States, shall enjoy entire liberty of conscience and shall be exempt from all disability or persecution on account of their religious faith or worship in either country. Cemeteries for sepulture of the dead, of whatever nativity or nationality, shall be held in respect and free from disturbance or profanation.

ARTICLE V.

The United States of America and the Emperor of China cordially recognize the inherent and inalienable right of man to change his home and allegiance, and also the mutual advantage of the free migration and emigration of their citizens and subjects, respectively, from the one country to the other, for purposes of curiosity, of trade, or as permanent residents. The High contracting parties, therefore, join in reprobating any other than an entirely voluntary emigration for these purposes. They consequently agree to pass laws making it a penal offense for a citizen of the United States or Chinese subjects to take Chinese subjects either to the United States or to any other foreign country, or for a Chinese subject or citizen of the United States to take citizens of the United States to China or to any other foreign country, without their free and voluntary consent, respectively.

ARTICLE VI.

Citizens of the United States visiting or residing in China shall enjoy the same privileges, immunities or exemptions in respect to travel or residence as may there be enjoyed by the citizens or subjects of the most favored nation. And, reciprocally, Chinese subjects visiting or residing in the United States, shall enjoy the same privileges, immunities, and exemptions in respect to travel or residence, as may there be enjoyed by the citizens or subjects of the most favored nation. But nothing herein contained shall be held to confer naturalization upon citizens of the United States in China, nor upon the subjects of China in the United States.

ARTICLE VII.

Citizens of the United States shall enjoy all the privileges of the public educational institutions under the control of the Government of China, and reciprocally, Chinese subjects shall enjoy all the privileges of the public educational institutions under the control of the Government of the United States, which are enjoyed in the respective countries by the citizens or subjects of the most favored nation. The citizens of the United States may freely establish and maintain schools within the Empire of China at those places where foreigners are by treaty permitted to reside, and reciprocally, Chinese subjects may enjoy the same privileges and immunities in the United States.

ARTICLE VIII.

The United States, always disclaiming and discouraging all practices of unnecessary dictation and intervention by one nation in the affairs or domestic administration of another, do hereby freely disclaim and disavow any intention or right to intervene in the domestic administration of China in regard to the construction of railroads, telegraphs or other material internal improvements. On the other hand, His Majesty, the Emperor of China, reserves to himself the right to decide the time and manner and circumstances of introducing such improvements within his dominions. With this mutual understanding it is agreed by the contracting parties that if at any time hereafter His Imperial Majesty shall determine to construct or cause to be constructed works of the character mentioned within the Empire, and shall make application to the United States or any other Western power for facilities to carry out that policy, the United States will, in that case, designate and authorize suitable engineers to be employed by the Chinese Government, and will recommend to other nations an equal compliance with such application, the Chinese Government in that case protecting such engineers in their persons and property, and paying them a reasonable compensation for their service.

.   .   .   .

REASSERTION OF THE MOST-FAVORED-NATION PRINCIPLE. SECRETARY SEWARD TO J. ROSS BROWNE, WASHINGTON, SEPTEMBER 8, 1868[4]

Under these circumstances [principles enunciated in Seward-Burlingame Treaty], the United States, refrain from initiating any proposals for a modification of the tariff and commercial articles in their Treaty with China. Nevertheless, if any such modifications shall be made in the contemplated revision of the British Treaty, it will then be not merely expedient, but absolutely necessary that the United States shall have for themselves an equal participation of all the benefits and advantages of such modifications. . . .

[4] *China Instructions,* Vol. II, No. 6.

TSANG KWOH-FAN ON CHINA'S FOREIGN POLICY, 1867-1868

THE GOVERNMENT of the Manchu Empire in 1867-68 was faced with the necessity of formulating a foreign policy. Since 1860, when the British and the French had exacted the Conventions of Peking, the spectacular had played but little part in China's foreign relations. Now after a lapse of ten years, the Treaties of Tientsin (British, French, American, and Russian), signed in 1858, would be subject to revision. The court at Peking feared that this would provide the occasion for the treaty powers to demand further commercial and social concessions. The Burlingame mission (1867-68) had been sent with the idea of forestalling these demands, and, if possible, of delaying revision. At the same time the throne sought the advice of the ablest viceroys and governors in the event that it should be forced to meet demands from the treaty powers. Among the reports received was that of Tsang Kwoh-fan, one of China's most gifted servants. Of equal interest are the comments of S. Wells Williams, at the time chargé d'affaires of the American legation in Peking, addressed to Secretary of State Seward.

A REPORT. TSANG KWOH-FAN HUMBLY BEGS THE "SACRED GLANCE"[1]

Tsang, the Acting Governor-general of the provinces of Kiangsu, Ngan hwui, and Kiangsi, reports to the Throne that, in obedience to the Imperial Will requiring previous consultations as to the points to be attended to in revising the treaties, he now reverently incloses a secret statement, upon which he humbly begs the Sacred Glance.

.   .   .   .

[Here Tsang quotes the Imperial Decree commanding important officers of the Empire to forward their views on the subject of treaty revision.]

In respect to the various points touched upon in the Decree which I have now received, I humbly beg to suggest that in all our intercourse with foreign nations, the most important things to be regarded are *good faith* and what is *right*,—and perhaps even above these should be placed *decision*. Those things which we cannot yield should, from first to last, be firmly declared, and not retracted under any circumstances; but those privileges which we can liberally yield might be made known to them in direct and plain terms.

Let our words be maintained when once spoken, and let no alternate con-

[1] *China Despatches*, Vol. XXIV, Incl. A in No. 16 of Williams to Seward.

cession and refusal be exhibited, which by its aspect of indecision and weakness will only open the door for the wily propositions and arguments of the other party.

It may be said in general that, during many centuries past, the inhabitants in Western lands have been striving to encroach on each others' Kingdoms; and in every case one has tried to possess itself of the profits of the others' trade as a preliminary to getting hold of its territory. They have established places of business throughout China, and trafficked or become carriers in all kinds of produce, simply that they may carry out their unscrupulous schemes of injury, which will end in depriving our merchants of their means of livelihood.

Since the time when we raised troops against them, our people have long suffered every grievous calamity. If we now open three or five more ports to their trade, and the entire length of the Yangtsz' River, it will daily add to the distress and indigence of our poor people, who, alas! are now nearly quite driven to the wall.

If we listen to the proposal of the foreigners to open the trade in salt, our own trade in and transportation of the article will presently be brought to nought. If we consent to their scheme of building warehouses [in the country], the occupation of those who now keep the inns and depots will likewise suffer. Their demand to have their small steamers allowed access to our rivers will involve the ruin of our large and small boats and the beggary of sailors and supercargoes. So also, if we allow them to construct railroads and set up telegraph lines, the livelihood of our cartmen, muleteers, innkeepers, and porters will be taken from them.

Among all the various demands which they make, however, that of opening coal mines should be excepted; for by working mines in the foreign way and employing machinery our own country would be permanently benefited, and it appears to me therefore worthy of a trial. The suggestions of Ying Pan-shi (now Intendant at Shanghai) upon this point in his minute seem to be feasible, and I have marked some notes upon it in approval.

In regard to the two proposals, of steamers going up all our rivers, and of building railroads, if foreigners are allowed to carry them on, the profits and advantages of our own country will gradually be carried off to other lands: and even if our own subjects join such enterprises, and get foreigners to conduct them, the rich and the strong will then engross the labor of the poor. Neither of them, therefore, are admissible.

In explanation of these points, I have already forwarded my own observations in the dispatches sent in care of Sun Sz'tah and his colleague, in which I have discussed each clearly in the interest of the thrift and livelihood of our own people, fortifying my positions with such arguments as cannot be gainsaid. If, however, the foreigners press for their adoption unceasingly, it will be desirable to let them know, that even if they should be able to force the Authorities at Peking to consent, the provincial rulers like myself and others would still resist their introduction with all our strength; and if, by some means, we too should be compelled to give our consent, there would still remain the myriads of common people, who in the extremity of their poverty would see how they could better themselves and rise to oppose the foreigners in a manner that all the Authorities in China could not curb or repress. The princes and magnates of the Middle Kingdom need have no lack of argument in pleading for the lives of their people; and even if our course should bring about a rupture, and we resort to force to preserve the rights and employments of our people, the struggle would not be owing to a mere empty discussion on things of no importance. On the one hand we could appeal to Heaven, Earth, and our sainted Emperors, and on the others to the inhabitants dwelling within every sea [for the justice of our cause]; we, in fact, between these parties ought to fear nothing as to the result, as after it we would have nothing to repent of.

Upon the questions of granting an audience, sending ministers to foreign courts, and permitting the propagation of religion, I did not make any observations in the dispatch forwarded to Peking. . . . Our Sacred Dynasty, in its love of virtue and kindness to those from afar, has no desire to arrogate to itself the sway over the lands within the boundless oceans, or require that their ministers should render homage; and it will be suitable, if, when your Majesty yourself takes the reins of government, they request an audience, to grant it. . . .

In regard to sending embassies abroad, the constant intercourse between us and other countries, with whom we have amicable relations, will constantly cause questions to arise. The risk of our envoys disgracing those who sent them, and the fear of involving ourselves in vast expenses, are both subjects of anxiety. . . . Seeing therefore, that this point has for its objects the honor and prosperity of his Majesty, and the smoothing over difficulties, it seems best on the whole to accede to it.

In respect to affording facilities for the propagation of religion, I may be allowed to observe that the Roman Catholics began their work by tempting men to join them from mercenary motives; but latterly most foreign missionaries have been poor, and as they could not hold out so many advantages their doctrines have not been believed. From the days of the Tsin and Han dynasties, the doctrines of Confucius and the sages have been rather obscured, so that Buddhism has got gradually the ascendant; yet Buddhism has been very greatly supplanted in India, its original country, by Mohammedanism. So too, Romanism, which arose in the Roman Empire, obtains the supremacy, but subsequently Protestantism has vigorously opposed it. From these facts it is evidently plain that all these different religions fluctuate, having their rise and fall; while the doctrines of Duke Chau and of Confucius suffer no attrition during the lapse of ages, but still suffice to regulate the government of China, correct the manners of its people, and exalt the dignity and institutions of the land. If, therefore, the adherents of these other doctrines take every method to promulgate them, they will after all get but few supporters and converts. As there are many churches in the districts and prefectures in every province already erected, there can be no want for allowing them to erect any more. Should the foreigners then at the coming revision of the treaty, persistently press their demands on this head, it will be enough to promise them that whenever occasion requires, protective orders will be issued in regard to this faith. It will not be necessary to add an additional article, and I think they will not ask further or often urge it.

These latter points, whose results are not likely to be very disastrous, need not be debated so as to cause bitterness, though they ought not to be instantly granted when asked for; but the other demands for railroads, steamers going up the rivers, opening the salt trade, and building warehouses in the interior— are so disastrous to the occupations of our people that they ought to be strenuously resisted. . . .

Should the day come when China gets the ascendant, and foreign nations decay and grow weak, we then should only seek to protect our own black-haired people, and have no wish to get military glory beyond the seas. Although they are crooked and deceitful, they yet know that reason and right cannot be gain-said, and that the wrath of a people cannot be resisted. By employing a frank sincerity on our part, we can no doubt move them to good ways, and then everything will be easily arranged to satisfaction.

.   .   .   .

COMMENTS ON THE REPORT OF TSANG KWOH-FAN. WILLIAMS TO SECRETARY SEWARD, PEKING, JULY [UNDATED], 1868[2]

Sir:

I have the honor to send you a careful translation, which I have made, of a secret memorial of Tsang Kwoh fan, the highest in rank among the provincial governor-generals of the Empire, and one of its most influential statesmen. It will repay perusal, not only as containing the opinions of an intelligent Chinese upon the various points on which his views were required, but from the importance of the matter, and the probable influence of his decision upon the policy of his Government during the coming decade. Tsang Kwoh fan is a Chinese, and regarded as one of the anti-foreign party, tho' he has not carried his opposition to the extent of resisting the orders of his Government connected with the position and rights of foreigners. He feels, no doubt, a loyal sympathy with the dangers which he thinks threatens his country thro' the craft and power of those who have thrice attacked it, and forced the gates of Peking. This fear of untoward consequences from yielding to the new demands now made upon his country, tinges this paper, and prevents him from candidly discussing their merits with his partial knowledge of their real bearings. He has been connected with the operations against the Taiping rebels during the last twenty years, and his capture of Nanking in 1864 gave him a commanding prestige that increased his influence in the empire. He is now over seventy years of age, and his long official life during four reigns adds weight to his opinion.

The stand-point from which he opposes the building of railroads and entry of steamers throughout the interior—that they will take the bread out of the mouths of the natives—has probably more weight in China than in any other country, and deserves our respectful consideration. The occupations of the Chinese are hampered by no legal restraints of any strength; every one is free to get his living in the best way he can. But when myriads of rustic hard-fisted people, trained to a single line of labor, like boating or carting are suddenly superseded by Steamers or locomotives, their privations from such forced idleness, may prove a serious calamity and real danger to their rulers. We have instances on record of their turbulence in other countries, one of which, cited by Josephus,—showing the violence of the forty thousand workmen set adrift after Herod's temple was finished,—will suffice, and those workmen were not unlike these Chinese in culture. These laborers are altogether too ignorant to understand the question, and go about to seek a livelihood in other directions, and here they find every other line of life occupied.

The opening of the River Yangtsz' to steamers in 1860 drove thousands of native craft off into its tributaries, and there they drove a strong competition with the boats already in those waters;—and in their strife hundreds

[2] *Ibid.,* No. 16.

of boatmen succumbed to want and temptation. Even the native merchants, who sent their freight on the Steamers, bemoaned the destitution of these boatmen thus suddenly turned out of their old course of life, and said that many of them had to join the rebels to get food.

If the introduction of steamers has been bad for the native boatmen (and in these vessels the greater part of the crews can be safely composed of these same boatmen)—how much worse would it be at first for the cartmen, muleteers, and cameleers superseded by a railroad. They could not be employed in making the road which was to take away their daily bread, for their services would be required up to the day of its completion; and then they would be thrown aside,—carts, wagons, mules, camels, inns, cartwrights, drivers, innkeepers, and all,—never more to be needed on that route.

In Europe the thousands who were thus superseded knew enough to turn to other occupations, or to emigrate to America, or to get work in the road itself; but no such resource is open to most of the labouring Chinese in their ignorance and misery. Between Peking and Tientsin, for instance, a distance of eighty miles, there are probably five thousand carts engaged in carrying passengers and produce whose owners and drivers would unite to make themselves heard by their rulers, if they should be left destitute on the completion of a railroad between these two cities, even if they did not resist its construction.

The question consequently comes up in this light to men in the position of Tsang Kwoh fan, who have to provide for and previse the future; and who must look at it very differently from ourselves. They may be more apprehensive of the dangers than there is ground for, but while they have not our experience of the results to the whole country of introducing a great improvement like this, it is also true that our experience, in the United States at least, is not applicable to a densely crowded country like China. Until more knowledge is introduced among the people, more strength infused into the government, and more tranquillity established throughout the provinces, it is a question whether it will be safe to attempt a railroad system.

The points which Governor Tsang approves in this paper are more feasible, and I am told that the Central Government has concluded to allow him to make an experiment of working the coal mines near Nanking or Chinkiang with foreign machinery. If once this experiment is tried, I think its success in developing a vast industry will prove a strong inducement to try other mines, as for instance those near Peking and north of Canton; and this source of wealth, being once opened prosperously, a rail or tram road to carry the coal to the boats or a market would follow under more promising inducements than can be now expected. It is worth mentioning in this connection, that the great stimulus to Stephenson in opening his railroad was also to get coal to a market.

The favourable view taken of granting an audience to foreign ministers, and its correlative of sending envoys to foreign countries, shows that the writer has begun to yield those antiquated notions of supremacy of the Emperor of China over all other human potentates in which he was educated, and to appreciate the benefits of an equal intercourse with other powers. In doing this, I think his position led him to be willing gracefully to accept the *fait accompli* as the best thing; while that change in his opinion illustrates the advantage, the members of the Foreign Office have in discussing these new steps, and advancing faster than their subordinates in the provinces.

His ideas respecting the diffusion of Christianity are the most singular, and indicate probably the average opinion of the literary and official class to which he belongs. As converts to a vital faith in Christ multiply, who show in their conduct and lives the power of the new principles they profess, this indifference and ignorance of our religion will give way to greater desire to know its tenets, and a determination to oppose or favor them by various high officials.

. . . .

While I send this paper to you as worthy of your regard, it may not be altogether irrelevant to compare the sentiments of this Chinese and pagan ruler in regard to what is best to adopt for his country's good, and the willingness he shows to uphold the rights already conceded by treaties to the citizens of the United States, with the unjust manner in which the Chinese have been treated in our own country, especially in California. . . .

XVI

THE CHINA POLICY OF J. ROSS BROWNE, 1868

ONE OF THE most vigorous spokesmen on the subject of American policy in China during the latter half of the nineteenth century was J. Ross Browne, American minister at Peking, March 11, 1868, to July 5, 1869. Browne's arrival in China coincided with the conclusion of the Seward-Burlingame Treaty. This treaty, implying as it did that the United States would bring no pressure to bear upon China looking to the adoption of Western improvements (railroads, telegraphs, etc.), was in part a threat to the co-operative policy of which Burlingame himself was likewise the author. It was, however, Burlingame's hope that all the treaty powers might use restraint in their demands for treaty revision, and thus that the co-operative policy might be preserved; but carried away somewhat by his own eloquence Burlingame had pictured a China whose major purpose was to grasp the fundamentals of Western civilization. It remained only to permit China to choose the time and the character of her reforms.

The principal contribution made by J. Ross Browne to American policy lies in his critical and penetrating analysis of, and attack upon, the Burlingame treaty. In Washington, Browne's views appear to have been regarded as too vigorous, yet in the main they formed the substance of the instructions received by his successor.

THE NEED OF THE CO-OPERATIVE POLICY. J. ROSS BROWNE TO SECRETARY SEWARD, PEKING, NOVEMBER 25, 1868[1]

An impression seems to have obtained in the United States that the Government of China is peculiarly friendly to our country, and that great advantages to our commerce are about to accrue from this preference. Enthusiastic expectations are entertained that the Empire, so long isolated from the world, is on the eve of being thrown open to American enterprise; that important concessions will soon be made granting special privileges to our citizens.

I need scarcely say these anticipations are without foundation. The Government of China may have preferences; but it has no special regard for any foreign power. The dominant feeling is antipathy and distrust towards all who have come in to disturb the administration of its domestic affairs. But little difference is recognized between one power and another. The concessions obtained by force of arms have been accepted by all.

[1] *China Despatches*, Vol. XXV, No. 7.

Nothing could be more fatal to China than an abandonment on our part of the cooperative policy. In this consist its chief security from unwarrantable aggressions. The United States and Great Britain have important commercial interests at stake; they have no sinister designs upon the territorial integrity of the Empire. So long as they can consistently act in concert, the less danger there will be of jealousy. Extraordinary favors or privileges granted to any one power might lead to demands from others who might esteem themselves equally entitled to consideration; and then instead of rival aspirations being held in check by a compact morally binding at least, there would be nothing to restrain each from seeking to indemnify itself in such way as it might deem proper.

.   .   .   .

INDUSTRIALIZATION AND THE OPIUM TRAFFIC. J. ROSS BROWNE TO SECRETARY SEWARD, PEKING, DECEMBER 5, 1868[2]

The great bane of society here, and the most demoralizing evil to all classes, is the use of opium. Already the poppy is cultivated in the provinces of Fuhkien, Szcheun, Shihli, extending even as far north as Manchuria. If the whole trade by sea were suddenly cut off, China would soon be supplied from its own soil and from India through the mountain passes of Thibet. This tremendous evil cannot be cured by prohibitive means, even if Great Britain and all other Christian nations were voluntarily to unite in an attempt to suppress it. An improved standard of morality based upon a higher appreciation of their own capacity and destiny is the only true remedy to which we can look for the reformation of the people; and this I think can best be attained by improving their industrial condition and enlarging the area of foreign intercourse, which would give efficiency to the labors of the missionaries and adequate protection to their proselytes. In other words railroads, telegraphs and the opening of the mines will tend more than all other means to remove existing prejudices, promote a good understanding between the races, and cause those civil, political and religious reformations essential to the enlightenment of the people.

[2] *Ibid.*, No. 11.

XVII

ROBERT HART AND J. ROSS BROWNE ON CHINA'S PROGRESS, 1869

SUGGESTIVE of the complexity of China's foreign relations is a correspondence between J. Ross Browne and Robert Hart, Inspector General of the Chinese Imperial Maritime Customs. Browne proposed to Hart, as perhaps the best informed of all foreigners in China, a series of questions:

(1) Was the Chinese embassy (the Burlingame mission) to the Western Powers a spontaneous movement on the part of the Peking government?

(2) What was its object as generally understood in Peking at the time of its departure?

(3) Had that object been fully and fairly represented by the public press of the United States and England?

(4) Were the Chinese authorities desirous of entering upon a career of public improvement?

(5) Were the Chinese authorities disposed to grant an imperial audience to the foreign ministers?

(6) Would the Seward-Burlingame Treaty induce the Chinese to enter upon a career of progress? etc.

The more significant sections of Hart's reply are printed together with the comments of Browne thereon.

THE STATUS OF CHINA'S FOREIGN AFFAIRS. ROBERT HART TO J. ROSS BROWNE, PEKING, JUNE 30, 1869[1]

1. Ever since my first arrival in Peking in 1861, I have been urging the Yamen to move in the direction of what the West understands by the word Progress, and on scarcely any point have I spoken more strongly or more frequently than on the necessity for the establishment of a resident mission at the Court of every Treaty Power. To show how diplomatic intercourse is conducted, I translated for the Yamen that part of "Wheaton's" relating to Rights of Legation, Treaties, &c. long before Dr. Martin came to Peking. I regarded representation abroad as of paramount importance, and as, in itself, progress: for while I thought I saw in it one of China's least objectionable ways of

[1] *China Despatches*, Vol. XXVI. [Unnumbered.]

preserving freedom and independence, I also supposed it would constitute a tie which should bind her to the West so firmly, and commit her to a career of improvement so certainly, as to make retrogression impossible. Availing myself of the approach of the time for treaty revision, I urged the point on the Yamen more strongly than ever. As a first step, and by way of demonstrating to the official Class, that the West can be safely visited, and that the journey is neither very fatiguing nor very dangerous, I induced the Yamen to send Lao-yeh Pin, and his party to Europe with me in 1866, and, on my return to Peking at the end of that year, I continued to argue for another forward movement. Thus it came to pass, that, in September and October 1867, the matter of representation abroad was talked of every time I went to the Yamen, and while Fau ta-jen told me that, in a week or two, a decision would be communicated to me showing that the Government was about to act at once on my advice, Weu-ta-jen added that, if I could be spared from Peking, it was in contemplation to appoint myself to accompany the Chinese official on whom their choice was most likely in the first instance to fall. Thus, so far as representation abroad, generally speaking, is concerned, the Embassy now in Europe can scarcely be said to have been a spontaneous movement on the part of the Imperial Rulers.

Towards the end of October, Mr. Burlingame went to the Yamen to pay his farewell visit, and in the course of it, I believe, he reminded the Prince, that, when formerly leaving Peking, he had been requested, if the opportunity occurred, to make certain explanations in connection with the disbandment of the Lay-Osborn Flotilla, and then went on to enquire whether he could do anything for the Yamen on the present occasion of leaving China.

The Prince replied by some such jocular remark as: "Why you might just as well be our Ambassador at once!" I style this remark jocular, because, for the moment, there was nothing more intended than a pleasantry. Dr. Martin was interpreting on that occasion, and he doubtless remembers what was said, and the manner of saying it. Some days after that, Mr. J. McL. Brown told me that the Yamen had it in contemplation to appoint Mr. Burlingame to be its representative to the Treaty Powers, and asked what I thought of it. I at once said that the notion ought to be supported, and, on the following day, I went to the Yamen and spoke very strongly in its favor.

Tung-ta-jen said to me: "We were already seven or eight parts inclined to do it, but now that you approve of it so fully, we really are twelve parts for it, (i.e. 'We thought well of it before; we think more than well of it now.')" At first the idea was that Mr. Burlingame should be invited to go alone or accompanied only by Mr. Brown, and the Yamen did not then appear to think that funds would have to be provided. I suggested that a Chinese Mission ought not to go without Chinese officials and that Mr. Dechamps should be associated with Mr. Brown, as Secretary of Legation, and arranged for the funds to support the party, fixing the rates of pay &c. Thus, although the establishment of Missions abroad was a step that had been urged on the Yamen for years, the selection of Mr. Burlingame may be said to have been spontaneous: i.e. he did not solicit the appointment; it naturally grew out of what at first was but a joke.

2. The object with which the Yamen despatched the Mission, as I understood it at the time, was to cultivate and conserve friendly relations by explaining to each of the Treaty Powers the many difficulties that China cannot

fail to experience in attempting to change existing conditions or to introduce novelties,—to bespeak forbearance and prevent in so far as possible, any resort to hostile pressure to wring from China concessions for which the Government did not as yet feel itself ready,—and to prepare the way generally for the day when China should not merely hear the words of foreign representatives in Peking, but should be able to address each Government in its own capital through a resident Chinese medium.

3. So far as newspaper reports go, the object of the Mission has been misinterpreted, and the public have regarded it as promising on the part of China the immediate performance of those very things which China sent the Mission to explain to the West are so difficult of performance; the impression created by the sending of such a Mission has besides been one that a generous, but ignorant and unreasoning public, has itself done much to puff into still falser dimensions. Nothing but complete ignorance of China could have permitted the public to assume that the vast changes now looked for are regarded as necessary and longed for by China herself, and nothing could well be more unreasonable than to suppose that such changes—even if felt by China to be called for—could be hurried forward, and given effect to it in the short time in which the West seems to expect them. . . . Thus, Mr. Burlingame's speech at New York, harshly criticised as it has been, is in the main defensible, when it is remembered that, without doing the speaker the injustice of putting a stern, matter of fact interpretation on every clause of each eloquent sentence, the burthen [burden?] of his address to a generous, sympathising audience, was: "Leave China alone, and all that you wish for will in its own good time follow."

That speech has been severely criticised, and it must be confessed that its language sounded strangely, read alongside of contemporaneous occurrences in China; it naturally suffers most when its parts are individually and separately commented on, and judged of from the standing point of fact in the past, rather than from its general drift which is to suggest hopefulness in the future; but taken as a whole,—and making allowance for the festive occasion on which it was delivered,—the speech was a true and telling one, when regarded as intended to *sum up what would result from* a policy of fair play and non-interference, *rather than to describe things as they now are,* and thereon to build a claim for fair play.

.   .   .   .

4. When asked if the Chinese Authorities are themselves desirous of entering on a career of improvement, and, if so, in what direction and within what definite period, a categorical reply would be as much an injustice to the Western public, were it in the affirmative, as it would be to China herself, were it in the negative. To the most of Chinese officials, the word *improvement* would convey no idea corresponding to that which is in the Western mind, when scrutinising the condition and prospects of China from the point of view that word suggests. From the memorials that appear daily in the Peking Gazette, it is abundantly evident that there is no lack of officials throughout the Empire who closely watch occurrences, who are desirous that wrongs should be righted, and bad ways abandoned for better, and who courageously and persistently give their opinions and offer their advice in the cause of improvement to the Emperor: but all such criticism relates to the internal affairs of China as distinguished from those affected by foreign inter-

course, and all such suggestions, appealing to past jurity (?) rather than to future advancement, founded on ethical precepts and ending in moral platitudes, fail to touch those points which the Western mind regards as at the base of all progress:—in a word, material improvement (in its widest sense, and suggestive of freedom of action in the development of resources and creation of industries) is never hinted at. But this cannot be wondered at; for the majority are ignorant and but few of the minority are appreciative in the little knowledge they do chance to possess.—Some forty officials in the provinces and perhaps ten at Peking, have a glimmering notion of what it is that the foreigner means, when he speaks in general terms of progress; but of those fifty, not one is prepared to enter boldly on a career of progress, and take the consequences of even a feeble initiative.

In this connection and at this point, I would call attention to a Memo. which accompanies this note, in which I argue that Progress *has* commenced and will flourish in China, reasoning much as follows:— . . .

"The condition of all progress is, that a want shall be felt; it is when a want is felt, that the mind seeks to supply it, and some wants are such, that, in the attempt to satisfy them, they create other wants:—there is a fountain want, which, once tapped, will make a channel for itself and rush onward in a vivifying stream. China has felt such a master want—the want of material strength, and, in national life, to feel that want is at the bottom of all wants —it is the parent of progress; she is attempting to satisfy that want: in that attempt to supply a want, to which she has become keenly alive, other wants are making themselves felt, and the number of wants will increase, and, just as she succeeds of herself in supplying one, so will China's determination to satisfy the others become keener, and be exercised after a more intelligent fashion."

"Thus, in her attempt to become strong physically, China has, to my mind, entered upon a career of improvement, and will, step by step, develop resources, create industries, and achieve progress materially, intellectually, and morally. I therefore am daily more inclined to believe that the true policy is to 'leave her alone:'—not that I am satisfied with the rate at which she progresses, but that I think—given the conditions which do exist and cannot be ignored—China is more likely to come to good in the end with benefit to herself and harm to none, if allowed to go along at her own rate, than if dealt with after a fashion, of which the chief characteristics would be constantly recurring acts of violence, and that foreign dictation which breeds revolt, and checks healthy growth and natural action."

Thus, without going the length of saying that the Chinese Authorities themselves consciously are desirous of entering upon a career of (what we style) improvement, I feel I can safely assert that China has commenced to improve, and that progress, although slow at the start, is certain to roll onwards with a daily increasing momentum, and in a daily increasing ratio.

5. As to the Audience question, there is no doubt that there is a growing feeling among certain officials who know of the existence of such a difficulty, in favor of its settlement by the reception of foreign representatives. But, even supposing some of the most influential advisers adopted and put forward the foreign view, I cannot with confidence predict a pacific solution of the question, (and I am of opinion, when it does come up, that Westerns will

either have to fight for it, and by carrying their point, place relations with China on a sure footing for ever, or withdrawing from the demand for an Audience, acquiesce in inaugurating a policy of which the sole aim will be to drive out the foreigner as speedily as possible.)

.   .   .   .

At the present moment, the Emperor's chief tutor is Wo-jen—an obstinate old man, ignorant of everything outside of China, and perfectly rabid against foreigners, and, however anxious Wen-Hsiang and his three or four colleagues may be to keep the peace, they will probably lose office, infl' ence, and life, if, on the subject of the Audience, they dare to initiate a propc sal to receive foreign representatives on the same terms as the members of the Embassy have been received in the United States and Europe. . . .

6. The event of the day, is of course, the publication of the additional articles negotiated with the United States. Those articles *may* be of use to Chinese in California (though indeed I hesitate to say so, knowing that such an opinion suggests, as at its foundation, the idea that the citizens of the United States do not treat Chinese fairly and is therefore the reverse of complimentary to either citizens or Government), but I question to what extent they will exercise a beneficial influence in inducing or encouraging China to press onwards in a career of improvement. . . .

7. As regards Article VIII [see p. 85] more particularly, whatever its other effects may be, I do not think it at all calculated to hasten progress: indeed, taking my view of progress in China, and regarding it as likely to be accelerated in proportion to the acuteness with which China feels the wants of material strength, I fancy, that, were all country[ies?] to join in making the same sort of a treaty, the result would be, that China's feeling of want of strength would be weakened, and her progress proportionately retarded, if not stopped. And, in this connection, it must not be forgotten that the feeling of want of material strength in China is attended now by a sister want: China is gradually feeling *how difficult it is, and yet how necessary, to acquit herself of her Treaty obligations,* and this feeling gives force to the power wielded by the perception of want of strength. Her central weakness goes hand in hand with her external; and her want of ability to give effect to her promises with her inability to oppose dictation give her reasons for growing strong externally; and she will become proportionately the more capable of performing her compacts internally. . . .

The West does not understand China, nor does China understand the West, and a just mean (?) is surely to be found between the view of the men of the day in China, who want everything done in their time, and of those who, far away from China, oscillate between extreme exertion and extreme quietude.

The best treatment for the future would seem to be found in that policy which insists that China shall scrupulously carry out her obligations, written and unwritten, to foreign powers, and which leaves her to develop internally after her own fashion; to insist on the first will accelerate improvement in the second, but to interfere in the second will introduce heterogeneous questions which are only too likely to work mischief for the first.

.   .   .   .

Notes and Comments on the Views of Robert Hart. J. Ross Browne to Secretary Fish [Undated][2]

A.—Mr. Hart was an employé in the Customs service. It was not strictly his duty to interfere in diplomatic affairs. When he was appointed Inspector General, it was made a condition of his appointment by Sir Frederick Bruce and Mr. Burlingame that he should not occupy a *quasi-diplomatic* position, but should reside at the treaty ports. His retention at Peking, with their consent and approval, can only be accounted for on the supposition that he labored to carry out their peculiar theories and that they found it expedient to have an intermediary agent. (See Mr. Burlingame's desp. Nov. 23d, 1863 and notes of interview, October 1867. Also Sir. F. Bruce's desp. Nov. 27th, 1863.)

B.—The acceptance of Dr. Martin's translation of Wheaton has been adduced as evidence of Chinese progress. Doubtless the Imperial government was quite willing to take advantage of any privileges or exemptions it might contain. There is no evidence that they ever contemplated accepting its obligations.

C.—Lao-Yeh Pin was a clerk (Shoo pan) in the Tsungli-Yamen—a man of no influence. On his return from Europe he made a report suited to the views of his employers, condemnatory of foreign improvements and demonstrating that such things were unsuited to China. In consequence of this, he was promoted.

.   .   .   .

H.—The object therefore was to *prevent* all progress inconsistent with Chinese isolation; to avoid the execution of treaties, and set aside the Foreign Ministers at Peking. The war of 1860 had resulted in the establishment of diplomatic relations at the capital, which was the only provision of the Treaties of Tientsin that the Chinese Government had strenuously resisted. Direct relations with the Imperial authorities had been resisted since the visit of Lord Macartney in 1793. An opportunity now offered to transfer the scene of future diplomacy beyond the boundaries of the Empire, by depriving the foreign ministers of all power to redress grievances or enforce the execution of treaties. With civilized governments bound together by common ties of race, religion and laws, and by facilities of intercommunication, a different interpretation might reasonably be attached to such a movement; but there is nothing in the history of China, since the beginning of foreign intercourse, to warrant the idea that the Imperial rulers had the slightest desire to enter into such relations as those contemplated under the law of nations. What they really wanted was time—time to repeat on a larger scale what they had done in the way of preparation to repel foreign intrusion at Canton from 1842 to 1857; and at Taku from 1858 to 1859; time to establish arsenals, build gunboats; poison the minds of the people throughout the Provinces; and in the end, when no longer able to postpone the execution of treaties, make a final attempt to drive every foreigner out of the country.

I.—The word "immediate" is ingeniously used by Mr. Hart to show how unreasonable the public are in expecting great reforms to be carried into effect at once, and how reasonable the Chinese are in desiring time to adapt themselves to the new order of things. The inference from all such expressions used in connection with Chinese affairs is utterly unwarranted by experience. The public understand well enough that it takes time to build railroads and

[2] *Ibid.*

telegraphs in all countries, and they never expected to see them *immediately* built in China; but there is a difference between doing a thing immediately and indefinitely postponing all experiment—even to the necessary preliminary steps.

Time is the essential element in all questions of progress. With China to postpone a measure is to evade it indefinitely—the day of preparation never comes. It behooves each generation, in our age and under a progressive civilization, to do its part; but the Chinese are content with what their ancestors did, and have no desire to better their own condition or bestow benefits upon their posterity. Mr. Hart would have expressed the truth more clearly had he said that the mission was sent to the West to explain not only how difficult it is to introduce improvements in China, but how utterly impracticable without material changes in the present system of government. Innovation strikes at the very root of the existing system. Whatever strengthens central authority destroys to a certain extent provincial responsibility; and this is precisely what the Imperial rulers have resisted since the beginning of foreign intercourse. . . .

J.—Mr. Hart is severe upon the public for believing the representations of the chief Ambassadors from China. If they manifested ignorance, who was better qualified to enlighten them than Mr. Burlingame? He had represented the government of the United States for six years in China; he now represented the government of China in the United States. It was the avowed object of his Mission to explain the condition of China. Surely it is unfair to blame the public for their confidence in the good faith and intelligence of the American Ambassador from the Court of Peking.

L.—Did Mr. Burlingame remind the press of these facts? Do his public speeches bear that interpretation? Do the published speeches of the leading statesmen and orators of the United States, made at Washington, New York and Boston on the occasion of the reception of the Chinese Embassy in response to his representations bear the interpretation that *"there is not a single man in the Empire prepared to advocate the introduction of Western improvements!"* . . . .

N.—All experience is to be rejected; the existing condition of affairs in China is to be disregarded; neither the past nor the present is to be taken .as a guide, but we are to build hopes for the future upon a policy not justified by any results hitherto obtained. If Mr. Hart's argument does not mean this, what does it mean? Mr. Burlingame's selection proves that the Chinese have had fair play since the war of 1860—otherwise why did they select him? As to non-interference, the only interference by foreign governments in the affairs of China since that date was to suppress the Taiping rebellion and prevent the overthrow of the Manchu dynasty. Surely this is not a legitimate subject of protest. What other interference has there been since 1860 except to ask for the execution of Treaties? The treaties have never yet been enforced. The diplomatic correspondence for the past eight years shows that they have been persistently evaded both by the central government and by the local authorities, and that neither the one nor the other has ever yet manifested a disposition to carry them out in good faith. Sir Frederick Bruce complained in June 1863 of the "general disregard of treaty provisions manifested at the Ports"—and said that "the central government if not unwilling shows itself unable to enforce a better order of things." (See his letter of that date to Prince Kung.)

Mr. Burlingame during the same year made similar complaints and said that the tergiversations of the officers who administered the government, rendered it difficult to hold relations with them without a sacrifice of personal dignity. Mr. Williams in 1866 said the effects of the lesson taught by the war of 1860 were passing away and the rulers were becoming more obstructive and impracticable than ever.

Sir Rutherford Alcock in 1868, protested in the strongest terms against the continued disregard of treaty stipulations, and complained that their most essential provisions were rendered nugatory by the *vis inertia* and shuffling evasions of the Imperial government. (See my despatch No. 7 with enclosures.) The whole diplomatic corps at Peking up to the present time, have during the whole term of their residence at the Capital, been chiefly engaged in making similar protests and remonstrances. The merchants at the Treaty ports, through their Chambers of Commerce have filled the archives of the Legations with proofs of the persistent manner in which trade has been obstructed and treaty rights violated; the Missionaries have written in vain from all parts of the country protesting against the indignities and abuses heaped upon them by the local mandarins in direct violation of treaty stipulations; in effect there is no difference of opinion on the subject among foreigners in China. Is this universal testimony to be disregarded? To whom are we to look for the truth if not to our own representatives and to all classes who hold intercourse with the Chinese. And yet the government of the United States in July 1868, adopted Additional Articles practically granting to the Chinese exemption from all existing obligations; and Lord Clarendon in December 1868 understood from Mr. Burlingame "that the Chinese government were fully alive to the expediency or even necessity, for their own interests, of facilitating and encouraging intercourse with foreign nations" &c; and admitted "that the Chinese government were entitled to count upon the forbearance of foreign nations." It might reasonably be asked what had been done by the Chinese to give them such an extraordinary claim to consideration and forbearance? All the testimony shows a persistent violation of treaties during a period of eight years, when there was no interference in their affairs beyond the existence of the treaties themselves, save to suppress a rebellion which threatened the overthrow of the government. With this experience before him, Mr. Hart thinks it quite justifiable to say "Leave China alone, and all that you wish for will in its own good time follow." . . .

O.—Mr. Hart is quite right in saying that the word *improvement* conveys to the mass of Chinese officials no idea corresponding to that which is in the Western mind. The difference is simply this: By *improvement* Western nations mean ameliorating the condition of the people; developing the resources of the country; increasing the profits of labor, and enhancing the comfort, freedom and happiness of all; in other words profiting by the experience of the past and advancing with ever-accumulating intelligence into the future. The Chinese mean the cultivation of memory and an adherence to time-honored usages; blindly imitating the past, and obdurately rejecting all reform. Progress with the one means going forward—with the other going backward. Arts are lost, sciences forgotten, the whole Chinese nation is far gone in demoralization and decay; and yet Mr. Burlingame thinks the prospect is cheering if we will only let them alone, and Mr. Hart thinks so too, but with the reservation that China may possibly disappoint public expectation by not progressing in the right direction.

. . . .

R.—Mr. Hart makes the encouraging announcement that voluntary progress has already commenced—*that a start has already been made.* When we analyze the grounds upon which this assertion is made, it appears that the Imperial government feels the want of material strength,—not to govern the Provinces and compel an observance of treaties on the part of the provincial mandarins,—(because that would be an innovation upon the time-honored principle of local responsibility); but to resist foreign intrusion or impose such onerous restrictions upon foreign intercourse as to narrow its limits to the treaty ports, and if possible regain that position of isolation which the Empire had enjoyed for so many centuries.

. . . .

S.—By far the most important part of Mr. Hart's communication is that relating to the Audience question. The revelations marked by himself in brackets are astounding. No man understands better than Mr. Hart the feeling of the Chinese rulers on this subject. He is in daily contact with them; his advice is sought on all important occasions (see notes of Mr. Burlingame's interview October 1867). He is constantly consulted upon questions of foreign policy. He speaks the Chinese language fluently, and has had many years experience of Chinese diplomacy. His statements cannot be regarded as mere conjectures. What he so confidently asserts is based upon personal knowledge. I refrain from an analysis of these extraordinary developments. They require no comment. If Western governments can see in them any evidence of a desire on the part of China to accept the obligations as well as the privileges of international law, or the slightest disposition to enter upon terms of equality into the family of nations, I can no longer understand the use of words, or the value of facts.

T.—Mr. Hart is a British subject and therefore may be supposed to have prejudices in favor of his own nationality. His statement however in regard to the absence of any preference on the part of the Chinese for Americans is attested by most of our diplomatic representatives and by all Americans resident in China. We are recipients of all the advantages gained by British and French arms, and are in the eyes of the Chinese accomplices in the acts of hostility committed by those powers. The ratification of the New Articles, though they were made in the interest of China, is postponed, partly because of the complications growing out of the favored nation clause in all the Treaties; but chiefly as I now believe because they regard all special tenders of advantages by foreign governments as covering some sinister project to open up the country. The mere mention of rail-roads and telegraphs fills them with visions of unrestricted intercourse. When they are told by a progressive and enterprising nation that these improvements will not be forced upon them, they naturally tax their ingenuity to find where, or in what form the new assault upon their established usages is going to be made.

. . . .

XVIII

THE CHARACTER AND EXPERIENCE OF CHINESE OFFICIALDOM, 1869

IN CONTRAST with the vigorous and at times unrestrained statements of J. Ross Browne are the more temperate but nonetheless critical appraisals of S. Wells Williams on the characteristics of Chinese and Manchu officialdom. The following document is the more significant because of Williams's understanding of and sympathy for the Chinese.

PEKING: ITS POPULACE AND OFFICIALDOM, 1869. S. WELLS WILLIAMS TO SECRETARY FISH, PEKING, SEPTEMBER 1, 1869[1]

I have the honor to acknowledge the receipt of your dispatches to Mr. Browne Nos. 37, 38 and 39. . . .

Your remarks in the first of these dispatches upon the completion of the Pacific Railroad, and the consequent increase of trade between China and the United States, as the facilities afforded by it and the ocean steamers are developed, have all been, in one form and another, made known to the Chinese officers. The course and length of the road, the details of its construction, the number of their countrymen employed upon it, and the influence it was likely to exert upon their state and nation, have all been illustrated and explained to them; but they are so unacquainted with such enterprises, and so imperfectly understand the reciprocal relations of nations, that all our efforts fail to interest them. All the officers with whom foreigners come in contact are old men, who have lived in or about the capital nearly all their lifetime, and some of them have never been out of this province. Prince Kung himself has never seen a steamer, and his chief advisers have none of them been on board one; and what is true of the Prince and his councillors, is still more applicable to other members of the Imperial Family—the young Emperor, the Empress-regents, and their kindred—and to other high officers in those departments of Government which have no direct intercourse with foreigners. With these we have no communication, and they take no measures to inform themselves directly of our views, or the condition of our countries.

Out of the nine gentlemen who have been connected with the Foreign Office since 1861, of whom four have been in it all the time, only two have ever invited a foreigner to their houses, and no one has ever been a guest at Prince Kung's or any of the Imperial Family. Chiefly through the trammels of official etiquette, but very much too, I think, from hauteur and ignorance, the Manchu princes and noblemen seclude themselves very much from the mass of Chinese who live in the capital, even from those of very high position; and this seclusion would of course be strictly maintained towards foreigners.

[1] *China Despatches*, Vol. XXVII, No. 61.

This class of Chinese consists very largely of aspirants for office from every province who flock to the capital, and of those who have attained their aspirations, and they together form another class of official society,—the élite of Chinese literati, whose tone of thought is adverse to further intercourse with us.

The population of Peking cannot be exactly stated, but I estimate it at between 800,000 and a million people. Of these, the Manchus and their immediate servants constitute rather less than one half, and the Chinese official class about a third of the remainder. The artisans, shopkeepers and laborers are nearly all Chinese; for the vicious system of enrolling all the Manchus in a military organization under banners, and half-supporting them on inadequate pay, fosters a spirit of pride and indolence that prevents all self-independence and progress. The lower classes of these Bannermen show very little antipathy to foreigners, not so much on the whole as the Chinese population, from whom they are further separated by laws tending to maintain their position as a peculiar, privileged class.

From these features of the social characteristics of the capital of China, you can readily infer how unfavorable the whole arrangement of things is for fitting its leading men to worthily govern the great empire under them. The location of the city, more than a hundred miles from the sea and inaccessible by water, does much to disable it from rapidly sympathising with other parts of the country, and exerting a commanding influence upon the provinces; and your remarks justly represent the need of railroads to strengthen this influence. This comparative isolation of Peking reacts upon the high Chinese officials in it, who, as they gradually rise in dignity and influence, become more and more identified with its community, and seldom return to their native provinces, in which they can hold no important post.

They do not keep up with the movements abroad, and are slow to appreciate what may be really feasible, or have that conviction of its advantages that will urge them on in the face of obstacles till it is adopted. Their whole lives having been spent in the routine of official duties, they can hardly be urged by any argument or pressure to leave the beaten track. Though nominally at the head of affairs, the central authorities are rather like superordinate advisory bureaus, and have no force at their disposal to compel the provincial officials to carry out orders; summary removal is their last resort in most cases. The reports they receive as to the real state of things do not supply the truth and life which personal observation would give them, but none of them can leave their posts and keep their commissions to make these observations. If this be the case with them in respect to matters in their own country, how much more is it likely to be in regard to foreign kingdoms; and how many more difficulties must appear to them in the way of introducing a railroad or steam machinery, than if they had seen their operation?

.   .   .   .

In addition to these remarks upon the position and training of the officers with whom we come into contact, as bearing upon the introduction of railroads, there is another idea gradually appearing as an opposing element, which will require time to show its unsoundness. This is the fear of the trading classes that the introduction of these novelties will take away the trade from them to transfer it to foreigners, who alone can manage them. This class is more powerful almost, than the official, and is made up of separate guilds and associations which over-rule the minutest details of trade, and generally thwart whatever they cannot manage.

The recent proposition to throw open the whole country to foreign merchants, and let these carry their goods by steam through every river, startled them; and they have not yet reached that intelligence derived from wide experience, which would enable them to see that they could easily control the inland traffic. I am of the opinion that the opposition to foreigners going into the interior to reside, which has recently been manifested against missionaries, had its origin and strength very much in this feeling. Very many of the literati and officials are indirectly connected with trade, (for degrees and rank are open in China to all,) and they would side with restrictive measures as the most likely to preserve their rights.

On the other hand this class is the most accessible to foreign ideas, its members are sooner and better able to judge of their merits, and self-interest and rivalry in trade tend to develop new things among them—all of which are interesting and encouraging features. During the last five years, the tendency of trade has decidedly been to pass into native hands, and make Hongkong and Shanghai the entrepôts for all imports, from whence native agents could supply themselves for the interior.

.   .   .   .

XIX

FREDERICK F. LOW AND THE TIENTSIN
MASSACRE, 1870-1872

THE SO-CALLED missionary question was during the latter part of the nineteenth century one of the most perplexing with which the foreign diplomats in China had to deal. Although in theory (and at times in practice) the Christian missionary was the agent of forces which were supposedly spiritual, moral, and humanitarian, he was likewise and inevitably in the Chinese mind associated with the impact of Western imperialism upon China. The legal status enjoyed by the missionary in China was a product of imperialistic wars and of treaties dictated at the cannon's mouth. The doctrines which the missionary expounded, questioned and in some cases condemned fundamental concepts of Chinese social and religious life. There was always the temptation for the missionary to appeal, on behalf of his converts, to the toleration clause of the treaties whenever his converts appeared to be subject to oppressive measures at the hands of local magistrates. To Chinese officialdom this was clear enough proof that the missionary was not only the propagandist of an alien and exclusive faith but also the political agent of one or other of the treaty powers. The development of antagonism was natural enough. It was the product of misunderstanding inseparable from the clash of opposing religious and political philosophies.

One of the most serious outbursts against the Christian missionary occurred in 1870 at Tientsin following closely upon the appointment of Frederick F. Low, of California, as American minister at Peking (December, 1869). Sections of the Chinese populace had been aroused by a revival of old charges that the Catholic orphanage was filled with kidnapped children whose hearts and eyes were extracted to compound direful drugs. The mob destroyed the cathedral, the orphanage, and the French consulate and pillaged a number of British and American chapels. A number of French nationals, including ten sisters and two priests, were killed. The total fatalities included likewise three Russians and more than thirty Chinese.

British, French, and American warships were sent to Tientsin. Diplomatic pressure from France was delayed, however, by reason of the Franco-Prussian War. China finally agreed to a settlement in which (a) the prefect and magistrate of Tientsin were exiled; (b) twenty rioters were condemned to death, and twenty-one banished; (c) China paid an indemnity and sent Chunghow, an imperial commissioner, on a mission of apology to France.

At the time of the settlement China proposed to the treaty powers a group of rules by which the actions of missionaries should be governed. Only the American minister was prepared even to discuss them. Had his sagacity been shared by his colleagues at Peking some of the unhappy events in which the missionaries were involved at the close of the century might have been avoided.

THE LEGAL AND SOCIAL STATUS OF THE MISSIONARIES. MINISTER LOW TO SECRETARY FISH, PEKING, DECEMBER 5, 1870[1]

In my opinion one of the great underlying causes of the unrest of the Chinese, which exhibits itself in hostility towards foreigners is to be found in the unwise action and illegal assumptions of the Roman Catholic Missionaries; which assumptions have, to a great extent, the countenance and support of the French Government.

To explain my views concerning the whole missionary question in China is the object of this despatch; and in order that the whole subject may be presented in as clear a light as possible it will be necessary to give some historical details of the various treaties entered into between China and Foreign Nations.

In 1858 Russia, the United States, Great Britain and France concluded treaties with this Empire at Tientsin. They were signed in the order in which the countries are named above. Each treaty contained a separate Article providing for the toleration of the Christian Religion; but, with the exception of an additional clause in the Russian and French treaties which permitted missionaries to travel with passports in the interior, all other privileges were restricted to the open ports, where they were placed on an equality with merchants and allowed to purchase land erect churches and schoolhouses, establish cemeteries &c. For an elaborate and able review of the whole question I beg to refer you to the despatches of Mr. Reed under dates of June 30 and July 29th, 1858. In the enclosures of these two despatches copies of all the treaties referred to may also be found.

A dispute arose in 1859 between the British and French Ministers and the Chinese authorities with reference to the route the Ministers should take to reach Peking which resulted in hostilities, and finally ended in the occupation of Peking by the British and French forces in 1860; where supplemental conventions were signed by the Ministers before referred to and Prince Kung. In

[1] *China Despatches*, Vol. XXIX, No. 40.

the British supplemental convention nothing was inserted except a provision for an increase of indemnity to cover the expenses of the war, and the opening of the Port of Tientsin to trade. The same stipulations were inserted in the French Convention, and an additional one concerning missionaries, which is contained in Article VI. Soon after the ratification of all the treaties, copies of the Chinese text of the French treaty of 1860 were obtained, translated and published. This was the only version of that particular treaty obtainable. For reasons which no one could then understand, but which are now apparent, no copies of the French text could be had, and all attempts by the other Legations to obtain them in Peking have proved unavailing until within a few weeks. It is believed that the British Government obtained copies at the time, or through the French Government in Paris, but if so none were sent to the Legation in Peking, or if sent were accompanied with instructions of a confidential character.

The Chinese text clearly conceded the right of the Missionaries to reside in all the Provinces, to acquire land, build churches schools &c, and to propogate their doctrines without let or hindrance. The Roman Catholic clergy, with the aid and protection of the French Government, have spread their missions in all parts of the Empire, so that at the present moment there are 20 Bishoprics in China proper, one in Mongolia, one in Manchuria, one in Corea and one in Thibet. Attached to these various missions are about five hundred priests.

The missionaries of this Religious Faith have, in addition to the right of residence as Bishops and Priests, assumed to occupy a semi-official position which places them on an equality with the native officers where they reside. They also claimed the right to protect the native Christians from persecution, which practically constituted the missionaries the arbiters of their disputes and the judges of their wrongful acts, and removed this class from the control of their native rulers. The absolute right of the Roman Catholic Clergy to exercise, in the name and by the authority of the French Government, a protectorate over native Christians was claimed as warranted by Article VI of the French treaty before referred to, and insisted upon by some of the earlier representatives of France in China. This assumption the Central Government most emphatically denied, and, during the discussion of the subject, Prince Kung and his associates clearly informed the Representative of France that, rather than yield to this demand they would accept a declaration of war instead, even though the issue of the war might involve the downfall of the Dynasty. It is believed by those who were here at the time and best able to judge, that the timely arrival of M. Berthemy prevented hostilities between France and China growing out of this question. He promptly withdrew the demand and, in unmistakable terms, informed the missionaries that their assumptions were not warranted either by treaty right or good policy. But notwithstanding this action of the French Minister it is asserted by the Chinese, with strong probability of its truth, that the missionaries still claim this right, and exercise it wherever local officials are found that can be frightened or coaxed into compliance. This they can do with impunity where there are no Consuls; and even where there are diplomatic or consular officers it is seldom the case that the united power of the clergy fails to silence opposition; and they are left untrammelled to gain all the power possible on the principle that, "the end justifies the means."

In making these observations I do not wish to be understood as impugning the motives which actuate the Catholic missionaries. They have undoubtedly been placed in positions to see and understand the persecutions to which native Christians are subjected for opinions' sake, and it is altogether likely the missionaries honestly believe that in no other way can an effectual remedy be applied. Many of our Protestant Missionaries take the same view, and are anxious that a stipulation shall be inserted in treaties placing native Christians under the protection of the Consular Courts. I have reason to believe that missionaries of all denominations are looking forward to the revision of the French treaty in 1871 hoping, and perhaps expecting, that this right will then be secured for native Christians.

The French missionaries having exercised the right to reside, purchase land, erect churches establish cemeteries &c anywhere in the country, the American and English missionaries of the Protestant faith claimed equal rights and privileges with the Catholics; although the claims of the Protestants scarcely assumed a practical form until within a few years by reason of their numbers being insufficient to justify the extension of their labors beyond the treaty ports. The question as to their right of residence has often been raised and referred to the Minister for his decision; and the uniform opinion of my predecessors has been that, conceding the Chinese text of the French treaty to be correct and authoritative, the stipulation contained in Article VI was only designed to provide for the restitution of the property which had been formerly owned and occupied by Christians, of which they had been deprived by persecutions and confiscations in former years, and that a fair construction of the Article in question in the light of previous history and surrounding circumstances, would not permit the permanent residence of missionaries in the interior beyond re-occupying the places from which they had been driven.

In reply to similar demands made by the English Missionaries they were informed by their Government that their right of residence away from the open ports must be sought for in treaties other than the English, and that as it was optional with any Government to avail itself or not of the "favored nation clause," it had been decided that no further claim would be made for the missionaries than is conceded to merchants; hence no governmental protection would be extended to either merchants or missionaries beyond the immediate vicinity of the open ports.

Within two or three years large additions have been made to the number of the American missionaries with a view of extending their field of operations and sphere of usefulness to points in the interior. Notwithstanding the decision of the Ministers regarding their treaty rights stations have already been established at Kalgan and some other points in this part of the country without serious opposition and with promise of good results, which stimulated exertions for further extension. In view of the increasing activity of the missionaries it appeared to me desirable that their legal status should be better defined and their rights fixed upon a more satisfactory basis than the restrictive construction given to the French treaty by my predecessors, for the missionaries, as a rule, declined to accept this as the proper construction of their treaty rights, and the result has been dissatisfaction at the course of the diplomatic representative and grave complaints at the lack of protection afforded them by their Government.

In the III Article of the French treaty of 1858 it is provided that when any discrepancy shall be found between the French and Chinese texts the original (French) shall govern in defining the proper meaning and intent. In view of this it seemed desirable, if not indispensable, that a copy of the French text should be obtained in order that the rights of our missionaries might be clearly understood. My application to the French Charge d'Affaires for permission to examine the official copy of the supplementary treaty of 1860 was granted, and I have the honor to send herewith an exact copy of the French text of Article VI and a careful translation in English of the Chinese text of the same. (enclosures A. B.) [not printed].

Your particular attention is requested to these two documents.

From rumors which had come to me from Chinese and other sources I expected to find a discrepancy which might vary the meaning somewhat, but I was not prepared to find so wide a difference as to preclude the possibility of its having occurred by accident or unintentional error. If the French text be considered authoritative, of which there can be no doubt, it follows that there is no authority in the treaty for residence in the interior; unless the provision for the restitution of the property of Christians indirectly confers the right of occupancy by its owners. With this version of the treaty before me there can be no doubt what the decision must be with reference to the questions which have arisen heretofore and which will come up again; and although I shall frankly state to the missionaries the facts, and give them, without reserve, my opinions with respect to their legal status, I do not consider it wise to give undue publicity to this remarkable discrepancy in the treaties at the present moment, nor shall I refer to it in any communication to the Chinese Government. Missionaries will continue to go into the interior whenever they can gain a safe footing, and I have no disposition to embarrass or hinder them. On the contrary I shall be glad to afford them all the moral aid and support possible whenever and wherever they can gain the goodwill of the people. But while doing this it is right and proper that they shall understand distinctly the limit of their legal right, beyond which their safety must depend upon the good faith and friendship of the Chinese among whom they live. Nor do I think the cause they are laboring to promote will lose anything by the practice of patience, conciliation and forbearance, which this knowledge will be likely to produce on the part of the missionaries.

.   .   .   .

The system of exterritoriality provided for in the treaties of all Western Nations with China seems, under existing circumstances, to be necessary for the protection of foreigners residing in China. It is however such an anomaly in international intercourse, and so difficult to carry out honestly and in good faith, that its extension must, sooner or later, end in the overthrow of the Government within whose jurisdiction it is exercised. This the officials begin to see and realize, which makes them disinclined to take any step which will be likely to increase the difficulty and embarrassment of their positions; any attempt to secure the rights which the missionaries desire touching native Christians will be resisted. Nor do I think it wise for foreign nations to ask, or even accept it if offered. It is wrong in principle and would be a constant source of irritation and trouble if attempted to be put into practical operation. Any extension of exterritoriality would lessen the dignity and influence of the native officials.

It is this consideration which makes them reluctant to see Foreign influence extended, and is the great obstacle in the way of procuring concessions, which if granted, would undoubtedly prove a great blessing to both Government and people. Prince Kung in a despatch to one of my predecessors states his view of the case so well that I quote an extract from it. He says: "But in the conduct of affairs it behooves every country carefully to watch the times and the tendencies, that its own power suffer no detriment, neither in the prerogatives of the Throne nor in the control exerted over the people. If these conditions can be maintained improvements can be adopted. This principle is applicable to all countries as well as the Middle Kingdom."

Any extension of the rights and privileges of foreigners undoubtedly extends their influence, and as a consequence lessens the power and influence of the Chinese officials; although it is likely that their ignorance and conservatism induce them to largely over-estimate the dangers that lie in their path. Their education and habits of thought totally unfit this people for appreciating in any proper sense the Christian Missionaries or their work. It is impossible for them to conceive that the Missionaries are isolating themselves among a strange people for the single purpose of teaching morality, with a view of improving the mental and spiritual condition of the human race. An ill-defined suspicion pervades the native mind that some political design lies beneath the honest exterior of the missionaries, and they are constantly watching with a suspicious eye for the hidden mystery which they can neither see nor understand. I regret to be compelled to say that the unwise action of the French Missionaries,—to say nothing of the French Government—has rather added to than lessened these suspicions.

If the Officials could be undeceived in regard to the real purposes of the missionaries, and if the missions in China could be conducted by really honest and sagacious men I doubt if anything more than a passive resistance would be met with, which would soon be overcome by friendly intercourse and mutual forbearance. But so long as the Roman Catholic missionaries, blinded by religious zeal, and forgetful of the ignorance and prejudices of this people, continue the illegal and unwarrantable assumptions which have characterized their course hitherto, so long may we expect to hear of the hostile attitude of the people towards them, which will occasionally take the form of insurrections riots and bloodshed, the destruction of missionary establishments and the ill treatment of native Christians,—in which Protestants will be likely to suffer also; and when these unhappy results occur, the moral sentiment of the civilized world will be shocked at the intelligence of *"religious persecutions,"* perpetrated by the Chinese without cause, provocation or excuse, deserving punishment and dire retribution.

Low's Policy on Missionaries Approved. Hamilton Fish to Frederick F. Low, Washington, March 2, 1871[2]

.   .   .   .

Your construction of the Treaty and of the limitation of the right of the residence of missionaries in the interior is approved by the Department; as is also your caution in withholding the public expression of your opinion on that subject in the existing state of things in China.

Your views of the proper relations between the missionaries and the native Christians are also regarded as sound . . . .

[2] *China Instructions,* Vol. II, No. 33.

"EQUALITY" AS UNDERSTOOD BY THE UNITED STATES AND BY CHINA. MINISTER LOW TO SECRETARY FISH, PEKING, JANUARY 18, 1872[3]

In compliance with an instruction contained in your No. 57 I have communicated the substance of that despatch to the Chinese Government. A copy of my note to Prince Kung is herewith enclosed.

Your views concerning the proper construction to be given to the treaties, and the duties of the Imperial Government with reference thereto are all embodied in my note. If it should appear that some of your statements of fact are omitted I beg to observe that I was induced to assume this responsibility for prudential reasons. Instead of strengthening and enforcing your arguments, as would be the case were I addressing a Christian Government they would, on the contrary, be seized upon as arguments by the Chinese Ministers to sustain their views. For instance you say that "it is the fundamental principle in the United States that persons of every sect, faith and race are equal before the civil law" &c &c. . . . "The United States ask no more in China than they confer at home."

Were I to repeat this the Chinese Government would question the correctness of the latter assertion, and affirm that we are not willing to place our citizens on an equality here. To prove this they would probably reiterate what they have before said to me: —"When Chinese subjects go to your country they become amenable to your laws; when your citizens come here they claim entire exemption from ours." The chief object aimed at in the memorandum, they would argue, was to remove this inequality so far as missionaries are concerned, and place on an equal footing all religious teachers in the Empire, whether they be Christian, Confucian, Taoist, or Mahommedan.

In our personal interviews heretofore when I have urged the relaxing of the restrictions so far as residence trade &c are concerned, Prince Kung has met my arguments with the assertion of his entire willingness to remove all restrictions upon the residence of foreigners providing they will place themselves on an equality with Chinese subjects and become amenable to Chinese law and the jurisdiction of the officials. The only response to this is, of course, that their laws are inferior to ours and not suitable for the government of our people, of the truth of which no argument will convince the high officials here. Such discussions only tend to irritate without serving any useful purpose, hence I deem it prudent to avoid them as much as possible.

I may add that ex-territoriality is at the present time a necessity for the safety and protection of our citizens residing here; nor will it be prudent to give up or relax our claims on that question until this nation is much farther advanced in modern civilization;—until their penal and civil codes are brought into something like agreement with those of Christian countries. On the other hand the entire exemption of foreigners from the operations of Chinese law impresses the Government with a sense of humiliation; it also is, and must continue to be a constant source of irritation to the officials, from the highest to the lowest.

With this explanation my action in this matter will, I trust, meet the approval of the Department.

[3] *China Despatches*, Vol. XXXI, No. 125.

THE MISSIONARY POLICY OF THE AMERICAN GOVERNMENT. MINISTER LOW TO THE CHINESE FOREIGN OFFICE, PEKING, JANUARY 18, 1872[4]

On the 13th of February last I had the honor to receive a note from the high ministers Wen Hsi-ang and Shen Kuei-fau covering a memorandum concerning Christian missions, and also the draft of eight rules for the regulation of missionary enterprises.

To this I returned a reply on the 20th of March in which the memorandum and the proposed rules were reviewed in detail. I gave it as my opinion that the rules are entirely unnecessary; nor did I think that they would be assented to, either in whole or in part, by the Government of the United States. Copies of the correspondence with the enclosures were sent to my Government without delay.

. . . .

In the opinion of the President the rights of American citizens are clearly defined by existing Treaties. Unless it be the desire of the Imperial Government to place restrictions upon the rights thus guaranteed additional rules and regulations appear to be superfluous and therefore unnecessary. If the proposed rules are intended to curtail the privileges granted by treaty, then I am instructed to say that they cannot be sanctioned or entertained.

In regard to Foreign Missionaries the Government of the United States neither expects nor asks for them exceptional rights or privileges over and above those granted to other American citizens residing in the Empire. If other Governments demand that Ecclesiastics be placed on a different footing from other foreign residents I am directed to inform your Imperial Highness that such demands will not have the sympathy or support of my Government. In case, however, such demands are made and assented to by His Imperial Majesty, the President reserved to himself the right to decide whether privileges intended to apply to ecclesiastics alone will not accrue equally to all citizens of the United States irrespective of their vocation, calling or profession, under and by virtue of the 30th Article of the Treaty of 1858.

With reference to subjects of His Imperial Majesty professing or teaching the Christian religion, the President confidently expects that the faith of the Empire pledged by treaty that they shall in no case be interfered with or molested on account of their religious faith will be kept, and that whatever may be the disposition of the turbulent and evil disposed portion of the population towards Christian subjects, he relies with confidence upon the Imperial Government to afford the full measure of protection guaranteed by Treaty to foreign Missionaries and native Christians alike.

But while insisting firmly upon this the President would see with regret any attempt to withdraw the native Christians from the jurisdiction of the Emperor without his full consent, or to convert the churches founded by the Missions into asylums for the refuge of desperadoes and criminals; and I am instructed to inform Your Imperial Highness that except so far as it may be found necessary to secure freedom from molestation on account of the profession or teaching of the doctrines of Christianity the officers of the United States in China will not be permitted to interfere between the Christian subjects of the Emperor and their rulers or participate in any attempt to disturb the natural relations that exist between His Imperial Majesty and his subjects.

[4] *Ibid.*, Incl. 1 in No. 125.

I am also instructed to reiterate what was said in my note to the Yamen, that the profession of Christianity cannot be considered as a protection against the just punishment for crime; nor will my Government allow American missionaries to shield or protect criminals, or permit ecclesiastical Asylums for the refuge of the lawless to be established by or through its agency or with its consent.

The Government of the United States has steadfastly observed its treaty engagements with China; it asks in return that the Government of the Emperor will do the same.

So long as the present treaties remain unchanged, if other Governments demand that unusual civil rights be conferred on foreign Ecclesiastics or advance pretensions inconsistent with the dignity of China as an independent power, my Government will not be a party to such proceedings; on the contrary the President will use his influence, so far as it can be exerted legitimately and peacefully, to prevent such demands and pretensions in case there should be reason to apprehend that they will be asserted.

. . . .

XX

THE AUDIENCE QUESTION, 1872-1873

ONE OF THE most difficult problems confronting the ministers of the treaty powers at Peking in the years 1870-73 was the question of audience before the emperor. The custom of audience, long accepted among Western states, had been requested at Peking as early as 1861, but the Manchu court had persistently refused on the ground that the emperor was a minor. When, however, in 1873 he came of age and assumed full powers, the ministers of the treaty powers, applying the co-operative policy through a joint note, brought united pressure to bear on the court, and the request for audience was granted. Although the Western Powers and Japan had thus won a decisive diplomatic victory, the Chinese were far from regarding themselves as defeated since they granted the audience in the Pavilion of Purple Light, which had long been used to receive bearers of tribute from vassal states.

The following despatches of Minister Low illustrate not only the reluctance of the Chinese to grant the audience, but also the difficulties of securing united action among the treaty powers.

FRANCE AND THE AUDIENCE QUESTION. MINISTER LOW TO SECRETARY FISH, PEKING, SEPTEMBER 13, 1872[1]

An examination of the papers which accompanied my No. 135 of 22d February last probably impressed you as they did me when I read them, that the French Government considered the Audience question above all others in importance, and that the discussion with reference to its immediate solution would be the first business of the new Minister after he should reach Peking. This impression has been generally entertained by all foreign residents in the Capital and at the ports. Such a belief was considerably strengthened by intimations coming from the French Legation to the effect that, unless audience of the Emperor be conceded to M. Geofroy upon his arrival his stay would be short in the Capital.

A few days since the French Minister called upon me, and, during the interview he alluded to the subject. He did this, he said, in order to correct an erroneous impression which seemed to be general, and in which I undoubtedly shared to a greater or less extent, as to his future course. He denied that there was any foundation for the reports referred to, and then proceeded to inform me of what had already occurred.

[1] *China Despatches*, Vol. XXXII, No. 186.

In accordance with the custom which had obtained hitherto (the United States alone excepted) a formal request was made for an audience of the Emperor for the purpose of presenting his letters of credence, and one from the President of the French Republic in reply to a letter which had been sent by the Emperor concerning the Tientsin massacre; that upon being informed by the ministers of the Yamen that the request could not, at the present time, be granted he did as all his predecessors had done;—left with Prince Kung a copy of the letter of credence, retaining the original and the letter of M. Thiers before referred to. These will not be delivered until an opportunity shall be afforded to present them to the Emperor in person.

From all that was said at the interview I infer that, while the French Government regards the solution of the audience question as of paramount importance there is no intention of forcing it prematurely, nor will France undertake to do it alone. M. Geofroy concurs in my opinion that a request to that effect made now by any one Government would be certainly refused; but that a joint or simultaneous demand made at the appropriate time by all the Treaty Powers represented here, would not be rejected.

The information he had obtained tended to make him sanguine that the Emperor would declare his majority at the same time as his marriage or immediately after; he was also of the opinion that as soon as the Regency is set aside there will be entire unanimity among European Powers as to the propriety of insisting upon a definite settlement of this vexed question.

. . . .

GERMANY AND THE AUDIENCE QUESTION. MINISTER LOW TO SECRETARY FISH, PEKING, DECEMBER 10, 1872[2]

Baron Von Rehfues, the German Minister, who has been absent on leave for eighteen months or more, returned to his post a few days since.

. . . .

With reference to the course which all foreign nations should pursue in order that a recognition of equality may be secured, the Minister's opinions are definite and decided, in accordance with which he is prepared to act when the appropriate time arrives, provided a majority of his colleagues will act in concert. He thinks that, as soon as the Emperor assumes power and authority as sovereign *de facto* the representatives of all the Treaty Powers should request a personal audience, according to the customs and forms usual in Christian countries, and that, if the demand be peremptorily refused, the Ministers should withdraw, leaving the Legations in the hands of Chargés d'Affaires. This proposition, you will observe, does not contemplate the interruption of diplomatic relations; nor would such a step be advisable at the present time in view of the .possible hardship it might work to individual interests and commercial affairs generally. If the withdrawal of the Ministers from Peking did not result in an invitation to them to return then foreign governments could consult and decide upon the course necessary to pursue.

In support of his view of the question the Baron argues that the failure of the foreign representatives to demand audience at the time referred to, will be construed into an admission of the inferiority of their Governments; if the demand be refused, some action more emphatic than verbal or written protests will be necessary, otherwise the Chinese Government would regard the result as a victory over the foreigner, which would render the Foreign Ministers' position here even more difficult and embarrassing than it now is. In his opinion it would be infinitely better that the demand were not made than to tamely and quietly submit in case of refusal.

So far as I can judge the opinions of the German Minister are shared in by all the representatives of foreign governments now in Peking. Whether they will be authorized to join in the action proposed I cannot, at this moment, say positively.

That the public recognition of entire equality between China and Western Governments in the manner proposed will be distasteful to the Court and all the high officials and that it will be resisted by all the arts known to diplomacy, no person well acquainted with Oriental traditions and customs can for a moment doubt; nor is it less true that nothing short of a fear of the consequences, which a positive refusal would be likely to entail upon the Government, will ever cause assent to be given to the proposition.

My views concerning this question have been given you in previous despatches. Of the propriety of making the demand there can be no question; nor do I believe that if it be made by all the Governments represented here it will be refused. But while I should anticipate a favorable result, no Government would, in my opinion, be justified in taking the step without deciding beforehand what it would do in case the Chinese Government declined absolutely to comply with the demand. A tame acquiescence in the refusal would prove a more serious damage than people at a distance, who are not familiar with Oriental arrogance and deceit, would imagine.

RUSSIA AND THE AUDIENCE QUESTION. MINISTER LOW TO SECRETARY FISH, PEKING, MARCH 13, 1873[3]

I am disposed to believe that the representative of Russia is not acting in good faith regarding the Audience question. If I am correct in these suspicions he will be likely to embarrass, if not defeat entirely, our efforts in that direction.

Ostensibly he is acting with his colleagues; really against them. I am not without reason for thinking that Russian policy is against it; and the Minister is trying to bring about a refusal by secretly advising the Chinese not to accede to the demand.

I have not been entirely satisfied of his good faith from the first, although I had no proof of his insincerity. Nor do I think he did anything at variance with his professions until within a day or two. And if he had found that the Chinese Gov't. was bent on refusing our request it is likely that he would have continued to refrain from interference. But as soon as the Chinese Ministers showed the slightest disposition to yield (which he undoubtedly thought he saw at our conference on the 11th) he then determined to weaken the force of our demand.

His first step was to announce at the close of the conference his intention of leaving in a day or two for Shanghai, to be absent three or four weeks, the ostensible object of his going is to meet the Grand Duke Alexis. This morning he took his departure. Yesterday he had a long interview with the Chinese Minister at the Yamen, to discuss, he said, questions of general business affecting Russian affairs; really, I believe, the interview had reference to the business which all have in hand.

[3] *Ibid.*, Vol. XXXIV. [Unnumbered.]

This erratic and apparently inconsistent course of my Russian colleague may be accounted for on either of the two hypotheses: viz.

1st. Russia undoubtedly expects sooner or later to absorb a portion or the whole of China: and to facilitate the carrying out of this plan it is her policy to keep China in *status quo* as nearly as possible, thus preventing other Western Powers from increasing the influence they already have; or

2d. It may be considered her best policy to induce China to adopt a course which will sooner or later provoke hostilities from some of the Treaty Powers, and when war comes to profit by the occasion to repeat what was done in 1860,—take another large slice of territory.

. . . .

OTHER THREATS TO THE AUDIENCE QUESTION. MINISTER LOW TO SECRETARY FISH, PEKING, MARCH 28, 1873[4]

Several unlooked for events have happened since the beginning of the discussion of the Audience Question, the effect of which already embarrasses our action, and may eventually defeat the object aimed at.

The first untoward occurrence was the departure of the Russian Minister from Peking with no other avowed object in view than to pay a visit of ceremony to the Grand Duke Alexis, who was expected in Shanghai sometime in March. His colleagues urged the necessity of all the signataries to the Collective Note asking for Audience remaining in Peking until a definite answer should be received, in order that our solid front *vis à vis* the Chinese might not seem to them to be broken or weakened, and pointed out to him the possible and probable damage which his absence at this time would do to the general question.

All our remonstrances and expostulations were, however, of no avail, and he took his departure on the 13th instant, two days after our first conference.

The first Shanghai newspapers received in Peking after the departure of the Russian Minister contained a London telegram announcing that M. Butzow, now Russian Chargé d'Affaires in Japan, had been transferred to Peking to relieve Genl. Vlangaly. Whether M. Butzow comes as Chargé or Minister the telegram did not state, and enquiries at the Russian Legation failed to elicit any information concerning the subject. If he comes as Chargé (which is not improbable) the name of the Russian representative will practically be withdrawn from the Collective note.

The newspaper before alluded to contained another telegram, saying that the Gladstone Ministry in England had, in consequence of an adverse note in the House of Commons, resigned. This news has had the effect to unsettle the plans of the British Minister; he is now not able to say one day what he can do the next, for he is likely to receive new and contradictory instructions any moment.

Added to all these difficulties, the German Minister informed me confidentially a day or two since, that he had just received by telegraph the assent of his Government to his request for leave of absence, made some months since on account of failing health. It will be necessary, he says, for him to leave Peking before the hot weather sets in.

In view of these adverse occurrences, I hazard little in saying that if this matter is allowed to drag along, as is usually the case when a decision is

[4] *Ibid.*, No. 243.

asked for concerning a difficult question, the causes above referred to will be likely to weaken our position so much that the Chinese will feel safe in interposing one objection after another and by this means postpone their decision indefinitely, or they may gather courage enough to send a peremptory refusal to our request.

If our present efforts fail to accomplish what in my judgement is of the first importance to all nations having relations with China, as well as the Chinese themselves, it will be the fault (if fault it be) of the Treaty Powers themselves or their representatives.

XXI

PROBLEMS OF DIPLOMACY IN A PERIOD OF PEACEFUL INTERCOURSE, 1875-1879

WHEN Benjamin P. Avery, United States minister to China, died at Peking in November, 1875, he was succeeded by George F. Seward, who since 1861 had been consul and later consul-general at Shanghai. He served as minister at Peking until 1880. Seward attacked problems of American policy in China with understanding and aggressiveness. In a detailed correspondence with the Department of State he dealt exhaustively with a wide and complex range of topics including, among others, treaty interpretation and revision, official intercourse, judicial procedure under extraterritoriality, taxation of foreign goods under the conventional tariff, the question of the opening of Korea, the coolie trade to Cuba and Peru, and the status of the Chinese in California.

A number of the more perplexing questions of the period were raised by signature in 1876 of the Chefoo Convention between Great Britain and China. This agreement proposed to alter materially the existing treaty settlement. It provided among other things in mixed civil cases for trial by an official of the defendant's nationality. *Likin* taxes on opium were to be paid with the import duty, after which the drug might be imported into the interior without further impost.

As a result of these various issues raised by the British minister, the Chinese Foreign Office requested the views of the ministers of the other treaty powers. This in turn led to a number of ministerial conferences, to a joint memorandum of views by the ministers, and to detailed comments by Seward directed specifically to American policy.

A JOINT MINUTE OF THE MINISTERIAL CONFERENCE. PEKING, DECEMBER 5, 1876[1]

The Undersigned, thinking it desirable to come to an understanding among themselves on certain questions raised in the Chefoo Agreement to which Her Britannic Majesty's Government may have drawn the attention of the Governments of Powers having treaties with China, have agreed upon the following.

The points to which reference is made in Part 1st of Section II. of the Chefoo Agreement may be divided into three heads:

1. *The Audience Question.*
2. *Intercourse between Foreign Representatives and Chinese Ministers.*
3. *Intercourse between Consuls and local Authorities.*

1st. With regard to the *Audience Question,* the Undersigned are of the opinion that it would be inopportune, for the present, to approach it. Practically, as far as foreign interests are concerned the situation is such that there is no pressing occasion to insist upon an audience; this being the case due regard can be paid to the peculiar circumstances now existing which would render difficult a satisfactory settlement of the ceremonial part of the question.

The point having been raised whether it would be desirable, while not asking for an audience, to take some step indicating that the foreign Representatives are not inclined to abandon the principle involved, it has been found advisable, in order not to provoke an embarrassing discussion to avoid, for the moment, all allusion to the question.

2nd. *The intercourse between foreign Representatives* and *Chinese Ministers* has been, so far as the relations with the Tsung li Yamen (Foreign Office) are concerned, on the whole, satisfactory.

With regard to such relations as might or ought to be entertained with other high Officials, the Undersigned are of opinion that the drawing up of a code of etiquette, such as proposed by the Chefoo Agreement would not be the best means of promoting the object. Improvement in this respect must be the work of time. The establishment of Chinese Missions abroad will go far to convince Chinese statesmen that closer relations with the foreign Representatives are in their own interest and in that of their country.

3rd. *The position of Foreign Consuls with regard to their relations to Chinese Officials,* is not satisfactory. Much depends, it is true, upon the tact of the individual Consul, as well as upon the personal feelings of the Chinese Official, but there can be no doubt that one of the principal causes of the unsatisfactory situation is to be found in the stipulations of some of the Treaties referring to the manner of correspondence and relative rank. (vide English Treaty of 1842. Art. XI.; English Treaty of 1858, Art. VII.; American Treaty of 1858, Arts. VII and X.; French Treaty of 1858, Art. IV.; Spanish Treaty of 1864, Art. II.)

Though probably not in the intention of the framers of the Treaties, these stipulations have nevertheless created a position of inferiority for the Consuls in their relations with the higher Provincial Authorities. In the opinion of the Undersigned, it would therefore be in the interest of the Treaty Powers to have such of the stipulations before mentioned, as are objectionable, abrogated.

[1] *China Despatches,* Vol. XLIII, Incl. 2 in No. 177.

It is essential that the Consuls should have free access to all the Provincial Authorities, the Governor and Governor General included, as the interests intrusted to them may require, without any persons or Boards being interposed between them, and without their being subjected to any ceremonial which would mark a degree of inferiority according to Chinese ideas.

Their correspondence with the Chinese Authorities should be upon a basis of perfect equality, and the terms "statement" or "memorial" (shen Chen —— [Chinese characters]) and "declaration" (Cha hsing —— [Chinese characters]) in use now for the designation of the correspondence between officers of different rank should be abolished, and replaced by the term "communication" (chao huei —— [Chinese characters]) for both sides.

The Undersigned believe that it would be possible to obtain this result much more easily by laying before the Chinese Government a semi-official statement of the impossibility of creating or maintaining a kind of hierarchical subordination between officials of different nationalities, than by making a grave political question out of it, and insisting upon the framing of a code of etiquette, which, as shown by the before-mentioned Treaty stipulations, is much more likely to do harm than good.

The Undersigned are, however, of opinion that while it would be possible to obtain certain concessions from the Chinese Government with regard to the position of *paid* Consuls, it would be necessary at the same time to draw a distinct line between *paid officials* of a Government, and *merchant Consuls*.

The appointment of the latter in China must be considered, at the best, a temporary expedient, and, in order to gain a better position for the official Consuls, it would become necessary to define more strictly than has been done heretofore, the rank and functions of *merchant* Consuls. To assign to them the position of Consular or Commercial Agents, with inferior rank and functions would facilitate, probably, very much, an arrangement with regard to paid Consuls, without being in any way contrary to the interests or the dignity of the Treaty Powers.

While, however, this part of the question cannot, in the opinion of the Undersigned, be taken up without specific instructions from their respective Governments, they will think it their duty to act, as much as possible, jointly in every case in which a Consular Officer has just cause of complaint against Chinese local Authorities.

Parts 2nd and 3rd of Section II of the Chefoo Agreement have reference to *jurisdiction in criminal matters, the mixed Court at Shanghai, the more perfect administration of justice at the open ports, and the presence of deputies of the Legation at trials of persons who have committed offences against British subjects.*

Jurisdiction in Criminal matters.

What is said in the agreement in regard to jurisdiction appears to have been intended to indicate that all criminal matters arising between British subjects and the Chinese within the territory of China must be heard and determined in the Court of the accused according to the laws of his country, and thus to set at rest a question which had been raised in regard to the meaning of Article XVI. of the British Treaty of Tientsin, which, has reference to this subject.

The Undersigned are of the opinion that the principle that criminal matters are to be tried in the natural Court of the accused, and according to the laws of his country is clearly stated in the treaties made between foreign Governments and the Government of China, and that no different principle should be adhered to.

The presence of officers at trials.

The first paragraph of part 3rd of Section II. provides that whenever a crime is committed, affecting the person or property of a British subject whether in the interior or at an open port, the British Minister shall be free to send officers to the spot, to be present at the investigation.

Paragraph 3rd of the same division speaks further of the presence of officials of the defendant's nationality, and declares that the purpose shall be to watch proceedings in the interests of justice, but if the officer so "attending be dissatisfied with the proceedings, it will be in his power to protest against them in detail."

The reservation of the right of the minister to send officers to be present at the trial of Chinese in the cases stated, may raise the presumption that British officers will attend trials only in those rare cases where the intervention of the Diplomatic Agent has been thought necessary.

It is essential to the right administration of justice in criminal cases in which Chinese are accused that the Consular Officer of the sufferer, or some representative of his Government, shall be admitted to the trial of the offender, and that he shall be permitted to present to the court such witnesses for his countryman as may not be otherwise called, and to assist in the examination of all witnesses. It would be inconvenient, therefore, and might defeat justice, if the right of the Consular officer to be present and to take such part in trials, should depend upon reference to the Legation.

The statement of a right to protest against the action of the sitting magistrates, as given in the Chefoo Agreement, is also of doubtful merit. The principle having been declared that criminal cases are to be tried in the Court of the accused, and according to the laws of his country, it follows that protests against the action of the given Court must take the form of appeal, or in the absence of a higher Court, of diplomatic representation to the Government.

It appears to the undersigned desirable to reach an understanding with the Chinese Government in regard to the rights and duties of officers present to watch the proceedings of courts in which their nationals are concerned. This understanding should follow, as nearly as may be, the views which have been expressed above.

The Mixed Court at Shanghai.

This is a court of first instance presided over by a deputy of the intendant of Circuit (Taotai). It has jurisdiction in minor criminal matters, for the districts of the so-called English and American settlements, and in civil matters of less concern between those foreigners who may choose to apply to it and Chinese defendants. A Consular officer representing one or another Consulate usually sits with the magistrate upon the trial of police cases, or of any others, civil or criminal, in which foreigners are concerned. His position is consultative only, and the term *mixed* court, is a misnomer.

That the mixed court fails to meet the wants of the great commercial community at Shanghai is undoubted. It may be questioned, however, whether it will be worth while to direct efforts specially to an improvement of it since an improvement of the native courts at the ports generally is needed, and because there is a question of principle to be settled, before efforts of the kind can well be undertaken, as will be seen from what follows.

The more perfect administration of justice.

Referring more particularly to matters of a civil nature, the undersigned meet, at once, the fact that there is a radical difference in the reading of the Treaties upon the point of jurisdiction. The representative of the United States is of opinion that the treaties concluded between the United States and China give, in effect, full jurisdiction in civil matters to the court of the defendant in all cases between Americans and Chinese arising within the territory of China, and states that this principle has been rigidly adhered to since the date of the first Treaty.

The Representatives of Russia, Germany, France, and Spain are of opinion that, under their Treaties all cases of a civil nature arising between Chinese and the subjects of their several Governments in China should be heard and determined by officers of the respective nationalities acting conjointly. They admit, however, that in practice, the state of affairs is different from that which is presented by their Treaties. In many cases the Chinese plaintiffs have submitted their grievances to the decision of foreign courts without asking the intervention of their own officials, while in those cases against Chinese, in which it has been found difficult for the Consular officer to reach an agreement with the Chinese magistrate, the course of the latter has seemed to be controled by an administrative rather than a judicial view of the issues involved.

Without desiring to prejudge in any way the reading of the Treaties by the respective Governments the Undersigned agree that it is most important that certain reforms and a uniform procedure should be arrived at.

There can be no doubt that the state of the Chinese judicial establishment, as it affects foreigners is unsatisfactory. No codes of procedure worthy to be called such exist. The magistrates' secretaries, and constables are often corrupt. Judgments are secured only after a great deal of exertion. Persistent efforts have to be made to procure their execution. Serious annoyances arise from the fact that it is often difficult to discover the officer who has jurisdiction in given cases, and to whom therefore the Consular officer should apply to secure a hearing for his countryman, and again because, so far as foreigners are concerned no Chinese appellate courts exist. For the latter reason, questions which should be decided by appeal can only be treated by political recourse, through the Diplomatic agents, and become the subject of long and annoying negotiations.

In order to effect a remedy of this state of things so far as may be possible and to bring about the best results which can be reached for the time being, the Undersigned advance the following suggestions.

1st. That the principle that civil cases shall be heard and determined in the court of the defendant, be uniformly adopted.

2nd. That the Chinese Government be asked to establish, at each open port, a court of first instance to hear the cases against Chinese in which foreigners are the plaintiffs, the Judges of these courts to be appointed by the Emperor, and also such of the clerks and other officers as may be determined upon.

3rd. The sittings of the courts to be public, and the right of Consular officers to be present and to assist in the examination of witnesses, and in the discussion of the merits of all cases to be admitted.

4th.   Clear rules of procedure to be provided for the guidance of the courts.

5th.   A court of appeal to be established at Shanghai or Peking, open to appeals from either side under suitable regulations, and especially a provision that no defendant may appeal without giving security for the satisfaction of the judgment of the higher court.

6th.   The laws of China in regard to matters which may be brought before the courts, to be made public.

7th.   It should be provided that criminal charges preferred by foreigners against Chinese, at the open ports, should be heard and determined in the courts of first instance and of appeal, which have been proposed above.

In view of these propositions, it may be said that a foreign officer sitting as cojudge with a Chinese magistrate, as the Treaties, or the greater number of them provide, cannot exercise, in the absence of Treaty stipulations of a more precise nature than those now existing, a greater authority than he would if his voice were considered consultative only.   Each officer has independent functions and responsibilities by reason of his separate allegiance and position, and directs his conduct accordingly.

Again judgements can be enforced, as matters stand, only under the forms of law to which the defendant, and the Judge of his nationality are subject.   It may be said even that in effect no judgement can be given that does not conform to the laws, or at least, to the system of equity of the defendants nation and that Chinese and foreign ideas of equity do not always fall within the same lines.

It is to be remembered moreover that subject to the principle of domicile the rule of courts and of Governments is to recognize the applicability of territorial laws to persons resident upon the soil.   It would be dangerous to recognize the laws of China this way.   As the Treaties stand, and are generally construed this must be done measurably (?) in many matters of private right including the condition of persons, property and obligations.

A reformation of matters then would involve practically a declaration of the broad principle that all cases are to be heard and determined in the court of the defendant and according to the laws of his country, or the adoption of a code for civil matters binding alike upon foreigners and Chinese in all mixed cases and taking the place of territorial laws in all those matters which are not otherwise provided for.

The Undersigned are not prepared to advise that efforts should be made to frame such a code for use here and to procure its adoption by China and the several Powers concerned.   Attempts of the kind which have been undertaken elsewhere show that they would be attended with many difficulties and these in the opinion of the Undersigned could not be surmounted here, at the present time.

It will not be easy indeed, to procure the assent of the Chinese Government to the simple plan which has been presented herein, and their active aid to carry it out.   But no other plan which has been suggested would present so few difficulties on the Chinese side.   And it is not to be forgotten that this system would fall in with legislation for China heretofore adopted by the different Governments and that no further legislation on the part of the greater number of Powers would be needed.

If the system proposed should be carried into execution, it would naturally form the basis for further reforms, and might even be expected to lead up to the eventual adoption of a Code for commercial and other matters of the kind which has been indicated.

The principal subject treated in Section III of the Chefoo Agreement, is that of the duties to be levied on imports carried inland, and on native produce carried to an open port for exportation.

The stipulations of the Treaties covering these points, regarding of course the most favorable stipulations of the several Treaties as applying to all of the foreign Powers, may be summarized thus:

Imports, on which the import duty has been paid can be sent inland without being subjected to any other tax than the Transit duties, which shall be levied according to the tariff in force at the time of the conclusion of the given Treaty, and shall not be raised in future.

On native produce, transported from the interior to an open port, or on imports sent inland, these Transit duties can be discharged in one payment.

The amount of such payment has been fixed for imports sent inland, and for produce bought inland by a foreigner for exportation, at half the import or export treaty tariff duty, or at 50% of the *ad valorem* duty on unenumerated goods.

With regard to imports the rights and privileges granted by the Treaties, attach to the goods themselves, and not to the person of the proprietor, whose nationality is of no importance.

All other taxes, Lekin included, must therefore be considered as illegal. The Transit duties, or their equivalent can only be levied on imports when sent outside of the Treaty port area, as such is to be considered the area between the nearest stations for the levying of Transit duties, which were in existence at the time of the conclusion of the Treaties.

It is certain that these stipulations have not always been observed by the Chinese Authorities; they have, on the contrary been often and persistently disregarded, but they constitute, at least, the situation as existing by right to which the Treaty Powers may, if convenient, appeal at any moment, in order to check taxation.

What, in the face of this situation, is the one created by the Chefoo Agreement?

The right of the Chinese Government to levy Lekin taxes on foreign imports is formally recognized; from the operation of this rule are to be excepted only the so-called foreign concessions, i. e. with the exception of that of Shanghai within which a certain number of Chinese live, and which may therefore be considered as possessing a local consumption of its own; the small areas, occupied exclusively by foreigners and, for certain ports, hardly more than the houses inhabited by them.

The Transit Pass system, more over, is rendered too severe, by the Chefoo Agreement. This will be understood when it is remembered that the transit charge is properly a commutation of the Transit duties only, while the Treaties expressly denounce as illegal the collection of any other dues on foreign goods or foreign owned native produce. If therefore the right to levy Lekin taxes is admitted, they can be levied on goods and produce without regard to Transit passes.

As to native produce the Agreement contains nothing new.

While, therefore, no advantage has been obtained by the Chefoo Agreement with respect to the complaints against the levying of illegal taxes, an approval of its stipulations would prove injurious to trade, and would deprive the foreign Powers of the right to protest against any unfair taxation; by such approval they would, on the contrary, bind themselves to recognize the unlimited imposition of Lekin by the Chinese Government.

On the other hand, it cannot be denied that the right to levy Lekin is of great importance to the Chinese Government, and that it will prove very difficult to protect foreign imports against it beyond a certain point. It may be considered therefore in the interest of both parties to come to an understanding on the Lekin question.

In the opinion of the Undersigned, the right to levy Lekin might be granted to the Chinese Government, under certain restrictions, and as a compensation for concessions made by them. These concessions, however, ought not to consist in the opening of ports, the Undersigned considering it as a mistake to allow the Chinese to imagine that the opening of a port is a sacrifice on their part, which justifies them in claiming a compensation. Such concessions should afford sufficient proof that the Chinese Government are prepared to abandon their old spirit of exclusiveness. The decision as to what they should be can be left to the future consideration of all the parties concerned. At the same time measures ought to be taken to prevent the levy of Lekin on foreign goods, and foreign owned native produce from burdening too heavily foreign trade while affording a financial advantage to China.

For this purpose the following arrangements appear necessary:—

1. A port area to be established for each open port within which no taxes, except the Treaty tariff duties may be levied on foreign imports.

2. The integrity of the Transit pass system to be acknowledged, (a) in regard to imports. That foreign imports, whether in foreign or native hands, and irrespective of ownership, may be sent inland free from any charges, Lekin or other of any kind whatsoever, during transit, excepting the half tariff commutation charge.

(b) in regard to exports.

That foreign owned produce intended for exportation, and covered by Transit pass, may be carried to the port, free from any charge, as before, other than the half tariff commutation charge, and exported upon payment of the tariff Duty.

In lieu of this an arrangement would be accepted, under which foreign owned native produce on its way to the port would pay all barrier dues and other taxes demanded, any part of which in excess of the half tariff commutation charge would be refunded at the Custom House on exportation.

3. The right of the Chinese Government to impose Transit dues and Lekin taxes upon foreign imports, and foreign owned native produce, not covered by Transit passes, outside of the port area to be recognized, subject to a provision that Transit dues and Lekin taxes only shall be levied, and that neither the one nor the other shall exceed a certain percentage of the tariff duty.

It is possible that the limitation of taxation proposed in the last paragraph may not prove of immediate value, but it will give to the Treaty Powers the very important right of watching over the taxation applied to foreign trade and of protesting against it, if it should prove excessive.

It seems to the Undersigned that the levy of Lekin taxes may be agreed to under such conditions, and in exchange for valuable concessions on the part of the Chinese Government.

Accord between all the Powers in a question of such importance is desirable, and for this reason it is to be hoped that the stipulations of the Chefoo Agreement on this subject will not be approved by Her Britannic Majesty's Government.

The term of three years accepted by the Chefoo Agreement (Div. V. Section III.) as that within which drawbacks may be claimed upon imports, in the place of the former unlimited period, can be considered as meeting the exigencies of trade; this concession ought, however, not to be made to the Chinese Government without their granting to foreign merchants the long claimed right to exchange the Drawback Certificates against cash.

Peking, 25th November, 1876.

(Signed)

> BUTZOW
> BRANDT
> GEORGE F. SEWARD
> VTE BRENIER DE MONTMORAND
> ESPANA.

COMMENTS ON THE RECOMMENDATIONS OF THE MINISTERIAL CONFERENCE. GEORGE F. SEWARD TO SECRETARY FISH, PEKING, DECEMBER 5, 1876[2]

I had the honor to advise you on the 22nd ultimo, that I was considering with my colleagues, the Ministers for Russia, Germany, Spain, and France, the agreement made at Chefoo last summer by the Plenipotentiaries of Great Britain and China, and on the 26th ultimo, I advised you by telegraph, via Berlin, that we had signed a joint statement.

It appeared very desirable that the Chefoo Agreement should be dealt with by my colleagues and myself in this way, for the reason that parts of it, in terms of the Agreement, are to be submitted to other Powers, by the British Government, and that various questions raised in it, in terms of the Agreement, are to be and, in fact, have already been submitted to the Diplomatic Body, by the Foreign Office, for joint consideration. In this connection, I beg leave to call your attention to the following words, which will be found in Part 6. of Section III of the Agreement:—"The date for giving effect to the stipulations affecting exemption of imports from *Lekin taxation,* within the foreign settlements, and the collection of *Lekin* upon opium, by the Customs Inspectorate, at the same time as the tariff duty upon it, will be fixed as soon as the British Government has arrived at an understanding on the subject with other Foreign Governments;" and to the following, which will be found in Part I of Section II. "To the prevention of further misunderstanding upon the subject of intercourse and correspondence, it is agreed that the Tsung li Yamen shall address a Circular to the Legations inviting foreign Representatives to consider with them a Code of Etiquette, etc"; and again to the following, in Part 2. of the same Section: "It is now understood that the Tsung li Yamen will write a Circular to the Legations, inviting foreign Representatives at once to consider, with the Tsung li Yamen, the measures needed for the more effective administration of justice at the open ports."

---

[2] *Ibid.,* No. 177.

As I have stated, and have fully reported in my despatch, number 134., the Foreign Office has addressed the Legations, regarding the matters which their plenipotentiary agreed should be submitted here. It is to be expected that the British Government, if they support their Minister, will make *"Lekin taxation"* the subject of correspondence with "other foreign Governments." It may happen, indeed, that the views of the British Minister may not be approved at London, and that the clauses of the Chefoo Agreement mentioned may not, for this or other reasons, be submitted to "other Powers." It will, however, be desirable, still, for the several Governments to be in possession of the views of their Representatives, because the questions indicated and particularly the general Lekin question, are important, while the questions which have been submitted to the Diplomatic Body, directly by the Foreign Office, are also important, and, in great part, cannot be treated by us, in the absence of instructions.

In dealing with the various points involved, my Colleagues and I found it more convenient to speak directly to the text of the Agreement, than to the several points at issue, as stated in the several letters which we have received from the Foreign Office. And it is to be said in this connection, that the Foreign Office, with a right appreciation of the dignity of "other Governments," did not leave the Lekin taxation questions to be referred to those Governments by that of Great Britain, but made it the subject of a special letter to the several Legations. This communication was transmitted with my despatch, number 134.

Section I. of the Chefoo Agreement, relates specially to the Yunnan matter, and of, this, we have, of course, said nothing in our joint statement.

In speaking of the questions raised, directly or otherwise, in Part I. of Section II., we have stated them under the following heads:—

1st. The Audience question.

2nd. Intercourse between foreign Representatives and Chinese Ministers.

3rd. Intercourse between Consuls and local Authorities.

The Audience question was referred by the several Governments to their Representatives here, more than a twelvemonth ago. The opinions of the Ministers upon it, should have been, returned long since.

I may say briefly that my Colleagues and I could not see that an Audience with the Emperor, who is only six years of age, would be of practical value to the interests confided to us. There is involved, of course a question of dignity, and of right procedure, and if the regents were men, we might and probably should have felt it necessary to advise that the right of Audience should be insisted upon. But as the regents are women, and as they, with the Emperor, grant Audiences to Asiatic representatives and their own high officials under forms of ceremony which we could not assent to, and which they could not depart from, without difficulty, we have considered that it is not necessary to advise that a positive attitude be taken up in regard to the matter.

At the same time we have thought that it is best, not to take a course which would embarrass our Governments, should they decide, now or hereafter, upon a different line of action. This was advisable, because there is no certainty that the present regency will last long. It is possible, though not probable, that, at any moment, the almost unprecedented control now exercised "from behind the curtain," that is to say, by women, may be put an end to, and the regency fall into male hands. In such case, we should probably advise our Governments to demand the Audience at once.

As you are aware, the several Ministers who are now here have not presented their Letters of Credence to this Government in any way. This has seemed to me, not only an abnormal condition of affairs, but one calling for some explanation, or remark, to the Foreign Office, and some of my Colleagues have held the same view. It has been manifest to us, however, on consideration, that we cannot speak to the Foreign Office about our Letters to the Sovereign, without incurring the danger of getting back a response to the effect that we shall be admitted to Audience, of course, when the Emperor takes the throne. We do not care, as has been stated, to contest this declaration at the moment, nor, on the other hand, to assent to it. It seems better, therefore, to take up a policy, which will save us from any risk of bringing about an embarrassing discussion, and which preserves all the advantages of the situation.

This, in brief, is the opinion held by the Ministers who have signed the joint statement, in regard to the Audience question in the form in which it now presents itself. The British Minister, who is absent from Peking, as I have heretofore stated, holds, I think, to the same opinion. I hope that it will meet your approval in all respects, and that of the Governments generally.

In dealing with the matter of intercourse between foreign Representatives, and the high Officials of the Chinese Government at the Capital and in the provinces, we have thought it necessary to say only that, so far as forms go, our relations with the members of the Foreign Office are essentially satisfactory, and that we do not think it desirable or wise to undertake to extend relations with Ministers of the Government by trying to establish a Code of Etiquette, as the British Minister proposes.

In my opinion, indeed, it would be idle to essay the preparation and acceptance of a Code which would meet the views of the Chinese, and would be satisfactory to us. We can differ, and we can pass by a great deal that is unsatisfactory, by a kind of tacit agreement not to see such things. But we cannot undertake to make a *Code* of Etiquette, unless we deal, in it, with all essential matters in a way which comports with our ideas of dignity. If we could succeed at all well, it would be at the expense of much irritation, which, after all would do us more harm than the Code would do good. In the words of our Minute; "Improvement in this respect, must be the work of time."

Our minute in regard to the intercourse of Consuls and the provincial Authorities with whom they have, or should have relations, points out that it is desirable to make the subject one of representation to the Chinese Government. It does not seem to us necessary to ask the Chinese Government to abrogate the Article of our Treaty containing the words which have led to a misapprehension of the independent position and functions of Consular Officers. There is a certain advantage indeed in defining the rank of our Officials, as it relates to the rank of Chinese Officers. But it does seem necessary to claim, for the Consuls, the right to address all Chinese Officials in the way in which Consuls elsewhere may address Officers of the State to which they are accredited, and to have access to them without being required to submit to any forms or ceremonies which are unbecoming. For nearly the whole term of my residence in Shanghai, I declined to hold correspondence with the Provincial Governor, and the Governor-General, for the reason that I was not willing to send up to them my documents in the form of petition or memorial, or to receive their responses in that of order, or instruction. Fortunately, I was never asked to submit to unpleasant forms when I made personal visits, and by doing my business with them in this way, I was able to avoid correspondence, without injury to the interests confided to me.

The issue then is one which needs attention, and I shall be glad to receive from you an instruction to deal with it as circumstances may admit, the result to be embodied in a correspondence with the Foreign Office, which shall modify or explain the words of the Treaty, as may be appropriate.

I may remark that I am now in correspondence with the Foreign Office in regard to the Trade Committee of Foochow, a body of middlemen who have been interposed there between the Consuls and the territorial Authorities. The minute contains a reference to the grievance involved, and my Colleagues are supporting me in the matter.

You will notice that the minute declares that it is desirable, in dealing with the general question, to acknowledge the inferior position of merchant Consuls. So far as we are concerned, this has been done already, that is to say, we have now no unpaid Consuls in China, saving Mr. Knight of Newchwang, the places where we have officers who are not paid, being specially declared to be Consular Agencies. There is a certain inconvenience in this, for the reason that our people are relieved from territorial control, and that we do not commit judicial authority to Consular Agents, and this may call, sooner or later, for legislation, under which the latter may be allowed jurisdiction in matters of less concern.

In speaking of Parts I. and II. of Section II. we divided them under the following heads:—

1st. Jurisdiction in criminal matters.
2nd. The Mixed Court at Shanghai.
3rd. The more perfect administration of justice at the open ports.
4th. Presence of deputies of the Legation at trials.

I have, heretofore stated that the stipulations of the Chefoo Agreement, in regard to judicial matters are valuable. I had reference, more particularly, to what I conceived to be a settlement of the question of jurisdiction in civil matters. In my Trade Report for last year, I spoke at length of a dangerous position which the Judge of the British Supreme Court at Shanghai had taken up. All trials of civil matters, in which Americans and Chinese have been concerned, have been heard and determined in the Court of the defendant. The same rule had been followed in cases between British subjects and Chinese, until the Judge mentioned, some two years ago, declared that cases between British subjects and Chinese, must be heard, under the Treaties, jointly, by native and foreign officers, acting together. The British Minister agreed with me that the Judge's decision was unnecessary, and that the former practice was defensible under their Treaty, and practically gave better results. The reading of the Chefoo Agreement led me to believe that he had settled this point, and conversation with him in which I must have expressed my satisfaction with his supposed action in a somewhat clear manner, did not draw from him a different statement.

It seems likely, indeed, that the British Minister did mean to promote this result. Why he should have referred to the "more perfect administration of justice at the ports," unless he intended to deal with civil matters in some way, it is difficult to understand, and, as I have indicated, he led me to believe that he considered the jurisdiction question very important. But the fact remains that there is nothing in his agreement in relation to the judicial question, which, in terms, refers to civil matters, and which, upon examination, does not seem, to relate, in terms, to criminal matters. It is upon this basis, then that my Colleagues and I have made our remarks upon this point of the Agreement.

In criminal matters, no question of the complete exterritoriality of foreigners has been raised since the Treaties were made, so far as I know, saving in one instance. This was the somewhat celebrated case of Fawcett, who killed a Chinaman near Chefoo, last year, accidentally, as he claimed, with intent, as the Chinese Officials declared, and about which, for reasons which need not be stated, a great deal of bad feeling was stirred up. It appears that the Chinese text of the Article of the Treaty which refers to such matters, contains a word which may be so construed as to justify a claim for the joint investigation of criminal cases. The English text, however, expresses clearly the doctrine of complete exterritoriality, and the same is true of the Chinese text, when it is read in right order.

In dealing with this part of the matter, my Colleagues and I have thought it unnecessary to do more than to state that the principle of exterritorial control in criminal matters is clearly set forth in the Treaties, and that no different system can be admitted.

I may recall your attention here to the curious fact which I have mentioned in another place, that China and Japan, the two countries, which, it might be assumed, would feel aggrieved at our adherence to the exterritorial system, have brought it into the Treaty recently made between themselves. And it may be of some significance to you to learn in this connection that a Corean who killed a Chinese lately within Chinese territory, was arrested and sent to Corea for trial. It does not appear that there is a treaty of exterritoriality between China and Corea, but, as has often been remarked, the principle receives a spontaneous acceptance among Asiatic peoples.

But while we must adhere to the exterritorial system in criminal matters, it is very necessary to make it clear to the Chinese that we are ready to have the proceedings of our Courts watched, and that we insist upon having the opportunity to watch their Courts when our people are concerned.

How true this is will be understood when I state that no lawyers are admitted to Chinese Courts, that there is no system of public prosecutors, and that the punishment of wrong doers generally, fails very often in China, where the sufferers are not able to force their grievances before the Magistrates. Chinese Officials are eminently respecters of persons and time servers. There is a proverb among Magistrates which runs: "Do not strike so hard with the bamboo that it will fly back into your face," meaning that the Magistrate must be careful not to punish over severely those who have the power to make him feel their resentment.

You will notice that the joint statement declares that it is necessary to insist that our Consular Officers shall be allowed to attend the trials of Chinese who have committed offences against our people, to produce witnesses on the foreign side, and to assist in the examination of all witnesses. Of course we must yield the same privileges to Chinese Magistrates in our Courts. This procedure is one which I claimed and acted on at Shanghai, and it will be well to authorize me to explain the matter to the Foreign Office, and to instruct our Consuls accordingly.

The so-called Mixed Court at Shanghai, does not perhaps, call for any remarks saving those made in the Minute. It will be very desirable to take steps to raise it to a higher place, so soon as the principle set forth in the next paragraphs has been accepted.

In regard to "the more perfect administration of justice at the open ports," I may say that while my Colleagues and I were unable to satisfy ourselves that the administration of justice in civil matters is intended, we yet thought it desirable to deal with that branch of the judicial question, for the reason that it may be brought in by implication, and because it is important and specially needs attention.

In reading what is set down under this head, you will remark, first, that a divergence of opinions exists as to the meaning of the Treaties, or in the wording of the Treaties. In effect, the divergence is in the construction of the Treaties, and the language of all of them, saving the Russian, is identical. Our own Treaty may be taken then as a sample of all, and although I have this connection, notably in my Trade Report for last year, and my notes on the German Treaty Revision scheme, I will repeat, briefly, the argument to which I adhere.

There are three Articles of our Treaty bearing upon the matter. The first is the XXIV. which reads: "When there are debts due by subjects of China to citizens of the United States, the latter may seek redress in law, and on suitable representations being made to the local authorities through the Consul, they will cause due examination in the premises, and take proper steps to compel satisfaction. And if citizens of the United States be indebted to subjects of China, the latter may seek redress by representation through the Consul, or by suit in the Consular Court."

This Article indicates, in unmistakeable language, that in matters of debt, the claimant must pursue the debtor before his, the debtors, natural Authorities, and must be content with such redress as he can procure in this way. It leaves the foreign debtor entirely exempt from the jurisdiction of the territorial Authorities, and subject only to the jurisdiction of those provided by his own Government.

The next Article having reference to the matter is the XXVII. which reads:—

"All questions, in regard to rights, whether of property or person, arising between citizens of the United States in China, shall be subject to the jurisdiction and regulated by the Authorities of their own Government. And all controversies occurring in China between citizens of the United States, and the subjects of any other Government, shall be regulated by the treaties existing between the United States and such Governments, respectively, without interference on the part of China."

This does not touch the case of disputes between Chinese and Americans, but makes very clear the principle that, in cases between Americans, and between Americans and other foreigners, the extraterritoriality of our people is perfect.

The next reference to jurisdiction, if it can be called such, is that contained in Article XXVIII. This declares the way in which citizens of the United States shall address the Authorities of China, and Chinese shall address our Officers, and then states "and if controversies arise between citizens of the

United States and subjects of China which cannot be amicably settled otherwise, the same shall be examined and decided conformably to justice and equity, by the public officers of the two nations acting in conjunction."

These clauses are taken from the Treaty of Tientsin. They are the same, in effect, as those contained in Mr. Cushing's Treaty. How Mr. Cushing regarded them, may be understood from the declaration of his despatch to the Secretary of State, dated the 5th of July, 1844, with which he transmitted the Treaty: "Americans in China are to be deemed subject only to the jurisdiction of their own Government, both in criminal matters, and in questions of civil right."

And this declaration is repeated again in his despatch of the 29th of September 1844, in these words: "In extending these principles to our intercourse with China, *seeing that I have obtained the concession of absolute and unqualified exterritoriality,* I considered it well to use in the Treaty terms of such generality, in describing the substitute jurisdiction, as while they hold unimpaired the customary or law-of-nations jurisdiction, do also leave to Congress the full and complete discretion to define, if it please to do so, what officers, instruments for the protection and regulation of the citizens of the United States.

The construction of our Treaty thus given by Mr. Cushing is rigidly adhered to by him, in his opinion, as Attorney General upon the Act giving judicial authority to our Officers in this Empire. In fact he treats the special question at much length in that opinion, and with characteristic learning and acumen. You will find what he says given at length in my Trade Report before mentioned, as well as the views of the English Judge. The quotation from Mr. Cushing's opinion begins with the paragraph which commences with the words: "As among the Nations of Christendom, etc."

I should say that Mr. Cushing could have made his argument stronger than he has by quoting the 24th Article of the Treaty, or rather the corresponding Article of his Treaty, the 16th. He does not even refer to it basing his opinion upon the less clear, although more general provision of his Article XXIV, which corresponds with Article XXVIII, of the Treaty of Tientsin. His 16th Article, as repeated in the Tientsin Treaty has been quoted and shows that matters of debt, at any rate, are to be prosecuted in the Courts to which the Defendants are subject. If therefore a different rule is to be set up in regard to "controversies," we have, in the same Treaty, unnecessarily and without explanation, two different systems provided for.

Before taking leave of Mr. Cushing's views in regard to this very interesting subject, I ought to call your attention to the very emphatic manner in which he has repeated it, in an opinion given under date of November 4, 1854, in regard to the authority of our Consuls, to celebrate marriages abroad. He uses these words:—

"This point (the exemption of our people from the local control) is determined very explicitly in our Treaty with China, which, in the most unequivocal terms, places all the rights of Americans in China, whether as to person or property, under the sole jurisdiction, *civil and criminal,* of the Authorities of the United States."

In the same opinion, Mr. Cushing quotes from Lord Stowell as follows:—

"Nobody can suppose that whilst the Mogul Empire existed, an Englishman (in Hindostan) was bound to consult the Koran for the celebration of his marriage. In most of the Asiatic and African countries indeed, the law is personal, and not local, as it was in many parts of modern Europe in the formative period of its present organization."

The same eminent jurist used the following words in his judgment in the "Indian Chief." "In the Western parts of the world, alien merchants mix in the society of the natives; access and intermixture are permitted; and they become incorporated to the full extent. But in the East, from the oldest times an immiscible character has been kept up; foreigners are not admitted into the general body and mass of the natives; they continue strangers and sojourners, as all their fathers were."

All this will indicate that the theory upon which Mr. Cushing acted was not held in an uncertain way by him, and that it is not a singular theory.

It is stated in our Minute that this theory has always been acted upon in cases arising between Americans and Chinese in China. In fact I know of no instance of a different sort in our practice. And my observation of the course pursued by British officers, up to the date of the ruling made by their Judge two years ago, authorizes a declaration that their practice was the same. Their cases and ours, would, together form more than nine cases out of ten, of all those which have happened.

It is notable that the Chief Judge's ruling was not made in view of any declaration of the Chinese Government, but entirely upon his own motion. I am not aware of any case in which the superior Authorities of China have asserted a different view of the Treaties from that which I have expressed. In one case, involving a large sum, the local Authorities did claim the right to hear the matter under the conjoint plan, but it was found to be so difficult to pursue the case in such manner, that they voluntarily abandoned it, and the claimant went into the British Court in the usual way. I refer to the celebrated case of the "Ocean."

You will not be surprised, after what has been said, that my Colleagues, while insisting upon a different construction of their Treaties, agreed with me that the course which I have advocated, was the better one, practically, and should be adopted. I beg leave to refer you to the Minute for their expressions upon this point, and for a statement of the considerations involved. I shall not attempt to review these, although they are set down in the briefest language which could have been used, for the reason that the fundamental principles involved, have already been touched upon, and that so far as the question is one to be decided by considerations drawn from practical experience, you will not expect more than the positive declaration given in our Minute, signed as it is by the several Ministers.

In one direction only, I wish to add a few words. Legislation is not easily procured in any country. If now the principle of joint hearings is to be adhered to, it will become our duty to provide legislation under which our Officers in China will be authorized to do their part in such joint hearings, and in the execution of the judgments arrived at. Perhaps this legislation can best take the form of special supplementary treaty stipulations. If this should be decided upon, we must seek to procure such a revision of existing treaty arrangements as will effect the purpose. In either case, we shall find it difficult to constitute the Courts in such a way that they will do satisfactory work, until we have provided a code of laws to be observed by them. I find myself sanguine very often of what may be done to put our intercourse with China upon a better footing, but I confess that I am not so sanguine as to believe that all this can be brought about in any near period.

On the other hand, if the rule be adopted that civil cases as well as criminal shall be tried and determined in the defendants Court, we have, comparatively, little to do to give effect to the system. Nearly every foreign Government has established Consular Courts here, and those who have not, can readily do so, on the model of existing Courts. Our immediate work is then done, and it will remain only to get the Chinese to provide as good a judicial establishment for the trial of matters in which our people are complainants and theirs defendants, as may be. To promote this object, we must move forward gradually, for in this matter, as in the matter of intercourse, time will be required. Today we may get them to declare what offices have jurisdiction in given cases. At another time, we can win their assent to a code of procedure, and, still later, we can induce them to provide legislation for this or that class of cases. A given structure must be built up here, as elsewhere, by the placing of stone upon stone.

I am by no means sure that this question will be readily appreciated by all the Governments. I shall hope, therefore, that if it comes to be considered between the different Cabinets and that of Washington, you will do what you can to put it before them in a clear way. Probably the first question which will be asked, if the business receives attention, will be: "Does our Government sustain the reading of our Treaty which is advocated by its Representative here?" This is a vital point, and, if answered affirmatively, may, in view of the opinions expressed by my Colleagues on the practical question involved, secure the adhesion of other Powers to the general scheme.

I shall hope for such action on your part, and also to receive from you an instruction that the tenor of the Minute and my views, as expressed in this letter, are approved generally, and authority to prosecute the matter, in such manner as may seem likely to procure the best results.

Section III. of the Chefoo Agreement relates to commercial matters, and more particularly to the matter of *Lekin* taxation.

It is with much satisfaction that I am able to point out to you that the expressions of the joint Minute accord entirely with the views which I have, at different times, laid before you in this connection. I have held consistently that all *Lekin* taxation is in contravention of the Treaties, but I have feared that, whether from apathy, or from a careless reading of the Treaties, this important fact would be lost sight of, or disputed, and that a main advantage guaranteed in existing Conventions with China would be allowed to fall.

For a more detailed statement of the views to which I have adhered in this connection I desire to refer you again to my Trade Report for last year, and to my notes on the German Treaty revision scheme.

I am able, however, to transmit to you, a far more elaborate argument upon this matter than any other which has fallen under my notice. I refer to the inclosed pamphlet written by Mr. Fergusson, a well known British merchant, resident at the port of Chefoo, and printed by the General Chamber of Commerce at Shanghai. It has come to hand since the joint Minute was prepared. In view of its full and careful statement of the matter, and the references to authorities which it contains, it does not seem necessary for me to extend remarks upon the subject.

I may inform you that the Ministers of the Foreign Office have intimated in conversation with the German Minister, since our joint statement was signed, that they would not look unfavorably upon a proposal to do away entirely with barrier and Lekin taxes, provided the tariff duties levied upon the importation or exportation of merchandise can be raised somewhat.

To my mind, this solution of the business would be a good one, provided we could assure ourselves that the Chinese would abide by their part of the contract. They will do this in all cases, *if we insist upon it*. Would we do so? Certainly the indifference which foreign Governments have exhibited to the violation of their rights under existing Treaties would appear to indicate that they are not likely to stand firmly in defense of rights which they may hereafter acquire. Yet it is to be said that there has been a doubt existing as to the meaning of existing stipulations, and, moreover, that China has been in the midst of revolution, and it has seemed unwise to bear too hardly upon her.

Whatever may be the best course to pursue in order to reach an equitable adjustment of the whole question, it is desirable that, as a preliminary step, the opinion expressed in the joint Minute of the tenor and effect of existing Treaty stipulations shall be confirmed by the several Governments. Beyond that, the matter may be left in the hands of the Representatives here, for discussion between themselves, and with the Imperial Government. A result satisfactory to all interests concerned may, perhaps, be reached in this way.

My Colleagues preferred to say nothing in regard to the opium clause of the Chefoo Agreement. I see no objection to it, provided it is understood that no argument shall be based upon it by which opium may be held to be freed from further taxation than that imposed when it is landed, and from such control as the Chinese Government, may see fit to exercise over its consumption by their people. I wrote to you on this subject from Chefoo.

The German Minister has had some conversation with the Foreign Office in regard to the drawback system, since the date of our Minute, and I understand from him that the Foreign Office have agreed to propose the arrangement of this question which is suggested in the Minute.

In review of the whole matter, I beg leave to suggest that, if the British Government shall apply to us to know whether we approve the general Lekin taxation clauses of the Chefoo Agreement, the answer shall be returned, in appropriate language that we hold that all such taxation of foreign merchandise in China is in contravention of the Treaties, and that similarly, the taxation of native produce, held by our people for exportation, and covered by transit passes is also illegal; that opium is, of course, on a different footing, and that we approve the new arrangement, on the understanding that it shall not be held to limit the right of the Chinese Government to deal with the drug, when it has reached the native consumers' hands in such manner as they may think necessary.

To this might be added the statement that the general Lekin matter will be made the subject of an instruction to the Representative of the United States to the effect that, while all taxation of the sort is held to be in contravention of the Treaties, he shall consider with his Colleagues, the Representatives of other Governments, what steps may best be taken for the adjustment of the whole business upon a basis acceptable to all concerned, and the suggestion of the hope that the British Government may be able to see its way to take the same course.

It is not likely that the British Government will ask whether any instructions are likely to be sent to me in regard to the ceremonial and judicial questions. If they should do so, it would appear to be sufficient to say that the United States Minister at Peking has discussed these matters with his Colleagues, and believes that it would not be wise to undertake the preparation of a code of etiquette; that better relations with Chinese Officials can only be wrought out gradually; and that, in the judicial matter, he has pointed out, in a very positive way, that it is necessary to adhere to the exterritorial system in its entirety. It would be well, I think, to treat the English Government in an open way, and to submit the joint Minute to them in case a fair opportunity offers, as affording a more perfect statement of the basis of the opinions which have been referred to.

The question whether the British Government will confirm the Chefoo Agreement is of much interest, for if they do, they will separate themselves from other Powers, as I believe, in the matter of Lekin taxation. They may think it necessary to do this, or to refuse to accept the opening of ports under the Agreement. They might, perhaps, be the less disposed to hesitate on that account, if they knew that the ports are likely to be opened irrespective of the Chefoo Agreement, under arrangements with the German Minister. This is not yet decided, but having a hope that the British Government may refuse to ratify the Agreement, I am doing what I can to induce the German Minister to put his matters in such shape that the opening of the ports may not fail in any event.

XXII

CONTROLLING CHINESE IMMIGRATION, 1880-1894

TWELVE YEARS after the signing of the Seward-Burlingame Treaty (1868), the United States sent to China a commission (James B. Angell, William H. Trescot, and John F. Swift) to substitute for Seward's cheap-labor treaty one which was to give the American government the right to regulate, limit, or suspend but not to prohibit the immigration of Chinese laborers. The instructions of Secretary Evarts to the commissioners are suggestive of the general commercial policy of the time and of the spirit in which revision of the immigration policy was sought. Negotiation of this new immigration agreement of 1880, which was soon to lead to the policy of Chinese exclusion, involved not only the delicate task of securing concessions from the Chinese government at a time when the Government of the United States had failed to protect adequately Chinese within its borders, but also the problem of harmonizing the views of the American commissioners as to the most effective and proper means of limiting Chinese immigration.

AMERICAN POLICY ON CHINESE TRADE AND IMMIGRATION. SECRETARY EVARTS TO THE COMMISSIONERS TO CHINA, WASHINGTON, JUNE 7, 1880[1]

In personal interviews I have been able, at some length, and in a manner both definite and comprehensive, to lay before you the views of the Department upon the topics which are to engage your attention in the important negotiations for the management of which you have been appointed and empowered by the President. It is my present design to give precision and support to the leading purposes to which you are to shape your efforts, by a brief outline of the treatment which these topics are to receive at your hand.

In the careful examination which I have made with you of the provisions of the treaty of 1844, concluded by Mr. Cushing, and that of 1858, concluded by Mr. Reed, which bear upon our Commercial intercourse with China, the point in which these provisions were to be modified or added to, seemed not to be numerous or important so far as any principles governing such intercourse are concerned. The elastic stipulations by which our merchants, our ships and our commerce are to receive the benefits that now are, or may hereafter be accorded by China to the most favored nations, require from you a circumspect examination of the existing treaty arrangements between that Empire and other Commercial nations and a vigilant observation of the working of their and our treaties upon commerce, as it shall exhibit itself

[1] *China Instructions*, Vol. III, No. 1.

to your intelligent scrutiny or shall be brought to your notice by the enterprising and experienced American merchants and the capable and faithful Consular officers with whom you may be put in communication. If this examination should show to your deliberate judgment any important advantages to be gained by a change in the text of the commercial articles of our existing treaties, by making our privileges more clear, more secure or more extensive, you will then entertain the consideration of the fitness of the time and circumstances for an attempt at such modifications, always having in view the more pressing subjects entrusted to your negotiations. These latter must neither be delayed nor embarrassed by waiting upon the solution of the more ordinary interests of commercial intercourse.

In regard to the main commercial topic now under consideration, if not under discussion, by the representatives of the treaty powers and the Imperial Government, the treatment of the subject by Minister Seward, in his communications to this Government, and his conferences with his diplomatic colleagues, has been submitted to your examination. This treatment has seemed to the Department to deserve its commendation for intelligence and ability. This subject pertains to the methods of taxation applied by the Chinese authorities to imported merchandise after it has paid the import duties fixed by the treaty tariff. You will readily understand that this question of internal taxation becomes especially interesting to the Chinese Government from the fact that the regulation of the duties on importations has been taken from their discretion by the firm stipulations respecting these duties in their treaties with us and other Powers. This peculiar position of the Imperial Government in respect of its revenue system you will not lose sight of, and you may not hesitate to exhibit a just and generous policy in the discussion and adjustment of these questions of taxation. A concurrence in judgments and in measures between yourselves and the representatives of the other treaty Powers is to be desired and aimed at. You will give your best attention to bring about such concurrence upon a basis of fair consideration of the exigencies and interests of China, as well as of the treaty Powers. You will, however, bear in mind that this country is the only one of the so-called Western Powers, that is a commercial Power of the Pacific Ocean, and that can by its geographical position, promise itself a constant enlargement of reciprocal trade with China for the consumption by each nation of the exportations of the other. Besides this, it is not too much to expect that the course of trade, by which the exportations of China and the East Indies are in so great part distributed to the American nations through European systems of trade and finance, will change its current and flow this way for distribution to the nations of Europe through our system of trade and finance.

The controlling idea to be pressed upon the Imperial Government is that it is of the essence of importation into a country, upon a system of imposts upon that transaction, that the duty when paid is for the importation, not into the territory, but into the consumption, of the country. It is an indispensable safe-guard of this principle that imported goods while they retain this quality, and are identified in form and condition of importation, not having been broken up or distributed into the mass of domestic property, are to be subjected to no further taxation antecedent to such distribution, and to no discriminating taxation, in their quality of foreign goods after such distribution. Any taxation under whatever motive of revenue, that pursues the goods and exacts further payments upon them *because* they are foreign, is in substance a further impost laid upon importation. If they can be followed for the collection of such a discriminating tax, they can be followed for protection against it.

The details of transit dues seem more manageable both in Imperial regulation and in local administration than the other forms of domestic taxation known as Leken taxes. The maximum of transit dues is fixed by the present treaty and firm adhesion to the above propostion will protect imported goods from being interrupted by cumulative taxation for transit, while they are passing into the consumption of the country and before their identification as foreign goods has been lost in their being mingled with the mass of domestic property in use or consumption.

While the subject of Leken taxes is not of as easy management, yet an adhesion to the principle I have asserted, will furnish the best guide for its practical treatment.

It would be premature to consider whether it would be possible to restore to the Imperial Government the control of the rates of imposts, upon imported goods, as an inducement and aid toward a just system of internal taxation, that should not by its new burdens frustrate the privilege of importation in its true sense, as purchased by the imposts paid upon the entry of foreign merchandise. If this were done by any or all of the Treaty Powers, it would need to be attended by from provisions covering these principal points. First, the Imperial Government would need to recognize the policy of general trade not to be suppressed by prohibitory duties, but to be encouraged and enlarged and burdened only for revenue. Second, no discrimination favorable to one foreign nation, directly or covertly, should be allowed in the adjustment of duties. Third, the principle that foreign goods, as such, should bear no other taxation of transit or otherwise, should be recognized and duly protected by treaty obligations capable of enforcement.

While not attempting to take so serious a step towards liberating the revenue system of China, from being hampered as it now is, by a treaty tariff, you will gain such information, and form such opinions as to the prospect of such a proposition being made compatible with a just regard to the interests of our commerce, as may be gathered from your intercourse with your colleagues and the Imperial Government.

The second subject that may engage your attention in your conferences with the Imperial government concerns the treaty relations between the two governments in regard to extra-territorial jurisdiction over American citizens in China in matters whether civil or criminal. I do not need to add particular instructions to the views considered between us while having under examination the text of the treaties and the dispatches of Mr. Seward showing the deliberations of himself and his colleagues on this subject.

This Government is disposed to treat with the greatest respect the desire of the Chinese Government to meet, if possible, the divergence between the Chinese and American systems of jurisprudence and procedure by some judicial establishment which will be more observant than the present of the principle that territory and jurisdiction are and should be co-extensive. The direction in which such an improvement of the footing of extra-territorial jurisdiction may be expected to occur is that of a treaty establishment of a mixed judicial system of greater permanence and dignity to replace, or at least to review the less solemn Consular tribunals.

I desire you to entertain any discussion on this subject the Imperial Government may promote, but to preserve, in any negotiation, a substantial participation by officers of this government in all judicial functions in civil and criminal cases in which an American citizen is defendant as impossible to be embarrassed or relinquished.

A treatment of this subject you will also make use of in such manner as to advance, but in no circumstance to retard the negotiations on the remaining topic for discussion between the two governments which I now proceed to consider.

I have no occasion to repeat here the reasons upon which this Government finds great public interests to require in our relations to China and the movement of its population to our Pacific coast, what may appear to be a modification of our universal hospitality to foreign immigration. The various discussions, through all the public channels of influence and opinion, and the important public action taken in the State most affected and in Congress, have brought into the public view, no less than your own, the traits of this movement of population to our territory which so clearly distinguish it from all the emigrations to this continent from the first colonial settlements to the present moment. The views of the Department, in this regard, have been fully unfolded in the conferences held with you on this interesting subject. You understand the energy of feeling in the communities where the Chinese population presses upon the observation the sentiments and interests of our people. You are also acquainted with the great commercial influences which are enlisted in the protection and extension of our commercial relations with China. You have weighed, too, and considered the widely diffused and, so to speak, natural sentiments of our people in favor of the most liberal admission of foreign immigrants who desire to incorporate themselves and their families with our society and mingle the stream of their posterity in the swelling tide of native population. You have, also, in mind the principal and manifold arguments by which the benevolent and devout elements of this religious nation protest against any limitations upon that "faith, hope and charity," which have been proclaimed as Christian duty for the benefit of all mankind. If, at any time, hereafter, I should think it useful to lay before you a more distinct exposition and array of the principal considerations bearing from one side and the other upon your negotiations on this subject, it will reach you in abundant season for your deliberations and conferences in shaping the actual provisions of any treaty you may find it in your power to conclude. I desire now, however, strongly to impress upon you the grave importance of your giving, in due proportion, weight to the various, and in some degree, conflicting interests and sentiments of different portions of our wide country, before concluding upon definite stipulations to control these international relations.

The subject itself includes the two-fold relations of the access of our people to and the freedom and security of their residence in China, and the regulation and conditions upon which the vastly more numerous Chinese movement of population to this country may be made compatible with our political institutions and the frame of our society.

The immense disparity between the stinted hospitality of China to the people of this country, led by the usual motives of trade and travel to desire to penetrate that country, and the wide privileges opened by the existing treaty arrangements to the admission and residence of Chinese here, is the most prominent feature of our present relations with China. It will be your principal duty to insist upon this disparity to the appreciation of the Imperial Government and to reduce it by modifications on both sides—tending to some common principle in which both Governments can, with equal respect to the other, concur.

As to an improvement, and greater security to our citizens, in privileges of trade, travel, education and missionary labor and of residence generally, it should be your purpose to obtain for the classes of our citizens resorting to China and their few numbers included in these classes as near an approach to the unrestricted freedom opened to Chinese subjects of these classes in this country as you shall find possible.

It will be, however, a question of delicacy and discretion how far an attempt in this direction may aid the principal end in view in your mission to China. Upon the best judgment I can form at this distance from the scene of your negotiations, it would seem to me that you might find it quite useful towards the restrictions you may have to ask upon the free flow of Chinese population to our coast, to expose the great inequality in privileges which would obtain, as between the subjects of the two governments, even after our privileges should be greatly enlarged and theirs very materially reduced.

The correspondence and conferences, as already conducted with the Imperial Government by Minister Seward, make it quite sure that you will find no great difficulty in securing firm provisions and practical guarantees against the importation into this country, under the guise of immigration of paupers, criminals, lewd women and laborers under pre-contract obligations, by which the trait of personal free choice on the part of the emigrant in seeking our coast and shaping his employments here would be substantially suppressed. Great attention to details in regulating this transportation will be necessary on your part to maintain in practice the advantages we desire from your negotiations even under this limited head.

A cardinal object with you should be to impose upon the Imperial Government strict obligations to see to it that expectant emigrants should be subjected to careful scrutiny by competent Chinese officers and that the Imperial Government should assume toward this Government, a definite responsibility, that would justify complaint on our part for surreptitious introduction of the prohibited immigrants and a reclamation for the expense of their return to China by the public authorities of this country.

In treating with the Imperial Government on the urgent question of the principles and methods upon which a continued hospitality to a true and permanent removal of its subjects to become members of our society, can be regulated, suitably to the interests and sentiments of the two nations, you will take care to sever that discussion from all considerations bearing upon the rights and privileges of the Chinese population already transferred to our territory under the actual or supposed permission of the Burlingame treaty. You will make it apparent that this population has and will continue to have, all the guarantees and protection of personal rights, before the law, that the institutions of the country provide for immigrants from other foreign countries and for our own population. While no extra-territorial jurisdiction and no special means of securing these Chinese subjects is provided by the treaty or is permissible in our policy, yet this neither springs from nor occasions any adverse discrimination to the disadvantage of the Chinese in our midst. The arrangements by which we secure to citizens and denizens alike the protection of our laws, if well understood by the Imperial Government, would relieve any apprehensions or misconceptions in regard to the equality of the condition of its subjects here in comparison with the general mass of our population, foreign and native, which it may have been led to entertain.

. . . .

ARGUMENTS ON TREATY PHRASEOLOGY. THE COMMISSIONERS TO SECRETARY EVARTS, PEKING, OCTOBER 26, 1880[2]

At the request of Mr. Swift, we have the honor to forward to you a record of a meeting of this Commission, with certain papers, to which the record refers, and which sufficiently explain themselves.

We also enclose a supplementary paper prepared by Mr. Swift which the other members of the Commission have agreed shall be submitted without further argument on their part.

SUMMARY OF DISCUSSION OF THE COMMISSIONERS. MEMORANDUM BY CHESTER HOLCOMBE[3]

At a meeting of the Commission held October 1st 1880., having read and compared the English and Chinese texts of the Memorandum to be submitted to the Chinese Commissioners—a discussion ensued upon the shape to be given to the articles to be presented to the Chinese Commissioners. Mr. Swift objected to the four articles (enclosure number 2) which had been drawn up by Mr. Trescot and Mr. Angell, and proposed to substitute an article drawn up by himself (enclosure number 3) and, in case of its rejection by the Chinese, to negotiate for the adoption of a second article (enclosure number 4).

Upon the rejection of his proposed articles by his Colleagues, Mr. Swift requested that all negotiation be suspended and that both sets of articles—No. 2, and Nos. 3 and 4 be transmitted by telegram to the Secretary of State with a request for instructions as to which should be made the basis of negotiation.

This being declined, Mr. Swift proposed that no articles be submitted to the Chinese Commissioners at the first meeting. It was finally agreed that none should be submitted at that interview unless in the course of the conference the Chinese Commissioners indicated a desire to have them, and in that contingency the proposition should be submitted in order to indicate with some precision the wishes of the Government.

Mr. Swift then expressed his wish to place upon the record his reasons for dissent from the conclusions of his Colleagues, which he did in the paper marked (enclosure 6). Messrs. Angell and Trescot also placed on the minutes in reply the papers marked (enclosure 7).

ARTICLES PROPOSED BY COMMISSIONERS ANGELL AND TRESCOT[4]

In order to indicate with somewhat more precision the wishes of the United States, the Commissioners now submit the following modification of Existing Treaty Provisions, subject to the consideration of the Chinese Government.

Art. I. The United States of America and the Emperor of China recognize the mutual benefit which results from the proper intercourse of the citizens and subjects of all nations and in order to encourage such intercourse

[2] *China Despatches*, Vol. LV, No. 9.
[3] Incl. in No. 9 of the Commissioners. [4] *Ibid.*

between the two countries agree, that citizens of the United States visiting or residing in China and subjects of China visiting or residing in the United States for the purposes of trade, travel, or temporary residence for the purpose of study or curiosity, shall enjoy in the respective countries all the rights, privileges, immunities or exemptions which are granted by either country to the citizens or subjects of the most favored nation.

Art. II. And the Emperor of China further agrees to consider favorably any opportunity for the extension of such intercourse as may seem upon due examination to conduce to the best interests of both countries and that the Emperor will receive with careful attention any representation of the Government of the United States as to such special extension of the area of trade intercourse which the United States may desire.

Art. III. Whenever in the opinion of the Government of the United States the coming of Chinese laborers to the United States or their residence therein affects, or threatens to affect, the interests of that country or to endanger the good order of the said country, or of any locality within the territory thereof, the Government of the United States may regulate, limit, suspend, or prohibit such coming or residence, after giving timely notice of such regulation, limitation, suspension, or prohibition, to the Government of China.

Art. IV. But it is distinctly understood between the contracting parties, that all Chinese subjects who under the faith of existing Treaties, have gone into or are now residing in the United States shall be guaranteed all the protection, rights, immunities, and exemptions to which they are now entitled under the provisions of said Treaties.

PROPOSED ARTICLE SUBMITTED BY COMMISSIONER SWIFT[5]

Art.

It is agreed between the Emperor of China and the United States that from and after the ratification and exchange hereof Chinese subjects are and shall be prohibited from immigrating to or residing in the United States or any territory thereof for any purpose except commerce, travel, education, curiosity, or religious teaching, and only while so occupied, until such time as the United States Government shall desire immigration for other purposes than above named, to be evidenced by the passage of an Act or resolution of Congress to that effect and until due notice of such desire shall be communicated to the Chinese Government.

The United States, on its part, engages to protect all Chinese subjects who have at any time lawfully entered its territories for any purpose under the faith of treaties in accordance with the terms of the treaties and laws in existence at the time of such entry.

ALTERNATE ARTICLE PROPOSED BY COMMISSIONER SWIFT[6]

Proposition presented by Mr. Swift as an alternative for the first and in case of its rejection.

Art.

It is agreed by and between the high contracting Powers that the citizens and subjects of China and the United States respectively visiting or residing in the territory of the other for any lawful purpose at the time of the exchange of the ratification of this treaty shall be guaranteed the right to continue and remain in such territory during their pleasure and while so remaining shall

[5] *Ibid.*   [6] *Ibid.*

be entitled to the protection of the treaties then in force. Provided however and it is further agreed that from and after exchange of such ratifications the citizens and subjects of either nationality shall be and are hereby prohibited from going to or remaining in the country of the other for any purpose except that of trade, travel, education, or religious teaching, and only while engaged in such occupations; until such time as the Power desiring the presence in its territory of such prohibited class shall by regulations duly made by its constituted authorities authorize the coming into its territory of such class.

ARGUMENTS OF COMMISSIONER SWIFT. SWIFT TO COMMISSIONERS ANGELL AND TRESCOT, PEKING, OCTOBER 1, 1880[7]

At the informal meeting held yesterday for the purpose of agreeing upon propositions to be made to the Chinese Commissioners as the basis of our negotiations, I had the honor to submit two proposed articles, copies of which accompany this—marked No. I. and No. 2.; the second being an alternative to be presented only in the event of the Chinese Commissioners refusing to agree to the first, which articles you decided to reject, while you adopted another providing, not for regulating and prohibiting Chinese immigration by positive stipulation in the treaty—as do both of mine—but simply authorizing Congress to do the same whenever in the future it shall deem such a course expedient.

I understand that your objections to my proposed articles do not go to any matter of form which I could amend, but that you are opposed on principle to any plan providing directly in the treaty and by its proper force for the immediate regulation, restriction, or prohibition of any class of Chinese immigration, even if the Chinese Government would consent to such a treaty, and that you propose to confine our negotiation strictly, at least so far as this question is concerned, to securing a modification of existing treaties so as to leave it in the power of Congress in its discretion to take such action in the future as it may deem advisable.

To this course I earnestly object. As I understand the instructions verbal and written of the State Department, to this Commission, the articles submitted, at least as to the disputed point between us, namely—the principle of regulating and restricting the obnoxious immigration by the direct force of the treaty itself, if such a concession can be obtained from China, more nearly represents the views of the Department, and is more in accordance with the wishes of the Country than your plan of leaving the question to be dealt with hereafter by Congress.

For, be it remembered that under my plan, Congress still has control of the question, and can remove all restrictions upon immigration at any time by an Act, or even by a simple resolution, and of course can regulate it in any way it desires. I base this opinion upon the following grounds—briefly stated.

While at Washington in May last I had many conversations with the Hon. The Secretary of State in which he endeavored to impress me with his opinions—and inform me of his purposes on the Chinese Question. That each of you had similar interviews and conversations with him, I have no doubt, and that you must have heard substantially the same language.

By these conversations I learned, in substance, that the Administration regarded the presence of the relatively great and increasing number of adult Chinese males in the states bordering on and contiguous to the Pacific Ocean

[7] *Ibid.*

as a great injury and danger to the well being of those communities, and a menace to our institutions, if not to our very civilization. That it was, as Mr. Evarts—(with a felicity of language quite his own) described it, "not an immigration in any sense but a labor invasion." That it was no more an immigration than would be the landing upon our shores of an equal number of foreign soldiers for temporary shelter, or even for purposes of agression and conquest. He described it as an "overshadowing evil" which the Administration thoroughly appreciated and was determined to check, restrain, and bring to an end as speedily as was consistent with our friendly relations with China, the just claims of commerce, and the rights of American citizens now residing in that country

To these conversations the Hon. Secretary of State calls our attention in direct terms in his first and most complete instructions yet sent us, as forming a part of the rules that are to guide our negotiations. In my judgment they were intended to be a very important part of them.

Since arriving in China we have received from him additional written instructions, notably the paper containing quotations from the respective platforms of the two great political parties into which our country is divided. In this last we are officially informed by the Hon. Secretary of State that the Republican party has declared through its National Convention that it regards "the unrestricted immigration of Chinese as an evil of great magnitude" and it invokes "Congress and the treaty making powers to restrain and limit the same."

In the same letter of instructions we are also told that the Democratic party is in like manner pledged, if in power, "to amend the Burlingame Treaty in such way that there shall be no more Chinese immigration, except for travel, education, and foreign commerce."

I am compelled to believe that these documents were sent to us for no idle or immaterial purpose, but that they are intended to remove any doubt that may rest in the mind of any Commissioner, of the purposes of the Administration as well as of the substantial unanimity of public opinion throughout the entire country upon this question.

I entertain the belief that the Administration desires, in accordance with the most intelligent opinion of the country expressed through these Conventions that Chinese immigration shall be, by Treaty if the Chinese Government will consent, brought at once under restraint and limited to those who come for the purposes of commerce, travel, education, and the prosecution of missionary work. I believe that if we can agree among ourselves, we can, by respectful discussion, convince the Chinese Commissioners, of the justice and propriety of these restrictions, and can obtain their consent to a treaty such as my articles indicate.

My plan if agreed to and placed in the form of a treaty with such matters of detail as would be necessary to perfect it, would set in operation immediately the remedy, slow enough at best, which in time, probably not less than a generation, would restore the Pacific States to the normal condition of healthy, well regulated, American communities, homogeneous in people, free from race conflicts, and marching abreast of their sister states upon the line of safe and durable progress.

My objection to the article proposed by you is that I fear the result will be to greatly postpone the relief which the Pacific States (up to this time the Chief sufferers by the Chinese evil) so much need, and to which in justice, in my opinion, and in the opinion, if I am correct, of the Administration, they are entitled. I do not wish to be understood, however in any sense, as objecting to the article proposed and agreed upon by you, in case those offered by myself should, for any reason, fail of being agreed upon. On the contrary I should and shall act with you, in doing all in my power tending to the success of your plan, and the perfection into treaty shape of the principles of your article.

In short, I regard your article as of great value, and one that I would gladly accept, if I did not hope and believe we could by making a united effort, do even better. But believing, as I do, that the country and especially the Administration expect us to come as nearly as possible to stopping Chinese immigration by force of the treaty, I feel that I cannot do less than respectfully insist that we make this effort, and not accept less than all we desire, till we find that the Chinese will not agree to our wishes.

Under these circumstances I have respectfully asked that we take the opinion of the Honorable Secretary of State upon the disputed point, before laying any definite proposition before the Chinese Commissioners. That this be done at once by telegraph.

Upon your denial of this request, and proceeding with the discussion as agreed upon between you, I formally but respectfully protest, and ask that under the rules, this paper be spread upon the minutes of the Commission.

I further request that this part of the proceedings be made the subject of a despatch and that the Secretary of State be requested to instruct us upon the point for our future guidance.

Reply of Commissioners Angell and Trescot to Commissioner Swift[8]

The undersigned, having given the most careful consideration to two propositions submitted by their Colleague Mr. Swift, as a substitute for their own and recognizing the right which he has exercised to place his protest against their rejection upon the minutes of the Commission, desire to put upon the record, the reasons which in their judgment prevent the adoption thereof.

Our proposition is that China shall recognize by modification of existing Treaties, the right of the United States Government to regulate, limit, suspend or prohibit the immigration of Chinese labor at its own will and pleasure.

The object of the two propositions submitted by Mr. Swift, seems to be to prohibit Chinese labor immigration absolutely unless the Government of the United States by some act of legislation shall open it, and as the Articles are constructed, immigration from China is to be prohibited by China. To ask one nation to adopt legislation subject to modification or abrogation by the independent legislation of another seems to us to ask too much. But waiving that we object—

1. Prohibition of immigration from China to the United States by China, will not prevent immigration from Hong Kong which is really and practically the point of immigrant departure. To make such a Treaty provision operative would require a Treaty with Great Britain and legislation on the part of the United States.

2. If in violation of such prohibition by the Chinese Government, Chinese laborers come to the United States, they will not unless the Government of the United States has prohibited their coming, have committed any punishable offence against the laws of the United States. Suppose for a moment that

[8] *Ibid.*

a European Nation should make such a prohibition, would either the law or the public opinion of the United States enforce it within their territory?

3. Such a prohibition by China, in a Treaty, could not be enforced in the United States without a law passed by Congress, so that the power given by our proposition to Congress would cover, only more fully and effectually the purpose of the proposed articles. This difficulty is even stronger in the alternative article which provides for mutual prohibition, for the undersigned cannot understand how under the previsions of the Constitution and the sentiment of our people a Treaty without legislative action, could prohibit an American citizen from leaving the United States, to go wherever he pleases.

4. If Congress having the power to limit and prohibit given in our Article, would not pass the laws requisite for the exercise of such powers, then it may fairly be presumed that the Senate would not ratify the Treaty which under these propositions, would have enacted the law for them.

5. If there is any doubt about what Congress would do we certainly have neither right nor power to bind its hands by Treaty stipulation and would, we fear, by attempting to do so, lay ourselves open justly to grave censure.

6. Being satisfied that the proposition would be rejected by China and that we would have to fall back on another, we are unwilling to commence by a proposition, giving up which, will encourage the Chinese Negotiators to believe that persistent rejection on their part will lead to renewed withdrawal on ours.

We cannot consent to suspend negotiation and ask for instruction. The delay would be too great, but what is worse, after the interview we have had with the Chinese Commissioners, to suspend further conference would be understood by them to mean a grave difference of opinion among ourselves, which would in our judgment be fatal to all hope of a successful negotiation. The provision in our Full Powers, that the consent of any two Commissioners is sufficient, was, we believe, meant to obviate any such necessity.

We will gladly at Mr. Swift's request submit the whole question to the Department in a despatch, but we cannot suspend action, the approval or disapproval of which of course lies with the Secretary of State and the responsibility of which we must take.

Supplementary Statement of Commissioner Angell[9]

The undersigned desires further to state as follows.

He is not prepared, as Commissioner to declare himself in favour of direct and complete arrest of Chinese emigration to the United States by treaty; even if such arrest is practicable. He believes that such emigration may proceed too rapidly or may become too great for the best interests of the nation and therefore that our Government should have the power to check it. But he is of the opinion that Congress representing the whole people is the proper body to judge when that power should be exercised.

He sympathises with the traditional policy of our Government to permit free emigration from other lands. He believes that restriction on it should be deemed the exception to our general rule and if the assent of any other nation to restriction of the immigration of its subjects is to be asked, it should be on the condition that positive and affirmative action of Congress declares the existence of an exigency which calls for this exceptional procedure.

[9] *Ibid.*

FINAL STATEMENT OF COMMISSIONER SWIFT[10]

I do not understand that there is any such thing as a right of emigration or of immigration disconnected from force or the right of the stronger. The entry of aliens into any country unless accompanied by strong hand (in which case the right is that of conquest) must always be subject to the approval of the country whose territory is intruded upon. The contrary doctrine laid down in the Burlingame Treaty not being based upon natural law cannot change the principle, and makes a new rule only between the signatory powers and as to them only during their good pleasure. Chinese and all other immigration into the United States depends upon positive law permitting it, and becomes unlawful and the immigrant an intruder when he comes without such permissive laws and especially when he comes in violation of positive enactments.

And while I do not understand that either of my Colleagues question these very elementary rules, yet it seems to me necessary to re-affirm them as the basis of my contention.

It is quite true that our Government being one of law, and permitting the executive and police authorities to exercise no power except as prescribed by the Legislature, it may be that the fact that an alien is unlawfully present in our country gives no one the right to molest or interfere with him. But such alien could be dealt with and at least ordered out of the country, whenever at any time the Legislature chooses so to do, and provides the necessary machinery for that purpose.

Even the 14th Amendment would not cover the case of an alien intruding upon our territory in violation of law; for I cannot believe, broad and comprehensive as that article seems to be, that it will ever be held that it confers upon the four hundred million Chinese still in China, the inchoate right to be sharers in the wealth of our land and to impress their habits and views upon its institutions whenever it may suit their convenience or pleasure to exercise the right by coming to it.

If therefore our Constitution confers no right upon non-resident aliens, as I believe it does not, and if a treaty duly made under our system becomes a part of the Supreme Law of the land about which there certainly can be no question, I see no reason why it is not competent for a treaty with China to render the coming to the United States of any Chinese subjects or class of subjects unlawful, and the individual so coming an intruder, to be expelled whenever there is a law to that effect and any competent authority to enforce such law.

Believing the coming of adult Chinese males to this country as it is now going on in the Pacific States to be an evil and that the Administration and the most intelligent opinion of the country is in accord with that view, I seek by treaty, as formulated in my proposed article, to render in the most direct and speedy manner possible that immigration unlawful.

I believe that if the Chinese of the objectionable classes once knew that they could not lawfully come to our country, and that if they did come against the provisions of the Treaty they could and possibly would be expelled as intruders—they would practically stop coming and the immigration, at least in its present proportion, would cease, almost from the adoption of the treaty. In short it is my opinion that the force and moral effect, of such a treaty as

[10] Ibid.

I propose, would substantially stop the immigration even before Congress could pass laws ancillary as it doubtless would, to make the result certain.

But if it did not operate as I believe it would, Congress could still go on and perfect a system that would produce the desired effect or send away those who had come in violation of law quite as well under my article as under yours.

As for the point made—that to stop the coming of Chinese from the British port of Hong Kong a treaty must first be made with Great Britain, I will only say that I do not so understand it.

It is not claimed that the Chinese embarking at Hong Kong are British subjects. They are Chinese who merely use that port as a convenient point for finding ships to transport them upon their voyage. I know of no treaty with Great Britain or any other power which confers the right upon any of its ports to ship, or its vessels to carry to this country any article or thing animate or inanimate which the Municipal law of the United States does not permit to enter or to remain in the country when brought.

British ships are accorded the right under existing treaties to engage in any lawful commerce between foreign ports and the ports of the United States. They may bring to our ports from foreign ports anything which the law of the land allows to come, in a word, anything which American ships or ships of the most favored nation may bring, and nothing more. To do more would be to surrender the sovereignty of the nation which I am sure has never been done.

It is true that until the law-making power provides a penalty for bringing to the country any unlawful commodity or thing and this is true of passengers, English ships and all others might still engage in such transportation without danger. But, as I have before said, I do not believe that the objectionable immigrants would come under such circumstances being liable to expulsion at the will of Congress, and if they did so, Congress could as easily impose a penalty upon the ship or upon the immigrant under my plan as under yours, and as mine is the most speedy and does not delay or impede yours, it ought to be tried if possible.

THE UNITED STATES AND CHINA. IMMIGRATION TREATY, NOVEMBER 17, 1880[11]

ARTICLES.

I. Suspension of Chinese immigration.
II. Rights of Chinese in the United States.
III. Protection of Chinese in the United States.
IV. Notification of legislation; ratification.

Whereas, in the eighth year of Hsien Feng, Anno Domini, 1858, a treaty of peace and friendship was concluded between the United States of America and China, and to which were added, in the seventh year of Tung Chih, Anno Domini, 1868, certain supplementary articles to the advantage of both parties, which supplementary articles were to be perpetually observed and obeyed:—and

Whereas the Government of the United States, because of the constantly increasing immigration of Chinese laborers to the territory of the United States, and the embarrassments consequent upon such immigration, now de-

[11] U. S. *Compilation of Treaties in Force*, pp. 118-120.

sires to negotiate a modification of the existing Treaties which shall not be in direct contravention of their spirit:—

Now, therefore, the President of the United States of America has appointed James B. Angell, of Michigan, John F. Swift, of California, and William Henry Trescot, of South Carolina as His Commissioners Plenipotentiary; and His Imperial Majesty, the Emperor of China, has appointed Pao Chün, a Member of His Imperial Majesty's Privy Council, and Superintendent of the Board of Civil Office; and Li Hungtsao, a Member of His Imperial Majesty's Privy Council, as his Commissioners Plenipotentiary; and the said Commissioners Plenipotentiary having conjointly examined their full powers, and having discussed the points of possible modification in existing Treaties, have agreed upon the following articles in modification.

ARTICLE I.

Whenever in the opinion of the Government of the United States, the coming of Chinese laborers to the United States, or their residence therein, affects or threatens to affect the interests of that country, or to endanger the good order of the said country or of any locality within the territory thereof, the Government of China agrees that the Government of the United States may regulate, limit, or suspend such coming or residence, but may not absolutely prohibit it. The limitation or suspension shall be reasonable and shall apply only to Chinese who may go to the United States as laborers, other classes not being included in the limitations. Legislation taken in regard to Chinese laborers will be of such a character only as is necessary to enforce the regulation, limitation, or suspension of immigration, and immigrants shall not be subject to personal maltreatment or abuse.

ARTICLE II.

Chinese subjects, whether proceeding to the United States as teachers, students, merchants, or from curiosity, together with their body and household servants, and Chinese laborers who are now in the United States shall be allowed to go and come of their own free will and accord, and shall be accorded all the rights, privileges, immunities, and exceptions which are accorded to the citizens and subjects of the most favored nations.

ARTICLE III.

If Chinese laborers, or Chinese of any other class, now either permanently or temporarily residing in the territory of the United States, meet with ill treatment at the hands of any other persons, the Government of the United States will exert all its power to devise measures for their protection, and to secure to them the same rights, privileges, immunities, and exemptions as may be enjoyed by the citizens or subjects of the most favored nations, and to which they are entitled by treaty.

ARTICLE IV.

The high contracting Powers having agreed upon the foregoing articles, whenever the Government of the United States shall adopt legislative measures in accordance therewith, such measures will be communicated to the Government of China. If the measures as enacted are found to work hardship upon the subjects of China, the Chinese Minister at Washington may bring the matter to the notice of the Secretary of State of the United States, who will consider the subject with him; and the Chinese Foreign Office may also bring the matter to the notice of the United States Minister at Peking and consider the subject with him, to the end that mutual and unqualified benefit may result.

In faith whereof the respective Plenipotentiaries have signed and sealed the foregoing at Peking, in English and Chinese, being three originals of each text of even tenor and date, the ratifications of which shall be exchanged at Peking within one year from date of its execution.

Done at Peking, this seventeenth day of November, in the year of Our Lord, 1880. Küanghsu, sixth year, tenth moon, fifteenth day.

JAMES B. ANGELL.   [SEAL.]

JOHN F. SWIFT.   [SEAL.]

WM. HENRY TRESCOT. [SEAL.]

PAO CHÜN.

LI HUNGTSAO

[SEAL.]

THE UNITED STATES AND CHINA. TREATY ON COMMERCIAL INTERCOURSE AND JUDICIAL PROCEDURE, NOVEMBER 17, 1880[12]

ARTICLES.

I. Commercial relations.
II. Importation of opium forbidden.
III. Equality of duties.
IV. Trials of actions in China.

The President of the United States of America and His Imperial Majesty the Emperor of China, because of certain points of incompleteness in the existing Treaties between the two governments, have named as their commissioners plenipotentiary:—that is to say

The President of the United States, James B. Angell of Michigan, John F. Swift of California, and William Henry Trescot of South Carolina;

His Imperial Majesty, the Emperor of China, Pao Chün, a Member of His Imperial Majesty's Privy Council and Superintendent of the Board of Civil Office, and Li Hungtsao, a Member of His Imperial Majesty's Privy Council, who have agreed upon and concluded the following additional articles.

ARTICLE I.

The Governments of the United States and China, recognizing the benefits of their past commercial relations, and in order still further to promote such relations between citizens and subjects of the two Powers, mutually agree to give the most careful and favorable attention to the representations of either as to such special extension of commercial intercourse as either may desire.

ARTICLE II.

The Governments of China and of the United States mutually agree and undertake that Chinese subjects shall not be permitted to import opium into any of the ports of the United States; and citizens of the United States shall not be permitted to import opium into any of the open ports of China, to transport it from one open port to any other open port, or to buy and sell

[12] *Ibid.*, pp. 120-122.

opium in any of the open ports of China. This absolute prohibition which extends to vessels owned by the citizens or subjects of either Power, to foreign vessels employed by them, or to vessels owned by the citizens or subjects of either Power, and employed by other persons for the transportation of opium, shall be enforced by appropriate legislation on the part of China and the United States; and the benefits of the favored nation clause in existing Treaties shall not be claimed by the citizens or subjects of either Power as against the provisions of this article.

ARTICLE III.

His Imperial Majesty, the Emperor of China hereby promises and agrees that no other kind or higher rate of tonnage dues, or duties for imports or exports, or coastwise trade shall be imposed or levied in the open ports of China upon vessels wholly belonging to citizens of the United States, or upon the produce manufactures or merchandise imported in the same from the United States, or from any foreign country; or upon the produce manufactures or merchandise exported in the same to the United States or to any foreign country, or transported in the same from one open port of China to another, than are imposed or levied on vessels or cargoes of any other nation or on those of Chinese subjects.

The United States hereby promise and agree that no other kind or higher rate of tonnage dues or duties for imports shall be imposed or levied in the ports of the United States upon vessels wholly belonging to the subjects of His Imperial Majesty, and coming either directly or by way of any foreign port, from any of the ports of China which are open to foreign trade, to the ports of the United States, or returning therefrom either directly or by way of any foreign port, to any of the open ports of China; or upon the produce, manufactures, or merchandise imported in the same from China or from any foreign country, than are imposed or levied on vessels of other nations which make no discrimination against the United States in tonnage dues or duties on imports, exports, or coastwise trade; or than are imposed or levied on vessels and cargoes of citizens of the United States.

ARTICLE IV.

When controversies arise in the Chinese Empire between citizens of the United States and subjects of His Imperial Majesty, which need to be examined and decided by the public officers of the two nations, it is agreed between the Governments of the United States and China that such cases shall be tried by the proper official of the nationality of the defendant. The properly authorized official of the plaintiff's nationality shall be freely permitted to attend the trial and shall be treated with the courtesy due to his position. He shall be granted all proper facilities for watching the proceedings in the interests of justice. If he so desires, he shall have the right to present, to examine and to cross examine witnesses. If he is dissatisfied with the proceedings, he shall be permitted to protest against them in detail. The law administered will be the law of the nationality of the officer trying the case.

In faith whereof the respective Plenipotentiaries have signed and sealed the foregoing at Peking in English and Chinese, being three originals of each text, of even tenor and date, the ratifications of which shall be exchanged at Peking within one year from the date of its execution.

Done at Peking this seventeenth day of November, in the year of our Lord, 1880. Kuanghsü, sixth year, tenth moon, fifteenth day.

JAMES B. ANGELL.	[SEAL.]
JOHN F. SWIFT	[SEAL.]
WM. HENRY TRESCOT.	[SEAL.]
PAO CHUN.	
LI HUNGTSAO.	
	[SEAL.]

THE UNITED STATES AND CHINA. CONVENTION REGULATING CHINESE IMMIGRATION, MARCH 17, 1894[13]

ARTICLES.

I. Immigration of Chinese laborers prohibited for ten years.
II. Regulations for return to the United States.
III. Classes of Chinese not affected.
IV. Protection of Chinese in the United States.
V. Registration of citizens in China.
VI. Duration.

Whereas, on the 17th day of November A. D. 1880, and of Kwanghsü, the sixth year, tenth moon, fifteenth day, a Treaty was concluded between the United States and China for the purpose of regulating, limiting, or suspending the coming of Chinese laborers to, and their residence in, the United States;

And whereas the Government of China, in view of the antagonism and much deprecated and serious disorders to which the presence of Chinese laborers has given rise in certain parts of the United States, desires to prohibit the emigration of such laborers from China to the United States;

And whereas the two Governments desire to co-operate in prohibiting such immigration, and to strengthen in other ways the bonds of friendship between the two countries;

And whereas the two Governments are desirous of adopting reciprocal measures for the better protection of the citizens or subjects of each within the jurisdiction of the other;

Now, therefore, the President of the United States has appointed Walter Q. Gresham, Secretary of State of the United States, as his Plenipotentiary and His Imperial Majesty, the Emperor of China has appointed Yang Yü, Officer of the second rank, Sub-Director of the Court of Sacrificial Worship, and Envoy Extraordinary and Minister Plenipotentiary to the United States of America, as his Plenipotentiary; and the said Plenipotentiaries having exhibited their respective Full Powers found to be in due and good form, have agreed upon the following articles:

ARTICLE I.

The High Contracting Parties agree that for a period of ten years, beginning with the date of the exchange of the ratifications of this Convention, the coming, except under the conditions hereinafter specified, of Chinese laborers to the United States shall be absolutely prohibited.

[13] *Ibid.*, pp. 122-124.

ARTICLE II.

The preceding Article shall not apply to the return to the United States of any registered Chinese laborer who has a lawful wife, child, or parent in the United States, or property therein of the value of one thousand dollars, or debts of like amount due him and pending settlement. Nevertheless every such Chinese laborer shall, before leaving the United States, deposit, as a condition of his return, with the collector of customs of the district from which he departs, a full description in writing of his family, or property, or debts, as aforesaid, and shall be furnished by said collector with such certificate of his right to return under this Treaty as the laws of the United States may now or hereafter prescribe and not inconsistent with the provisions of this Treaty; and should the written description aforesaid be proved to be false, the right of return thereunder, or of continued residence after return, shall in each case be forfeited. And such right of return to the United States shall be exercised within one year from the date of leaving the United States; but such right of return to the United States may be extended for an additional period, not to exceed one year, in cases where by reason of sickness or other cause of disability beyond his control, such Chinese laborer shall be rendered unable sooner to return—which facts shall be fully reported to the Chinese consul at the port of departure, and by him certified, to the satisfaction of the collector of the port at which such Chinese subject shall land in the United States. And no such Chinese laborer shall be permitted to enter the United States by land or sea without producing to the proper officer of the customs the return certificate herein required.

ARTICLE III.

The provisions of this Convention shall not affect the right at present enjoyed of Chinese subjects, being officials, teachers, students, merchants or travellers for curiosity or pleasure, but not laborers, of coming to the United States and residing therein. To entitle such Chinese subjects as are above described to admission into the United States, they may produce a certificate from their Government or the Government where they last resided viséd by the diplomatic or consular representative of the United States in the country or port whence they depart.

It is also agreed that Chinese laborers shall continue to enjoy the privilege of transit across the territory of the United States in the course of their journey to or from other countries, subject to such regulations by the Government of the United States as may be necessary to prevent said privilege of transit from being abused.

ARTICLE IV.

In pursuance of Article III of the Immigration Treaty between the United States and China, signed at Peking on the 17th day of November, 1880, (the 15th day of the tenth month of Kwanghsü, sixth year) it is hereby understood and agreed that Chinese laborers or Chinese of any other class, either permanently or temporarily residing in the United States, shall have for the protection of their persons and property all rights that are given by the laws of the United States to citizens of the most favored nation, excepting the right to become naturalized citizens. And the Government of the United States reaffirms its obligation, as stated in said Article III, to exert all its power to secure protection to the persons and property of all Chinese subjects in the United States.

ARTICLE V.

The Government of the United States, having by an Act of the Congress, approved May 5, 1892, as amended by an Act approved November 3, 1893, required all Chinese laborers lawfully within the limits of the United States before the passage of the first named Act to be registered as in said Acts provided, with a view of affording them better protection, the Chinese Government will not object to the enforcement of such acts, and reciprocally the Government of the United States recognizes the right of the Government of China to enact and enforce similar laws or regulations for the registration, free of charge, of all laborers, skilled or unskilled, (not merchants as defined by said Acts of Congress), citizens of the United States in China, whether residing within or without the treaty ports.

And the Government of the United States agrees that within twelve months from the date of the exchange of the ratifications of this Convention, and annually, thereafter, it will furnish to the Government of China registers or reports showing the full name, age, occupation and number or place of residence of all other citizens of the United States, including missionaries, residing both within and without the treaty ports of China, not including, however, diplomatic and other officers of the United States residing or travelling in China upon official business, together with their body and household servants.

ARTICLE VI.

This Convention shall remain in force for a period of ten years beginning with the date of the exchange of ratifications, and, if six months before the expiration of the said period of ten years, neither Government shall have formally given notice of its final termination to the other, it shall remain in full force for another like period of ten years.

In faith whereof, we, the respective plenipotentiaries, have signed this Convention and have hereunto affixed our seals.

Done, in duplicate, at Washington, the 17th day of March, A. D. 1894.

WALTER Q. GRESHAM [SEAL.]
YANG YÜ.   [SEAL.]

XXIII

COMMODORE SHUFELDT'S INDICTMENT OF CHINA, 1882

COMMODORE Robert W. Shufeldt, who negotiated the American treaty with Korea (1882), owed the success of his mission in part to assistance received from Li Hung-chang. The Chinese viceroy frequently consulted Shufeldt on naval affairs, and may have contemplated appointing him to a responsible post in the Chinese Navy. These considerations, however, did not prevent Shufeldt from entertaining views on China which Secretary Frelinghuysen characterized as brutal in their frankness. They are contained in a letter which Shufeldt wrote at Tientsin in January, 1882, to his friend Senator Aaron A. Sargent of California. Through some means this letter found its way to the press, a fact which proved most embarrassing to the administration in Washington. With the following draft of the Shufeldt letter are printed the comment and criticism thereon of Chester Holcombe, secretary of the American legation in Peking.

AN INDICTMENT OF CHINA. COMMODORE SHUFELDT TO SENATOR SARGENT, TIENTSIN, JANUARY 1, 1882[1]

My Dear Sir,—You know me well enough to understand that the current of my sympathies for the human race has always been in favour of the "downtrodden" people of the earth. The African or the Asiatic, whether at home or as slave or emigrant upon foreign shores, has always seemed to me more or less the victim of oppression, and I have fired my indignation upon the oppressor with a force never equal to my zeal and with a sincerity never greater than my convictions. I have, indeed, rarely analysed the causes, but always warmed up over the effects; in other words, I have all my life suffered under a sort of sentimentalism—an unquestioning sympathy for the "under dog."

With reference to the Eastern nations, I have charged foreigners dwelling therein with prejudice of race, with arrogance of power, with ignorance of customs, with contempt of religious faith—never crediting them with forbearance, charity or sympathy for an inferior people. To me, the merchant seemed to force his wares and the missionary his creed, upon a passive and long suffering community.

[1] *China Despatches*, Vol. LX, Incl. in Holcombe's No. 108. Also published in the *North China Daily News*, Shanghai, May 9, 1882.

There is an underlying truth in these sentiments, but as a practical idea the view is inapplicable to the relations, both commercial and political which connect Asia with Europe or America.

Six months residence in this city, the political centre of the Chinese Government, and an intimacy rather exceptional with the ruling element, has convinced me that deceit and untruthfulness pervade all intercourse with foreigners; that an ineradicable hatred exists, and that any appeal across this barrier, either of sympathy or gratitude, is utterly idle. The only appeal or argument appreciated is that of *force*. If justice is done to these people, it must be for the sake of itself, not expecting appreciation. If justice is exacted, it must be unrelentingly. All sympathy will be construed into weakness, all pity into fear. Above all things necessary, is tenacity of national dignity. The least condescension fosters conceit and provokes insolence.

It is quite true, however, that Europe only permits or encourages "Western civilization" in China to the extent of subordination. It fosters the pretext of strength, sells guns and ships, knowing that it is not in the genius of the Chinese to handle them; that in time of war they simply become easy prizes to the first European enemy. But commercially, England alone controls China. Eighty-six per cent. of the foreign trade is English. The Imperial Customs, which collects all duties upon foreign imports, is managed by an English Inspector-General. Under him is a corps of foreign officials, which controls the Custom Houses, commands the gunboats and revenue cruisers and maintains the lighthouse system. In fact, almost everything which filters into China from the outside world goes through this strange excrescence upon its body politic.

Diplomatically, also, England rules China. Recognizing the hard logic of facts, she has infused a wholesome dread of her power by always following the word with the blow. The murder of Margary, for instance, on the westernmost confines of the country, outside of all visible protection, among an insubordinate people, was avenged on the demand. Sir Thomas Wade, H.B.M.'s Minister, said, "Do this, or I will haul down my flag." No squirming could evade the command; no lies deceive. He insisted upon the trial of the murderers in the presence of a British officer, and it was done.

I do not go into the equity of this case, or the zeal and responsibility of the Peking Government, but I am convinced that acting with such decision always when right, and even sometimes when wrong, is the only means by which foreigners can live in China with security to life and property. It is only a question between this and the right to live here at all.

But the United States, standing, or endeavouring to stand, upon a higher plane than that of mere physical force, pursues in China a policy of moral suasion, which neither convinces nor converts the Chinaman to the doctrines of a common brotherhood of men or nation—for, high as the heavens are above the earth, so high is his conceit, as deep as the waters of the sea is the measure of his contempt for the "outside barbarian."

Any high moral ground in the field of diplomacy—any appeal to the motives which ordinarily govern nations—indeed, any argument unaccompanied by the outward and visible sign of force, is used only for the purpose of delay, which in the end is equivalent to victory. Yet the United States has interests in China destined in the future to be greater than those of any other nation—possessing as we do the Pacific Ocean as a common highway—

geographically with reference to the continents, politically with reference to Europe, and commercially with reference to each other. These interests should be reciprocal, but China does not care to realise this fact—does not desire any identity of interests. She would to-day, if she could, exclude every article of foreign manufacture from her shores. She is slowly learning the Western arts, in order that by means of them she may some time not only exclude foreign goods, but the foreigner himself from the country. "China for the Chinese," is more than ever the motto of every Mandarin in the Empire. Our policy, therefore, should be positive, and governed, to the extent of moral law, by American interests alone, and followed up by the argument which they understand—the argument of force, pressure, not persuasion.

Li Hung-chang, Senior Guardian of the Emperor, Grand Secretary, Commander-in-Chief of eighteen provinces, Commissioner of Coast Defense, etc., sits in his viceregal chair at Tientsin, the gate of the capital of China, regulates the ingress and the egress of foreign diplomats to the Court, and defines the foreign and dictates the domestic policy of the country. Li Hung-chang is, therefore, the absolute and despotic ruler of 400,000,000 of people. Yet such is the system of this Government that he lives upon the mere breath of the Empress, an ignorant, capricious and immoral woman. A word from her and his power would vanish with the morning mist, and his courtiers would shrink from him as a man with the plague.

He is fifty-nine years of age, six feet two inches in stature, has a cold, clear, cruel eye, and an imperious manner. He is a thorough Oriental and an intense Chinaman. This implies contempt for Western nations and hatred for all foreigners. Li Hung-chang, the Viceroy of Chihli, is the Bismarck of the East. He keeps together an incongruous Empire and an effete dynasty by the repressive force of an indomitable will. He suppresses rebellions by decapitation, and quiets the turbulent with the bamboo. Yet he is great, not because he is so much in advance of his countrymen, but because he is not so far behind as they are in an appreciation of the arts, political and physical, which govern the modern world. He at least recognizes the value of these forces; he buys ships of war, contructs forts, experiments in torpedoes, and drills troops with modern arms. He has learned that despite the protestations of civilization, the sword yet remains the arbiter of nations, and that China, to be respected, must be armed. But he does not know that standing in the way of his military and naval aspirations is the fact that in China there is no military spirit.

Antedating all other nations in her traditions—standing, as it were, upon this "Rock of Ages"—China has taught her people to believe that there is something derogatory to honour in the character of a soldier—that the road to true glory lies through the fields of literature, and to emolument by the paths of commerce. Throughout these centuries generations have been imbued with these ideas, until, by the doctrine of a survival of the fittest, all martial spirit has died out of the race. The Chinese will suffer and endure; will, if cornered, fight; will rise against local oppression; but, under these circumstances, their wars become mere murders or retaliations, shocking from their cruelty. There is absolutely no chivalry, which makes the soldier an agent of civilization—no *esprit de corps,* which creates heroes and national leaders. The only idea of discipline is the fear of corporal punishment.

The bamboo is the dread alike of the General and the private. The civil button of the Mandarin takes precedence over military rank and defines relative subordination.

Under such a system there can be no *organization*—none of that spirit which distinguishes an army from an armed mob. Li-Hung-chang, as the Viceroy of the Imperial Province, guards and garrisons with his own provincial army the capital city of Peking. He has a partially trained force of about 35,000 men, armed with breech-loaders, and a complement of field-pieces. He has also in store 200,000 or 300,000 stands of arms and several hundred pieces of artillery. His forts on the seaboard of the Gulf of Pechili are of modern construction, and are armed with heavy ordnance. But, although his troops have been more or less drilled and organized by foreign officers, they are at all times liable to be dispersed for labour upon the public works, thus continually destroying what their instructors are endeavouring to create in them, viz., the *élan* and spirit of a military corps.

Over these men the Viceroy appoints the Generals and perhaps the Colonels, but the subordinate officers are simply hired by the month, and degraded or bambooed at the caprice of their superiors. The men are obedient, apt, and only insubordinate when not paid. They are pure volunteers, and paid as coolie labourers would be, by the month. There is no code of justice, and no such thing as court-martials.

But this small force forms no type of the immense mass of men which has been and can be collected into a so-called army; nor is it even a nucleus for a well drilled force. The first and almost insurmountable obstacle, in addition to what has already been stated, is the absence of any consolidated national feeling or love of country as a whole. The political divisions of the Empire have cut through every stratum of society, have established customs or created languages or dialects, making each of the nineteen provinces not only distinct, but hostile nationalities. Besides, each of these provinces is governed by a Viceroy almost independent of Peking, and only bound to it and to each other by the mythical tie of a common Emperor, who rules as the "Son of Heaven." It is impossible to convince these antagonistic people that they can have any common cause or move them by any common motive. For these reasons it will be seen how difficult it would be to create a national army.

As it is with the army, so with the navy. There are four distinct naval fleets, each independent of the others, and although nominally under the control of two "Commissioners of Coast Defence," of which Viceroy Li Hung-chang is one, and the Viceroy of Nanking the other, yet there is no combination or unity. A few years ago the Foochow Arsenal fleet, under the able administration of Mr. Giquel, a French officer, gave promise of forming at least the nucleus of an Imperial naval force, after twenty years of labour that gentleman has gone away, and now both the arsenal and fleet are lapsing into decay.

Under the pressure of a war imminent with Russia, Viceroy Li undertook to form a squadron for the protection of the approaches to Peking. Within a year or two he has collected a force of about twelve ships—six of these are gunboats of unique type—being remarkable for carrying the heaviest gun (35 tons) on the smallest displacement of any vessel afloat. Two others of similar type, but larger, and with very high speed, carry two guns each of

20 tons. These were all built by Sir William Armstrong. The other vessels of the squadron are composite, built at Foochow, and armed with light guns of French pattern. Besides these there is being built in Germany two iron-clads of the "Sachsen" class of the German Navy. Every modern appliance in the art of naval warfare has been placed on these new ships—guns with large calibre and high velocity, moved by hydraulic power, machine guns, electric lights, torpedoes and torpedo boats, engines with twin screws, steel rams, etc. etc. Indeed, the material of this squadron is complete, yet it is evident that in order to be really effective, it needs an intelligent personnel and a thorough organization.

It represents, indeed, a large amount of money expended, and has deluded the Chinese Government, and to some extent the world, into the belief, that China is really in possession of a navy. But the vices and weaknesses of the Chinese system of administration pervade and permeate it. The absence of naval rank and consequently of *esprit de corps*—of maritime experience and knowledge of the outside world among the officers—incongruous crews from different provinces, wanting in that pluck and dash which a national feeling and a national flag only can create—deep-seated and ineradicable financial corruption—all these combine to neutralize the qualities of the ships and to render them valueless as a fighting force.

To increase the inherent defects of this organization and, under the semblance of strength, in reality to add to its weakness, are the intrigues and jealousies of foreign officers both in and about the service. The Inspector-General of the Customs, an Englishman, in addition to his great power in that office, would also like to administer the navy. The ships were built in England under his contracts. Since their arrival in China the Commissioner of Customs at Tientsin—a German—has managed to secure their control. Three Englishmen—"quasi" officers of the Royal Navy, but now belonging to the Imperial Customs services afloat—are on board of the ships as "advisers" to the Chinese Admiral and Captains. Two ex-officers of the French Navy, employed at high salaries for some purpose never yet specified, make up three nationalities, each jealous of the other, and all despising the Chinese, while aspiring to control its naval service. With such discordant parts it will be easily seen how difficult it is to create a harmonious whole. The Viceroy, astute in all things but in the wisdom of the outside world, is more or less a victim to the flatteries or the arts of these ambitious men, who persuade him that he has a navy.

But the Ministers of the Western Powers, who watch every movement of the Chinese toward the acquisition of military or naval strength, and who are determined that they shall go thus far and no further—know that—sold at large profit by their constituents and officered by their countrymen—it is only a toy to amuse His Excellency, the Viceroy, in time of peace and a prize to be captured in time of war.

When we consider the enormous power of these 400,000,000 of people if turned in any intelligent direction—unrestrained by any moral obligation, unhindered by any physical obstacle from overrunning countries, exterminating races—I am forced to agree with the experienced diplomats, that Chinese progress in the arts of war is a thing to be checked, rather than accelerated by Western nation[s].

But notwithstanding the heavy hand which the representatives of Europe lay upon China whenever it attempts to move, contrasted with the scarcely perceptible pressure of American influence, China is really more in sympathy with Europe than with America. Russia, with a long, continuous border, exerts great power over its foreign policy, rendered easy by the assimilation of race and forcible by the dread of aggression.

But it is to our form of government that China is most antagonistic. The Mandarins are beginning to understand that if by the force of our example, liberal principles should be introduced in the Empire, there would be an end to the "heaven-born" dynasty, as well as to the taxation and tyranny upon which they now fatten and flourish. This fact has been illustrated lately by the treatment of the Chinese students peremptorily brought back from the United States before their educational course was completed. Wherever these youths have been distributed in the public service, they seem to have been regarded as the embodiment of "Americanism," and the determination has been shown to repress it, even by the cruelest means. They have fallen upon evil times, yet thoroughly imbued as they are with the spirit of free institutions, it is not likely that even the bamboo will entirely drive out of them the knowledge of these better things. But to-day they are the victims of oriental hatred to popular institutions, and the innocent cause of dislike on the part of the Mandarins for everything American.

The visit of General Grant to China was dramatic, rather than real, in its effect. Li Hung-chang was pleased to meet a man whom he could consider his peer, both as a soldier and a statesman, and, at the same time, one who, like himself, had risen to greatness by virtue of his own genius. The prominent visitors coming to China from Europe have usually been the mere scions of royalty—immature boys or wandering Princes—but General Grant had been the ruler of a great people and, more than that, the Viceroy expected he would be again. It was this, indeed, which give the General's visit its authority. The Russian bear was growling on the borders of China, and the English lion, inspired by the Imperial policy of Beaconsfield, was crouching for a spring upon anything or anywhere that threatened English trade or supremacy, while the friendship of the United States, personified in General Grant, was easily secured by the outstretched hand, no more of friendship than diplomacy, of the astute Viceroy.

But it would be a mistake to think that the visit had any permanent effect upon the foreign policy of China. The good it really did was to draw the attention of the United States to that country, with its immense possibilities for American commerce. During our war China had been almost forgotten and our trade almost annihilated. General Grant's visit revived these memories—indeed, around the world his journey had this significance. It reminded both the West and the East that America still lived. General Grant represented a character which, abroad, many of his countrymen are ashamed to confess—a *Republican* by conviction and an *American* at all times, whether in courts or camps.

As an adjunct to the army and navy, China has four arsenals—at Foochow, Shanghai, Tientsin and Nanking. At the first three are docks and plant for building and repairing small ships of war and engines, and distributed among them are factories for making powder, metallic cartridges, torpedoes, steam launches, etc. At Shanghai heavy ordnance is fabricated for the navy, and at Nanking field pieces for the army. All of these establishments have been or are more or less under foreign supervision, but it is at Tientsin alone that at present—under the vigorous determination of Li Hung-chang to arm China—there are any signs of vitality. The others are in a state of gradual decadence.

With such warlike means and methods, and under the condition I have enumerated, China is growing into fictitious strength and keeping imaginary pace with Western improvements. Concomitant with these is an increasing and undying feeling of hostility to foreigners all and every nationality.

Under these circumstances—portrayed without prejudice, but without sentiment—I am of the earnest conviction that the policy of the United States in China, and towards the Chinese in America, should be with us as it is with them—*purely selfish*—coming, as it ought to, under the universal law of right and justice, but by no means governed by the fallacious idea of international friendship, or even the broader ground of a common brotherhood.

. . . .

CRITICISM OF THE SHUFELDT-SARGENT LETTER. CHESTER HOLCOMBE TO SECRE-
TARY FRELINGHUYSEN, PEKING, MAY 22, 1882[2]

I have the honor to enclose herewith a printed copy of "an open letter to Hon. A. A. Sargent"—written by Commodore Shufeldt and recently reprinted at Hongkong and Shanghai.

It is not within my province or desire to pass any criticism upon the motive or state of mind which prompted the preparation of this letter or which led its author to consent to its being made public. Indeed I should not feel called upon to address the Department at all upon the subject were it not that the letter has come to the knowledge of the Ministers of the Foreign Office here and the Viceroy at Tientsin where it has very naturally aroused much unpleasant and even angry feeling towards its author and towards the country of which he is both a Diplomatic and a Naval Representative.

It is most fortunate that the letter was not made public here until after Commodore Shufeldt's departure for Corea. For had it come to the knowledge of the Chinese Government earlier, it would in all probability have resulted in the withdrawal of China from her position as mediator in the Corean negotiations, and made our efforts to execute a treaty fruitless for the present, at least with the author of this letter as our Envoy.

Without attempting an exhaustive review of the contents of the document, I must at least say that, in my opinion, one half of it is composed of truths which had better not have been made public by an officer of our Government, while the other half is made up of erroneous impressions.

That part of it which relates to the Chinese naval and military organization is substantially correct, though, in my opinion, the Commodore exaggerates the difficulties which the provincial peculiarities have placed in the way of a consolidated and efficient army and navy.

The incidental remarks which the letter contains in reference to Mr. Hart, are, in my opinion, neither just as regards either that gentleman, the Customs Service as a whole, or the Government of China.

Nor is it true in any sense of the term that the Viceroy Li is "the absolute and despotic ruler of 400,000,000 of people." Otherwise the portrait of that

² *China Despatches*, Vol. LX, No. 108.

distinguished officer is fairly correct. No criticism is needed of the language with which, in this connection, the Commodore characterizes the Empress Regent of China.

Passing from these points, there are three or four sweeping assertions in the letter which ought not to go unnoticed.

First among these is the declaration that "the only appeal or argument (appreciated by the Chinese) is that of force," and the natural sequence which is derived from this false premise, that the policy of the United States towards China—"a policy of moral suasion"—is a failure.

Both of these assumptions are entirely untenable. The whole drift and tendency of the Chinese mind is opposed to war and demonstrations of force. As Commodore Shufeldt himself remarks, very correctly—"China has taught her people to believe that there is something derogatory to honor in the character of a soldier—that the road to true glory lies through the fields of literature, and to emolument by the paths of commerce." And he might have added with entire truth that there is no country on earth in which the *role* of a "peace-maker" is held in such respect and honor between man and man, and so constantly and universally practised, as in China. It by no means follows that, because we were obliged to open this country to foreign intercourse with the edge of the sword forty years ago, nothing but the same weapon will serve any valuable purpose here today. Of all the powers maintaining treaty relations with China, only two have secured those relations by war, and, as a matter of fact, this Government looks with peculiar suspicion and distrust upon those same two powers, *because* of the force employed at the inception of their relations. It is a remark constantly made by the highest officers of the Chinese Government that they repose particular trust and confidence in the United States, and have no distrust of us, *because* our relations have always been those of peace and we have sought and gained what we wanted by peaceful arguments and friendly persuasion.

Nor is a practical proof and illustration of the truth of this assertion wanting. In 1880, the United States sent a Commission to this Empire to negotiate in regard to the vexed and embarrassing question of Chinese immigration. When one bears in mind the intense national pride of the Chinese, it is easy to see that few questions would have been so likely to stir up unfriendly feeling and provoke determined opposition on the part of the Government of China as that with which the Commissioners were intrusted. The entire foreign community of China, including all the Diplomatic Representatives in Peking, prophesied utter failure of the Commission. Yet the Commission was in Peking only 60 days, during which time nothing but kind words and friendly arguments were used, and all that could in reason be sought was granted, and granted as cordially and gracefully as could have been desired. And nothing on our part was given in exchange for that which we sought. Our forbearance, our "policy of moral suasion," stood us in good stead and secured what, in my opinion, would not have been granted to any other Power without some substantial equivalent.

And in this negotiation the United States gained the end desired, mainly because, without arrogant demonstration of force and avoiding carefully any appearance of a disposition to trifle unnecessarily with existing treaty stipulations, it sent its Commission to consult in good faith and in a friendly spirit with the Chinese Government, thus recognizing, as no application of force does recognize, the right of China to an equal voice in the business in hand.

It is of course true that England has, commercially, the largest foreign influence in this Empire. But this is the result of certain other factors of the situation here with which the Department is entirely familiar and has nothing to do with the question at issue.

But it is most emphatically *not* true that "diplomatically also England rules China." Her war and opium policy in the past and present is a serious weight upon her diplomatic influence, and I question whether there are not at least three Powers now represented in Peking any one of which has a greater influence with China than Great Britain.

At least, in my opinion, the United States has no reason to question the wisdom of its policy of "moral suasion" with this Empire, or to shrink from any comparison between its diplomatic influence here and that of other foreign Powers.

A policy of force if persisted in would result in the inevitable dismemberment of China, which certainly is the last thing we could desire. A firm, persistent, yet kindly policy of "moral suasion," requires much patience and forbearance, and its results are perhaps tardy in development, yet they are permanent and far reaching and quite justify the means by which they are secured.

The second assumption which need be noticed is the following:—"But it is to *our* form of Government that China is most antagonistic." The Commodore illustrates this assertion by referring to the recall of the Chinese students, the treatment which they are receiving here, and adds—"today they are the victims of Oriental hatred to popular institutions, and the innocent cause of dislike on the part of the mandarins for everything American."

Here the Commodore makes an assertion which is entirely erroneous and illustrates it by a fact which has no connection therewith. It is well known here that the recall of the Chinese students grew out of an unfortunate jealousy on the part of the late senior Minister to the United States towards his junior Yung-Wing; that the Foreign Office and the Viceroy Li were adverse to the recall, but could not prevent it at the moment; and are now concerting measures to return a portion of them to the United States.

As to any peculiar antagonism felt by China towards our form of Government, I am thoroughly convinced that such a sentiment has, in point of fact, no existence. On the contrary the system of Government in China has very many and very close points of resemblance to our own, and these points are well known and often pleasantly commented on by the high Chinese officials.

The Government of China today is more nearly a "government of the people, by the people and for the people" than many systems upon the continent of Europe. This may seem an extravagant statement but careful examination and comparison will bear it fully out.

The last general statement made by Commodore Shufeldt, requiring notice is that in which he declares that there is in China "an increasing and undying feeling of hostility to all foreigners of every nationality."

If a residence of thirteen years in this Empire, coupled with a knowledge of the language, a constant intercourse with all classes of the people in all parts of the country, may count for anything, then I may be allowed to assert that the opposite of this is true, and that the old feeling of hostility to foreigners is slowly but surely disappearing as the two classes come into more intimate association and mutual acquaintance each with the other.

Having written thus in criticism of some of the more important statements made by Commodore Shufeldt, I may be allowed to say in conclusion, that I am in no sense a lover of the Chinese, or blind to the glaring defects in their individual and national character. Their officials are intensely proud, inclined to be overbearing, mendacious as a rule and not as an exception, narrowminded and suspicious to an extreme degree, and naturally given to tortuous and deceptive lines of conduct rather than to such as become persons called upon to bear grave responsibilities. Their habits of procrastination and evasion are calculated to test the patience and exasperate those who are accustomed to prompt and straightforward dealing. A long patience, a cool brain, indomitable persistency and imperturbable good nature are necessary qualifications to the success of any person who may come into official relations with them.

XXIV

CONFLICTS OF CONFUCIAN THEORY AND INTERNATIONAL LAW, 1882-1883

DURING the closing decades of the nineteenth century China lost the control which at various times she had exercised over neighboring "vassal" states, such as Korea and Indo-China. China's position in these areas had been based on Confucian concepts of the elder and younger brother. With the impact of Western nations in the Far East this Confucian or "natural" relation was opposed by the West's legal concepts of international law. In the case of Korea, China insisted that this state was independent, yet claimed an overlordship which, however, would not accept responsibility for the acts of the "vassal" or younger brother. There was of course no place for this ancient relationship in the language of modern Western international law. In terms of the treaties concluded between Korea and Japan (1876), and between Korea and the United States (1882), this Oriental kingdom was an independent state. It was not, however, until 1895 that China was forced by treaty to recognize this new status. From the beginning of this controversy, the United States assumed that its treaty of 1882 disposed effectively of any claim China might have to suzerainty in the Korean peninsula. The fact that there was no point of contact between China's Confucian theories and Western concepts of international law is illustrated in the discussions of the American minister, John Russell Young, with Li Hung-chang.

KOREA REGARDED AS AN INDEPENDENT STATE. SECRETARY FRELINGHUYSEN TO MINISTER YOUNG, WASHINGTON, AUGUST 4, 1882[1]

The Treaty of May 22, 1882, with Corea, which was negotiated by Commodore Shufeldt, was sent to the Senate by the President on the 29th ultimo. I am not in a position to inform you as to the probability of its approval by that body.

.   .   .   .

An interesting point may be raised as to how far the dependency of Corea upon China may affect the execution of the Corean treaty under the Chinese Immigration Act. The fact of such dependency is ignored in the

[1] *China Instructions*, Vol. III, No. 30.

Treaty itself, but a letter from the King of Corea to the President declares that Corea is a dependency of China, although "the management of its government affairs, domestic and foreign, has always been vested in the sovereign." In the past, the Chinese government has not admitted that the Empire is responsible for, or internationally represented Corea. Our former employment of force toward Corea, as though it were wholly independent, and without remonstrance on the part of China, will be remembered. In view of all the circumstances, I cannot but regard the administrative independence of Corea as a pre-established fact, abundantly recognized by the events of the past few years, and not created by or recognized by the conclusion of our treaty.

It is to be borne in mind that the somewhat anomalous position of Corea has long been a cause of jealous ill-feeling between China and Japan, which has not been allayed by the action of the U. S. and other powers in negotiating treaties with Corea through the good offices of Chinese authorities. It is undesirable that the recent course of the United States in initiating such negotiations, should foment any existing ill-will. It should be a part of your duty to aid in dispelling such feeling. In your intercourse with the Chinese authorities, you should make it clear, whenever a proper occasion may offer to do so, that we have not regarded the aid lent to us by Chinese officials in bringing about this treaty as in any way an assertion of China's administrative rights over Corea, to the waiver of which we became a party; but that we regarded Corea as *de facto* independent, and that our acceptance of the friendly aid found in China was in no sense a recognition of China's suzerain power. For, if we had regarded, or were constrained by any action of China to regard Corea as dependent upon the Empire, we should look to the execution of our treaties with China for the preservation of the rights of our citizens on the Corean Peninsula.

A Reassertion That Korea Is Independent. The Acting Secretary of State John Davis to Minister Young, Washington, January 22, 1883[2]

I have to acknowledge the receipt of your No. 50 of October 31, 1882. It is a very interesting despatch and has been read with care and attentively considered. Your endeavors to prevent a rupture between China and Japan and to preserve the cordial relations which exist between those Governments and the U. S. meet with the approval of this Department.

I observe that you state that you have conversed with some of your colleagues as to whether China's action in arresting and punishing high Corean dignitaries would compel the treaty powers to ask the Emperor of China to approve the conventions made with Corea.

Out of abundant caution and not because it is believed that you have any doubt on the subject, I would remark that this government does not deem such an approval necessary. No where in the treaty or elsewhere have we admitted that the relations of Corea with China are such as to require the ratification of the latter government to add force to any treaty concluded with the former. Were Corea so dependent upon China as to make such an approval necessary, no treaty with that country would be required, as you justly remark, for the existing treaties with China would suffice upon an extension of their operation to Corea.

² *Ibid.,* No. 81.

In their negotiations with Corea the United States availed themselves of the good offices of China, which were tendered in a spirit of friendship and good will, but thereby this government did not commit itself to any recognition of a lack of independence in Corea. On the contrary, as is well known to you that point was expressly guarded against in the treaty and negotiations.

That China claims some right of suzerainty over Corea is understood, but when the Corean King expressly states that full sovereignty has been exercised by the Kings of Chosen in all matters of internal administration and foreign relations (as will more fully appear by a reference to Mr. Holcombe's No. 133 of June 26, 1882) the effect of that claim is not apparent. It is, moreover, understood that it has no greater force than the claim heretofore made in relation to Siam and is not such as to affect the treaty relations of either Corea or Siam with foreign powers.

As you will learn by an instruction which goes to you by this mail, the treaty with the King of Chosen has been ratified by the Senate, which has thereby recognized the independence of Corea in its relations to the Government of the United States.

LI HUNG-CHANG AND JOHN RUSSELL YOUNG DISCUSS POLITICS. MINISTER YOUNG TO SECRETARY FRELINGHUYSEN, PEKING, AUGUST 8, 1883[3]

I have the honour to report for the information of the Department certain transactions and conversations with the Grand Secretary Li Hung Chang. . . .

I happened to be in Shanghai on a domestic errand. The Grand Secretary knowing of my presence, sent an urgent message, asking me to await his arrival, as he specially wished to see me. I found him rather worn from the rites of mourning and seclusion, which he had undergone, according to Chinese custom for his mother's death. I was sorry to meet him in an unfortunate temper, towards all foreigners, notably Frenchmen. Our country was not excepted from the general sway of denunciation. This conversation, will, I think have value to the Department, because it is the only occasion since I have been minister, when any member of the Government has discussed our Immigration Bill.

After words of courtesy and personal inquiry, the Viceroy expressed his thanks to me for awaiting him in Shanghai. He was troubled about affairs. There seemed to be a conspiracy against China among the Western nations, especially the European. "China" said His Excellency, "had to look the fact in the face, that she had no friends. Here was Russia menacing her on the north. Germany had invaded her territory at Swatow. Japan had taken the Loo-Choo islands. England held Hongkong, and was forcing upon her a traffic in opium that meant the misery and ruin of her people. France was sending an expedition to dismember her empire. The United States had passed an act excluding Chinese from her soil, Chinese, alone, of all the races in the world."

I said "that so far as the United States was concerned His Excellency should not regard the Immigration Bill as unfriendly. Before the measure was passed, my Government sent a special embassy to China, an embassy composed of three distinguished citizens, and made known to China all the embarrassments attending the immigration of Chinese. We asked the Imperial Government to unite with us in a plan for solving the problem, and the result was a treaty, in which China and the United States, united, and under its terms the immigration act was passed. I could not see how His Excellency could regard that as an unfriendly proceeding. On the contrary, we had shown to China the highest consideration."

"America," he replied, "is large enough for all the nations in the world, who choose to go there. Why is she not large enough for the Chinese? Are the Chinese worse than other people?"

I again reminded His Excellency "that all these questions had been discussed with his Government by my predecessor Mr. Angell, as well as by Mr. Trescot and Mr. Swift that a treaty had been signed, and I was not instructed to enter into their consideration. I was instructed however, to say, that the American Government felt the deepest interest in China, wished to see her resources developed, her commerce extended, and the two nations always as friends. We had never made war on China, nor craved an inch of her dominions. On the contrary we believed in her independence". . . .

"Remember," he said, interrupting, and laying his hand on mine—"remember, that I am not complaining of you, or your President, or your Secretary for foreign affairs, or of your predecessors, who have been my good friends, as you are my good friend, and as General Grant is likewise. I know your great men, your President, your Secretary, and those in authority have good hearts for China. But why is it not shown as you show it to Japan? . . . . You know Japan is our enemy, and I cannot endure to have Japan receive a recognition that is not given to us. As to Corea, I have no anxiety. I have no fear of Japan's influence there. I am," he said with a smile, "King of Corea, whenever I think the interests of China require me to assert that prerogative. I am not afraid of Japan. I was ready to fight her last summer, when she sent her troops to Corea, and am ready now. I do not wish to meddle with the king of Corea's affairs, nor to menace his independence. That is not China's policy. But I shall not permit Japan to do so. Corea is the gateway to China, and its possession by an aggressive power like Japan, would be a danger to China."

I replied "that I knew His Excellency's views on this subject, and had never ceased to cherish the hope that there would come such an understanding between China and Japan as would remove all causes of ill-will and suspicion."

"Then," he said, "let Japan stop taking Chinese territory. She tried to do it in Formosa, would like to do it in Corea, has done it in Loo-Choo. Your colleague Mr. Bingham, and Sir Harry Parkes, have both expressed their opinions on the Loo-Choo case, and held that Japan has no business there."

I said, "that Mr. Bingham was an eminent and learned man, who had experience in foreign as well as home affairs, and any expression of his opinion would be of value. But it seemed to me a hardship, a cruelty I might say for two nations like China and Japan to allow the possession of these few islands to be a constant provocation to war. China is now one of the largest empires in the world. For the ownership of a dominion about which she never cared, which she never governed, which is of no value to her, she would lose more lives than there are inhabitants in Loo-Choo."

"There is the principle," said His Excellency. "China does not want

Loo-Choo. She wants the sovereign restored. The United States has made treaties with him as a King, and you should insist upon his restoration."

I answered "that I was not instructed to enter upon the merits of the Loo-Choo case, and really had never given the subject attention enough to have as clear an opinion upon it, as had been expressed by Mr. Bingham. It always seemed to me to be too small a matter to be allowed to imperil the peace of Asia."

"Small matters sometimes lead to great wars," said His Excellency. To which historical proposition, I could not demur.

I then said "that His Excellency should consider that there was another side to these questions. Had not China invited controversy and aggression by her own uncertain policy? Why did not the emperor define the actual limits of China and say to the world that this was his territory, and he would defend it. The world would respect such a declaration. But China claimed dependencies, and then declined the responsibility of governing them. In Formosa when the Japanese asked for reparation because of the murder of Japanese seamen by Formosan savages China answered that she was not to blame for the acts of savages. Japan sent an expedition to punish the authors of the outrages, and China at once came forward and paid an indemnity to Japan to leave the country. In the West we should call that an ignoble act."

"If Formosa were Chinese territory, why submit to the indignity of a foreign army invading the soil? The same thing happened in Corea. The crew of an American ship was murdered by Coreans. My predecessor Mr. Low asked redress from the Yamen. He was informed that China was not responsible for Corea. We were compelled to deal with Corea in our own way. Why does not China define her territory?"

The Viceroy said "that the limits of the empire were well defined. There was China, and there were the tributaries of China. These tributaries were self governing, except in the fact that they owed the emperor an allegiance, which was satisfied by acts of tribute and ceremony. These offices done, the emperor never interfered in the internal affairs. At the same time their independence concerned China, and he could not be insensible to any attack upon it."

I replied "that in modern times and under the forms of civilization which now prevailed, there were no such institutions as tributary states. A colony was as much a part of the empire as the capital. In the United States we have many states, and outlying territories, one far away to the north, isolated, Alaska. But if any foreign power placed a soldier in Alaska, with an unfriendly purpose, it would be as much an act of war as landing ten thousand men in New York, and would be so regarded. This is the rule of civilized nations. China should follow it, and save herself embarrassments by consolidating her empire, and having the world know the exact limits of her territory."

His Excellency said "that he saw no reason why the outside nations should destroy relations that had existed between China and these outlying nations for ages. They had gone on well together, doing each other good, and why should France come in and disturb them? It was an act of aggression, and only convinced him that China had no friends among the nations."

"Your Excellency," I replied, "would be more accurate, I think, if you said that China had no enemies among the nations. China is not an aggressive power. Her civilization is venerable, picturesque, respected. The character of her people, of her literature and her historical traditions excite sympathy and respect. No one wishes to fight China, and there could be no motive for doing so, except a motive of aggrandizement. I was happy to indulge the hope that as our civilization advanced, wars for mere motives of gain were coming to an end. So far then from China thinking that the nations were unfriendly, it was her true policy to regard them as friends, throw open her ports, remove the barriers to trade, and abandon the policy of reaction which had recently been seen in Peking."

The Viceroy asked, "Why did not foreign nations if they were friendly to China, deal with China as they did with themselves? Why have one kind of treaties with his empire and another kind with other empires?"

I said "that I hoped the time would come when China in the matter of treaty stipulations would stand among the most favoured nations. That was my most earnest wish. But China must lead the way to that. She must first show the world that she had a Government. There was now no government in Peking. Instead of dealing with foreign powers, it was in matters of business simply trifling. Plain necessary questions, concerning trade, that might be settled in an hour, linger for months and months, with no result. The Yamen shows no desire to encourage diplomatic relations and the result was alienation and irritation when there should be friendship and a cordial understanding. I had no hesitancy in speaking to His Excellency frankly on this point because I knew his enlightened mind and that he was a statesman with whom it was pleasant to transact business. But when he complained of the apathy or the unkindness of foreign powers, he should ask how far was his own government to blame."

His Excellency replied "that affairs in Peking were to be explained partly by the long illness of Prince Kung and the fact that the emperor was an infant. Of course, there were reactionary tendencies, because there were parties in China, as in other countries, and parties here turned unfortunately, upon the question that most interested China, namely, opening her country to foreigners and foreign influence. He himself did not dread the foreigners, although some of his experiences with them had not been encouraging". . . .

XXV

POLITICAL DESTINIES CONTROLLED BY THE STARS, 1882-1884

CHINA's advancement in the acceptance of Western ideas and institutions was frequently hampered by the unenlightened character of her rulers. Even in cases where intelligent men were appointed to the foreign office their efforts were nullified by intrigues of their antiforeign colleagues, the jealousies of their rivals, and the baneful superstitions of the censors.

RETIREMENT OF WANG WEN-CHAO. MINISTER YOUNG TO SECRETARY FRELINGHUYSEN, PEKING, DECEMBER 21, 1882[1]

An event of importance in its bearings upon foreign relations has recently occurred here in the retirement from office of Wang Wen Chao, a Member of the Privy Council, Minister of the Foreign Office, and Vice President of the Board of War.

His Excellency came to the Capital in 1878. from Hunan of which Province he had previously been Governor. He was at once appointed to the Foreign Office, and to the other posts named above. Since the death of His Excellency Shen-Kuei-fun which occurred in February 1881. and was reported in Mr. Angell's despatch number 109. to the Department, he has been, under His Imperial Highness Prince Kung virtually the managing head of the foreign affairs of China.

By his genial and pleasant manners, his marked ability and intelligent conception of the true interests of China, and, as a natural sequence, his progressive ideas, he had won a high place in the esteem and kind regard of all the members of the Diplomatic Body here, who regard his retirement from public life as a very serious loss not only to China but to all Powers having relations with her.

And, as will be seen, the manner of his retirement, serves to intensify this feeling of regret. Some months since a Censor memorialized the Throne accusing Wang Wen Chao and Ching lien, another Minister of the Foreign Office and President of the Board of War, of receiving presents and bribery in connection with military expenditures in the Province of Yunnan. It was generally believed at the time, and subsequent developments have confirmed this belief, that the accusation was trumped up by the reactionary party, under the management of Tso Chung Fang, to ruin the influence of Wang Wen Chao and to punish him for entertaining progressive and so called pro-foreign ideas. This line of policy has been frequently adopted in recent years by the conservative party, and with almost unvarying success. The case of Chung How is a striking illustration in point.

[1] *China Despatches*, Vol. LXIII, No. 83.

As Ching Lien is a member of the conservative party, his name was only brought into the accusation incidentally, and to preserve a show of justice. The charges against him were not pressed. But those against Wang Wen Chao were, and, after a struggle lasting some four months, the reactionists have, as usual, conquered, and by a recent Decree, "Wang Wen Chao is permitted to retire to his native village to recruit his shattered health." As he is still in middle life and has not been ill, the Decree tells its own story between the lines and deceives no one.

This incident will be of interest to the Department as serving to show the nature of the political struggle which is constantly going on here between the friends and the enemies of progress in China, and the means resorted to by the latter to accomplish their purposes.

RETIREMENT OF WANG WEN-CHAO. MINISTER YOUNG TO SECRETARY FRELINGHUYSEN, PEKING, FEBRUARY 21, 1883[2]

In my despatch No. 83 I reported the retirement from the Yamen of Wang Wen Chao, a most useful and enlightened member of that body, with the reasons which, so far as the Legation could learn led to his withdrawal.

I have now the honour to enclose for your information an extract from the Peking Gazette, preferring against Wang the charges which prompted his resignation. This memorial is from the superintending censor of the Yunnan circuit. It is a quaint and interesting specimen of the supernatural influence which plays so important a part in Chinese government. What led the censor to look into the condition of affairs, at Peking, was the fact that "a comet had arisen in the east, like a piece of silk in form, with a tail several *chang* long, stretching away to the southwest, while at the dawn its brightness vies with that of the rising sun."

Now although the censor does not claim to a knowledge of the science of divination, and cannot give an authoritative explanation of the Divine purposes implied in the cometary visit, history shows clearly from all records that "such phenomena appear alone as a consequence of misgovernment below." The censor thereupon recites in detail certain charges of bribery against Wang, and he asks his dismissal, along with another equally guilty official. These charges he concludes by saying are not only universally made but he "sees them confirmed by celestial portents."

The official result of the inquiry, so far as the guilt or innocence of Wang on the bribery charge has not been made known. It is generally felt, however, that the accusation was a pretext, and that he was forced from public life by the influence of the reactionary party whose power has been steadily on the increase for some time past.

To hear of statesmen, whose rise and fall are governed by the movements of the planetary bodies, is like reading some Arabian fable. But a memorial like this, which might easily pass as a chapter from a fairy story, is not without interest from a political view when we remember that these childlike, fantastic, romantic theories about comets, stars, and good government, are the profound convictions of men who rule the most populous empire on the globe.

[2] *Ibid.*, Vol. LXIV, No. 136.

CONFLICT IN CHINESE POLITICS: A MEMORIAL OF CHANG CHIH-TUNG. MINISTER YOUNG TO SECRETARY FRELINGHUYSEN, PEKING, JANUARY 31, 1884[3]

I have the honour to enclose for your information a copy of a secret memorial to the throne, by Chang Chih-Tung, at present Governour of the Province of Shansi. This official came into notice in 1880, as will be seen in a despatch No. 32, dated, May 15th, 1880, addressed by Mr. Consul General Denny to Mr. Payson. He was then a sub-reader in the Han-lin, a position which indicated high scholarship without any special rank. The despatch of Mr. Denny enclosed a memorial to the throne from Chang Chih Tung assailing the treaty concluded between Russia and the unfortunate Chung How. I quote as an enclosure an expression of opinion from that memorial shewing the temper of the writer towards foreign nations and especially Russia—and, throwing light upon any opinions he may now express.

This memorial is the opinion of an official of high rank; and what I am afraid are the opinions of the party which holds sway in the Imperial Councils. The writer believes in War and assails the Peace Party. "The Peace Party," he says, "are only anxious, in their selfishness for their own comforts. They simply wish to perform their official duties in peace and laziness." He adds, "that for years the arsenals in the several provinces have expended millions, for the purpose of manufacturing munitions of war." He asks the pertinent question. "If now we do not put them to use, to what ultimate use can they be destined?"

This statement read between the lines will be understood as a reflection upon Li Hung Chang. That statesman is criticized by the impetuous spirits in China because he did not make war last year. The gravamen of the accusations is that he has spent millions of dollars in preparing for war and now when China has an enemy, and a cause for enmity he is not ready. The criticism on Li, is emphasized in the comparison drawn by the memorialist between Li, and his great rival Tso Tsung Tang, the Nanking Viceroy.

"Tso," he says, "is a man of great experience, and there is no ground for doubt, but that he has matured all his plans, in the event of hostilities."

Li is censured by implication in what follows: "Tientsin is the nearest to the sacred capital. It is important, therefore that talented men should be placed there, to lead the troops stationed there, and who can also plan strategic measures."

When we remember that Tso is a very old man, burdened with bodily infirmities, and no more fitted to take the field, than was our own illustrious General Scott when the Rebellion came upon us;—and that Li, although advancing in years is in the prime and vigour of manhood, the animus of this allusion is plain. Li commands at Tientsin and has been there for fourteen years. To suggest that "talented men" should be in command who would show the activity and foresight of Tso, means that Li wants in talents, and does not compare in energy and forethought with his venerable and worn out colleague.

How far the councils of this impetuous memorialist will govern the Yamen events will shew. So far as we can understand the "peace policy" of statesmen like Prince Kung and Li Hung Chang, it means that they know that China is not ready—that France can master her, and that war means disaster. If the councils of these statesmen had been followed years ago, say in the time

[3] *Ibid.*, Vol. LXVIII, No. 344.

of awakening which my distinguished predecessor Mr. Burlingame did so much to bring about, China could now be the formidable antagonist of any Western power. The men who are clamoring for war; for immediate war against one of the greatest and most perfectly organized civilizations in the family of nations have hitherto been the perverse opponents of progress. They have kept China helpless, have dwarfed her, and now complain because she is not able to do a strong man's work.

It is true that large sums have been expended in naval and military preparations, and the memorialist may well ask "If now we do not put them to use, to what ultimate use can they be destined?" But I am afraid that only a small portion of these sums ever reached the purpose for which they were intended. The governmental system in China has so degenerated in the high qualities of authority, such as diverting the public treasure to the public good, that no confidence can be felt in the soundness of any military or naval organization. What Li, or Tso may have done towards strengthening the country can only be regarded as spasmodic and futile efforts, and not the outcome of a firm, generous, comprehensive policy, emanating from the throne, pervading the whole empire, and in the end enabling China to be, what she should be, a strong, wise, and civilized nation.

This, however, opens a field of speculation which my despatch does not contemplate, involving deep and far reaching considerations. My purpose is to send you, as an important phase in Chinese politics this noticeable memorial, with such comments as may shew the impression it has made upon the Legation.

THE MEMORIAL OF CHANG CHIH-TUNG[4]

A Secret Memorial from the Futai of Shansi.

Chang Chih-tung, Futai of Shansi, on bended knees presents the following Memorial, with reference to making a Tributary State secure, and preventing cruel persecutions against it; whereby, making war in one day, peace may be secured for ten thousand years. From former times until now, all dissensions in that State which the Government of the Tributary may not be able to quell itself, have been tranquillised by the Greater Empire. Hence we have smoothed her difficulties many times. Now, since year by year Annam has paid in her tribute without fail, we should not at last neglect her.

This matter of tribute is known throughout the Ten Thousand Kingdoms of the World, but France in her spirit of aggression has brow beaten the weaker state (of Annam). Supposing the case that Annam had offended France, then she should first notify the fact to the Heavenly Dynasty (China); France ought by no means, brooding mischief, to have attempted to encroach upon Annam. Nor can such a procedure be within the spirit of the International Law. Where, then, is the inborne nature of justice, in France?

It is the duty therefore of the Sacred Dynasty to explain the injustice of the French to the World, and then collect its armies to punish these cruel persecutions. There should be no hesitation in the matter, nor should there be any spirit of self-depreciation to the effect that we are useless in war. Those who urge for peace say that "France is like a whale, which, opening its mouth, wishes to swallow up (Annam), and that if China helps her, France would surely declare war against us; moreover the Treasury of the Empire is not full, how then would it be possible to go to war?"

[4] Incl. in Young's No. 344.

But according to the Memorialist's ideas there can be no cause for fear. *The Peace Party are only anxious, in their selfishness, for their own comfort. They simply wish to perform their official duties in peace and laziness.* Now even supposing the Government Treasuries be empty, if we devise plans to fill them it is not so impossible as to be sure of failure. The Peace Party also say, "the French have strong ships and formidable guns, and are always prepared for war. What, then, can China do if the French ships of war keep continually warring against her?"

The Memorialist is of opinion that no fear on this account ought to be entertained. *For years the Arsenals in the several provinces have expended millions each year for the purpose of manufacturing munitions of war. If now we do not put them to use, to what ultimate use can they be destined?*

The French must come with much trouble and privation from afar, while we await them at our leisure. We shall be fighting on our own ground, whence recruiting will be exceedingly easy, whereas the French as strangers will not have this advantage. The difference therefore will be immeasurable.

If we do not go to war, what possibility will there be hereafter for China to uphold her name as a strong Power amongst other nations? And, moreover, how can she protect her tributaries? When it was determined to send soldiers to Annam to protect her from injustice, the minds of all men were glad, and numbers came voluntarily to enroll themselves as soldiers. Moreover, the French troops have been beaten in succession; hence we should take the opportunity and attack them. If, however, the French army, having received their reinforcements, be collected together, it will be hard to conquer them.

The Memorialist suggests three plans, should war be declared against France. The first is to infuse the nature of the case into the hearts of the people; the second is to consult upon plans for self-defence; the third is to settle upon the necessary generals to lead the armies. Now, with reference to the first. The people all know how cruel the French are, and now that France has warred against Annam, a tributary state of China; it is an instance of despising the Suzerain; hence the people are unanimous for war.

The Memorialist therefore hopes that an Imperial Decree will be forwarded to the High Officials of the Border Provinces directing them to explain the rights and wrongs of the matter to the people, who will then be prepared for war; then rewards for good conduct can be first granted to the deserving, so that, when the time comes for fighting, the people will be enthusiastic for battle, and also know the Justice and Augustness of the Emperor.

With reference to the second plan, measures must be consulted for the defence of Fuhkien, Kuangtung, Kuangsi, Yunnan, Kiangnan and Tientsin. Yunnan is the nearest to the seat of war, and hence it is the most important. But even if Yunnan be a large province, still most of it consists of wild places, and hence it is fit for the battle fields of our Dynasty. Should the French, therefore, come by land, they will be lost in the passes of an unknown country. Yunnan therefore will have no cause for fear. Fuhkien and Kuang-tung being on the sea-coast, it would be easy for the French ships of war to enter their ports; the Throne therefore should quickly send a Decree directing the High Officials of those provinces to order the military officials to construct forts at the most important spots for their defence, and also order out our ships of war to give the necessary assistance. Hence, all being prepared, they can await the arrival of the enemy.

Kiang-nan possesses the largest number of ships of war. Tso Tsung-tang is a man of great experience, and there is no ground for doubt but that he has matured all his plans in the event of hostilities. Kiang-nan therefore, is sufficiently protected.

Tientsin is the nearest to the Sacred Capital; it is important, therefore, that talented men should be placed there to lead the troops stationed there, and who can also plan strategic measures. The French coming from a distance of a thousand li, will, in this case, surely be conquered.

With reference to the third place, Tsen Yu-ying is well known in Yunnan and Kueichow, and feared by the people. The French also admire and revere him. The Memorialist, therefore, prays that the Throne will command that Viceroy speedily to raise troops for the rescue of Annam. The French, having recently suffered defeat, will then be unable to withstand a numerous and fresh army.

The military sage Sun says, "We must not say that we are sure to conquer before we fight; after the battle is over and we are victorious, then it will be time enough to say so."

If we do not fight against France, and the despatches coming to and fro speak of peace and nothing but peace, then China will be put to great derision before other countries, and thus be proportionately browbeaten hereafter. There will be no more plans for China, nor can she even be rescued into safety.

Now if we go to war and be victorious, all countries will know the strength and majesty of our soldiers, and in consequence that of our Emperor. Therefore by warning [warring?] in one day, we will be able to secure a peace of ten thousand years, and Annam be rescued. The Memorialist does not venture to boast, nor is he happy in the prospect of war; but he sees that things are changing in the world, and everything is being made more difficult. For this reason he dares to tell his opinion to the Empress Dowager and the Emperor, and reverently prays that his Memorial may be sent to the High Officials of all the Provinces and consulted upon, and that they be directed to pay attention to the expressions of the Memorialist, whereby he displays on the one hand his solicitude for his country and on the other his indignation at the procedure of France. He therefore prays that the Sacred Glance may be cast upon his reverential Memorial.

.   .   .   .

XXVI

LIKIN TAXATION AND FOREIGN TRADE, 1885

To THE FOREIGN merchants engaged in China's import and export trade, taxes imposed by the Chinese authorities were a matter of primary importance. The import and export duties were of course determined by the conventional tariff. Goods which were imported and which had paid the duty might likewise be shipped into the interior (without further imposition) by payment at the port of entry of an additional tax (one half the duty), for which a transit pass was given. However, in practice, goods designed for export or import were usually subject to a local Chinese internal revenue tax known as *likin*. Although the payment of this tax was protested by foreigners, it was too valuable a source of revenue to be surrendered by the local Chinese authorities. Minister Denby's memorandum of 1885 summarized the principal issues involved in the question of *likin* taxation.

A MEMORANDUM ON LIKIN TAXATION. CHARLES DENBY TO SECRETARY BAYARD, PEKING, DECEMBER 18, 1885[1]

I.

Between 1843 and 1844 the Government of China, desiring to cover the losses arising to the public exchequer from the necessity of having to remit the land tax, wholly or partially, in the disturbed districts, and in view of the absolute necessity of raising funds for the pay of the soldiery (decree September 23, 1879) instituted the "likin" tax, or a tax of .001 on the tael.

It might be supposed, if we consider but the name (*li*, .001 of a tael, *kin*, money coin), that it was an ad valorem duty; but such does not appear ever to have been its character. In its present form, which dates from about 1860, when it became a universal tax, it is a specific rate per bale, piece, or picul, as the case may be. Originally of a temporary character (decree February 11-12, 1882), it has become a permanent and universal tax, which has gradually become intolerably burdensome to native and foreign trade alike.

The amount and mode of the collection of likin varies in the different provinces, in each of which this service is under the direction of the provincial high authorities. In each province there is a likin central office (*Tsung Likin Chii*) under the direction of a high official, and he establishes subsidiary stations throughout the province along the routes frequented by trade, and entrusts the management of each to a deputy *(wei-yüan)*, who reports to the central office, and is independent of the local officials. Each deputy transmits

[1] *Foreign Relations*, 1886, No. 57, pp. 66-73.

his accounts to the central office, and there does not appear to be any means of controlling them. In many cases, especially at the large ports, the collection of likin on a certain article of trade is farmed out, the contractor paying a fixed sum per annum to the provincial authorities, generally a very small percentage of the sums collected, and retaining the balance for himself.

The likin barriers have gradually increased until they are thickly distributed throughout the provinces, the number of deputies *(wei-yüan)* deputed to manage them is excessive, and the expenditure thus unnecessarily incurred is very large.

.   .   .   .

The imperial commands have been issued directing governors-general and governors to apply themselves with genuine zeal to the task of withdrawing or amalgamating these collectorates. Habit and long custom have, however, in many instances, prevailed, and the desire of standing well with their subordinates has often induced their chiefs to help them with appointments to these collectorates. (Decree December 29, 1884; see also decree September 23, 1879.)

Great Britain, by the treaty of Nanking (August 29, 1842, Article X), founded the transit pass system, which has since been adopted by all of the treaty powers in China, the object of which was to exempt by the payment of a transit duty (fixed at half the tariff duty) all foreign goods from all inland taxation.

This system would have been of the greatest assistance to foreign trade, as well as to native, but for the determined opposition of the provincial authorities.

.   .   .   .

A few of the irregular or arbitrary modes of procedure of the local authorities in connection with foreign goods under transit pass may here be mentioned, and among these I will not even consider the categorical refusal of the local authorities (as at Kini Chan) to recognize transit passes, "upon the arrival inland of any merchandise protected by a transit pass the likin officials at the place of designation proceed at once to exact a 'consumption tax,' and it must be paid by either the seller or the buyer before the goods can be transferred. This tax is quite arbitrary, and upon bases quite unknown to the seller. It may be light and not appreciably advance the cost of the goods. It may also be and often is exorbitant, and amounts to a prohibition of sale without actual loss.

When the goods have arrived at the terminus indicated in the pass, they become 'uncertificated,' and, if forwarded further inland, must pay likin at every barrier passed. If twenty such barriers intervene between the point indicated in the pass and some city further inland to which it is desirable to transport the goods for a market, at every one of the twenty barriers likin must be paid.

There are yet to be adduced evils in the system certainly not less than the foregoing. They are the uncertainty in valuation and the apparently arbitrary way in which rates are decided upon.

.   .   .   .

Receipts for payment are refused, * * * so that there can be no proof of illegal exactions, if complaint is made.

.   .   .   .

While the taxing of uncertificated goods certainly appears irregular, still it is a right claimed by China, as may be seen by reference to the memorandum of the Tsung li Yamên to the Chinese ministers abroad, in March, 1878, quoted further on.

.   .   .   .

A proof of the baneful effect of likin taxation over foreign trade may be shown by the recent increase in the amount of likin levied on kerosene oil at Canton.

Under the tariff the import duty on kerosene oil is fixed at 5 per cent. per case, but since 1882 a likin has been levied on kerosene at Canton of 40 cents per case, on the grounds set forth in the annexed proclamation, by which the petitioner is granted the right to collect this likin in consideration of the annual payment to the provincial authorities of $31,000. In the latter part of 1884, or the commencement of 1885, another likin tax was imposed upon kerosene of 30 cents per case, thus making at the port of entry alone a total tax of 47½ per cent. as against 7½ per cent. as contemplated by the treaty for import tax and transit dues.

This case serves also to show how thoroughly worthless is the system, for supposing the normal importation of kerosene oil into Canton to be 500,000 cases, and this is believed to be a close approximation, the extra tax of 40 cents per case would yield the monopolist $200,000 per annum, whereas he only pays $31,000 *per annum* to the Government or about 6 per cent., the balance being retained by him.

One of the chief grievances which the Chinese authorities have against the transit pass system is the abuse which foreign merchants make of the privileges which the passes accord them, and the facilities they afford Chinese merchants, whose agents they are, of bringing from the interior under transit pass goods which they have no intention of exporting, and in the ownership of which the foreign merchant has no part.

.   .   .   .

Putting aside the question of foreign trade, and only considering the likin question as part of the internal revenue system of China, we find that as a whole it works most unsatisfactorily, and that the abuses in connection with the stations for the collection of likin are very numerous. (Decree November 13, 1879.)

.   .   .   .

II.

The position taken by the Chinese Government in regard to the likin question is clearly set forth in a memorandum sent by the Tsung-li Yamên to the Chinese ministers abroad in March, 1878, and which they communicated to the different Governments to which they were accredited.

As regards likin the memorandum says: "Likin is continually objected to by foreigners. But is it not just as well known that Chinese merchants are opposed to it too, and that the Government regards it only as a temporary expedient? "Independent powers must be guided by national necessities in fixing their taxation. In these troublesome times the demands on the Government are very heavy, and it is impossible to avoid having recourse to special measures; we maintain that all such matters should be left to be determined by China herself, and that the foreigner has no more right to interfere with or object to them than China would have to interfere with or criticise the action of a foreign Government in raising loans are increasing taxes. If foreign merchants desire to escape the likin they can escape it. All they have to do is to supply themselves with transit certificates when taking foreign goods into the interior or bringing native produce out of the interior; if they do not carry transit certificates they must pay the likin, for in the absence of transit certificates all goods are alike and indistinguishable and must in the interior pay likin according to the rule of the locality."

And farther on the same paper, summarizing the position taken up by China on the question, says: "In the matter of likin and taxation generally we hold that China, as an independent state, has the right to levy whatever taxes she pleases, in whatever manner she may think best, and we consider it unfair on the part of other Governments to question our proceedings or put difficulties in our way, seeing that we only collect special taxes because special circumstances call for them."

To the arguments put forth by China it may be replied that, if China, in claiming the sovereign right to levy whatever taxes she pleases, and, in such a way as best suits her purposes, asserts her right to interpret as she pleases the agreements by which she has entered the commercial union of nations, we must categorically deny it her, for this right belongs to none of the contracting parties. If, moreover, we admit her claim to subject foreign goods on which the full duty at the port of entry has been paid to such additional taxation as she may choose to impose, it is as if we allowed her the right to tax *ad libitum* foreign goods and virtually suppress foreign trade.

Referring to the transit question, the same memorandum remarks:

"In a word, as we understand the inward transit privilege, a certificate only protects goods from charges *en route* from port to place; but this is already a great privilege, for on payment of transit dues the foreigner can at pleasure send his goods tó any market, however distant, without further liability to taxation."

This right of taxing foreign imports when they have become uncertificated cannot be admitted by foreign powers. It takes away nearly all the advantage of the transit pass system, and allows China to levy in very many cases likin on foreign imports to such extent as she sees fit, and thus exclude them from the market.

The position held by foreign powers is, that the transit dues once paid the goods are free from all other inland taxation of whatever nature it may be. They have been willing to see this transit duty increased to 5 per cent., but it must be the sole duty leviable from the moment the merchandise leaves the port of entry until it enters the consumer's hands. "The duties once paid on goods at the port of discharge, their owners should have a right to carry them to the interior wherever they liked; so that wherever found the presumption would be that the goods were there rightfully, and that the customs officials were neither guilty of negligence or corruption in permitting them to pass duty free." (O. M. Denny, U. S. Consul at Tientsin, to Minister Seward, No. 29, December 24, 1879.)

III.

The history of the negotiations between the foreign representatives, at Peking, and the Chinese Government in reference to the likin question is, briefly, as follows: In 1876 the German minister, Mr. von Brandt, brought up before the Tsung-li Yamên, the question of the right of China to levy likin within the foreign settlement of Shanghai (the only settlement at the time with defined limits) on foreign merchandise, having paid regular duty prior to its being entered for transit. This was a right claimed by China on the ground that local authorities at each of the treaty ports were allowed to levy dues, and that foreign concessions at the several open ports were still Chinese territory. (*Précis* of conversation between Mr. v. Brandt and the foreign office, 17th June, 1876.)

The negotiations resulted in the Chinese Government agreeing that "from and after the 1st day of the 1st moon of the 3d year Kuang Hsii (February 13, 1877), no likin taxes should be levied upon bona fide foreign merchandise imported by foreign merchants within the limits of the foreign settlements at Shanghai, whether sold to Chinese or foreigners. (Prince Kung to Minister Seward, December 12, 1876.)

By this agreement it appears that China did not intend to relinquish her right to levy likin on opium within the limits of any of the settlements at treaty ports; and she has exercised this right down to the present day with the approval and sanction on different occasions of the British and German ministers. (Article XLVI, British treaty of Tientsin, clause 3, section 3, Chefoo convention. Mr. v. Brandt to foreign office, 22d day, 10th month, 2d K. S.)

The issuance, August, 1885, by the Shanghai consular body, of legitimation tickets to likin runners has been a further acknowledgment on the part of the treaty powers of this right. The question has, however, been again brought under discussion by the British consular authorities asserting that the levy of likin on opium within the settlement was an infringement of treaty rights.

The new opium convention between Great Britain and China will settle the question by the levy of a commutation tax of 60 taels per chest (exclusive of 30 taels import duty), which is to free the drug [from] all further taxation.

On March 20, 1877, Mr. von Brandt addressed a note to the Tsung-li Yamên, in which he requests it (1) to take the necessary steps in order that on German goods conveyed into the interior *without a transit pass*, no other duties be levied than those which existed at the time of the conclusion of the treaty; (2) to take care that in the district within the nearest customs station in existence, no other duties be levied but the import duties. To this note the Tsung-li Yamên replied on the 25th March, 1877, stating that Article XXVIII of the English treaty of 1860 is observed by all treaty powers. This stipulates that if merchants desiring to convey imports inland pay a single duty (shui) at the different secondary barriers (tze kow), no further duties shall be levied. Under *tze kow* in the treaty all customs stations and barriers are to be understood. Consequently, if merchants do not desire to make the one payment they must pay *shui* at every customs station and likin at every barrier. Article I of the general regulations for open ports for 1861 also declares this. It is further said that goods to be conveyed inland, unless provided with a duty certificate, must pay on the way likin and other duties.

As to the second demand of Mr. von Brandt, the Yamên states that nowhere in the treaties is it claimed that the limits of the port extend to the nearest customs station.

Mr. von Brandt, in his reply to this note (April 11, 1877), states that he does not wish to commence negotiations on the questions referred to, and that Germany would prefer to settle the question of the levying of taxes on foreign goods together with the other treaty powers by a joint arrangement with the Chinese Government.

On the 23d of September, 1879, the diplomatic representatives of England, Germany, the United States, Holland, Peru, Italy, Japan, Russia, Belgium, Spain, and France held a meeting at Peking and decided to discuss, in common with the Chinese Government, the questions of likin taxes, the transit pass system, the judicial system, and official intercourse. (Minister Seward to Secretary Evarts, No. 482, September 24, 1879.)

On the 22d November, 1879, the foreign representatives presented to the Tsung-li Yamên a list of twenty grievances to which foreign trade was subjected. The grievances which have their source in the system of likin taxation are:

(1) That taxes of different kinds are levied on foreign imports at some ports as soon as they pass into native hands.

(2) That levies are made on foreign imports in the interior which are not properly transit duties, or are in excess of the transit duties, which were levied when the treaties were made.

(3) That at several of the open ports, inward transit passes are either not issued at all or that the issue is fettered by arbitrary and unnecessary conditions.

(4) That inward transit passes when issued at the port are not respected in the interior of the Empire.

(5) That foreign imports forwarded inland under transit passes are often vexatiously detained by the officers at the stations in order to extort illegal fees or to further the interests of Chinese guilds who have made special arrangements with likin collectors or other Chinese officers.

(6) That the protection of the transit-duty certificate is denied to imports when they have passed the barrier nearest the inland market to which they may be consigned under the certificate.

(7) That the exercise of the right of foreigners to visit the interior for purposes of trade is unfavorably affected by the want of proper regulations for the temporary storage or transport of their goods.

(8) That all over the Empire tax stations are constantly opened without due authority.

(9) That the tariffs under which inland duties are levied are neither published nor for sale.

(10) That very frequently no receipts are given for duties levied.

(11) That officials guilty of levying illegal taxes are rarely, if ever, punished.

(12) That the recovery of illegally levied duties, even if the fact itself be acknowledged by the Chinese authorities, is, if not impossible, at least very difficult, and in the best case attended with vexatious and unnecessary delay.

(13) That difficulties are frequently thrown in the way of foreigners asking for transit passes to bring down Chinese produce from the interior, and that [in] many instances such passes are either entirely refused or granted under conditions arbitrarily imposed.

(14) That on native produce, and especially on silk, duties are levied after sale and before the goods are delivered to the purchaser, and that the levy of these duties is farmed out to certain companies, which are enabled thereby to monopolize the trade in certain articles.

This list was followed on the 22d December by a note from Her Britannic Majesty's minister, Sir Thomas Wade, the chairman of the committee on likin, requesting the Yamên to appoint a day for the discussion of the questions referred to in the list of grievances. The Yamên allowed the whole question to drag, but finally replied that they begged the foreign representatives to wait until they had answered the note of November 22, 1879, before asking them to appoint a day for the discussion of the questions involved.

On the 19th January, 1880, the Tsung-li Yamên sent its reply to the note of November 22, 1879. The Yamên states that "more than half of the twenty grievances mentioned in their excellencies' note refer to the collection of the duties and transit dues. This Yamên has three plans in mind upon the subject:

"(1) The present regulations may be carried into effect. The high provincial authorities will, on the one hand, be instructed by this Yamên to direct their officials to act in good faith in obedience to them, and, on the other hand, your several consular officers and merchants will be instructed by your excellencies to scrupulously obey them.

"(2) The regulations heretofore agreed upon between this Yamên and his excellency the British minister, Sir Rutherford Alcock, may be put in force.

"(3) The stipulations in the several treaties that foreigners shall not be subject to Chinese jurisdiction may be stricken out, and foreigners in China shall be subject to Chinese authority at all places and always, and be dealt with as Chinese subjects."

On March 20, 1880, Minister Seward writes to Secretary Evarts (No. 632) that no progress has been made in the negotiations. "The foreign representatives appear disposed to believe that the present moment is inopportune to press matters, because of the assumed strength of the reactionary party." Mr. Seward thinks it better to proceed with the discussion, and to draw away from it at a later moment if it should seem necessary for reasons to be advanced by the representatives.

On the 9th of April, 1880, the Tsung-li Yamên express their willingness to meet the foreign representatives whenever convenient, and the latter fix the 20th instant. At this meeting the diplomatic body stated the conference was not so much to define the intent of existing stipulations as to reach a basis for further stipulations which would be satisfactory to both sides. The Yamên agreed to take up the conference on these lines. (Minister Seward to Secretary Evarts, No. 665, April 23, 1880.)

Her Britannic Majesty's minister, Sir Thomas Wade, who had been chosen chairman of the committee on likin, after several conferences with the Tsung-li Yamên on the question of the inland taxation of imports, reached the conclusion that China would be willing to assent to the imposition of a fixed duty (higher than the existing tariff), on the payment of which the goods imported would be exempted from all further taxes of every kind, no matter into what part of the Empire they might be carried. The rate of duty would probably be between 7½ and 12½ per cent.

Sir Thomas expressed, however, the fear that likin would nevertheless be laid to a greater or less extent on foreign goods so long as it should be laid on native goods. (Minister Angell to Secretary Evarts, No. 58, November 30, 1880.)

On the 13th December, 1880, the Tsung-li Yamên wrote to Sir Thomas

Wade and proposed that the duty on foreign imports be fixed at 11.5 taels (11½ per cent.). On the 4th January, 1881, the foreign representatives rejected this proposition as unsatisfactory.

In the meanwhile the negotiations with the Yamên on the question of inland taxation of native produce under transit pass outward were being conducted by Mr. von Brandt. He had suggested to his colleagues that the Chinkiang rules of 1877 be taken as a basis, and he drew up the annexed scheme, which was accepted as a basis of discussion by the Yamên, who asked that time might be given them to refer the project to the high provincial authorities for their opinion on the question.

. . . .

Mr. von Brandt seemed to be on the verge of a tolerably satisfactory agreement with the Yamên, when suddenly the Yamên came forward with so important and unacceptable modifications that the diplomatic body, in the meeting of July 11, 1881, agreed that it was useless to prolong negotiations on such a basis.

The Tsung-li Yamên insisted on two concessions: (1) Foreign goods admitted free of duty, shipped coastwise, should pay coast-trade duty; (2) Goods manufactured from native produce bought at the port should be subjected to the same restrictions as goods manufactured from produce brought down under transit pass.

While these negotiations between Mr. von Brandt and the Yamên were going on, Sir Thomas Wade was busy with the likin question. On July 7, 1881, he wrote to the Yamên that the foreign representatives could not accept the 10 per cent. import duty in lieu of likin, to which the Yamên had finally agreed, unless certain other provisions asked for in the collective note of the 22d November, 1879, were conceded. The diplomatic body was of opinion that if certain safeguards could be secured it would have been worth the while to have tried as an experiment, say for five years, the scheme proposed. But it deemed it necessary to have some sort of court of reclamation in which redress could have been claimed if likin had really been assessed. "But it must be confessed," writes Minister Angell to Secretary Blaine (No. 217, September 24, 1881), "that it is very doubtful whether for some time to come the Government can prevent the levying of likin. The people hate the tax and would gladly be rid of it. But it is extremely convenient for the local authorities, and the whole weight of the influence of the provincial officials will be thrown in favor of the continuance of it."

On August 1, 1881, the Tsung-li Yamên answered Sir Thomas Wade's note of July 7, and stated that while they had agreed to the 10 per cent. duty, still, in view of the foreign representatives insisting on certain other provisions for the protection of trade in the collective note of the 22d November, 1879, any provisional experiment of the 10 per cent. duty scheme would be premature.

After this little or no progress was made in the negotiations. On September 18, 1881, Mr. von Brandt writes to Prince Kung that he is willing to continue the negotiations if they are carried on with a view of removing the Yamên's complaint as to the illegal use of transit passes outward, and those of his colleagues and himself in regard to the illegal attempts of local authorities to ignore the stipulations of the treaties referring to the treatment of duty free foreign imports and native produce, and the use or exportation of goods bought or manufactured in the port.

Under date September 29, 1881, Prince Kung replying to the above note, lays down as a general principle that "neither liberties nor restrictions on trade, inasmuch as they have not been expressly stipulated in the treaties, can be simply and positively claimed by way of inference by the one or the other party on the ground of one-sided opinions; far from this, it is rather necessary that an agreement should be arrived at on the ground of mutual deliberation before it is permitted to act accordingly." (Prince Kung to Mr. von Brandt, September 29, 1881.)

After this nothing of any importance has occurred in the way of a settlement of the pending difficulties. Minister Young, writing to Secretary Frelinghuysen under date June 13, 1884 (No. 462), remarks: "The whole (transit pass) system sadly needs revision and readjustment, but it is too much to expect that the Government of China will take official measures to put an end to the violation of the treaties by the local officers in this direction until it has a practical assurance that foreign powers will no longer permit abuses of the privilege by their people."

Again, Mr. Young, under date August 6, 1884 (No. 492), writing to Secretary Frelinghuysen, remarks: "The general question of likin concerns all interests in China, and must be a matter of joint action. I doubt if there will be any settlement until we have a new treaty, and one which will be unmistakable as to all questions of manufacture and trade."

On the 30th of September, 1884, Mr. Secretary Frelinghuysen (No. 344), acknowledging Minister Young's dispatch No. 492, writes: "In view of the long-standing controversy as to likin * * * it certainly appears desirable that some conclusion shall be reached which will remove the merits of the question from the domain of doubt.

"In case you find the way favorably open for the discussion of a special treaty engagement which shall concede what we have always claimed in the premises, you should use your good endeavors to promote such a result."

On April 27, 1885, the diplomatic body at Peking had a conference at which the transit-pass system outwards was discussed, as well as the practice of levying taxes on foreign goods at the ports of entry for municipal and other purposes. The failure of the Chinese Government to observe treaty stipulations in these particulars was admitted, but as all communications hitherto made to the Yamên had produced no result, it was deemed best that the representatives of all the foreign powers at Peking should refer to their respective Governments for instructions, with a view of securing a modification of the present treaties or their more rigid enforcement. (Mr. Chargé d'Affaires ad interim Smithers to Secretary Bayard, No. 11, May 1, 1885.)

Summing up the results of six years' negotiations between the foreign representatives at Peking and the Chinese Government, we find that with the exception of the more rigid observance of some of the treaty stipulations in regard to transit passes, China has not abandoned one of the rights she has always claimed, and that under existing treaties nothing materially advantageous to foreign trade can be arrived at.

The recent opium convention between Great Britain and China, by which a duty of 110 taels per chest of opium is to exempt the drug from all further taxation, is a step in the way of the 10 per cent. duty on foreign goods proposed by the conference in 1880. An opportunity will thus be afforded us, in case the arrangement comes into force, of ascertaining whether this system can prove a permanent solution of the likin difficulty. The experience of late years teaches us that as long as the provincial governments of China are strongly opposed to a measure, the central Government is not in a position to enforce it, and we know that any measure which will occasion a reduction in the revenues which they derive from likin has and always will meet with their determined opposition.

A partial solution of the difficulty might be the abolition throughout China of likin on miscellaneous goods, but, for the reasons offered above, this would very probably work in a most unsatisfactory manner, even if meeting with the full assent and aid of the Peking Government. This, moreover, would be a concession to foreign trade greater than could be expected, for it would only foster foreign trade to the prejudice of the native one, which would still be subject to the likin taxation.

The natural solution of the difficulty is in the adoption by China of Western financial and commercial methods, which will give that elasticity to her revenue system which it most utterly lacks at the present moment. Unless China adopts a liberal and progressive policy, and, putting aside some of her prejudices and dislike for ideas and methods of which she has not been the originator, freely takes from civilized nations the means which they can offer her of developing the natural resources of the land and increasing its wealth, all suggestions in the way of radically ameliorating her condition will prove useless.

XXVII

OBSTACLES TO THE INTRODUCTION OF RAILROADS, 1886

DURING THE latter half of the nineteenth century, the opposition of the Chinese government and the populace to the introduction of railroads was proverbial. The first foreign-built road from Shanghai to Woosung was purchased by the Chinese in 1877 and the rails were removed. Nevertheless, the decade of the eighties witnessed increasing efforts on the part of foreign promoters to introduce railroads in China. To China's native opposition there were now added the rivalries of international politics. These coupled with the conservative and at times corrupt character of the Peking administration proved an almost insurmountable obstacle to railroad construction. Minister Charles Denby wrote voluminously on the subject.

CONFLICTS BETWEEN AMERICAN AND GERMAN RAILROAD PROMOTERS. MINISTER DENBY TO SECRETARY BAYARD, PEKING, JANUARY 14, 1886[1]

I have the honor to report that I called on the Tsungli Yamên yesterday with Captain Higginson and Ensign Atwater. These gentlemen are officers of the United States Man-of-War "Monocacy" which is now stationed at Tientsin. We were received in a very friendly manner by His Highness Prince Ching and their Excellencies. After some pleasant conversation on ordinary topics, I broached a subject about which for some time I have desired to talk to the Yamên. I have not been able to do so hitherto on account of the absence of Prince Ching, caused by the death of his wife. I said to the Prince that I had heard from various sources that Mr. von Brandt, the German Minister, had appeared before the Yamên and had complained that Americans were being employed in railroad enterprises in China. I had also understood that Mr. von Brandt had advised the Yamên not to enter upon the construction of railroads at this time. The Prince denied that Mr. von Brandt had made such representations. I stated that I was very glad to learn that I was mistaken; that I regarded it as my duty to answer any attack made from any source on Americans. I further stated that our treaty provided that we would on the request of China furnish engineers to build railroads, and that it would afford me great pleasure at any time to advise the Yamên on that subject and to carry out the treaty. I further asked leave to make a few observations on the general question. I stated that the United States was about the size of China, that we had built nearly, if not quite, one hundred and twenty six thousand English miles of railroads, which were equal to three hundred and seventy eight thousand Chinese miles, that this mileage was probably equal to that of all other countries. I further stated that we had the best and most experienced engineers in the world; that owing to the vast distances in the two countries, China and our own, our system was perfectly adapted to China. I further stated that I had understood that Mr. von Brandt had argued before the Yamên that railroads would not pay at this time. That it might be true that new lines would not pay dividends immediately to their shareholders, but that experience in India was that the value of property had been increased three fold, and this experience was general wherever railroads had been constructed. His Highness again assured me that Mr. von Brandt had not made the observations imputed to him, but that the people of China were at present opposed to building railroads. I am bound to take as true the statements of the Prince. But my information was not derived simply from the papers, which are full of it, but also from one of my colleagues, and from a confidential adviser of Li Hung Chang. It tallied also with a discussion which I, myself, had with Mr. von Brandt, in which he advanced nearly the same ideas, and which I combatted to the best of my ability. There is vast opposition to the building of railroads, coming chiefly from the Censors and the Board of Revenue. Officially I have nothing to do with the question, but personally, in conversation with Chinese Officials, I have endeavored to show the advantages of railroads. . . .

EFFECTS OF CORRUPT GOVERNMENT ON RAILROAD ENTERPRISE. MINISTER DENBY
TO SECRETARY BAYARD, PEKING, FEBRUARY 24, 1886[2]

I have the honor to report that in order to understand the condition of the questions involving the inauguration of public improvements in China it is necessary to comprehend the Governmental conditions which exist here. I have received several communications from men of prominence in the United States touching the building of railroads. They seem to assume that either there is a certainty or a very great probability that a grand system of public improvements will be inaugurated. I cannot enter into a full and free discussion of these questions with any person. But I can indicate my views to you to be used in your own discretion.

The Chinese Government is the most corrupt in the world. There is scarcely a day that the Peking Gazette does not contain decrees degrading and punishing officials for corrupt practices. Very lately it was reported that all the clerks in the Revenue Office had been detected in robbing. The system of "squeezing" is universal from the throne to the body servant. Small salaries are paid to officials. They are expected to steal and to share their stealings with the higher officials. A regular system of tribute is paid at the Peking gates. A Taotai or other officer coming to Peking must pay so many thousands of taels into the Imperial Exchequer. If he fails to pay tribute he is degraded and punished. Let one example of very late occurrence illustrate the species of government which exists here. A few weeks ago a retired Hoppo was living at Peking, where he had built a fine house. Prior to the Chinese New Year he set off a few sky-rockets. The sticks fell in the yard of the Chief Eunuch. The Eunuch complained but the Hoppo insisted that he had a right to set off his fireworks. The Eunuch said he would get even with him. The Eunuch reported to the Empress that the man was very wealthy and ought to be assessed. The Empress ordered him to pay two hundred thousand taels. He was utterly unable to raise the sum but did raise fifty thousand taels. He was told that that sum would not do. The Empress also said to him that she had seen through a spy-glass that he had a fine house. She wanted that house and he must move out of it in three days. He begged for five days in which to move, and before the five days expired he committed suicide. This event among thoughtful men has created some consternation. It indicates that China is being governed by the Eunuchs who govern the Empress. It reduces the government to a rule controlled by whims.

Now when I am asked what China intends to do about the construction of railways I answer that no man can tell. It is plain that at some period of time railways will be built. When the Indian Railway System reaches China through Burma it will no doubt be extended. On the other hand the Emperor, when he takes the reins of government into his own hands, a year or two from now, may inaugurate a policy of improvement. Or at any day a whim may seize the Empress and she may issue an Imperial Edict to that effect. Opposition to railways seems to be increasing. The great leader of progress, Li Hung Chang, seems to be afraid to propose innovation. He seems to realize the uncertain and whimsical character of the Government and to dread the contest which would follow the introduction of western progress.

While I am willing unofficially to aid in matters of introduction and civility any American who comes to China I can not hold out any inducements of present success in business ventures. The question is very doubtful.

.   .   .   .

XXVIII

THE POSITION OF MISSIONARIES IN CHINA, 1886

THE PECULIAR mixture of legal and of spiritual considerations affecting the position of the missionary in China is illustrated in the following dispatch of Minister Denby.

THE MISSIONARY PROBLEM. CHARLES DENBY TO SECRETARY BAYARD, PEKING, OCTOBER 9, 1886[1]

SIR: Owing to the notoriety of the two recent cases of riots in which missionary property has been destroyed in China, the time seems opportune for some discussion of the rights of missionaries in China. This discussion runs through the archives of this legation, occurring now and again. My observations will not be new to the Department, but may, possibly, serve some good purpose if brought to the knowledge of missionary organizations in the United States. In their preparation I recognize my obligation to my predecessors generally, and particularly to Governor Low, who exhaustively discussed some of the questions sixteen years ago.

The treaties with China which provide for the toleration of the Christian religion with the great Powers, Russia, the United States, Great Britain, and France, were concluded in 1858. The Russian and French treaties went farther than the others, in this, that they contained provisions that the missionaries of those countries might travel in the interior on passports.

In the other treaties the missionaries were allowed the same privileges as merchants who were confined to the open ports. In those ports they might purchase land and erect houses.

After the occupation of Peking by the French and English in 1860, a new clause, the celebrated sixth clause, was inserted in the Chinese text of the French treaty. The last sentence is this:

It is in addition permitted to French missionaries to rent and purchase land in all the provinces and to erect buildings thereon at pleasure.

No such words are contained in the French text. There are no similar words, no language, which, by any construction, can seem to have been made the basis of the actual translation from French to Chinese.

Our own missionaries have often cited this clause to me, and Mr. John Russell Young, in 1885, in one of his dispatches, cites it as being some sort of a basis for the right to go into the interior. But my predecessors have very generally construed this clause differently. They have almost universally held that even if the Chinese text is authoritative it must apply to rights which existed before it was adopted, thereby restoring to the French the right to return to the localities which they formerly occupied but conferring no new rights.

[1] *Foreign Relations*, 1886, No. 221, pp. 96-100.

The English Government distinctly adopted this construction, and declined in any event to avail itself of the right to adopt this clause under the favored-nation clause, even if the right existed.

It has never been definitely known how the clause, touching which the French text is absolutely silent, became a part of the Chinese text.

. . . .

It must be remarked, also, that the third article of the French treaty of 1858 provides that the French text shall govern in defining the true meaning of the treaty. This rule, therefore, does away with the alleged Chinese text.

It must be assumed, therefore, as the construction placed by all the nationalities on the treaty in question, that the right to settle at will in the interior does not exist. But, for fear of misapprehension, let it also be distinctly said that the treaties guarantee peace and protection to foreigners who are lawfully anywhere in China. It follows that, if the zeal of missionaries leads them to locate in the interior, and if the local authorities consent to such location, allow them to buy land and erect buildings, the United States would not submit to their being ejected by violence or without due process of law.

There is an element affecting the right of foreigners to locate in the interior to which proper consideration has been rarely given. It is the effect of the extraterritorial jurisdiction which is claimed and exercised with the utmost strictness by the foreign powers. It is frequently said that the Chinese have in the United States much greater rights and privileges than the Americans have in China. Looked at in the general this is true. The Chinese in the United States may, when once he has lawfully landed, take up his residence at pleasure in any one of the thirty-eight States and eight Territories. Possibly in some of the States, and perhaps all the Territories, under late legislation, he cannot become the owner of land in fee. But with this exception he enjoys all the rights of the native-born citizen, except the right of participating in the government of the country by voting. And he has none of the ordinary liabilities which accompany citizenship. He cannot be compelled to serve on juries or in the militia, or be conscripted in the Army. He enjoys all the privileges of residence without any burden upon him either to his own country or to that of his residence. He may engage in all species of business on the same terms as a citizen. It would seem at the first blush that he has greatly the advantage of the American in China, who is restricted to the selection of a residence in the open ports, is not allowed to engage in any manufacturing enterprises, and cannot travel anywhere without a passport. It is held that the passport when granted is confined in its use to the territory described in it.

But the foreigner has one very remarkable advantage which is far-reaching in its effects. The foreigner in China is amenable only to his own laws as far as mode of trial extends and measure of punishment. He can be tried by his own consul only, and by no other tribunal. He is thus protected from the imposition of the severe and barbarous penalties such as the Ling-Chih, or death by the slow process, torturing, bambooing, and bastinadoing, which are daily inflicted on the Chinese by their own courts. For debt or crime he must be proceeded against according to the laws of his own nationality.

This concession of extraterritorial jurisdiction necessarily restricts the area of its exercise. If the foreigner is amenable to no court but his own there should be a convenient forum in which he might be tried. Foreigners are by no means perfect in their conduct in China any more than they are at home. It is evidently impracticable to create such a tribunal at every locality in China. The only other remedy is to restrict foreigners in their residence to such localities as may furnish the necessary tribunals. Besides this system is an anomaly.

.   .   .   .

It is on principle only defensible because it is a necessary part of self-defense, a doctrine which is the supreme law of civilized communities.

But the Chinese are becoming day by day more jealous of its exercise. Japan, to avoid its effect, is about to adopt a code in accordance with the codes of western countries. She will then, perhaps successfully, appeal to the world to renounce the extraterritorial claims in her borders.

If all foreign powers all over this vast Empire exercised practically the extraterritorial jurisdiction, and if, by reason of the location of many foreigners all over the Empire, its exercise became a common and usual matter, plainly the authority of the Chinese Government would be seriously shaken. No nation can be expected to surrender willingly its inherent power over all the people residing in its territory.

It is further to be observed that there are many foreigners now residing in China who are to all intents permanent residents. They retain their distinctive national character because it is advantageous to them in many ways. But for the protection assured by their own Governments they render no equivalent, and they are beyond the pale of liability to China. They escape the burdens of society and the obligations of citizenship to any and all Governments. I do not make this suggestion with any purpose of criticizing unfavorably this relation, and I do not recommend any modification of this condition as far as China is concerned. It is perhaps an anomaly in international relations that a citizen of the United States can deliberately take up his permanent residence abroad and retain all the rights of citizenship in his old home and escape all its obligations. But in semi-civilized countries, at least, there seems no remedy for these inconsistencies.

If there were correlative naturalization laws prevailing in all countries some solution might be had. But there is no solution as far as China is concerned which occurs to me. As the United States has deliberately denied citizenship to the Chinese while allowing them residence, she, at least, cannot raise this question.

The foreign powers make no difference in China between the treatment of missionaries and any and all other classes. The missionary is simply a citizen, and the sacred character of his object and purposes does not enter into the question of the determination of his rights.

It is impossible for men to shut their eyes to the peculiar employments of their fellows, and as in Christian communities a large amount of sympathy is accorded to those persons who have exiled themselves to do "God's work" and not man's, it is probable that a consideration of the religious and charitable character of missionary work might form the basis of some solution of the right of the missionary to go into the interior. Practically these considerations do enter into the treatment of the missionaries. No manufacturer or merchant would be allowed to settle in Kalgan or other points in the interior where there are flourishing missionary stations. If any distinction, therefore, between missionaries and other classes of citizens were possible under the laws and Constitution of the United States the vexed question of residence in the interior might be solved. The first element in such broad recognition of the duties, obligations, and purposes of the missionaries would be the impression on the minds of the Chinese of the fact that there is no purpose in their coming to China save the honest open one of the spread of religious principle and the practice of pure charity. It should be mentioned incidentally that there are twenty-three great hospitals now in operation under the missionaries in China. Neither foreigner nor Chinese disputes the patent fact of the great good which they accomplish. But the observer in China must recognize that there is great mistrust of the missionaries. To say, as is usually said, that this mistrust is confined to the literati and gentry and does not extend to the common people, does not alter the fact. These two classes control all others.

That the religious representatives in China of all sects have furnished, of late years at least, no cause for this mistrust, I believe is true. It used to be charged that the Catholics assumed some temporal power, but I have seen no proof of any tendency in that direction. The Catholics number, probably, 1,200,000 adherents, and in late years they have done very little proselyting, but have confined their labors to the spiritual needs of Catholic families.

The natural increase has made them powerful and numerous.

Here, then, is the long, slow, tedious work before the missionary to convince the Chinese by his conduct that he has no object to accomplish but their own welfare, to remove prejudice and to win confidence.

The means are apparent and have been used by missionary laborers with rare ability, courage, and industry. They are to educate the young and heal the sick. This great country, owing to its peculiar language, its dense population, its ancient conservatism, moves slowly. But when we realize that mission work under favorable auspices only commenced after the treaty of 1858, and the occupation of Peking by the English and French in 1860, and when we see what has been accomplished in twenty-six years, we must admit that great progress has been made and we must look hopefully to the employment of missionary agencies in the future.

I think no one will deny the beneficent effect of mission work in Japan in civilizing that country and educating that people. Why, then, should some praise not be accorded to missionaries in China for the immense work in the same line that they have done?

I offer no observation on the religious side of this work. It does not come within the purview of the diplomatic agent to discuss the spiritual nature of this labor. If an American Buddhist or Mohammedan or Jew were to come to China to pursue the work of preaching his doctrine, he would undoubtedly receive at the hands of his country's representatives the same protection that is vouchsafed to the Christian. It may be asked, what has diplomacy to do with a question which is so largely confined to the spread of religious doctrine. The answer is that the diplomatic agent recognizes that the complete civilization of a people means the increase of trade and commerce with the rest of the world. Any line of conduct which throws open new continents to intercourse with the great producing and creating countries is beneficial to them. Here in China it cannot be denied that the educational labors of the missionaries, the preparation and publication of innumerable books, the introduction of new medicines and inventions in surgery have all tended to improve the natives. Civilization means commerce, trade, a market for manufactured articles.

It is idle to inquire whether war would have produced the same results, or the merchant alone would have done as much. The ardent zeal, the supreme self-denial, the utter self-sacrifice that characterize missionaries are not found in the votaries of commerce.

Diplomacy, finding the representatives of the various nationalities here, steps in to supplement their labor. It has its field of education no less pertinent than theirs. It educates the diplomatists of the country. It teaches international law. It insures protection to all honest labor. Its efforts are not directed to the aggrandizement of individuals, but to the promotion of the general welfare of the various nations. In some cases, as luminously in our own country, it antagonizes baleful commercial enterprise, like the opium traffic. And here again the missionaries by their influence aid the efforts of diplomacy. Diplomacy makes both the merchant and the missionary secure.

In my trip over China I visited every mission school and hospital, and made the acquaintance of every missionary. I am persuaded that their work is being pushed with diligence and intelligence. I demand of them the exercise of prudence and forbearance. I demand that they shall insist on no doubtful rights—that their zeal shall not outrun their discretion. Their warrant to preach the Gospel to all nations must be construed with the context, which enjoins obedience to the powers that be. If they remain in the fair scope of their exalted employment this legation will always be found in sympathy with their just rights.

XXIX

ANTIFOREIGNISM AND THE PROTECTION OF FOREIGNERS, 1891

A DECADE before the culmination of antiforeignism in the Boxer Rebellion serious outbreaks had occurred in China, threatening and in some cases destroying the lives and property of foreign residents, particularly missionaries. The problems created thereby and the measures taken by the foreign representatives to deal with the situation are suggested in the following dispatch from Minister Denby.

THE CO-OPERATIVE POLICY AGAIN APPLIED. CHARLES DENBY TO SECRETARY BLAINE, PEKING, AUGUST 14, 1891[1]

SIR: I have the honor to inclose herewith a copy of a joint communication [not printed] from all the foreign representatives at Peking which was sent to the foreign office on the 13th instant. This document was called forth by statements made by the Chinese representatives in Europe that China had substantially done all it could do in the matter of quelling the recent riots and in punishing the rioters. These statements were communicated to the British, French, and German ministers here and called forth a denial from these gentlemen. It appears that these governments then issued instructions to their representatives to demand more stringent action on the part of China. The paper now inclosed recites the shortcomings of China in matters connected with the recent riots, and a general failure to properly protect foreigners, and embodies various specific demands for appropriate action. As this paper was originally drawn it contained the statement that all the foreign representatives had been specifically instructed to make the charges and demands therein stated. As I had received no such instructions, I procured a modification to be made, which made no change in the force of the paper. It may in the future, however, be necessary to urge that the action that the ministers may deem it necessary to take has been dictated by their governments. I ask authority to that effect, and that I be so informed by cable. In passing upon the propriety of the charges and demands made in the inclosure it must be borne in mind that this is an absolute and autocratic Government; that every official holds his office at the sole will of the Emperor; and that there are no self-governing divisions of the Empire, but all parts are ruled in all respects by one imperial head.

In view of the fact that the inclosure was signed by the representatives of all foreign powers in China, it must be remembered that united action is absolutely necessary on the part of foreigners in China for self-protection. The Chinese mob knows nothing about race or nationality. It regards all foreigners as enemies, and destroys all alike. It is true that the recent riots were chiefly directed against Catholics, but two Englishmen were murdered at Wusieh, and many injuries have been done to English chapels. Americans slightly suffered, but in various places the missionaries were compelled to flee for their lives. I have had no hesitation, therefore, in joining with my colleagues in earnest demands for redress of wrongs, punishment of offenders, and better assured protection to foreigners.

The time is now appropriate for a definite settlement of the rights of foreigners in China. If it comes to be understood by the people that rioting may be indulged in without fear of punishment, the residence of foreigners in China must cease. It must not be imagined that the Government of China favors or foments riots. The Emperor thoroughly understands that these outrages are injurious to his dignity and power, and he is impressed also with the idea that the ringleaders are looking to the destruction of the Manchu dynasty. Very excellent proclamations have been issued, but, as the inclosure states, there has been little actual repressive or punitory work done. I sincerely hope that the Yamên will respond favorably to the demands made in the inclosure, and thus avoid complications which may possibly lead to hostile acts on the part of the powers that are most aggrieved.

THE OPEN DOOR POLICY, 1899-1902

FUNDAMENTAL to all American policy in China since the time of John Hay has been the principle of equal opportunity for trade and commerce, commonly referred to as the open door. In examining the character of this policy it is important to note not only the contribution of W. W. Rockhill, regarded in the State Department in 1899 as the best informed man on China, but also of Alfred E. Hippisley, an Englishman and a member of the Chinese Imperial Maritime Customs Service, on whom Rockhill relied for advice. The memoranda of these men, together with the drafts of the first Hay open door note (to Great Britain) and the Hay circular directed to the Powers in July, 1900, at the time of the Boxer uprising, give the major aspects of the open door concept as it existed in 1899-1900. Its more specific amplification is found in the Hay memorandum to Chinese Minister Wu in 1902 at a time when Russia was seeking exclusive privileges in Manchuria. These statements on the open door should be compared with the treaty definition given to the doctrine in the Nine-power Treaty of 1922 (see p. 281).

DOCUMENTARY BASES OF THE OPEN DOOR POLICY

Hippisley Memorandum[1]
Memorandum on the "Open Door" in China

The mercantile communities of the United States and Gt. Britain, realising the important field for their enterprise which under existing conditions is afforded by China, and the vastly extended field for it which they might legitimately look forward to under improved conditions in the future, earnestly desire the maintenance of the "open door," *i.e.,* of the rights possessed under the existing treaties of Tientsin. In other

Rockhill Memorandum[1]
Memorandum

No one person has done more within the last few months to influence public opinion in the United States on the Chinese question than Lord Charles Beresford, by his book "The Break-Up of China," and by the speeches he has made in the United States. By these means he has sought to prove the identity of interests of our two countries and the necessity of an Anglo-American policy in China. It seems desirable to

[1] Papers of W. W. Rockhill as quoted by A. Whitney Griswold, *The Far Eastern Policy of the United States* (New York, 1938), pp. 475-491. Reprinted with permission of the publishers, Harcourt, Brace & Co.

words, they ask that they be assured the equality of opportunity which all nations alike have hitherto enjoyed under those treaties for (a) commerce, (b) navigation, and (c) exploitation of mines and railroads.

preface the following remarks by examining the data supplied by Lord Charles, endeavoring to control his views, and to show, if possible, the truth or fallacy of his conclusions.

For one who has devoted the better part of his life to the study of Chinese affairs, the book of Lord Beresford comes as an agreeable surprise—so far as regards foreign commercial relations with China, and is on the whole rather encouraging than dispiriting. The volume of foreign trade has steadily increased, and everywhere signs are not wanting of its further extension; the Chinese Government has not failed to fulfill any of its pecuniary obligations to foreigners, and is endeavoring, in a clumsy, uncertain way it is true—but that is not entirely its fault, to take some further steps in the direction needed for its internal development. If, on the other hand, the Empire is in a disturbed condition, and if foreign interests suffer thereby, this is entirely due to the unseemly haste of some of the Treaty Powers in their scramble for commercial advantages and acquisition of territory. This they lament but do not seek to remedy.

Lord Beresford's interviews with the various foreign mercantile organizations at the treaty ports of China bring clearly before us the fact that they have not in the last twenty years had any new ground for complaint against the Chinese Government, that they are to-day suffering, not perhaps even quite so severely as years ago, from the existence of certain restrictions, especially those resulting from internal revenue taxes, which have been the subject of endless correspondence between the diplomatic representatives in Peking and the Chinese Government for the last quarter of a century and with which every one interested in affairs in that Empire must by this time be pretty familiar.

The grievances of which the foreign mercantile class in China has to complain and a remedy to which lies with the Chinese Government, are all proper subjects for diplomatic discussion and no one can doubt that if within the last two years steady and united pressure had been brought to bear on it by the Treaty Powers, some of them would be in a fair way to settlement at the present time.

Take for example *likin*. In the rush for concessions to foreigners in China and the necessity for that country to find funds to insure the payment of interest on the loans she has been forced to contract to carry out more or less urgent public works recommended by them, the Treaty Powers have compelled her to increase her internal revenue taxes and have permanently fastened on the country this very tax *(likin)* they had for twenty-five years and more been trying to have suppressed. Again take the transit pass system by which foreign goods are allowed to be carried throughout the Empire on payment of one-half the import duty, and which system the British merchants claim is an utter failure, we know by the successful endeavors of the French government in enforcing this right under the treaties for goods imported into southwestern China, that if failure it is in other parts of the Empire, the fault lies with the foreigners themselves.

Lord Beresford's opinion that it is primarily necessary for the development of China to make a military and naval power of that Empire, is, I think, the weakest part of his work, and his opinion is at variance with that of all those who know best China and the Chinese. So far as the protection of foreign interests is concerned, the Chinese Government is, and has been since the suppression of the Taiping rebellion, able to protect them whenever and wherever it has chosen to, as innumerable cases familiar to the Department can show.

In the various memoranda submitted to Lord Beresford by the British merchants of China and published in his book, the need for China to increase her armament to insure their security, is no where hinted at, but in all of them we find the cause of the present stagnation of trade attributed, and rightly to my mind, to the vaccillating policy of the home Governments, frequently brought about by apathy and lack of knowledge regarding Chinese affairs, the resulting ability of the Chinese Government to escape the performance of its treaty obligations, and to the jealousies and lack of concerted action of the Powers in treating questions of general interest.

No more representative foreign body can be found in China than the China Association at Shanghai. In its memorandum to Lord Beresford, we read: "It seems plain that such security (as foreign trade requires) can only be found in the entire reform of the present corrupt state of Chinese government. The undertaking of such a task, no doubt, bristles with difficulties, and entails responsibilities which will necessarily be complicated by international jealousies; it is, nevertheless, clear that unless the situation be boldly faced, still greater difficulties and still greater international trouble will have to be faced in the near future. . . . The establishment of a government in Peking, which is not only strong, but which is in sympathy with the wishes and feelings of the nation at large, is, we believe, a first necessity if China is to be saved from partition. . . . Weakness in Peking must inevitably mean disruption and partition of the Empire. . . . We say, then, that the one thing wanted for the development of trade, for the protection of capital, and for the extension of enterprise in China is security, which can only be effected through pressure from without. . . ."

That the task of strengthening the central government is a comparatively easy one, the history of China's progress in the last fifty years conclusively shows. The introduction of telegraphic lines throughout the Empire, the Maritime Customs service, the more recent organization of a system of imperial railways and their withal successful working, and a variety of other reforms are all operating in the same direction, so that Lord Beresford's statement (p. 231) "no reforms . . . can possibly be brought about in a country so hopelessly corrupt as China until the first and initial step is taken of giving authority to those in power which only an effective military and police can supply," is a hasty and erroneous conclusion.

That the existence of a strong and well officered and disciplined army and navy in China might assist that country to ward off the attacks of a foreign foe, is likely; that, in the absence of such a force, and with the present aggressive policy of some of the Treaty Powers, the creation of "spheres of interest" (or influence) easily reached by rail or by the sea by the interested Power from its own territory, should be held to be the only way of insuring China against complete partition, is comprehensible; but that the United States should lend a hand to the carrying out of either of these two policies seems absolutely suicidal to our vast and growing interests in that part of the world.

Last year when the British Govt. was energetically insisting on the necessity of maintaining the "open door" in China, Mr. Balfour's speeches foreshadowed a policy which, though nominally aiming at that object, conceded to the various

British writers on Chinese questions, and especially Lord Beresford, have advocated in the strongest terms the "open door policy" or equality of treatment and opportunity for all comers, and denounce in the strongest terms the system of "Spheres of

Powers the possession of spheres of influence or interest in which they would enjoy special rights and privileges in respect of railroad and mining enterprises: and the undertakings entered into by Gt. Britain with Germany as regards Shantung and with Russia as regards Manchuria go to show that this is the policy which the British Govt. has definitely adopted to govern its relations with other Powers in China. A policy the object of which is to maintain the "open door" and at the same time to recognise spheres of interest with special, and practically exclusive, rights as regards mines and railroads, is possibly feasible; but it certainly is feasible only on the condition that adequate steps are taken to prevent the special mining and railroad rights being so stretched as to include territorial jurisdiction and the power to impose discriminating taxation in any form.

In any case the undertakings above referred to have already practically deprived Britishers of equality of opportunity as regards mines and railroads in certain important districts of China, and would appear to render it difficult for other nationalities to insist on the maintenance of their equality of opportunity as regards those enterprises in the districts concerned—though the importance of this curtailment of previously existing rights is much reduced by the facts that the concessions for mines and railroads already granted in China will require years to fulfil, even if they do not require a larger amount of capital than is likely to be forthcoming for investment in that country, and that these concessions are distributed among all of the wealthy nations.

Influence" (or interest); but such spheres have now been recognized by Great Britain as well as by France, Germany and Russia, and *they must be accepted as existing facts.*

But while adopting the policy of spheres of interest, which, we will admit, political reasons may have forced it to do, Great Britain has tried to maintain also the "open door" policy, the only one which meets with the approval of its business classes, for by it alone can they be guaranteed equality of treatment in the trade of China. In this attempt to minimize the evils brought about by the necessities of her foreign policy, Great Britain has been, however, unable to secure to her people perfect equality of opportunity, for she has recognized special and exclusive rights first of Germany and then of Russia in their areas of activity, more particularly those relating to railways and mines. What these rights may eventually be claimed to include, no one can at present foretell, though it would not be surprising if the exercise of territorial jurisdiction and the imposition of discriminating taxation were demanded under them—at least by

France. Should such rights be conceded, our trade interests would receive a blow, from which they could not possibly recover.

To sum up then, we find to-day in China that the policy of the "open door," the untrammeled exercise of the rights insured to Treaty Powers by the treaty of Tientsin, and other treaties copied on it or under the most favored nation clause, is claimed by the mercantile classes of the United States and other powers as essential to the healthy extension of trade in China. We see, on the other hand, that the political interests and the geographical relations of Great Britain, Russia and France to China have forced those countries to divide up China proper into areas or spheres of interest (or influence) in which they enjoy special rights and privileges, the ultimate scope of which is not yet determined, and that at the same time Great Britain, in its desire not to sacrifice entirely its mercantile interests, is also endeavoring to preserve some of the undoubted benefits of the "open door" policy, but "spheres of influence" *are an accomplished fact,* this cannot be too much insisted on. This policy is outlined by Mr. Balfour in his Manchester speech of January 10, 1898.

Equality of opportunity as regards (c) having practically then already gone by the board, it would seem that the utmost that can now be attempted is to safeguard equality of opportunity as regards (a) and (b)— commerce and navigation. To do this it appears essential that the nations in favour of the "open door" policy should bind themselves, and secure undertakings from the other powers, to the effect that each in its respective spheres of interest or influence

(1) will in no way interfere with any treaty port in such sphere or with the interests vested in it:

(2) will promise that, unless the

Such then being the condition of things, and in view of the probability of complications soon arising between the interested powers in China, whereby it will become difficult, if not impossible, for the United States to retain the rights guaranteed them by treaties with China, what should be our immediate policy? To this question there can, it seems, be but one answer, we should at once initiate negotiations to obtain from those Powers who have acquired zones of interest in China formal assurance that (1°) they will in no way interfere within their so-called spheres of interest with any treaty port or with ports opened to trade in it are declared free ports, the Chinese treaty tariff as existing or as hereafter amended shall apply to all merchandise landed or shipped, no matter to what nationality such merchandise may belong; and that the dues and the duties so leviable shall be collected by the Chinese Govt.: and

(3) will levy no higher harbour dues on vessels of another nationality frequenting any port in such sphere than shall be levied on vessels of its own nationality, and no higher railroad charges on merchandise belonging to subjects of other Powers transported through such sphere than shall be levied on similar merchandise belonging to its own nationals transported over equal distances.

Such an arrangement would go far to secure an open market for merchandise in China and to remove dangerous sources of international conflict: and it is not anticipated that any serious difficulty would be experienced in attaining it. If the declarations of responsible British statesmen mean anything, they should ensure hearty support from Gt. Britain. Germany by her enlightened policy in sanctioning the establishment of a Chinese Customs-house at Kiaochow and in rendering it all possible assistance—in marked contrast to the narrow, unjust, and shortsighted policy of Gt. Britain in expelling the Chinese Customs-house from the Kowloon extension, inev-

vested rights in it of any nature; (2°) that all ports they may open in their respective spheres shall either be free ports, or that the Chinese treaty tariff at the time in force shall apply to all merchandise landed or shipped, no matter to what nationality belonging, and that the dues and duties provided for by treaty shall be collected by the Chinese Government; and (3°) that they will levy no higher harbor dues on vessels of other nationalities frequenting their ports in such spheres than shall be levied on their national vessels, and that they will also levy no higher railroad charges on merchandise belonging to or destined for subjects of other powers transported through their spheres than shall be levied on similar merchandise belonging to its own nationality.

In other words, we should insist on absolute equality of treatment in the various zones, for equality of opportunity with the citizens of the favored powers we cannot hope to have, in view of the well known methods now in vogue for securing privileges and concessions, though we should continually, by every proper means, seek to gain this also.

Such understandings with the various Powers, and it is confidently believed that they could be reached at present, would secure an open market throughout China for our trade on terms of equality with all other foreigners, and would further remove dangerous sources of irritation and possible conflict between the contending powers, greatly tend to re-establish confidence, and prepare the way for concerted action by the Powers to bring about the reforms in Chinese administration and the strengthening of the Imperial Government recognized on all sides as essential to the maintenance of peace.

Great stress has been laid by British writers on the role of Russia in itably to the enormous increase of smuggling—shows that little opposition is to be anticipated on her part. The doubtful Powers have hitherto been Russia and France, but the Ukase issued by the Czar on the 15th inst. declaring "Talien-wan a free port during the whole period of the treaty for the merchant ships of all nations" removes all doubt as to Russia's attitude and justifies the expectation that she would cooperate in such an undertaking as that proposed; and it is little likely that France would refuse to listen to Russia's advice—opposed though it is to her traditional policy in China of insisting that, whenever in any degree possible, territorial jurisdiction is included in any rights conceded—and so stand out in opposition alone.

China which they contend is a "purely political and military conquest" and who, "though she may mean to eventually build up a commerce, only wants for the present the Chinese seaboard and ports for strategic purposes." (Colquhom. *"China in Transformation."* 326.) Lord Beresford says (32) that he was told at Niuchuang by the British residents that "they regarded Manchuria as really a Russian province . . . that though the Russians might not impose a tariff on goods just at present, they were placing themselves in such a powerful military position that they would be able to do so in the near future, . . . and the merchants considered their trade threatened by such exhibition of military power." In the face of these apprehensions of the British merchants at Niuchuang, who were but feeling in their persons the discomforts and restrictions which all foreigners may sooner or later have to experience when settled in the sphere of influence of some rival power, it is agreeable to have to record the opening of the port of Talien-wan (near Port Arthur and an infinitely better port than Niuchuang, being below the line of winter and ice), to the merchant ships of all nations during the whole of the lease under which it is held by the Emperor of Russia's ukase of August 15th of this year. This I conceive will greatly help to allay fears and doubts as to Russia's attitude in China, and justifies the belief entertained that she would cooperate in bringing about such international understanding as is here outlined. The recent statement of a Russian writer inspired by a personage enjoying for years the friendship of the Emperor of Russia, that "the independence and integrity of China is a fundamental principle of Russia's policy in Asia" (*N. A. Rev.*, July, '99, p. 16), may or may not be absolutely correct; at all events, it may well be taken as indicating the present trend of Russia's policy, and seems to insure the friendly consideration at St. Petersburg of the arrangement here suggested. Whatever the ulterior object of Russia may be, its present one is unquestionably conciliation, for any haste might prove the spark which would cause the explosion by which the Chinese Empire would be shattered.

Nor does the assent of Germany to the proposed agreement seem very doubtful; she has declared Kiaochao a free port and allowed a Chinese custom house to be established there, in pleasing contrast by the way with the illiberal and shortsighted policy of Great Britain which has expelled the Chinese custom house from the Kowloon extension in front of Hongkong, and while she has insisted on certain exclusive mining and railroad rights in her sphere of interest, it seems highly probable that as German capital flows slower and slower into these enterprises, as it undoubtedly will as the vast requirements for long years to come of the already granted concessions are more exactly determined, she will find it greatly to her advantage to encourage and foster the enterprises of other nations.

No reference has been made to the way in which the Japanese Government would consider the propositions here suggested, because these measures are so clearly advantageous to Japan and so much in line with its own policy in China, that it must meet with its hearty approval.

It is particularly important for obvious reasons of both domestic and foreign policy that the initiative for these negotiations should be taken by the United States. Such a policy cannot be construed as favorable to any power in particular, but is eminently useful and desirable for the commerce of all nations. It furthermore has the advantage of insuring to the United States the appreciation of Chinese Government, who would see in it a strong desire to arrest the disintegration of the Empire and would greatly add to our prestige and influence at Peking.

France is the only doubtful country from whom some opposition might be anticipated, it being her well known policy in China to claim all implied jurisdictional rights wherever possible, but it is little likely that in this question, as in others, she would decline to listen to Russia's advice and stand out in opposition alone.

The issue of the Czar's ukase just referred to opens the door for *pourparlers* on this subject and renders the present a specially opportune moment for entering on them.

A. E. H.
17-viii-99

The prospect seems bright therefore *at the present moment* of bringing to a successful conclusion the negotiations needed to attain the ends here indicated and which will, it is thought, relieve our commercial world from the just apprehension and perturbation in which recent events have thrown it, giving it equal treatment so far as commerce and navigation go, with the subjects of any other Power.

Respectfully submitted,
W. W. Rockhill
Washington, 28th of August, 1899.

THE OPEN DOOR NOTES

Rockhill Draft[2] Wash. Sept. 1899 The Sec. of State to Mr. Choate London.	Final Draft[3] Department of State, Washington, September 6, 1899.
Sir:	Sir:
The Government of H.B.M. [having] has [repeatedly] declared that its policy and its very traditions precluded it from using any privileges which might be granted it in China as a weapon for excluding commercial rivals [from China], and that freedom of trade for Great Britain	The Government of Her Britannic Majesty has declared that its policy and its very traditions precluded it from using any privileges which might be granted it in China as a weapon for excluding commercial rivals, and that freedom of trade for Great Britain in that Empire meant

[2] Rockhill Papers. Quoted by Griswold, *op. cit.*, pp. 494-500.
[3] *Foreign Relations*, 1899, pp. 131-133.

in that Empire meant freedom of trade for all the world alike. While [recognizing] conceding by [convention] formal agreements first with Germany then with Russia the possession of spheres of influence or interest in China in which they are to enjoy special rights and privileges, most especially in respect [to] of railroads and mining enterprises, H.B.M. Government has *therefore* sought to maintain at the same time what is called the "open door" policy, [or] to insure to the commerce of the world in China equality of treatment within said spheres for their commerce and navigation. This latter policy is *alike* urgently demanded [not only] by the British mercantile [classes] communities [but also] *and* by those of the United States, as is held by them to be the only one which will improve existing conditions, enable them [can] to maintain their positions in the markets of China and [allow them to extend their] and extend their [oppor] operations in the future. While the Government of the United States [is in] will in no way commit[ted] itself to a recognition of exclusive rights [or control] of any power within or control over [the limits of the Chinese Empire and] any portion of the Chinese Empire under such agreements as have within the last year been made, it cannot conceal its apprehension that under existing conditions there is a possibility, even a probability, of complications [soon] arising between the Treaty Powers [in China] which may imperil the rights insured to the United States under our treaties with China. This Government is Animated by a sincere desire that the interests of our citizens may not be prejudiced through [any] exclusive treatment by any of the controlling Powers within their so-called "spheres of interest", [and in the hope that]

freedom of trade for all the world alike. While conceding by formal agreements, first with Germany and then with Russia, the possession of "spheres of influence or interest" in China in which they are to enjoy special rights and privileges, more especially in respect of railroads and mining enterprises, Her Britannic Majesty's Government has therefore sought to maintain at the same time what is called the "open-door" policy, to insure to the commerce of the world in China equality of treatment within said "spheres" for commerce and navigation. This latter policy is alike urgently demanded by the British mercantile communities and by those of the United States, as it is justly held by them to be the only one which will improve existing conditions, enable them to maintain their positions in the markets of China, and extend their operations in the future. While the Government of the United States will in no way commit itself to a recognition of exclusive rights of any power within or control over any portion of the Chinese Empire under such agreements as have within the last year been made, it can not conceal its apprehension that under existing conditions there is a possibility, even a probability, of complications arising between the treaty powers which may imperil the rights insured to the United States under our treaties with China.

This Government is animated by a sincere desire that the interests of our citizens may not be prejudiced through exclusive treatment by any of the controlling powers within their so-called "spheres of interest" in China, and hopes also to retain there an open market for the commerce of the world, remove dangerous sources of international irritation, and hasten thereby united or concerted action of the powers at Pekin in favor of the in China, and hope[ing] also to [receive] *retain* there an open market for the [merchandise] *commerce* of the world, [in China and to] remove dangerous sources of international irritation *and* [to] *hasten thereby united or concerted action of the Powers at Peking in favor of the administrative reforms so urgently needed for strengthening the Imperial Government* [by which alone] *and maintaining the integrity of China in which the whole western world is alike concerned, can be brought about.* [and] It believes[ing] that such a result may be greatly assisted by a declaration [by the of intentions] by the various Powers claiming "spheres of interest" in China of their intentions as regards [for] treatment of foreign trade therein. [this] The present moment seems a particularly opportune one for [calling submitting to] *informing* H.B.M. Government *of* the sincere desire of the United States to see it [give its support lend its support to obtaining bind itself] *make* [give] *a formal* [assur] *declaration* and to lend its support in obtaining similar [assu formal assurances] *declarations* from the various Powers claiming "spheres of influence" in China to the effect that each in its respective spheres of interest or influence

1. Will in no way interfere with any treaty port or any vested [rights] interest within any so-called "sphere of interest" or leased territory it may have in China.

2. That the Chinese treaty tariff of the time being shall apply to all merchandise landed or shipped to all such ports as are within said "sphere of interest" (unless they be "free ports"), no matter to which nationality it may belong, and that duties so leviable shall be collected by the Chinese Government.

3. That it will levy no higher harbor dues on vessels of another nation-

administrative reforms so urgently needed for strengthening the Imperial Government and maintaining the integrity of China in which the whole western world is alike concerned. It believes that such a result may be greatly assisted by a declaration by the various powers claiming "spheres of interest" in China of their intentions as regards treatment of foreign trade therein. The present moment seems a particularly opportune one for informing Her Britannic Majesty's Government of the desire of the United States to see it make a formal declaration and to lend its support in obtaining similar declarations from the various powers claiming "spheres of influence" in China, to the effect that each in its respective spheres of interest or influence—

First. Will in no wise interfere with any treaty port or any vested interest within any so-called "sphere of interest" or leased territory it may have in China.

Second. That the Chinese treaty tariff of the time being shall apply to all merchandise landed or shipped to all such ports as are within said "sphere of interest" (unless they be "free ports"), no matter to what nationality it may belong, and that duties so leviable shall be collected by the Chinese Government.

Third. That it will levy no higher harbor dues on vessels of another ality frequenting any port in such "sphere" than shall be levied on vessels of its own nationality, and no higher railroad charges over lines built, controlled or operated within its "sphere" on merchandise belonging to citizens or subjects of other nationalities transported through such "sphere" than shall be levied on similar merchandise belonging to its own nationals transported over equal distances.

The recent ukase of His Majesty the Emperor of Russia declaring the port of Ta-lien-wan open to the [commerce] merchant ships of [the world] all nations during the whole of the lease under which it is *to be* held by Russia, removing as it does all uncertainty as to the liberal and conciliatory policy of that Power together with the assurances given this Government by Russia, justifies the expectation [H. M. Russia]—will cooperate in such an understanding as is here proposed, and our Ambassador at the Court of St. Petersburg has been instructed accordingly to submit the proposition above detailed to H.I.M. and ask their early consideration. Copy of my instructions to Mr. Tower is herewith enclosed for your *confidential* information.

The action of Germany in declaring the port of Kiao-chao [is] a "free port" and the aid [to] the Imperial Government has given [the] China in the establish[ment] there of a Chinese Customs-house [indic] coupled with the *oral* assurances [given] *conveyed* the United States by Germany that our interests within its "sphere" would in no wise be affected by its occupation of this portion of the Province of Shan-tung, tend to show that little opposition [is to] may be anticipated from that Power to the desired declaration—

The interests of Japan, the next most interested Power in the trade of China, will be so clearly served by

nationality frequenting any port in such "sphere" than shall be levied on vessels of its own nationality, and no higher railroad charges over lines built, controlled, or operated within its "sphere" on merchandise belonging to citizens or subjects of other nationalities transported through such "sphere" than shall be levied on similar merchandise belonging to its own nationals transported over equal distances.

The recent ukase of His Majesty the Emperor of Russia, declaring the port of Ta-lien-wan open to the merchant ships of all nations during the whole of the lease under which it is to be held by Russia, removing as it does all uncertainty as to the liberal and conciliatory policy of that power, together with the assurances given this Government by Russia, justifies the expectation that His Majesty will cooperate in such an understanding as is here proposed, and our ambassador at the court of St. Petersburg has been instructed accordingly to submit the propositions above detailed to His Imperial Majesty, and ask their early consideration. Copy of my instruction to Mr. Tower is herewith inclosed for your confidential information.

The action of Germany in declaring the port of Kiaochao a "free port," and the aid the Imperial Government has given China in the establishment there of a Chinese custom-house, coupled with the oral assurance conveyed the United States by Germany that our interests within its "sphere" would in no wise be affected by its occupation of this portion of the province of Shantung, tend to show that little opposition may be anticipated from that power to the desired declaration.

The interests of Japan, the next most interested power in the trade of China, will be so clearly served the proposed arrangement, and the declarations of its statesmen within the last year are so entirely in line with the views [entertained by this Government] here expressed, that its hearty co-operation is confidently counted on.

[Another argument in favor of the policy here outlined may be found in the]

You will at as early a date as practicable submit the above [suggestions] considerations to H.B.M. Principal Secretary of State for Foreign Affairs and request their immediate consideration.

I enclose herewith a copy of the instructions sent to our Ambassador at Berlin bearing on the above subject.—

I am, etc.,
Rockhill papers.

The above is written entirely in Rockhill's handwriting including revisions. Brackets denote deletions, italics insertions.

by the proposed arrangement, and the declaration of its statesmen within the last year are so entirely in line with the views here expressed, that its hearty cooperation is confidently counted on.

You will, at as early date as practicable, submit the considerations to Her Britannic Majesty's principal secretary of state for foreign affairs and request their immediate consideration.

I inclose herewith a copy of the instruction sent to our ambassador at Berlin bearing on the above subject.

I have the honor to be, etc.,
JOHN HAY
For. Rel., 1899, pp. 131-133.

THE INTEGRITY OF CHINA. SECRETARY HAY TO THE GREAT POWERS, WASHINGTON, JULY 3, 1900[4]

In this critical posture of affairs in China it is deemed appropriate to define the attitude of the United States as far as present circumstances permit this to be done. We adhere to the policy initiated by us in 1857, of peace with the Chinese nation, of furtherance of lawful commerce, and of protection of lives and property of our citizens by all means guaranteed under extraterritorial treaty rights and by the law of nations. If wrong be done to our citizens we propose to hold the responsible authors to the uttermost accountability. We regard the condition at Pekin as one of virtual anarchy, whereby power and responsibility are practically devolved upon the local provincial authorities. So long as they are not in overt collusion with rebellion and use their power to protect foreign life and property we regard them as representing the Chinese people, with whom we seek to remain in peace and friendship. The purpose of the President is, as it has been heretofore, to act concurrently with the other powers, first, in opening up communication with Pekin and rescuing the American officials, missionaries, and other Americans who are in danger; secondly, in affording all possible protection everywhere in China to American life and property; thirdly, in guarding and protecting all legitimate American interests; and fourthly, in aiding to prevent a spread of the disorders to the other provinces of the Empire and a recurrence of such disasters. It is, of course, too early to forecast the means of attaining

[4] *Ibid.,* 1900, p. 299.

this last result; but the policy of the Government of the United States is to seek a solution which may bring about permanent safety and peace to China, preserve Chinese territorial and administrative entity, protect all rights guaranteed to friendly powers by treaty and international law, and safeguard for the world the principle of equal and impartial trade with all parts of the Chinese Empire.

You will communicate the purport of this instruction to the minister for foreign affairs.

HAY.

THE OPEN DOOR IN MANCHURIA. SECRETARY HAY TO MINISTER WU (CHINA), WASHINGTON, FEBRUARY 3, 1902[5]

MY DEAR MR. MINISTER: I have the honor to communicate to you herewith a memorandum expressing the views of the United States in regard to the proposed convention and arrangement between China and Russia respecting Manchuria, the substance of which has been cabled to the American representatives at Peking and St. Petersburg.

I am, etc.,

JOHN HAY.

_____

[Inclosure.]

Memorandum respecting Manchuria—February 1, 1902.

DEPARTMENT OF STATE
Washington, February 1, 1902.

An agreement by which China cedes to any corporation or company the exclusive right and privilege of opening mines, establishing railroads, or in any other way industrially developing Manchuria, can but be viewed with the gravest concern by the Government of the United States. It constitutes a monopoly, which is a distinct breach of the stipulations of treaties concluded between China and foreign powers, and thereby seriously affects the rights of American citizens; it restricts their rightful trade and exposes it to being discriminated against, interfered with, or otherwise jeopardized, and strongly tends toward permanently impairing the sovereign rights of China in this part of the Empire, and seriously interferes with her ability to meet her international obligations. Furthermore, such concession on the part of China will undoubtedly be followed by demands from other powers for similar and equal exclusive advantages in other parts of the Chinese Empire, and the inevitable result must be the complete wreck of the policy of absolute equality of treatment of all nations in regard to trade, navigation, and commerce within the confines of the Empire.

On the other hand, the attainment by one power of such exclusive privileges for a commercial organization of its nationality conflicts with the assurances repeatedly conveyed to this Government by the Imperial Russian ministry of foreign affairs of the Imperial Government's intention to follow the policy of the open door in China, as advocated by the Government of the United States and accepted by all the treaty powers having commercial interests in that Empire.

[5] *Ibid.*, 1902, pp. 275-276.

It is for these reasons that the Government of the United States, animated now, as in the past, with the sincerest desire of insuring to the whole world the benefits of full and fair intercourse between China and the nations on a footing of equal rights and advantages to all, submits the above to the earnest consideration of the Imperial Governments of China and Russia, confident that they will give due weight to its importance and adopt such measures as will relieve the just and natural anxiety of the United States.

XXXI

SETTLEMENT OF THE BOXER UPRISING, 1901

THE POLICY of the Powers, including the United States, toward China at the beginning of the twentieth century is exemplified in terms of the Protocol of September 7, 1901, embodying the settlement of the Boxer Rebellion. The policy of the United States is to be observed principally in Article VI (the indemnity), Article VII (the legation quarter), Article VIII (destruction of the Taku forts), and Article XI (revision of the commercial treaties).

AUSTRIA-HUNGARY, BELGIUM, FRANCE, GERMANY, GREAT BRITAIN, ITALY, JAPAN, THE NETHERLANDS, RUSSIA, SPAIN, THE UNITED STATES, AND CHINA. FINAL PROTOCOL FOR THE SETTLEMENT OF THE DISTURBANCES OF 1900 [THE BOXER REBELLION]. SEPTEMBER 7, 1901.[1]

[Extracts]

· · · · · · · · · · · · · ·

ARTICLE 6.—By an Imperial Edict dated the 29th of May, 1901 (Annex No. 12), His majesty the Emperor of China agreed to pay the Powers an indemnity of four hundred and fifty millions of Haikwan Taels. This sum represents the total amount of the indemnities for States, companies or societies, private individuals, and Chinese referred to in Article VI of the note of December 22nd, 1900.

(a) These four hundred and fifty millions constitute a gold debt calculated at the rate of the Haikwan tael to the gold currency of each country, as indicated below.

Haikwan tael—marks	3.055
Austro-Hungary crown	3.595
gold dollar	0.742
francs	3.750
pound sterling	3s.od.
yen	1.407
Netherlands florin	1.796
gold rouble (17.424 dolias fine)	1.412

This sum in gold shall bear interest at 4 per cent per annum, and the capital shall be reimbursed by China in thirty-nine years in the manner indicated in the annexed plan of amortization. (Annex No. 13.)

Capital and interest shall be payable in gold or at the rates of exchange corresponding to the dates at which the different payments fall due.

The amortization shall commence the 1st of January, 1902, and shall finish at the end of the year 1940. The amortizations are payable annually, the first payment being fixed on the 1st of January, 1903.

Interest shall run from the 1st of July, 1901, but the Chinese Government

[1] U. S. Treaty Series, pp. 279-284.

shall have the right to pay off within a term of three years, beginning January, 1902, the arrears of the first six months, ending the 31st of December, 1901, on condition, however, that it pays compound interest at the rate of 4 per cent per annum on the sums the payments of which shall have thus been deferred. Interest shall be payable semi-annually, the first payment being fixed on the 1st of July, 1902.

(b) The service of the debt shall take place in Shanghai, in the following manner:

Each Power shall be represented by a delegate on a commission of bankers authorized to receive the amount of interest and amortization which shall be paid to it by the Chinese authorities designated for that purpose, to divide it among the interested parties, and to give a receipt for the same.

(c) The Chinese Government shall deliver to the Doyen of the Diplomatic Corps at Peking a bond for the lump sum, which shall subsequently be converted into fractional bonds bearing the signatures of the delegates of the Chinese Government designated for that purpose. This operation and all those relating to issuing of the bonds shall be performed by the above-mentioned Commission, in accordance with the instructions which the Powers shall send their delegates.

(d) The proceeds of the revenues assigned to the payment of the bonds shall be paid monthly to the Commission.

(e) The revenues assigned as security for the bonds are the following:

1. The balance of the revenues of the Imperial maritime Customs after payment of the interest and amortization of preceding loans secured on these revenues, plus the proceeds of the raising to five per cent effective of the present tariff on maritime imports, including articles until now on the free list, but exempting foreign rice, cereals, and flour, gold and silver bullion and coin.

2. The revenues of the native customs, administered in the open ports by the Imperial maritime Customs.

3. The total revenues of the salt gabelle, exclusive of the fraction previously set aside for other foreign loans.

The raising of the present tariff on imports to five per cent effective is agreed to on the conditions mentioned below.

It shall be put in force two months after the signing of the present protocol, and no exceptions shall be made except for merchandise shipped not more than ten days after the said signing.

1.° All duties levied on imports "ad valorem" shall be converted as far as possible and as soon as may be into specific duties. This conversion shall be made in the following manner: The average value of merchandise at the time of their landing during the three years 1897, 1898, and 1899, that is to say, the market price less the amount of import duties and incidental expenses, shall be taken as the basis for the valuation of merchandise. Pending the results of the work of conversion, duties shall be levied "ad valorem."

2.° The beds of the rivers Peiho and Whangpu shall be improved with the financial participation of China.

ARTICLE VII.—The Chinese Government has agreed that the quarter occupied by the legations shall be considered as one specially reserved for their use and placed under their exclusive control, in which Chinese shall not have the right to reside and which may be made defensible.

In the protocol annexed to the letter of the 16th January, 1901, China recognized the right of each Power to maintain a permanent guard in the said quarter for the defense of its legation.

ARTICLE VIII.—The Chinese Government has consented to raze the forts of Taku and those which might impede free communication between Peking and the sea; steps have been taken for carrying this out.

. . . .

ARTICLE XI.—The Chinese Government has agreed to negotiate the amendments deemed necessary by the foreign Governments to the treaties of commerce and navigation and the other subjects concerning commercial relations, with the object of facilitating them.

. . . .

ARTICLE XII.—An Imperial Edict of the 24th of July, 1901 (Annex No. 18), reformed the Office of foreign affairs (Tsungli Yamen), on the lines indicated by the Powers, that is to say, transformed it into a Ministry of foreign affairs (Wai-wu Pu), which takes precedence over the six other Ministers of State. The same edict appointed the principal members of this Ministry.

. . . .

NOTE.[2]—The Boxer indemnity was divided as follows:

	(Taels)	Per cent of total
Russia	130,371,120	29.
Germany	90,070,515	20.
France	70,878,240	15.75
Great Britain	50,620,545	11.25
Japan	34,793,100	7.7
United States	32,939,055	7.3
Italy	26,617,005	5.9
Belgium	8,484,345	1.9
Austria-Hungary	4,003,920	.9
Netherlands	782,100	.2
Spain	135,315	
Portugal	92,250	.1
Sweden	62,820	
Other claims	149,670	
	450,000,000	100.0

[The tael was then valued at $0.742 gold.]

The United States, in 1908, having paid all claims and retained $2,000,000 for possible future adjustments, remitted $10,785,286 of her indemnity. China was still to make the regular payments, but the extra amounts would be as regularly remitted. The Chinese government announced its intention to use the returned indemnity payments for the education of students in the United States. When China entered the World War the payments to Germany and Austria-Hungary ceased, and the other indemnity powers engaged in the war agreed to waive their payments for five years, Russia, however, only agreeing in respect to one third of her installments. By the peace treaties Germany and Austria-Hungary were forced to relinquish their shares of the indemnity.

[2] Payson J. Treat, *The Far East* (New York, 1935), pp. 358-359. Reprinted with permission of the publishers, Harper and Brothers.

By this time the favorable results of the American remission of a part of her indemnity were widely recognized. Great Britain, in 1922, decided to remit the balance due her. Such a bill was passed in 1925, but an investigation as to the use to which it should be put delayed immediate action. France, about the same time, would use her balance to rehabilitate a defunct bank in China and for education. Japan followed suit in 1923, and created a fund into which should go the moneys received from the Shantung Railway, mines, and government properties as well as the indemnity balance, and which would be used for cultural purposes. The next year Russia, by treaty, relinquished her remaining share, and the United States waived the balance of $6,137,332. The Netherlands, in 1925, would use her balance for the improvement of the Yellow River, and Italy, the same year, for education, philanthropy, and public works, the materials for which should be bought in Italy. While China, in every case where the indemnity was remitted, would continue to pay the original amounts, the sums would then be returned to be used for the purposes announced by the respective powers.

XXXII

RESTATEMENT OF PRINCIPLES AND POLICY, 1903

IN 1903 THE United States concluded with China a commercial treaty significant because of its reference to a number of important phases in the relations of the two countries. In this treaty the United States agreed to relinquish extraterritoriality conditional on the meeting by China of certain conditions. The treaty status of missionaries was likewise restated.

THE UNITED STATES AND CHINA. TREATY FOR THE EXTENSION OF THE COM-MERCIAL RELATIONS BETWEEN THEM. OCTOBER 8, 1903[1]

. . . .

ARTICLE I.—Diplomatic representatives; rights and privileges.—In accordance with international usage, and as the diplomatic representative of China has the right to reside in the capital of the United States, and to enjoy there the same prerogatives, privileges and immunities as are enjoyed by the similar representative of the most favored nation, the diplomatic representative of the United States shall have the right to reside at the capital of His Majesty the Emperor of China. He shall be given audience of His Majesty the Emperor whenever necessary to present his letters of credence or any communication from the President of the United States. At all such times he shall be received in a place and in a manner befitting his high position, and on all such occasions the ceremonial observed toward him shall be that observed toward the representatives of nations on a footing of equality, with no loss of prestige on the part of either.

The diplomatic representatives of the United States shall enjoy all the prerogatives, privileges and immunities accorded by international usage to such representatives, and shall in all respects be entitled to the treatment extended to similar representatives of the most favored nation.

English text authoritative.—The English text of all notes or dispatches from United States officials to Chinese officials, and the Chinese text of all from Chinese officials to United States officials shall be authoritative.

ARTICLE II.—Consular officers; rights and privileges.—As China may appoint consular officers to reside in the United States and to enjoy there the same attributes, privileges and immunities as are enjoyed by consular officers of other nations, the United States may appoint, as its interests may require, consular officers to reside at the places in the Empire of China that are now or that may hereafter be opened to foreign residence and trade. They shall hold direct official intercourse and correspondence with the local officers of the Chinese Government within their consular districts, either personally or in writing as the case may require, on terms of equality and reciprocal respect.

[1] U. S. *Treaty Series* [Unnumbered]. See also MacMurray, *Treaties and Agreements with and concerning China* (New York, 1921), pp. 423-432.

These officers shall be treated with due respect by all Chinese authorities, and they shall enjoy all the attributes, privileges and immunities, and exercise all the jurisdiction over their nationals which are or may hereafter be extended to similar officers of the nation the most favored in these respects. If the officers of either government are disrespectfully treated or aggrieved in any way by the authorities of the other, they shall have the right to make representation of the same to the superior officers of their own government who shall see that full inquiry and strict justice be had in the premises. And the said consular officers of either nation shall carefully avoid all acts of offence to the officers and people of the other nation.

On the arrival of a consul duly accredited at any place in China opened to foreign trade it shall be the duty of the Minister of the United States to inform the Board of Foreign Affairs, which shall, in accordance with international usage, forthwith cause the proper recognition of the said consul and grant him authority to act.

ARTICLE III.—American citizens in China; their rights.—Citizens of the United States may frequent, reside and carry on trade, industries and manufactures, or pursue any lawful avocation, in all the ports or localities of China which are now open or may hereafter be opened to foreign residence and trade; and, within the suitable localities at those places which have been or may be set apart for the use and occupation of foreigners, they may rent or purchase houses, places of business and other buildings, and rent or lease in perpetuity land and build thereon. They shall generally enjoy as to their persons and property all such rights, privileges and immunities as are or may hereafter be granted to the subjects or citizens of the nation the most favored in these respects.

ARTICLE IV.—Likin and other transit dues to be totally abolished.—The Chinese Government, recognizing that the existing system of levying dues on goods in transit, and especially the system of taxation known as *likin,* impedes the free circulation of commodities to the general injury of trade, hereby undertakes to abandon the levy of *likin* and all other transit dues throughout the Empire and to abolish the offices, stations and barriers maintained for their collection and not to establish other offices for levying dues on goods in transit. It is clearly understood that, after the offices, stations and barriers for taxing goods in transit have been abolished, no attempt shall be made to re-establish them in any form or under any pretext whatsoever.

Surtax on tariff rates granted in compensation.—The Government of the United States, in return, consents to allow a surtax, in excess of the tariff rates for the time being in force, to be imposed on foreign goods imported by citizens of the United States and on Chinese produce destined for export abroad or coastwise. It is clearly understood that in no case shall the surtax on foreign imports exceed one and one-half times the import duty leviable in terms of the final Protocol signed by China and the Powers on the seventh day of September, A. D. 1901; that the payment of the import duty and surtax shall secure for foreign imports, whether in the hands of Chinese or foreigners, in original packages or otherwise, complete immunity from all other taxation, examination or delay; that the total amount of taxation, inclusive of the tariff export duty, leviable on native produce for export abroad shall, under no circumstances, exceed seven and one-half per centum *ad valorem.*

China's right to levy taxes.—Nothing in this article is intended to interfere with the inherent right of China to levy such other taxes as are not in conflict with its provisions.

Keeping these fundamental principles in view, the High Contracting Parties have agreed upon the following method of procedure.

Likin barriers to be abolished. Native customs offices to be retained in certain localities.—The Chinese Government undertakes that all offices, stations and barriers of whatsoever kind for collecting *likin,* duties, or such like dues on goods in transit, shall be permanently abolished on all roads, railways and waterways in the nineteen Provinces of China and the three Eastern Provinces. This provision does not apply to the native Customs offices at present in existence on the seaboard, at open ports where there are offices of the Imperial Maritime Customs, and on the land frontiers of China embracing the nineteen Provinces and the three Eastern Provinces.

Wherever there are offices of the Imperial Maritime Customs, or wherever such may be hereafter placed, native Customs offices may also be established, as well as at any point either on the seaboard or land frontiers.

Surtax on duties on foreign imports.—The Government of the United States agrees that foreign goods on importation, in addition to the effective five per centum import duty as provided for in the Protocol of 1901, shall pay a special surtax of one and one-half times the amount of the said duty to compensate for the abolition of *likin,* of other transit dues besides *likin,* and of all other taxation on foreign goods, and in consideration of the other reforms provided for in this article.

Revision of foreign export tariff.—The Chinese Government may recast the foreign export tariff with specific duties, as far as practicable, on a scale not exceeding five per centum *ad valorem;* but existing export duties shall not be raised until at least six months notice has been given. In cases where existing export duties are above five per centum, they shall be reduced to not more than that rate.

Surtax on exports; how levied.—An additional special surtax of one-half the export duty payable for the time being, in lieu of internal taxation of all kinds, may be levied at the place of original shipment or at the time of export on goods exported either to foreign countries or coastwise.

Certificate of origin.—Foreign goods which bear a similarity to native goods shall be furnished by the Customs officers, if required by the owner, with a protective certificate for each package, on the payment of import duty and surtax, to prevent the risk of any dispute in the interior.

Junk-borne goods.—Native goods brought by junks to open ports, if intended for local consumption, irrespective of the nationality of the owner of the goods, shall be reported at the native Customs offices only, to be dealt with according to the fiscal regulations of the Chinese Government.

Machine-made goods in China; treatment of.—Machine-made cotton yarn and cloth manufactured in China, whether by foreigners at the open ports or by Chinese anywhere in China, shall as regards taxation be on a footing of perfect equality. Such goods upon payment of the taxes thereon shall be granted a rebate of the import duty and of two thirds of the import surtax paid on the cotton used in their manufacture, if it has been imported from abroad, and of all duties paid thereon if it be Chinese grown cotton. They shall also be free of export duty, coast-trade duty and export surtax. The same principle and procedure shall be applied to all other products of foreign type turned out by machinery in China.

Maritime Customs to oversee native customs affairs.—A member or members of the Imperial Maritime Customs foreign staff shall be selected by the Governors-General and Governors of each of the various provinces of the Empire for their respective provinces, and appointed in consultation with the Inspector General of Imperial Maritime Customs, for duty in connection with native Customs affairs to have a general supervision of their working.

Complaints; how investigated. Responsibility for enforcement of provisions of treaty.—Cases where illegal action is complained of by citizens of the United States shall be promptly investigated by an officer of the Chinese Government of sufficiently high rank, in conjunction with an officer of the United States Government, and an officer of the Imperial Maritime Customs, each of sufficient standing; and, in the event of it being found by the investigating officers that the complaint is well founded and loss has been incurred, due compensation shall be paid through the Imperial Maritime Customs. The high provincial officials shall be held responsible that the officer guilty of the illegal action shall be severely punished and removed from his post. If the complaint is shown to be frivolous or malicious, the complainant shall be held responsible for the expenses of the investigation.

Edict to be published when article becomes operative.—When the ratifications of this Treaty shall have been exchanged by the High Contracting Parties hereto, and the provisions of this Article shall have been accepted by the Powers having treaties with China, then a date shall be agreed upon when the provisions of this Article shall take effect and an Imperial Edict shall be published in due form on yellow paper and circulated throughout the Empire of China setting forth the abolition of all *likin* taxation, duties on goods in transit, offices, stations and barriers for collecting the same, and of all descriptions of internal taxation on foreign goods, and the imposition of the surtax on the import of foreign goods and on the export of native goods, and the other fiscal changes and reforms provided for in this Article, all of which shall take effect from the said date. The Edict shall state that the provincial high officials are responsible that any official disregarding the letter or the spirit of its injunction shall be severely punished and removed from his post.

ARTICLE V.—Tariff on American imports. Most favored nation treatment.— The tariff duties to be paid by citizens of the United States on goods imported into China shall be as set forth in the schedule annexed hereto and made part of this Treaty, subject only to such amendments and changes as are authorized by Article IV of the present convention or as may hereafter be agreed upon by the High Contracting Parties hereto. It is expressly agreed, however, that citizens of the United States shall at no time pay other or higher duties than those paid by the citizens or subjects of the most favored nation.

Conversely, Chinese subjects shall not pay higher duties on their imports into the United States than those paid by the citizens or subjects of the most favored nation.

ARTICLE VI.—Bonded Warehouses.—The Government of China agrees to the establishment by citizens of the United States of warehouses approved by the proper Chinese authorities as bonded warehouses at the several open Ports of China, for storage, re-packing, or preparation for shipment of lawful goods, subject to such necessary regulations for the protection of the revenue of China, including a reasonable scale of fees according to commodities, distance from the custom house and hours of working, as shall be made from time to time by the proper officers of the Government of China.

ARTICLE VII.—Mining regulations to be revised and operations encouraged. —The Chinese Government, recognizing that it is advantageous for the country to develop its mineral resources, and that it is desirable to attract foreign as well as Chinese capital to embark in mining enterprises, agrees, within one year from the signing of this Treaty, to initiate and conclude the revision of the existing mining regulations. To this end China will, with all expedition and earnestness, go into the whole question of mining rules; and, selecting from the rules of the United States and other countries regulations which seem applicable to the condition of China, will recast its present mining rules in such a way as, while promoting the interests of Chinese subjects and not injuring in any way the sovereign rights of China, will offer no impediment to the attraction of foreign capital nor place foreign capitalists at a greater disadvantage than they would be under generally accepted foreign regulations; and will permit citizens of the United States to carry on in Chinese territory mining operations and other necessary business relating thereto provided they comply with the new regulations and conditions which will be imposed by China on its subjects and foreigners alike, relating to the opening of mines, the renting of mineral land, and the payment of royalty, and provided they apply for permits, the provisions of which in regard to necessary business relating to such operations shall be observed. The residence of citizens of the United States in connection with such mining operations shall be subject to such regulations as shall be agreed upon by and between the United States and China.

Any mining concession granted after the publication of such new rules shall be subject to their provisions.

ARTICLE VIII.—Drawback certificates.—Drawback certificates for the return of duties shall be issued by the Imperial Maritime Customs to citizens of the United States within three weeks of the presentation to the Customs of the papers entitling the applicant to receive such drawback certificates, and they shall be receivable at their face value in payment of duties of all kinds (tonnage dues excepted) at the port of issue; or shall, in the case of drawbacks on foreign goods re-exported within three years from the date of importation, be redeemable by the Imperial Maritime Customs in full in ready money at the port of issue, at the option of the holders thereof. But if, in connection with any application for a drawback certificate, the Customs authorities discover an attempt to defraud the revenue, the applicant shall be dealt with and punished in accordance with the stipulations provided in the Treaty of Tientsin, Article XXI, in the case of detected frauds on the revenue. In case the goods have been removed from Chinese territory, then the Consul shall inflict on the guilty party a suitable fine to be paid to the Chinese Government.

ARTICLE IX.—Protection of trade-marks.—Whereas the United States undertakes to protect the citizens of any country in the exclusive use within the United States of any lawful trade-marks, provided that such country agrees by treaty or convention to give like protection to citizens of the United States:—

Therefore the Government of China, in order to secure such protection in the United States for its subjects, now agrees to fully protect any citizen, firm or corporation of the United States in the exclusive use in the Empire of China of any lawful trade-mark to the exclusive use of which in the United States they are entitled, or which they have adopted and used, or intend to adopt and use as soon as registered, for exclusive use within the Empire of China. To this end the Chinese Government agrees to issue by its proper authorities proclamations, having the force of law, forbidding all subjects of China from infringing on, imitating, colorably imitating, or knowingly passing off an imitation of trade-marks belonging to citizens of the United States, which shall have been registered by the proper authorities of the United States at such offices as the Chinese Government will establish for such purpose, on payment of a reasonable fee, after due investigation by the Chinese authorities, and in compliance with reasonable regulations.

ARTICLE X.—Protection of patents.—The United States Government allows subjects of China to patent their inventions in the United States and protects them in the use and ownership of such patents. The Government of China now agrees that it will establish a Patent Office. After this office has been established and special laws with regard to inventions have been adopted it will thereupon, after the payment of the prescribed fees, issue certificates of protection, valid for a fixed term of years, to citizens of the United States on all their patents issued by the United States, in respect of articles the sale of which is lawful in China, which do not infringe on previous inventions of Chinese subjects, in the same manner as patents are to be issued to subjects of China.

ARTICLE XI.—Protection of copyright.—Whereas the Government of the United States undertakes to give the benefits of its copyright laws to the citizens of any foreign State which gives to the citizens of the United States the benefits of copyright on an equal basis with its own citizens:—

Therefore the Government of China, in order to secure such benefits in the United States for its subjects, now agrees to give full protection, in the same way and manner and subject to the same conditions upon which it agrees to protect trade-marks, to all citizens of the United States who are authors, designers or proprietors of any book, map, print, or engraving especially prepared for the use and education of the Chinese people, or translation into Chinese of any book, in the exclusive right to print and sell such book, map, print, engraving or translation in the Empire of China during ten years from the date of registration. With the exception of the books, maps, etc., specified above, which may not be reprinted in the same form, no work shall be entitled to copyright privileges under this article. It is understood that Chinese subjects shall be at liberty to make, print, and sell original translations into Chinese of any works written or of maps compiled by a citizen of the United States. This article shall not be held to protect against due process of law any citizen of the United States or Chinese subject who may be author, proprietor or seller of any publication calculated to injure the well-being of China.

ARTICLE XII.—Navigation of inland waters.—The Chinese Government having in 1898 opened the navigable inland waters of the Empire to commerce by all steam vessels, native or foreign, that may be specially registered for the purpose, for the conveyance of passengers and lawful merchandise,—citizens, firms and corporations of the United States may engage in such commerce on equal terms with those granted to subjects of any foreign power.

In case either party hereto considers it advantageous at any time that the rules and regulations then in existence for such commerce be altered or amended, the Chinese Government agrees to consider amicably and to adopt such modifications thereof as are found necessary for trade and for the benefit of China.

Mukden and Antung opened to foreign trade.—The Chinese Government agrees that, upon the exchange of the ratifications of this Treaty, Mukden and Antung, both in the province of Sheng-king, will be opened by China itself as places of international residence and trade. The selection of suitable localities to be set apart for international use and occupation and the regulations for these places set apart for foreign residence and trade shall be agreed upon by the Governments of the United States and China after consultation together.

ARTICLE XIII.—Uniform national coinage.—China agrees to take the necessary steps to provide for a uniform national coinage which shall be legal tender in payment of all duties, taxes and other obligations throughout the Empire by the citizens of the United States as well as Chinese subjects. It is understood, however, that all Customs duties shall continue to be calculated and paid on the basis of the Haikuan Tael.

ARTICLE XIV.—Christianity; its teachers and followers not to be discriminated against. Rights and duties of missionaries.—The principles of the Christian religion, as professed by the Protestant and Roman Catholic Churches, are recognized as teaching men to do to others as they would have others do to them. Those who quietly profess and teach these doctrines shall not be harassed or persecuted on account of their faith. Any person, whether citizen of the United States or Chinese convert, who, according to these tenets, peaceably teaches and practices the principles of Christianity shall in no case be interfered with or molested therefor. No restrictions shall be placed on Chinese joining Christian churches. Converts and non-converts, being Chinese subjects, shall alike conform to the laws of China; and shall pay due respect to those in authority, living together in peace and amity; and the fact of being converts shall not protect them from the consequences of any offence they may have committed before or may commit after their admission into the church, or exempt them from paying legal taxes levied on Chinese subjects generally, except taxes levied and contributions for the support of religious customs and practices contrary to their faith. Missionaries shall not interfere with the exercise by the native authorities of their jurisdiction over Chinese subjects; nor shall the native authorities make any distinction between converts and non-converts, but shall administer the laws without partiality so that both classes can live together in peace.

Property; land purchased by missionary societies.—Missionary societies of the United States shall be permitted to rent and to lease in perpetuity, as the property of such societies, buildings or lands in all parts of the Empire for missionary purposes and, after the title deeds have been found in order and duly stamped by the local authorities, to erect such suitable buildings as may be required for carrying on their good work.

ARTICLE XV.—Reform of judicial system. Extra-territoriality to terminate.— The Government of China having expressed a strong desire to reform its judicial system and to bring it into accord with that of Western nations, the United States agrees to give every assistance to such reform and will also be prepared to relinquish extra-territorial rights when satisfied that the state of the Chinese laws, the arrangements for their administration, and other considerations warrant it in so doing.

ARTICLE XVI.—Prohibition of importation of morphia.—The Government of the United States consents to the prohibition by the Government of China of the importation into China of morphia and of instruments for its injection, excepting morphia and instruments for its injection imported for medical purposes, on payment of tariff duty, and under regulations to be framed by China which shall effectually restrict the use of such import to the said purposes. This prohibition shall be uniformly applied to such importation from all countries. The Chinese Government undertakes to adopt at once measures to prevent the manufacture in China of morphia and of instruments for its injection.

ARTICLE XVII.—Treaties to remain in force except as here modified.—It is agreed between the High Contracting Parties hereto that all the provisions of the several treaties between the United States and China which were in force on the first day of January A. D. 1900, are continued in full force and effect except in so far as they are modified by the present Treaty or other treaties to which the United States is a party.

The present Treaty shall remain in force for a period of ten years beginning with the date of exchange of ratifications and until a revision is effected as hereinafter provided.

Revision.—It is further agreed that either of the High Contracting Parties may demand that the tariff and the articles of this convention be revised at the end of ten years from the date of the exchange of the ratifications thereof. If no revision is demanded before the end of the first term of ten years, then these articles in their present form shall remain in full force for a further term of ten years reckoned from the end of the first term, and so on for successive periods of ten years.

English text authoritative.—The English and Chinese texts of the present Treaty and its three annexes have been carefully compared; but, in the event of there being any difference of meaning between them, the sense as expressed in the English text shall be held to be the correct one.

This Treaty and its three annexes shall be ratified by the two High Contracting Parties in conformity with their respective constitutions, and the ratifications shall be exchanged in Washington not later than twelve months from the present date.

In testimony whereof, we, the undersigned, by virtue of our respective powers, have signed this Treaty in duplicate in the English and Chinese languages, and have affixed our respective seals.

Done at Shanghai, this eighth day of October in the year of our Lord one thousand nine hundred and three, and in the twenty ninth year of Kuang Hsü eighth month and eighteenth day.

EDWIN H. CONGER. [SEAL]

JOHN GOODNOW. [SEAL]

JOHN F. SEAMAN. [SEAL]

Signatures and seal of Chinese Plenipotentiaries.

[LÜ HAI-HUAN.]

[SHENG HSÜAN-HUAI.]

ANNEX I.

As citizens of the United States are already forbidden by treaty to deal in or handle opium, no mention has been made in this Treaty of opium taxation.

As the trade in salt is a government monopoly in China, no mention has been made in this Treaty of salt taxation.

It is, however, understood, after full discussion and consideration, that the collection of inland dues on opium and salt and the means for the protection of the revenue therefrom and for preventing illicit traffic therein are left to be administered by the Chinese Government in such manner as shall in no wise interfere with the provisions of Article IV of this treaty regarding the unobstructed transit of other goods.

.   .   .   .

XXXIII

CHINA'S ANTI-AMERICAN BOYCOTT, 1904-1906

THE FIRST major boycott employed by China was directed against the United States. The origins of this movement of 1905 are to be found in the legislative program by which the United States sought to enforce the policy of Chinese exclusion. The treaty of 1894 (see p. 156), which provided for the exclusion of all Chinese laborers for a period of ten years, lapsed in 1904. China refused to renew its provisions, insisting that the exclusion policy be modified. Chinese claimed that regulations for the exclusion of their people were enforced with undue harshness. They were irritated likewise by extension of the exclusion acts to Hawaii and the Philippine Islands. It was also claimed that the boycott was furthered by Chinese brokers at Canton seeking profits through the importation of coolie labor. The boycott was finally brought to an end through the protests of the American government and of the merchants of Shanghai. Problems involved in the enforcement of the exclusion laws are illustrated in the extracts from a report of the Commissioner-General of Immigration, submitted to the House of Representatives, May 18, 1906. The policy of the American government toward the boycott is given in the notes of Minister Rockhill to the Chinese Foreign Office, and to the Secretary of State.

BEGINNINGS OF THE BOYCOTT. MINISTER ROCKHILL TO THE SECRETARY OF STATE, PEKING, JULY 6, 1905[1]

Sir: When I arrived in Shanghai on May 20, last, on my way to my post, I was informed by our consul-general that a few days previously the leading native merchant guilds of that place had held meetings for the purpose of declaring a general boycott against all American goods and persons residing in China for the purpose of forcing the Government of the United States to amend its laws concerning the exclusion of Chinese. The Chinese public was told that our government was attempting to force that of China to sign a treaty highly detrimental to Chinese interests and that the people of China ought by means of the proposed boycott to resist America's demands. Telegrams were sent by the meeting to some twenty cities in China, all interested in the American trade, urging them to take the proposed action, which was to be put in force on or about August 1 next.

[1] *Foreign Relations*, 1905, pp. 205-206.

Our consul-general, while not believing that the proposed anti-American agitation could have very series [serious?] results, was nevertheless anxious about it, and asked me to see the heads of the native guilds, which he had asked to meet him at the consulate-general for the purpose of talking the matter over with them.

I agreed to Mr. Davidson's request, and on May 21, I met the committee of representative merchants and bankers of the local guilds and explained to them that they had been misled and were evidently not aware of the true state of the negotiations now pending between the two governments, otherwise they would have refrained from taking the hasty action they had, which could only tend to create bad feeling and embarrass trade without any object. I then read to them the memorandum of which I enclose a copy. I asked them to make it known to their guilds. This they promised to do, and they left assuring me that they were perfectly satisfied with my explanation.

A couple of days later, the local native press continuing to print inflammatory articles against our country and encouraging the proposed boycott, I suggested to Mr. Davidson that he should see the taot'ai and ask him to put a stop to such foolish and lawless agitation. Mr. Davidson saw the taot'ai, but no action was taken by him.

On my arrival in Peking I found numerous telegrams and dispatches from our consuls and citizens, reporting that the movement had spread to Foochow, Amoy, Canton, Hankow, Tientsin, and to several interior towns of this province, and fears were expressed that the ignorant people of the interior might commit acts of violence against foreigners if the Chinese Government did not take prompt action to check the movement and state the true conditions of the negotiations for a new treaty.

I therefore asked the Prince Ch'ing in the first interview I had with him on June 3 to take prompt action to put a stop to the agitation. This he promised to do, but as the inflammatory articles continued to appear, particularly in the Peking native press, I felt obliged to call his attention to the matter in a note. This having remained unanswered for a week, I wrote him again, and the day before yesterday I received the inclosed reply [not printed], which tends to strengthen my belief that the movement was with official approval, if not actually at official suggestion. The action of the foreign office would probably not have been taken yet had it not been that the energetic viceroy, Yuan Shih-k'ai, saw the possible danger lurking in it and took prompt and radical action to suppress it. He also wired to the foreign office here advising it strongly to instruct the viceroys and governors of the various provinces to use their efforts to arrest the movement. I have thanked the Viceroy Yuan for his prompt and wise action, during a visit I paid him at Tientsin a few days ago.

· · · · · · · · · · · ·

MEMORANDUM. MINISTER ROCKHILL TO THE CHINESE GUILDS[2]

In 1894 the governments of China and the United States, animated by the desire to amicably settle the question of the coming of Chinese laborers into the United States, which previous treaties had either left in an unsatisfactory condition or which previous experience had shown required change and amendment, concluded a new treaty for a period of ten years.

[2] *Ibid.*, pp. 206-207.

The last article of this treaty of 1894 provided that, if six months prior to the date on which it expired (7th of December, 1904) neither of the signatory powers had declared its desire to terminate it, it should be in force for another period of ten years.

The Chinese Government informed the American Government during the summer of 1904 that it did not wish to see the treaty of 1894 extended beyond the date fixed for its termination; that is to say, December 7, 1904. At the same time it declared its willingness to begin negotiations for the conclusion of a new treaty regulating the subject of the entry of Chinese laborers into the United States. In August of last year—that is to say, about seven months ago—the Chinese Government, through its minister at Washington, submitted a first draft of a treaty for the consideration of the American Secretary of State. This was to serve as a preliminary basis for negotiations.

This first draft was carefully considered by the Secretary of State of the United States, and, in due course of time, a reply was sent to the Chinese minister, Liang Ch'eng, with a counter draft, in which the proposals made by China in its draft were embodied with such changes as were deemed necessary, to the end that the treaty when concluded should in no wise conflict with the laws of the United States, while at the same time they met all the wishes of the Chinese Government.

These proposals of the American Government were translated by the Chinese minister to his government at Peking, and some three months later—that is to say, the early part of this year—a new draft, embodying some of the modifications suggested by the United States, was received by the American Secretary of State from the Waiwu Pu.

This last draft is still before the American Government and is now the basis on which negotiations between the two governments are being conducted. It is confidently believed that it will enable the two governments who are equally animated by an earnest and sincere desire to remove this question from the field of discussion, and who are conducting the negotiations in the most amicable manner, to reach a final settlement both just and satisfactory to the two nations.

Although it would not be proper at the present stage of the negotiations to disclose the provisions which in one form or another will be incorporated into the treaty when finally agreed upon between the two countries, it may be categorically and emphatically stated that neither by word nor implication has the United States sought to in any way impede the return to the United States of Chinese laborers rightfully entitled so to do, nor to put burdensome restrictions in the way of Chinese subjects not belonging to the laboring classes who may wish to visit the United States or to reside therein for purposes of pleasure or of study. On the contrary, it is the earnest desire of the President and the people of the United States to extend to this latter class of visitors all such courtesies and facilities as they may desire, to become better acquainted with our country, its resources, its industries, its mode of thought, its method of administration, by which knowledge, better than all other means, the relations with China may become closer and even more friendly than they have ever been. It is believed that the proposals which are now being considered by the United States and China looking to this most desirable end will fulfill our expectations and realize the friendly wishes of our President and our people.

CHINA HELD RESPONSIBLE FOR LOSSES TO AMERICAN TRADE. MINISTER ROCK-
HILL TO THE SECRETARY OF STATE, PEKING, AUGUST 17, 1905[3]

Sir: In further confirmation of my cable dispatch of the 12th instant, informing you that I had, under the authority given me by the Department,
informed the Chinese Government that the United States would hold it
directly responsible for all losses our trade or other interests may have incurred
or may hereafter incur on account of its failure to protect us in the rights
guaranteed us under Article XV of our treaty of 1858 [see p. 52]. I inclose
herewith copy of the note addressed to Prince Ch'ing.

I also informed our consuls-general at Shanghai, Canton, and Chefoo of
what I had done, and authorized them to use this information as they deemed
necessary and expedient.

Under date of the 14th instant I again addressed a note to Prince Ch'ing,
demanding that the prime mover in the boycott, a man by the name of Tseng
Shao-ching, president of the Fu-Kien Merchants' Guild of Shanghai, and
holding the rank of prefect (taot'ai), be deprived of his rank and otherwise
punished.

On the same date I also addressed a letter to the foreign office, declining
to further discuss a tentative draft of treaty for regulating the coming of
Chinese to the United States, to be submitted to you, until the present campaign of intimidation was completely put an end to.

I have not at this date received replies to any of the above communications,
but will probably within the next few days.

Our consul-general at Shanghai tells me he has informed the public of my
note of the 14th instant to the foreign office, and that it had produced an
excellent effect. I inclose a Shanghai editorial on this matter, also one from
Chefoo, showing that it has also been well received there.

I beg that the Department will not attach importance to the statements
being made in the ports and in the United States press that the Japanese
Government has had anything to do with encouraging the present anti-
American movement. The conduct of the Japanese Government has been not
only friendly throughout, but their foreign office has done all in its power
to arrest the movement and control the Japanese controlled papers published
in China.

CHINA'S GOVERNMENT ENCOURAGES THE BOYCOTT. MINISTER ROCKHILL TO
PRINCE CH'ING, PEKING, AUGUST 7, 1905[4]

YOUR HIGHNESS: I had the honor in interviews with you in the last two
months of drawing your earnest attention to the very serious nature of the
movement then being openly organized in Shanghai, Canton, and other large
cities of China to interfere with, and, if possible, completely impede American
trade as a means of intimidating the United States Government, which is
seeking to meet with your wishes for a new treaty regulating the coming of
Chinese into the United States and for forcing upon us a repeal of our laws
concerning the exclusion of Chinese laborers.

In several communications which I addressed to you I also insisted on the
danger which might result from failure on the part of the Imperial Government to arrest the movement, which, if carried into effect, would greatly disturb and possibly cause serious loss to trade, breed a spirit of enmity between

[3] *Ibid.*, pp. 212-213. [4] *Ibid.*, pp. 213-214.

the peoples of our respective countries, and perhaps even result in acts of violence.

In conversations with His Excellency Na-tung I have also on several occasions dwelt on the growing gravity of the situation in Shanghai, Canton, and Amoy, and urged on him, as I had on you, that the Imperial Government should take prompt and radical measures for putting an end to the ever-increasing menace to our trade and the perfect cordiality and friendliness which characterized our relations so markedly.

I was answered by your note of July 1 that the high provincial authorities had been urged by you to use their influence with the people to dissuade them from the contemplated organized interference with our trade, but you also stated therein, much to my astonishment:

My board finds upon investigation that this movement has not been inaugurated without some reason, for the restrictions against the Chinese entering America are too ong, and American exclusion laws are extremely inconvenient to the Chinese. The Coolies immigration treaty has been abrogated, but, though the treaty is null and void, the exclusion restrictions are still in force. The great inconvenience suffered by Chinese merchants has thus led to this movement, but if the restrictions can be lightened by your government and a treaty drawn up in a friendly manner then this agitation will of its own accord die out.

I was constrained to conclude from this passage that the movement had a certain amount of sympathy from your highness's government. It is also to be presumed that the orders you informed me had been given out to the provincial authorities in this manner were not of such an emphatic nature as the gravity of the situation required, for the movement went on openly under the guidance and active participation of high officials, and the organization, with the help of threats of violence against the lukewarm and by the use of other methods of pressure, developed rapidly and has now been put in force, especially at Shanghai, Canton, and Amoy.

Recently, on the 24th of July, in an interview with His Excellency Na-tung, when calling his attention to an outrage committed on the premises of our consulate at Amoy on the 18th of July (the day on which the boycott against American trade was put in operation at Shanghai and Amoy), I urged in the most pressing manner that the proclamations should be issued in all localities which had taken up or might later take up this movement to effectively put a stop to it. He promised to confer with you and to urge the adoption of this course; but I have heard nothing from the Waiwu Pu on the matter, neither have I learned that proclamations or any general measures had been taken, either by the Imperial Government or the provincial authorities, adequate to arrest the trouble in time. I must except, however, the Province of Chihli, where measures adopted by the provincial high authorities appear to have arrested it before it could be put in force.

Your highness must be perfectly aware that the prime movers in the agitation are men holding high official positions. I need only cite among them Taot'ai Tseng, the president of the Chamber of Commerce of Shanghai, who has given much time and money to strengthen and develop the movement and has done probably more than any other individual to intensify the feeling of hostility toward my government and people by his false and malicious statements in his eagerness to bring about the boycott. Other officials could be named who, in Shanghai and elsewhere, have taken active part in this campaign of slander and falsehood, but it seems needless at this time to do so. I only refer to the active participation of officials in the movement to show how easy it would have been for the central government to have had stringent orders for the suppression of the movement carried out, if it had been earnestly desirous of doing so.

The President of the United States, justly surprised at the extraordinary supineness the Imperial Government has shown in this matter, which agrees so little with the friendliness he thought he had reason to expect of it, directs me to inform your highness that the Government of the United States will hold it directly responsible for any loss our interests have sustained or may hereafter have to bear through the manifest failure on the part of the Imperial Government to stop the present organized movement against us, which the President considers is allowed to continue in open violation of the rights guaranteed to us by China in Article XV of our treaty of 1858.

COMPILATION OF FACTS CONCERNING THE ENFORCEMENT OF THE CHINESE-EXCLUSION LAWS. SUBMITTED TO THE HOUSE OF REPRESENTATIVES, MAY 18, 1906, BY SECRETARY V. H. METCALF, DEPARTMENT OF COMMERCE[5]

[Extract]

CHAPTER I

Introduction

Prior to the passage of the act of Congress approved June 6, 1900 (31 Stat., 588-611), making appropriations for sundry civil expenses, and for other purposes, by which the Commissioner-General of Immigration was charged, in addition to his other duties, with the administration of the Chinese exclusion laws, the enforcement of the treaty and statutory provisions in which were embodied the exclusion policy of this country was vested in the office of the Secretary of the Treasury. As most of the duties of enforcing the laws devolved upon collectors and deputy collectors of customs located at the various ports of this country, at first the division of customs of the office of the Secretary of the Treasury was invested with general supervisory powers; but at a later date, it is understood because of the extensive character of the other duties with which the said division was charged, this general supervisory power was transferred by the Secretary of the Treasury to the division of his office known as the division of special agents, the supervising special agent being constituted the chief administrative officer, under the Secretary of the Treasury. By this arrangement the various details of administering the laws remained in the hands of the collectors of customs, and it was only in a very general way that the division of special agents exercised its supervisory powers.

The Chinese exclusion laws were then recognized, as they still are, notwithstanding certain changes which have been made in them, as among the most difficult on the statute books to enforce. This condition arose from three causes: First, under the arrangement above described there was a divided responsibility, due to the disconnected official agencies through which the laws were administered, and it was not possible to effect the organization and systematization necessary for even a reasonably thorough enforcement of the

[5] H. Doc. 847: 59-1 (4990).

laws; second, a certain element of the citizenship of this country has never believed in the exclusion policy, being actuated either by strictly interested motives or by the missionary spirit, and the persons forming that element are never willing to assist, and are often ready and glad to oppose, the enforcement of the law; third, the laws relate to a people who, according to all recognized authorities, are deficient in a sense of the moral obligation of an oath, and who in their political views hold caste in higher esteem than law, and are "clannish" to the highest degree.

.   .   .   .

CHAPTER II

Conditions in General

.   .   .   .

Difficulties in Enforcement of Laws.

The reasons which contribute to the difficulty of enforcing the Chinese-exclusion laws are briefly stated in the introductory chapter of this paper (pp. 5, 6.) The experience of the Bureau and its field officers has led them to the conviction that there is a secret but powerful influence always at work in the United States with the object of importing coolies into this country. As pointed out on pages 79 to 80 of the Commissioner-General's last annual report, this obstacle to the enforcement of the laws is all the more serious because it can not be located with precision, nor can the individuals or organizations through which it exerts itself be identified. That it exists there can be no question, for there is no Chinese steerage passenger so destitute that money practically without limit cannot be commanded to pay for his landing in the United States, and he can command legal advice of the most expensive counselors, can purchase witnesses to testify to any state of facts which it is desired to establish, and, if he is rejected, can carry his case through all of the ordinary judicial tribunals, and in many instances into the United States Supreme Court itself.

.   .   .   .

Chinese Compared with Other Aliens

Each year, under the immigration laws, aliens of all nationalities to a number infinitely in excess of the total arrivals of Chinese are annually returned to their native countries, and yet the administrative officers experience practically no difficulty with the deportation of such persons, as compared with the bitterness and persistency with which the rejection of Chinese is always met. Moreover, under the Chinese exclusion laws persons of that race found in this country engaged as laborers and not having in their possession the certificates required by the registration acts must be arrested on warrants sworn out before judicial officers, and are allowed a judicial hearing of their cases, the privilege of appeal to the courts of highest resort being granted, even though the Government itself can not appeal from a decision rendered in favor of the Chinamen by a United States commissioner; whereas, under the immigration laws, aliens of other nationalities found in this country in violation thereof are arrested upon departmental warrants and are granted a hearing before administrative officers, their right of appeal and delay, with its consequent opportunities for preparing a defense, being limited to a review of the hearings by the Department. In this manner, during the last fiscal year, for instance, 845 aliens were arrested and expelled from the United States, almost entirely at the cost of the transportation lines by which they had originally been brought here, and during the same period the United States Government expended approximately $68,000 in deporting 621 Chinese laborers who had been given the benefit, at an additional heavy expense to the United States, of judicial trials.

· · · · · · · · · · · ·

"Safe" Districts for Chinese.

· · · · · · · · · · · ·

During 1904, in conducting several investigations in a district of the "Middle West," a number of Chinamen of the unlawful class were found residing therein, and several arrests were made; but the decision rendered by the district court in one of those cases in September last has resulted in turning that district into a safe one for the Chinese also, for in the said case the court laid down such a broad ruling as to what constitutes a merchant that any Chinese laborer working in a laundry or a restaurant can remain in the district as a member of the mercantile class. An appeal has been taken from that decision, as it was rendered by a district court, not by a commissioner. (Bu. Im. file No. 12016 C.)

· · · · · · · · · · · ·

Commissioners' Certificates of Citizenship

Another serious phase of the situation is the fact that such a large number of Chinamen have been declared by United States commissioners, especially in the districts lying along the Canadian and Mexican borders, to be American citizens by birth, and have been furnished with what are known as "commissioners' certificates," namely, a paper reciting the fact that a Chinaman of such and such a name was brought before them on a certain date and adjudged to be lawfully within the United States, and the fact that so many of these papers have been transferred from hand to hand, altered, forged, and even counterfeited, that it is impossible to determine in many instances whether the holder of such a paper is entitled thereto or not.

· · · · · · · · · · · ·

Opinion of Commissioner-General.

In closing the chapter the following quotation from the annual report of the Commissioner-General for the fiscal year 1905 seems appropriate (pp. 78-79):

In no branch of its widespread activities does the Bureau believe that it has so thoroughly succeeded in carrying into effective operation the purpose of the laws committed to its charge as in the exclusion of Chinese of the classes which it is the professed desire of both this Government and the Empire of China to keep out of the United States. As pointed out in former reports, there are many serious obstacles, both in the circumstances to be dealt with by administrative officers and in the opposition of many citizens of this country to the policy of selecting the Chinese alone as subjects for exclusion, that exact of the Bureau a degree of vigilance and resourcefulness unexampled, it is believed, in the administration of any other legislation on the statute books. Representatives of the large missionary interests do not hesitate to express openly their disapproval of the law or to denounce those whose duty it is to administer the law. The commercial interests of the country, while more prudent and self-restrained in their utterances on the subject, are equally opposed both to the policy and to the means necessarily used to make that policy effective. A large and somewhat vociferous element sympathizes with the foregoing classes. This element is composed in part of those who can not see any greater risk at stake than the probable reduction of the price of labor in this country, of those who are persuaded that Chinese would engage in agricultural labor in the Southern States and constitute a more reliable system than that now available there, and of those who hold the illogical opinion that because alleged undesirable aliens of other races are being allowed to enter the United States this country is compelled by some fancied rule of consistency or propriety to admit other undesirable aliens of the Chinese race.

Of course it is not questioned that all of these persons are entitled to entertain such views, or any views, but the only proper means of giving them expression in law is by a resort to Congress. The course pursued, however, is denunciation of the officers who enforce the law and misrepresentation of their acts, either made in willful disregard of the truth or in ignorance, and published abroad either through the public press or by any other means which promises to secure such frequent repetition as may serve to invest falsehood with a semblance of truth.

.   .   .   .

CHAPTER IV

The Exempt Classes

Section 6 "Merchants"

It is this class, and the next one discussed, "Students," the "harsh treatment" of which it was at first claimed resulted in the boycott. That many so-called "merchants" supplied with section 6 certificates have been rejected is not denied; in fact, the only cause for regret connected with the matter, from the standpoint of an efficient enforcement of the laws, consists in the fact that it was not possible to controvert some certificates held by applicants who were undoubtedly coolies. That any real merchant has been refused admission under a properly issued and viséed certificate has not been shown by any one of the complainants, and it is confidently believed can not be shown.

.   .   .   .

Admission of Students.

With regard to the Chinese students who apply for admission to this country, and concerning whose cases there has been such extensive newspaper comment, it is interesting to know that of 128 such persons applying for admission to this country during the fiscal years 1903, 1904, and 1905, 116 were admitted and 12 were denied landing. Several of those denied were rejected under the provisions of law relating to all aliens found afflicted with loathsome or dangerous contagious diseases, and the remainder were refused admission on grounds similar to those existing in the much more numerous cases of alleged merchants, viz. because their own testimony and personal appearance showed that the certificates were fraudulent.

There are several reasons why the student claim has not been used as extensively as the merchant claim in the endeavor to defeat the laws. In the first place, as is pointed out in the chapter on "Regulations" (p. 33), it became necessary, at an early stage of the enforcement of the law, to define and restrict the term "student"; and, in the second place, it requires a Chinaman of much more intelligence to pose as a student than as a merchant. Cases are not lacking, however, of violations and attempted violations of law by such means. . . .

CHAPTER V

Domiciled Merchants.

.   .   .   .

The subject of the so-called domiciled merchant very early engaged the attention of administrative officers, and has always been a source of difficulty and embarrassment in the endeavor to properly enforce the exclusion laws, and thereby prevent the entry to or residence in this country of Chinese laborers, and at the same time administer no injustice toward the real merchant living in the United States and conducting a bona fide business as such. The following is copied from the annual report of the Commissioner-General of Immigration for the fiscal year ended June 30, 1901 (p. 51):

Of those expressly mentioned among the excepted classes there is perhaps more difficulty with such as claim to be merchants than with the others. Their extravagant and apparently improbable claims to large interests in mercantile houses in China are hard to reconcile with their frquent lack of money or apparent provision of means for their support here. Of the resident merchants, moreover, who seek readmission, much the same statement may be made. Every conceivable device of ingenuity is used to establish a mercantile status. Certificates alleging such status are signed often as a mere matter of accommodation by the white witnesses required by the law, and a nebulous interest in alleged mercantile firms with trivial supplies on hand and numerous partners, all possessing interests of $1,000 each or multiples thereof, lead to the inevitable conclusion that unless the law is amended by requiring more specific evidence, or the term "merchant" is defined more narrowly, the opening made by this exception is wide enough to let in almost any adult Chinaman.

.   .   .   .

Trade in Coolies.

It has also been demonstrated in many instances that Chinese firms in this country are used, not only in the manner above indicated for the purpose of covering the unlawful return to this country of persons already illegally here, but for the purpose of importing laborers from China under the guise of membership therein; in fact, the experience of administrative officers has led them to believe that the chief business of many of these so-called "mercantile houses" is the importation of coolies, from which trade a much larger profit can be derived than by importing Chinese merchandise. The following is copied from page 96 of the Annual Report of the Commissioner-General of Immigration for 1905, from a letter received from the inspector in charge of the district of Texas, with headquarters at El Paso:

In view of recent criticism as to the attitude of immigration officials toward members of the exempt classes, attention is called to the fact that the great majority of those claiming to be exempts are not such in fact; at least such is the case at this station. It is true that there are a number of alleged mercantile establishments whose members are ever ready to file complaints as to their ill treatment by immigration officials. With one or two exceptions, however, it can safely be said that the sole occupation of such firms in El Paso consists of selling opium to members of their own race and unfortunate Americans who have been seduced into the habit, conducting gambling establishments, and dealing in coolies at a profit of about $200 on each one placed in the United States.

Inasmuch as all Chinese persons in El Paso are engaged directly or indirectly in the smuggling of coolies, it is not seen how even those claiming to belong to the exempt classes can be allowed to secrete coolies in their establishments without subjecting themselves to "domiciliary" visits by inspectors. To hold to the contrary would be placing a premium upon smuggling and herding coolies in El Paso by every Chinese person or firm, of any class, owning or renting any kind of an establishment.

The conditions existing in El Paso, as above indicated, while perhaps more general there than in interior localities, are by no means confined to such border towns. In fact, investigations have shown time and again that the chief business of these mercantile houses is the conduct of gambling, lottery, and opium-smoking institutions, in addition to their trade in Chinese coolies.

Importing Prostitutes.

Another nefarious practice which has been detected, although apparently not as extensively engaged in by the alleged domiciled merchant as by the alleged native, is the importation of women from China for sale as slaves to houses of prostitution in this country. A notable case of this character is one which is at the present writing pending at one of the Pacific ports, in which a prominent merchant returned to this country after a visit to his native land accompanied by a woman whom he claimed was his wife. He was not able to establish his marriage to this woman, and while the latter was being held pending the submission by the merchant of further evidence, she made a confession to the effect that she had never been married to him, but that he had purchased her from a house of ill fame in China, and had told her that he intended to bring her to the United States where he would sell her for enough money to pay for the smuggling of his brother into this country, and when he and his brother had accumulated more money they would repurchase her; also, that the said merchant had three wives, all living, in China. This confession was corroborated by an investigation in China, conducted by the vice-consul-general at Canton. (Bu. Im. No. 13830 C.)

.   .   .   .

CHAPTER XI

The Boycott

Character of Boycotters.

The boycott, according to the contention of all parties concerned therein, was organized and carried on by the students and merchants of China because of "harsh treatment" accorded those classes, especially the former, by the officers of this Government. On this point it is not necessary to do more than refer to the figures and accompanying comments, appearing under the two headings "Merchants" and "Students" in the chapter on "The Exempts" (pp. 55, 57, respectively), and further to call attention to the fact that in the section of China from which most of the students come to this country (i.e., northern China), the boycott has amounted to nothing, while in the section from which hail practically all the laborers now in the United States, and who are constantly endeavoring to obtain admission by smuggling or other fraudulent means, the boycott has been actively and effectively operated. It is from the Canton (or Kwong Tung) Province, also, that the most of the so-called mercantile class of this country come—the class which (as shown at p. 60) is so largely interested in the importation of coolies. And, finally, attention is directed to the statements made in the preceding chapter on "Complaints" (p. 125), where each specific instance of alleged harsh treatment is discussed in detail. It is an easy matter, of course, for any person or class of persons to make the general charge that harsh measures have been enforced in an inexcusable manner. To such a general charge it is only possible to enter a general denial. If specific instances are given, the opportunity will be welcomed by the Government to investigate, and in every instance in which the complaint is not shown to be unjustified by the facts (as the majority of those already given have been, and it is confidently believed the most, if not all, that can now by any means be brought forward will be) a punishment appropriate to the offense will be immediately accorded to the guilty parties.

In the light of the contents of this paper, and of the various items of information of an apparently authentic character which have appeared in the public press since the issuance of the last annual report of the Commissioner-General of Immigration, there does not seem to be any good or sufficient reason for modifying in any degree, unless in the direction of making the statement more emphatic, the following comment appearing on page 81 of said report:

In concluding these prefatory remarks, the Bureau expresses the firm conviction that whatever the original source of the present agitation against the enforcement of the exclusion laws may be, the purpose in view will not be content with any modification of present modes of administration, however extensive. An influence sufficiently potent, by using the boycott against a great nation, to secure the relaxation of regulations which have been enforced for years, which are believed to be just and necessary, and which have successfully passed ordeals before the judicial branch of the Government, will have secured assurance that it may likewise influence the legislation of the nation and will be emboldened to demand all it wants—the emasculation, if not repeal, of the exclusion policy.

XXXIV

THE ROOT-TAKAHIRA EXCHANGE OF NOTES, 1908

On November 30, 1908, the United States and Japan exchanged an expression of their identic views regarding policy in the region of the Pacific Ocean and especially regarding China. This exchange was occasioned by a threatened conflict of American and of Japanese interests in Manchuria. Later years were to reveal difficulties in the application of the Root-Takahira policy. Like the later expressions of policy contained in the Lansing-Ishii Notes (1917) and in the Nine-Power Open Door Treaty, it was expressed in the form of principles whose definition and application were to raise unforeseen difficulties.

THE JAPANESE NOTE. AMBASSADOR TAKAHIRA TO SECRETARY ROOT, WASHINGTON, NOVEMBER 30, 1908[1]

SIR:

The exchange of views between us, which has taken place at the several interviews which I have recently had the honor of holding with you, has shown that Japan and the United States holding important outlying insular possessions in the region of the Pacific Ocean, the Governments of the two countries are animated by a common aim, policy, and intention in that region.

Believing that a frank avowal of that aim, policy, and intention would not only tend to strengthen the relations of friendship and good neighborhood, which have immemorially existed between Japan and the United States, but would materially contribute to the preservation of the general peace, the Imperial Government have authorized me to present to you an outline of their understanding of that common aim, policy, and intention:

1. It is the wish of the two Governments to encourage the free and peaceful development of their commerce on the Pacific Ocean.

2. The policy of both Governments, uninfluenced by any aggressive tendencies, is directed to the maintenance of the existing status quo in the region above mentioned and to the defense of the principle of equal opportunity for commerce and industry in China.

3. They are accordingly firmly resolved reciprocally to respect the territorial possessions belonging to each other in said region.

4. They are also determined to preserve the common interest of all powers in China by supporting by all pacific means at their disposal the independence and integrity of China and the principle of equal opportunity for commerce and industry of all nations in that Empire.

5. Should any event occur threatening the status quo as above described

[1] United States, *Treaty Series* [Unnumbered].

or the principle of equal opportunity as above defined, it remains for the two Governments to communicate with each other in order to arrive at an understanding as to what measures they may consider it useful to take.

If the foregoing outline accords with the view of the Government of the United States, I shall be gratified to receive your confirmation. . . .

THE AMERICAN NOTE. SECRETARY ROOT TO AMBASSADOR TAKAHIRA, WASHINGTON, NOVEMBER 30, 1908

EXCELLENCY:

I have the honor to acknowledge the receipt of your note of to-day setting forth the result of the exchange of views between us in our recent interviews defining the understanding of the two Governments in regard to their policy in the region of the Pacific Ocean.

It is a pleasure to inform you that this expression of mutual understanding is welcome to the Government of the United States as appropriate to the happy relations of the two countries and as the occasion for a concise mutual affirmation of that accordant policy respecting the Far East which the two Governments have so frequently declared in the past.

I am happy to be able to confirm to Your Excellency on behalf of the United States, the declaration of the two Governments embodied in the following words:

1. It is the wish of the two Governments to encourage the free and peaceful development of their commerce on the Pacific Ocean.

2. The policy of both Governments, uninfluenced by any aggressive tendencies, is directed to the maintenance of the existing status quo in the region above mentioned, and to the defense of the principle of equal opportunity for commerce and industry in China.

3. They are accordingly firmly resolved reciprocally to respect the territorial possessions belonging to each other in said region.

4. They are also determined to preserve the common interests of all powers in China by supporting by all pacific means at their disposal the independence and integrity of China and the principle of equal opportunity for commerce and industry of all nations in that Empire.

5. Should any event occur threatening the status quo as above described or the principle of equal opportunity as above defined, it remains for the two Governments to communicate with each other in order to arrive at an understanding as to what measures they may consider it useful to take. . . .

XXXV

THE KNOX NEUTRALIZATION PROPOSAL FOR MANCHURIAN RAILWAYS, 1909

LATE IN 1909 Secretary of State Philander Knox sought a solution of the so-called Manchurian problem through what is usually referred to as his neutralization proposal. It was his hope to end the predominant position of Japan and Russia in Manchuria by enabling China to purchase from these powers the Japanese-owned South Manchuria Railway and the Russian-owned Chinese Eastern. He hoped likewise to ease Russian and Japanese resentment occasioned by the proposal of British and American interests to construct a railroad from Chinchow to Aigun, the obvious purpose of which was to compete with the Japanese and Russian lines. The formal character of the Knox proposal, an unsuccessful venture in the sphere of dollar diplomacy, is given in the following note to Great Britain.

THE KNOX NEUTRALIZATION PROPOSAL. SECRETARY KNOX TO AMBASSADOR REID, WASHINGTON, NOVEMBER 6, 1909[1]

In reply to Sir Edward Grey's inquiries reported in his telegram of October 20, Mr. Reid is instructed to present to the foreign office textually the following memorandum:

Now that there has been signed and ratified by an unpublished imperial decree an agreement by which the American and British interests are to cooperate in the financing and construction of the Chinchow-Tsitsihar-Aigun Railroad, the Government of the United States is prepared cordially to cooperate with His Britannic Majesty's Government in diplomatically supporting and facilitating this enterprise, so important alike to the progress and to the commercial development of China. The Government of the United States would be disposed to favor ultimate participation to a proper extent on the part of other interested powers whose inclusion might be agreeable to China and which are known to support the principle of equality of commercial opportunity and the maintenance of the integrity of the Chinese Empire. However, before the further elaboration of the actual arrangement, the Government of the United States asks His Britannic Majesty's Government to give their consideration to the following alternative and more comprehensive projects: First, perhaps the most effective way to preserve the undisturbed enjoyment by China of all political rights in Manchuria and to promote the development of those Provinces under a practical application of the policy of the open door and

[1] *Foreign Relations*, 1910, p. 234.

equal commercial opportunity would be to bring the Manchurian highways, the railroads, under an economic, scientific, and impartial administration by some plan vesting in China the ownership of the railroads
through funds furnished for that purpose by the interested powers willing
to participate. Such loan should be for a period ample to make it reasonably certain that it could be met within the time fixed and should be upon
such terms as would make it attractive to bankers and investors. The plan
should provide that nationals of the participating powers should super-
vise the railroad system during the term of the loan and the governments
concerned should enjoy for such period the usual preferences for their
nationals and materials upon an equitable basis inter se. The execution
of such a plan would naturally require the cooperation of China and of
Japan and Russia, the reversionary and the concessionaries, respectively,
of the existing Manchurian railroads, as well as that of Great Britain and
the United States, whose special interests rest upon the existing contract
relative to the Chinchow-Aigun Railroad. The advantages of such a plan
to Japan and to Russia are obvious. Both those powers, desiring in good
faith to protect the policy of the open door and equal opportunity in Manchuria and wishing to assure to China unimpaired sovereignty, might well
be expected to welcome an opportunity to shift the separate duties, responsibilities, and expenses they have undertaken in the protection of their
respective commercial and other interests, for impartial assumption by the
combined powers, including themselves, in proportion to their interests.
The Government of the United States has some reason to hope that such
a plan might meet favorable consideration on the part of Russia and has
reason to believe that American financial participation would be forthcoming. Second, should this suggestion not be found feasible in its entirety,
then the desired end would be approximated, if not attained, by Great
Britain and the United States diplomatically supporting the Chinchow-
Aigun arrangement and inviting the interested powers friendly to complete
commercial neutralization of Manchuria to participate in the financing and
construction of that line and of such additional lines as future commercial
development may demand, and at the same time to supply funds for the
purchase by China of such of the existing lines as might be offered for
inclusion in this system. The Government of the United States hopes that
the principle involved in the foregoing suggestions may commend itself to
His Britannic Majesty's Government. That principle finds support in the
additional reasons that the consummation of some such plan would avoid
the irritations likely to be engendered by the uncontrolled direct negotiations of bankers with the Chinese Government, and also that it would
create such a community of substantial interest in China as would facilitate a cooperation calculated to simplify the problems of fiscal and mon-
etary reforms now receiving such earnest attention by the Imperial Chinese
Government.

XXXVI

THE FINANCIAL POLICY OF THE UNITED STATES IN CHINA, 1913

PRESIDENT WILSON, on March 18, 1913, made a declaration of United States policy regarding China which altered radically the course which had been followed by the Taft administration. The conditions in which the Taft administration was prepared to give its support to American bankers in the Six-Power Consortium were regarded by the Wilson administration as endangering its conception of the so-called open door policy.

PRESIDENT WILSON AND THE SIX-POWER CONSORTIUM. THE ACTING SECRETARY OF STATE (ADEE) TO CERTAIN AMERICAN DIPLOMATIC OFFICERS, WASHINGTON, MARCH 19, 1913[1]

[Telegram]

Only for your information and guidance, I quote the following statement issued by the President:

"We are informed that at the request of the last administration a certain group of American bankers undertook to participate in the loan now desired by the Government of China (approximately $125,000,000). Our Government wished American bankers to participate along with the bankers of other nations, because it desired that the good will of the United States toward China should be exhibited in this practical way, that American capital should have access to that great country, and that the United States should be in a position to share with the other powers any political responsibilities that might be associated with the development of the foreign relations of China in connection with her industrial and commercial enterprises. The present administration has been asked by this group of bankers whether it would also request them to participate in the loan. The representatives of the bankers through whom the administration was approached declared that they would continue to seek their share of the loan under the proposed agreements only if expressly requested to do so by the Government. The administration has declined to make such a request, because it did not approve the conditions of the loan or the implications of responsibility on its own part which it was plainly told would be involved in the request.

"The conditions of the loan seem to us to touch very nearly the administrative independence of China itself, and this administration does not feel that it ought, even by implication, to be a party to those conditions. The responsibility on its part which would be implied in requesting the bankers to undertake the loan might conceivably go the length in some unhappy con-

[1] *Foreign Relations*, 1913, pp. 170-171.

tingency of forcible interference in the financial, and even the political, affairs of that great oriental State, just now awakening to a consciousness of its power and of its obligations to its people. The conditions include not only the pledging of particular taxes, some of them antiquated and burdensome, to secure the loan, but also the administration of those taxes by foreign agents. The responsibility on the part of our Government implied in the encouragement of a loan thus secured and administered is plain enough and is obnoxious to the principles upon which the government of our people rests.

"The Government of the United States is not only willing, but earnestly desirous, of aiding the great Chinese people in every way that is consistent with their untrammeled development and its own immemorial principles. The awakening of the people of China to a consciousness of their responsibilities under free government is the most significant, if not the most momentous, event of our generation. With this movement and aspiration the American people are in profound sympathy. They certainly wish to participate, and participate very generously, in the opening to the Chinese and to the use of the world the almost untouched and perhaps unrivaled resources of China.

"The Government of the United States is earnestly desirous of promoting the most extended and intimate trade relationship between this country and the Chinese Republic. The present administration will urge and support the legislative measures necessary to give American merchants, manufacturers, contractors, and engineers the banking and other financial facilities which they now lack and without which they are at a serious disadvantage as compared with their industrial and commercial rivals. This is its duty. This is the main material interest of its citizens in the development of China. Our interests are those of the open door—a door of friendship and mutual advantage. This is the only door we care to enter."

XXXVII

CONDITIONS OF CONSULTATION BETWEEN THE UNITED STATES AND JAPAN RELATIVE TO AFFAIRS IN CHINA, 1914

THE OUTBREAK of the World War and Japan's ultimatum to Germany relative to Kiaochow occasioned a correspondence between the State Department and its diplomatic representatives in Tokyo and Peking which clarified the character of American policy with special reference to the Root-Takahira Notes of 1908.

THE UNITED STATES AND THE WAR IN THE FAR EAST. SECRETARY BRYAN TO AMBASSADOR GUTHRIE (JAPAN), WASHINGTON, AUGUST 14, 1914[1]

[Telegram]

Your cipher telegram of August 15, midnight. In reply to the statement of the Japanese Minister for Foreign Affairs you will communicate to him textually the following:

The American Government, while regretting that differences have arisen between the Imperial Japanese Government and the Imperial German Government which may eventuate in war, does not, in accordance with its policy of strict neutrality in relation to disputes between other nations, express any opinion as to the merits of the differences. It, however, notes with satisfaction that Japan, in demanding the surrender by Germany of the entire leased territory of Kiaochow, does so with the purpose of restoring that territory to China, and that Japan is seeking no territorial aggrandizement in China in the movement now contemplated, but is acting in strict pursuance of the alliance with Great Britain. It is recalled that one of the aims of that alliance is declared to be "the preservation of the common interest of all powers in China by insuring the independence and integrity of China and the principle of equal opportunities for the commerce and industry of all nations in China." Should disturbances in the interior of China seem to the Japanese Government to require measures to be taken by Japan or other powers to restore order, the Imperial Japanese Government will no doubt desire to consult with the American Government before deciding upon a course of action. This would be in accordance with the agreement made in the exchange of notes on the 30th of November, 1908 [see p. 243] by His Excellency, Baron Kogoro Takahira, then Japanese Ambassador to the United States, and Hon. Elihu Root, the American Secretary of State.

Repeat to Peking as strictly confidential for information only.

[1] *Foreign Relations*, 1914 (Supplement), p. 172.

MacMurray Interprets the Root-Takahira Notes. The U. S. Chargé in China to the Secretary of State, Peking, September 10, 1914[2]

.   .   .   .

This matter of maintaining its sovereignty, as involved in the question of neutrality, has been one of much solicitude and anxiety to the Chinese Government. It would seem that, during the first weeks of the war, even the more serious and responsible of the Chinese were deluded by the rumors which were disseminated from Japanese sources to the effect that the American Government was preparing to act in opposition to Japanese interests in China; and upon that delusion they founded extravagant hopes that the United States would undertake to guarantee China against any territorial aggression or disregard of its sovereignty. The publication, in the Reuter News Service, of the substance of the note with which the American Government acknowledged the Japanese communication of the ultimatum to Germany (embodied in the instruction to the Tokyo Embassy, August 19, 2 p.m.) synchronized with a sudden and almost complete cessation of the anti-American agitation in the press controlled by Japanese influences. On the other hand, the suggestion of consultation between the American and Japanese Governments, in pursuance of the Root-Takahira exchange of notes of 1908, seems to have been interpreted in some Chinese quarters as indicating a determination on the part of our Government to insist upon its approval as a condition precedent to any Japanese action in Chinese territory. On the 27th ultimo Dr. V. K. Wellington Koo, of the Wai Chiao Pu, called upon me informally, professedly at the instance of the President, to inquire as to the precise terms and purport of the American note. I enclose herewith a copy of the paraphrase which I subsequently furnished to him in accordance with the Department's telegraphic authorization of August 27, 5 p.m. In discussing the matter with me, Dr. Koo strongly intimated the view that the Root-Takahira exchange of notes established in favor of the United States a right to be consulted with respect to any action contemplated by Japan in Chinese territories, as though to imply that such rights were held by our Government in trust for the Government of China; and he specified the possible landing of an expeditionary force in Shantung (beyond the limits of the zone of condominium established by the treaty of lease of the Kiaochow territory) as constituting a question in regard to which the Japanese Government would thereby be required to seek the approval of the United States. Not knowing how peremptorily our Government is disposed to insist upon its suggestion that the Japanese Government would doubtless desire to consult our own in the event that it should judge the situation here to require action, I pointed out to Dr. Koo that that suggestion in terms concerns only the case of internal disorders in China; and I furthermore reminded him that the Root-Takahira exchange of notes, although frequently referred to for convenience as an agreement, was in fact simply a joint declaration of policy rather than a convention establishing a legal status which either party might invoke against the other.

.   .   .   .

[2] *Ibid.*, pp. 186-187.

MacMurray's Interpretation of the Root-Takahira Notes Confirmed.
The Acting Secretary of State (Lansing) to the Minister in China
(Reinsch), Washington, November 4, 1914[3]

.   .   .   .

Mr. MacMurray's analysis of the situation appears to the Department to be quite correct. While regretting that the wars which have unfortunately broken out in Europe have involved the Far East in hostilities, the Department realizes that the belligerents could hardly hope to keep their leased territories in China free from attack, since they partake of the nature of military bases. The international settlements, however, at the open ports of China, are regarded as belonging to an entirely different category. These settlements with their cosmopolitan population, the Department believes should be by general consent entirely excluded from the field of military operations.

In view of the possibilities of internal disorders in China threatening the safety of life and property in these settlements, the American Government desires to do what it can with the consent of other interested powers to assist in the protection of these settlements, but the Legation must realize that the forces at the disposal of the Government for such purposes are limited.

.   .   .   .

Reference was made in the despatch under acknowledgment to the Department's telegraphic instruction to Tokyo of August 19, 2 p.m., in reply to the communication notifying the United States of Japan's ultimatum to Germany. Mr. MacMurray, in his conversation with Dr. Koo, interpreted very correctly the reference to the Root-Takahira exchange of notes. The Department had reason to fear that the military operations undertaken against Tsingtao might lead to misunderstandings or that the revolutionists who were reported to be planning to take advantage of the situation might foment disturbances elsewhere in China and that a condition of affairs might arise which would invite, if not require, foreign intervention to restore order and therefore in its reply to the Japanese memorandum, it recalled the Root-Takahira exchange of notes to assure the Japanese Government that should the *status quo* in China be threatened the Department relied in full confidence upon Japan's willingness to consult with the United States.

With respect to other questions raised in the despatch you are instructed that, while the Department desires, of course, to safeguard all American rights in China, to protect all legitimate American interests there and to promote by all proper methods the development of American trade, it is at the same time anxious that there shall be no misunderstanding of its aims by the Chinese Government. The United States desires China to feel that American friendship is sincere and to be assured that this Government will be glad to exert any influence, which it possesses, to further, by peaceful methods, the welfare of the Chinese people, but the Department realizes that it would be quixotic in the extreme to allow the question of China's territorial integrity to entangle the United States in international difficulties.

[3] *Ibid.*, pp. 189-190.

XXXVIII

TREATY PROVIDING FOR A PERMANENT INTERNATIONAL COMMISSION, 1914

On September 15, 1914, a treaty for the advancement of the general cause of peace was concluded between the United States and China. This treaty provided in certain cases for investigation and report by a permanent international commission.

The United States and China. Treaty for the Advancement of the General Cause of Peace. September 15, 1914[1]

ARTICLE I.

Any disputes arising between the Government of the United States of America and the Government of the Republic of China, of whatever nature they may be, shall, when ordinary diplomatic proceedings have failed and the High Contracting Parties do not have recourse to arbitration, be submitted for investigation and report to a Permanent International Commission constituted in the manner prescribed in the following article.

The High Contracting Parties agree not to resort, with respect to each other, to any act of force during the investigation to be made by the Commission and before its report is handed in.

ARTICLE II.

The International Commission shall be composed of five members appointed as follows: Each Government shall designate two members, only one of whom shall be of its own nationality; the fifth member shall be designated by common consent and shall not belong to any of the nationalities already represented on the Commission; he shall perform the duties of President.

In case the two Governments should be unable to agree on the choice of the fifth commissioner, the other four shall be called upon to designate him, and failing an understanding between them, the provisions of article 45 of The Hague Convention of 1907 shall be applied.

The Commission shall be organized within six months from the exchange of ratifications of the present convention.

The members shall be appointed for one year and their appointment may be renewed. They shall remain in office until superseded or reappointed, or until the work on which they are engaged at the time their office expires is completed.

Any vacancies which may arise (from death, resignation, or cases of physical or moral incapacity) shall be filled within the shortest possible period in the manner followed for the original appointment.

[1] S. Doc. 348: 67-4 (8167), pp. 2514-2517.

The High Contracting Parties shall, before designating the commissioners, reach an understanding in regard to their compensation. They shall bear by halves the expenses incident to the meeting of the Commission.

ARTICLE III.

In case a dispute should arise between the High Contracting Parties which is not settled by the ordinary methods, each Party shall have a right to ask that the investigation thereof be intrusted to the International Commission charged with making a report. Notice shall be given to the President of the International Commission, who shall at once communicate with his colleagues.

In the same case the President may, after consulting his colleagues and upon receiving the consent of a majority of the members of the Commission, offer the services of the latter to each of the Contracting Parties. Acceptance of that offer declared by one of the two Governments shall be sufficient to give jurisdiction of the case to the Commission in accordance with the foregoing paragraph.

The place of meeting shall be determined by the Commission itself.

ARTICLE IV.

The two High Contracting Parties shall have a right, each on its own part, to state to the President of the Commission what is the subject matter of the controversy. No difference in these statements, which shall be furnished by way of suggestion, shall arrest the action of the Commission.

In case the cause of the dispute should consist of certain acts already committed or about to be committed, the Commission shall as soon as possible indicate what measures to preserve the rights of each party ought in its opinion to be taken provisionally and pending the delivery of its report.

ARTICLE V.

As regards the procedure which it is to follow, the Commission shall as far as possible be guided by the provisions contained in articles 9 to 36 of Convention 1 of The Hague of 1907.

The High Contracting Parties agree to afford the Commission all means and all necessary facilities for its investigation and report.

The work of the Commission shall be completed within one year from the date on which it has taken jurisdiction of the case, unless the High Contracting Parties should agree to set a different period.

The conclusion of the Commission and the terms of its report shall be adopted by a majority. The report, signed only by the President acting by virtue of his office, shall be transmitted by him to each of the Contracting Parties.

The High Contracting Parties reserve full liberty as to the action to be taken on the report of the Commission.

ARTICLE VI.

The present treaty shall be ratified by the President of the United States of America, with the advice and consent of the Senate of the United States, and by the President of the Republic of China.

It shall go into force immediately after the exchange of ratifications and shall last five years.

Unless denounced six months at least before the expiration of the said period of five years, it shall remain in force until the expiration of a period of twelve months after either party shall have notified the other of its intention to terminate it.

In witness whereof the respective plenipotentiaries have signed the present treaty and have affixed thereunto their seals.

Done at Washington this 15th day of September, in the year nineteen hundred and fourteen, corresponding to the 15th day of the ninth month in the third year of the Republic of China.

[SEAL]   WILLIAM JENNINGS BRYAN.

Signature and seal of Chinese Plenipotentiary.

[KAI FU SHAH]

XXXIX

THE OPEN DOOR PRINCIPLE VERSUS "SPECIAL RELATIONS" AND "SPECIAL INTERESTS," 1915-1919

SINCE 1915 it has been increasingly difficult for the United States and Japan to reconcile their policies toward China. Both nations professed to adhere to the popular principle called the open door. In 1915, however, the United States conceded that Japan possessed "special relations" with contiguous portions of Chinese territory. The Lansing-Ishii Notes (1917) referred to Japan's "special interests" in China. Japanese governments have tended to interpret these phrases as conceding to Japan a special "political" interest. The United States has insisted that they implied nothing more than a natural interest depending on geographical contiguity. The fullest statement of the American view is contained in the Bryan note of March 13, 1915, relative to Japan's Twenty-one Demands.

THE UNITED STATES AND THE TWENTY-ONE DEMANDS. SECRETARY BRYAN TO THE JAPANESE AMBASSADOR, WASHINGTON, MARCH 13, 1915[1]

EXCELLENCY: On February 8 last your excellency left with me at the Department a memorandum setting forth the demands which the Imperial Japanese Government felt obliged to make upon China, and on the 22d of the same month your excellency delivered to me an additional memorandum presenting certain "requests" affecting the relations between the two countries which the Imperial Government has urged China to consider.

The American Government is glad to learn from these two communications of the Imperial Government that the "requests" were not presented to China as "demands" but that they were but "wishes" for which "friendly consideration" was asked on the part of China. The American Government understands from this distinction between the "demands" and the "requests" that the latter are not to be pressed if the Chinese Government should decline to consider them.

Inasmuch as these requests appear to have a bearing upon the traditional attitude of both the United States and Japan towards China, I desire to present to your excellency the following considerations of the Government of the United States relative to the effect which, it is thought, these demands and requests may have upon the relations of the United States with the Chinese Republic.

Reciprocating the frank and friendly character of the statements of the Imperial Japanese Government, the Government of the United States of

[1] *Foreign Relations*, 1915, pp. 105-111.

America believes that an expression of its views with respect to these matters will be received by the Imperial Government in the same friendly spirit in which it is offered.

It will be recalled that in the year 1899 the Government of the United States requested the Governments of France, Germany, Great Britain, Italy, Russia and Japan to give their formal consent to three proposals:

First. They will in no way interfere with any treaty port or any vested interest within any so-called "sphere of interest" or leased territory they may have in China.

Second. The Chinese treaty tariff of the time being shall apply to all merchandise landed or shipped to all such ports as are within said "sphere of interest" (unless they be "free ports"), no matter to what nationality it may belong, and that duties so leviable shall be collected by the Chinese Government.

Third. They will levy no higher harbor dues on vessels of another nationality frequenting any port in such "sphere" than shall be levied on vessels of their own nationality, and no higher railroad charges over lines built, controlled, or operated within such "sphere" on merchandise belonging to citizens or subjects of other nationalities transported through such "sphere" than shall be levied on similar merchandise belonging to their own nationals transported over equal distances.

On December 26, 1899, the Minister for Foreign Affairs addressed a note to the American Minister at Tokyo assuring the Minister—

that the Imperial Government will have no hesitation to give their assent to so just and fair a proposal of the United States, provided that all the other Powers concerned shall accept the same.

A similar acceptance was given on behalf of the other Powers approached.

On July 3, 1900, having been consulted by other Powers as to the course to be pursued in China as a result of the Boxer disturbances, this Government expressed its views in a circular communication to Austria-Hungary, France, Germany, Great Britain, Italy, Japan and Russia, stating that—

the policy of the Government of the United States is to seek a solution which may bring about permanent safety and peace to China, preserve Chinese territorial and administrative entity, protect all rights guaranteed to friendly Powers by treaty and international law, and safeguard for the world the principle of equal and impartial trade with all parts of the Chinese Empire.

In reply the Minister for Foreign Affairs of the Imperial Government expressed through the American Minister at Tokyo views in accord with those of the United States Government.

In the following month Great Britain and Germany signed an agreement defining their mutual policy in China:

I. It is a matter of joint and permanent international interest that the ports on the rivers and littoral of China should remain free and open to trade and to every other legitimate form of economic activity for the nationals of all countries without distinction, and the two Governments agree on their part to uphold the same for all Chinese territory so far as they can exercise influence.

II. Her Britannic Majesty's Government and the Imperial German Government will not on their part make use of the present complication to obtain for themselves any territorial advantages in Chinese dominions and will direct their policy towards maintaining undiminished the territorial conditions of the Chinese Empire.

This agreement being communicated by those Powers to Japan was acknowledged by the Imperial Government in a note containing the following language:

The Imperial Government having been assured by the contracting Powers that in adhering to the agreement in question they would be placed in relation to it in the same position as if they had been a signatory thereto, do not hesitate to declare formally their adherence to the said agreement and their acceptance of the principles embodied therein.

In 1901, when the Manchurian Convention was being negotiated by the Russian and Chinese Governments, involving the grant of certain exclusive privileges relating to the opening of mines and the building of railroads in Manchuria, the Japanese Minister called on the Secretary of State of the United States and said that the Japanese Government considered that the convention was a most undesirable thing because it was a violation of the understanding among all the Powers that the integrity of the Chinese Empire should be preserved, and that the Japanese Government was anxious that some means should be taken by the different Powers to induce China to delay the final signature of the convention beyond the period assigned by Russia as an ultimatum for signing.

On the same subject a circular note was sent by the United States to Belgium, China, France, Germany, Great Britain, Italy, Japan, the Netherlands, Russia and Spain, as follows:

An agreement by which China cedes to any corporation or company the exclusive right and privilege of opening mines, establishing railroads, or in any other way industrially developing Manchuria, can but be viewed with the gravest concern by the Government of the United States. It constitutes a monopoly, which is a distinct breach of the stipulations of treaties concluded between China and foreign Powers, and thereby seriously affects the rights of American citizens; it restricts their rightful trade and exposes it to being discriminated against, interfered with or otherwise jeopardized, and strongly tends towards permanently impairing the sovereign rights of China in this part of the Empire, and seriously interferes with her ability to meet her international obligations. Furthermore, such concession on the part of China will undoubtedly be followed by demands from other Powers for similar and equally exclusive advantages in other parts of the Chinese Empire, and the inevitable result must be the complete wreck of the policy of absolute equality of treatment of all nations in regard to trade, navigation, and commerce within the confines of the Empire.

On the other hand, the attainment by one Power of such exclusive privileges for a commercial organization of its nationality conflicts with the assurances repeatedly conveyed to this Government by the Imperial Russian Ministry of Foreign Affairs of the Imperial Government's intention to follow the policy of the open door in China, as advocated by the Government of the United States and accepted by all the Treaty Powers having commercial interests in that Empire.

It is for these reasons that the Government of the United States, animated now, as in the past, with the sincerest desire of insuring to the whole world the benefits of full and fair intercourse between China and the nations on a footing of equal rights and advantages to all, submits the above to the earnest consideration of the Imperial Governments of China and Russia, confident that they will give due weight to its importance and adopt such measures as will relieve the just and natural anxiety of the United States.

The foregoing constitute the beginnings of the policy of the United States and other Powers interested in the welfare of China for the maintenance of the territorial integrity and administrative entity of China, and equal opportunities in commerce and industries in her behalf. To this policy the Powers have generally given their formal acceptance and support.

It is only necessary to refer to the British-Japanese Treaty of 1902, the Japanese Declarations at the opening of the Russo-Japanese war, the British-Japanese Treaty of 1905, The Russo-Japanese Treaty of Portsmouth, of 1905, the Franco-Japanese Entente of 1907, and the Russo-Japanese Treaty of 1907, in which Japan confirmed her special interest in maintaining the political independence and territorial integrity of the Empire of China, and in securing equal opportunities to all nations in the commercial and industrial development of China.

Finally, the United States and Japan declared their policy in the Far East by an exchange of notes on November 30, 1908, between the Honorable Elihu Root, then Secretary of State, and Baron Kogoro Takahira, the Ambassador of Japan. These notes contain the following language:

4. They are also determined to preserve the common interest of all Powers in China by supporting by all pacific means at their disposal the independence and integrity of China and the principle of equal opportunity for commerce and industry of all nations in that Empire.

5. Should any event occur threatening the status quo as above described or the principle of equal opportunity as above defined, it remains for the two Governments to communicate with each other in order to arrive at an understanding as to what measures they may consider useful to take.

I assume that it is because they wish to act in the spirit of this agreement to communicate with each other in reference to any event which may threaten these principles that your excellency's Government has informed this Government of the above-mentioned proposals which have been made to China. It is with the same purpose also, and on the further ground that the United States feels itself under a moral obligation to the Powers whose pledges are deposited with it not to pass over in silence any threatened violation of these pledges, that I address this communication to you with a view to carrying out the agreement of 1908 in accordance with that mutual regard and friendship which inspired it.

The United States, confident that the principle of mutuality will be preserved by Japan, believes that it may rely upon the often repeated assurances of your excellency's Government relative to the independence, integrity and commerce of China, and that no steps will be taken contrary to the spirit of those assurances.

For two generations American missionaries and teachers have made sacrifices in behalf of religious and educational work in China. American capital has been invested and industries have been established in certain regions. The activity of Americans has never been political, but on the contrary has been primarily commercial with no after thought as to their effect upon the governmental policy of China. As an outgrowth of these two interests Americans have become concerned in the legitimate participation in the economic development of China along broader lines. Many projects which in other countries are left to private enterprise are in China conducted necessarily under government direction. United States citizens and capital are thus engaged in certain public improvements, such as the Huai River conservancy, the Hukuang Railway project, etc. A fourth matter of great moment to the United States is its broad and extensive treaty rights with China. These in general relate to commercial privileges and to the protection of Americans in China. In view of these treaty rights and its increasing economic interests in China, this Government had noted with grave concern certain of the suggestions which Japan has, in the present critical stage of the growth and development of the new Republic, considered it advisable to lay before the Chinese Government. While on principle and under the treaties of 1844, 1858, 1868, and 1903 with China the United States has ground upon which to base objections to the Japanese "demands" relative to Shantung, South Manchuria, and East Mongolia, nevertheless the United States frankly recognizes that territorial contiguity creates special relations between Japan and these districts. This Government therefore, is disposed to raise no question, at this time, as to Articles I and II of the Japanese proposals. Further, as to Article IV, and Article V, paragraphs 2, 5 and 7, this Government perceives no special menace to the existing rights and interests of the United States or of its citizens, in China. On the other hand Article V, paragraph 4, restricting the purchase of arms and ammunition to purchases from Japan, and paragraph 6 contemplating a monopoly of the development of the province of Fukien, the United States Government considers, would, if they should become operative, be violations of the principle of equal opportunity for the commerce and industry of other nations. American citizens may claim a right to share in the commercial development not only in Fukien but in other provinces as well. The United States is not unmindful that many serious disadvantages would result to its commercial and industrial enterprises if special preference is given to one nation in the matter of concessions. An example is shown in the operation of the South Manchuria Railway whereby discriminations have been made for some time against freight brought into Manchuria in other than Japanese vessels. This case indicates the embarrassing results of concessions of a broad preference or option. The United States, as well as every other nation, has the right to have its citizens free to make contracts with the Central and Provincial Governments without having the exercise of their rights interrupted or regarded as unfriendly by a third power; for each American enterprise in China is treated on its own merits as to its usefulness and prospective benefit, and without any regard to the possible effect it might have on China's future political status in the Orient.

The rights and privileges, which are set forth in these two paragraphs and which Japan seeks to obtain from China, are in conflict with rights of Americans secured by treaties between the United States and China.

Article XV of the Treaty of 1844 reads as follows:

The former limitation of the trade of foreign nations to certain persons appointed at Canton by the Government and commonly called Hong-merchants, having been abolished, citizens of the United States, engaged in the purchase or sale of goods of import or export, are admitted to trade with any and all subjects of China without distinction; they shall not be subject to any new limitations, nor impeded in their business by monopolies or other injurious restrictions.

Article XXX of the Treaty of 1858 reads as follows:

The contracting parties hereby agree that should at any time the Ta Tsing Empire grant to any nation or the merchants or citizens of any nations, any right, privilege or favor, connected either with navigation, commerce, political or other intercourse which is not conferred by this treaty, such right, privilege and favor shall at once freely enure to the benefit of the United States, its public officers, merchants and citizens.

Article VIII of the treaty of 1868 reads as follows:

The United States, always disclaiming and discouraging all practices of unnecessary dictation and intervention by one nation in the affairs or domestic administration of another, do hereby freely disclaim and disavow any intention or right to intervene in the domestic administration of China in regard to the construction of railroads, telegraphs or other material internal improvements. On the other hand, his Majesty, the Emperor of China, reserves to himself the right to decide the time and manner and circumstances of introducing such improvements within his dominions. With this mutual understanding it is agreed by the contracting parties that if at any time hereafter his Imperial Majesty shall determine to construct or cause to be constructed works of the character mentioned within the empire, and shall make application to the United States or any other western Power for facilities to carry out that policy, the United States will, in that case, designate and authorize suitable engineers to be employed by the Chinese Government, and will recommend to other nations an equal compliance with such application, the Chinese Government in that case protecting such engineers in their persons and property, and paying them a reasonable compensation for their service.

Articles III and VII of the Treaty of 1903 read as follows:

Article III.   Citizens of the United States may frequent, reside and carry on trade, industries and manufactures, or pursue any lawful avocation, in all the ports or localities of China which are now open or may hereafter be opened to foreign residence and trade; and, within the suitable localities at those places which have been or may be set apart for the use and occupation of foreigners, they may rent or purchase houses, places of business and other buildings, and rent or lease in perpetuity land and build thereon. They shall generally enjoy as to their persons and property all such rights, privileges and immunities as are or may hereafter be granted to the subjects or citizens of the nation the most favored in these respects.

Article VII.   The Chinese Government, recognizing that it is advantageous for the country to develop its mineral resources, and that it is desirable to attract foreign as well as Chinese capital to embark in mining enterprises, agrees, within one year from the signing of this treaty, to initiate and conclude the revision of the existing mining regulations. To this end China will, with all expedition and earnestness, go into the whole question of mining rules; and, selecting from the rules of the United States and other countries regulations which seem applicable to the condition of China, will recast its present mining rules in such a way as, while promoting the interests of Chinese subjects and not injuring in any way the sovereign rights of China, will offer no impediment to the attraction of foreign capital nor place foreign capitalists at a greater disadvantage than they would be under generally accepted foreign regulations; and will permit citizens of the United States to carry on in Chinese territory mining operations and other necessary business relating thereto provided they comply with the new regulations and conditions which will be imposed by China on its subjects and foreigners alike, relating to the opening of mines, the renting of mineral land, and the payment of royalty, and provided they apply for permits, the provisions of which in regard to necessary business relating to such operations shall be observed. The residence of citizens of the United States in connection with such mining operations shall be subject to such regulations as shall be agreed upon by and between the United States and China.

Any mining concessions granted after the publication of such new rules shall be subject to their provisions.

It is manifest that these articles including "most favored nation" treatment entitle Americans to claim from China the same rights as those which Japan now seeks to have granted exclusively to her subjects.

It remains to call attention to Article III forbidding the alienation or lease of any port, harbor or island on the coast of China, and to Article V, paragraph 1, requiring China to employ competent Japanese subjects as advisers for conducting administrative, financial and military affairs, and paragraph 3 suggesting the joint policing of China, "where it is deemed necessary."

With reference to the first of these three proposals, Baron Kato has explained to the American Ambassador at Tokyo that Japan has no desire for a naval station on the coast of China, either at Tsingtau, or south of that point, as it would be valueless to her, but that it would however object to another nation having such a station. With reference to the employment of advisers the United States believes it may be assumed that the Chinese Government will not discriminate unfairly in their selection, although it should be pointed out that this Government understands that Japan has six out of twenty-five advisers to the Republic representing eight nations. In respect to the proposed joint policing of certain places where there has been some friction between Japanese and Chinese, this Government feels apprehensive that this plan, instead of tending to lessen such friction might create greater difficulties than those which it is desired to remove.

But what is more important is the fact that these proposals, if accepted by China, while not infringing the territorial integrity of the Republic, are clearly derogatory to the political independence and administrative entity of that country. The same is in a measure true of Paragraph 4 of Article V relative to the purchase of arms. It is difficult for the United States, therefore, to reconcile these requests with the maintenance of the unimpaired sovereignty of China, which Japan, together with the United States and the Great Powers of Europe, has reaffirmed from time to time during the past decade and a half in formal declarations, treaties and exchanges of diplomatic notes. The United States, therefore, could not regard with indifference the assumption of political, military or economic domination over China by a foreign Power, and hopes that your excellency's Government will find it consonant with their interests to refrain from pressing upon China an acceptance of proposals which would, if accepted, exclude Americans from equal participation in the economic and industrial development of China and would limit the political independence of that country.

The United States is convinced that an attempt to coerce China to submit to these proposals would result in engendering resentment on the part of the Chinese and opposition by other interested Powers, thereby creating a situation which this Government confidently believes the Imperial Government do not desire.

The United States Government embraces this opportunity to make known that it has viewed the aspirations of Japan in the Far East with that friendship and esteem which have characterized the relations of the two nations in the past. This government cannot too earnestly impress upon your excellency's Government that the United States is not jealous of the prominence of Japan in the East or of the intimate cooperation of China and Japan for their mutual benefit. Nor has the United States any intention of obstructing or embarrassing Japan, or of influencing China in opposition to Japan. On the contrary the policy of the United States, as set forth in this note, is directed to the maintenance of the independence, integrity and commercial freedom of China and the preservation of legitimate American rights and interests in that Republic.

The Bryan "Nonrecognition" Policy. Secretary Bryan to Ambassador Guthrie (Japan), Washington, May 11, 1915[2]

[Telegram]

Please call upon the Minister for Foreign Affairs and present to him a note textually as follows:

"In view of the circumstances of the negotiations which have taken place and which are now pending between the Government of Japan and the Government of China, and of the agreements which have been reached as a result thereof, the Government of the United States has the honor to notify the Imperial Japanese Government that it cannot recognize any agreement or undertaking which has been entered into or which may be entered into between the Governments of Japan and China, impairing the treaty rights of the United States and its citizens in China, the political or territorial integrity of the Republic of China, or the international policy relative to China commonly known as the open door policy.

"An identical note has been transmitted to the Government of the Chinese Republic."

[2] *Ibid.,* p. 146.

JAPAN's VIEW OF "SPECIAL INTERESTS." THE JAPANESE AMBASSADOR (SATO) TO THE SECRETARY OF STATE, WASHINGTON, JUNE 15, 1917[3]

This paper bears the following marginal note: "This the Japanese Amb. read to me as an oral communication. It is not to be considered a document. June 15/17 RL"

That, Japan has special and close relations, political as well as economic, with China, is well and has long been understood by the American Government. In a note dated March 13, 1915, [see p. 255] addressed to Viscount Chinda, my predecessor, by Mr. Bryan, the then Secretary of State, he recognized this state of affairs and declared that the activity of Americans in China had never been political. Reposing confidence in this statement, the Japanese Government has attached no importance to the recent rumor repeatedly finding its way to the press despatches from China to the effect that the American Minister at Peking [Paul S. Reinsch] was more or less involved in the present political crisis in China. Again, with regard to the recent important representations made by the American Government to the Chinese Government relative to the political situation in China without previously consulting Japan, the Japanese Government does not entertain the slightest doubt as to the fair and unselfish motives of the United States Government. However, it is constrained, much to its regret, to recognize as a fact that, since the Japanese public is specially sensitive toward Chinese problems, this action of the American Government, in conjunction with the rumor aforementioned, has generated in the minds of a certain part of the people a feeling of uneasiness. In such circumstances, the Japanese Government believes that if the United States Government sees its way by some appropriate means to confirming the statement made by Mr. Bryan and clearly reasserting its friendly attitude toward Japan in respect of Chinese problems, it would leave a good impression on the minds of the Japanese public and would certainly contribute in no small measure to the friendly relations between our two nations, and accordingly it now communicates its conviction most frankly to the American Government and desires to be informed of the latter's opinion.

LANSING's VIEW OF "SPECIAL INTERESTS." THE SECRETARY OF STATE (LANSING) TO THE JAPANESE AMBASSADOR, WASHINGTON, JULY 6, 1917[4]

As evidence of the friendly attitude of the United States toward Japan in respect to questions relative to China, the American Government is pleased to remove any doubts which may arise as to its purposes by reaffirming the statements made in the note of Secretary Bryan to Viscount Chinda, dated March 13, 1915. In that note Secretary Bryan, after reviewing what he termed the

beginnings of the policy of the United States and other Powers interested in the welfare of China for the maintenance of the territorial integrity and administrative entity of China and for equal opportunities in commerce and industries in her behalf,

[3] *Ibid.*, 1917, p. 259. On June 4, the United States had informed China that her entry into the war against Germany was secondary to her need for establishment of a united and responsible government (*ibid.*, pp. 48-49).   [4] *Ibid.*, pp. 260-262.

and after pointing out in what respects the proposals made by Japan to China in 1915 (in so far as the objects and purposes of those proposals were known and understood by the United States Government at the time) were in derogation of the policy mentioned as well as of the understanding based upon the exchange of notes of November 30, 1908, and the treaty rights of the United States in China, said in conclusion:

The United States, therefore, could not regard with indifference the assumption of political, military, or economic domination over China by a foreign Power, and hopes that your excellency's Government will find it consonant with their interests to refrain from pressing upon China an acceptance of proposals which would, if accepted, exclude Americans from equal participation in the economic and industrial development of China and would limit the political independence of that country.***

The United States Government embraces this opportunity to make known that it has viewed the aspirations of Japan in the Far East with that friendship and esteem which have characterized the relations of the two nations in the past. This Government cannot too earnestly impress upon your excellency's Government that the United States is not jealous of the prominence of Japan in the East or of the intimate cooperation of China and Japan for their mutual benefit. Nor has the United States any intention of obstructing or embarrassing Japan, or of influencing China in opposition to Japan. On the contrary, the policy of the United States, as set forth in this note, is directed to the maintenance of the independence, integrity and commercial freedom of China and preservation of legitimate American rights and interests in that Republic.

I desire to direct your excellency's attention to the fact that, while Mr. Bryan's note thus expressed the views of the United States in regard to international relations in the Far East, I do not find that it anywhere went to the extent of stating or recognizing that Japan has special and close relations, political as well as economic, with China as a whole, as your excellency stated at our interview on June 15 last. Mr. Bryan merely said that the United States recognized that territorial contiguity created special relations between Japan and the districts of Shantung, Southern Manchuria and East Mongolia, but he did not admit that the United States might not in the future be justified in expressing its views in regard to Chino-Japanese relations involving even these districts. This view is borne out by the fact that Mr. Bryan felt justified in his communication of May 11, 1915, in declining to recognize any agreement or understanding entered into then or thereafter between Japan and China impairing the treaty rights of the United States, the political or territorial integrity of China, or the international policy of the open door.

As the official memorandum which your excellency handed me on June 15 referred to Japan's interests both political and economic in China as "paramount," and as Mr. Shidehara informed the American Chargé at Tokyo that your excellency had telegraphed to your Government that I had expressed myself as quite in accord with the deep sense of the memorandum, I feel that in this restatement of the attitude of the United States Government I ought to make it clear to your excellency that I had no intention in our conversation of June 15 to convey the impression that this Government recognized that Japan possessed in China a paramount interest. It was my intention to vary in no way the formal declaration of Mr. Bryan, and, as I recall my language, I did not employ the word "paramount" but spoke of "special" interest in the same sense in which the term was used in the note of March 13, 1915.

The United States has no political ambitions in respect to China, but its historic interest in the welfare of the Chinese people and the territorial and administrative integrity of the Republic, its treaty relations and extensive commerce with China, render it impossible for the United States to be indifferent to matters affecting these interests, which the civil dissension in China, according to reports, threatened to do. As, however, the factional difficulties did not seem to threaten the *status quo* in the region of the Pacific and the principle of equal opportunity, there would seem to have been no necessity under the Agreement of 1908 to communicate to the Japanese Government the intention of the United States Government to express to China its views on the internal dissension in that country and its interest and hope in the composing of the political difficulties, but with the purpose of avoiding any possible misunderstanding on the part of your excellency's Government as to the motives of this Government, the subject of the proposed communication to China was promptly brought to the attention of the Japanese Government, notwithstanding the fact that the Japanese proposals of 1915 were made to China several weeks before Japan acquainted the United States with them in accordance with the exchange of notes in 1908. In the case of the Japanese demands growing out of the Cheng Chia Tun trouble, the United States was not informed of the action of Japan until after inquiry had been made by this Government.

In taking the action which has led to the representations by the Japanese Government the United States Government is of the opinion it has departed in no way from its traditional policy towards China or from the views expressed by Mr. Bryan in 1915, in neither of which has the United States claimed the prerogative to control China's political development nor recognized the right or paramount interest of any other country to extend political influence over China.

AMERICAN POLICY RELATIVE TO "SPHERES OF INFLUENCE." THE SECRETARY OF STATE (LANSING) TO THE BRITISH AMBASSADOR, WASHINGTON, AUGUST 24, 1917[5]

[Memorandum]

The American Minister at Peking, on July 14, telegraphed to the Department that he had been informed by the British Chargé d'Affaires that his Government had authorized a protest against the construction of American railways in the provinces of Hupeh and Hunan on the ground that, on September 9, 1905, the Viceroy, Chang Chih-tung, gave to the British Consul General at Hankow a letter promising that in case foreign capital should be needed for railway building in these provinces, application would be made first of all to British concerns. On the 9th instant the American Minister informed the Department that the protest had been filed.

It appears that the letter of the Viceroy, Chang Chih-tung, to the British Consul General in 1905 has never been published and therefore can not be held to defeat a *bona fide* public concession by the Central Government.

[5] *Ibid.*, pp. 191-192.

The reservation of whole provinces and larger areas in China for railway construction, for mining or for other industrial enterprise by any one Power, appears to the American Government to be decidedly at variance with the policy of the "open door" and equality of commercial opportunity to which the British Government has subscribed.

It is the opinion of the American Government that none but agreements or contracts for specific enterprises can be held to be of force under the policy of the "open door," and that such contracts if not executed within a reasonable period, ought not to operate to prevent the necessary development of the region concerned.

The recognition of the claims of any one Power to a monopoly of railway building or other industrial enterprise in extensive regions of China must result in the recognition of similar claims of other Powers in other regions and thus create a large number of spheres of interest in that country which would make a mockery of the "open door" policy and tend to destroy the territorial integrity and administrative entity of China, to the preservation of which both the American and British Governments are pledged.

The interests of the United States and Great Britain in China are identical in this respect and require that an interpretation of the "open door" policy be agreed upon that will protect *bona fide* contracts and still preserve equality of commercial opportunity. The attention of His Britannic Majesty's Ambassador is invited to this matter as one of urgent importance. It is hoped that His Britannic Majesty's Government will be disposed to concur in the views herein expressed.

THE LANSING-ISHII EXCHANGE OF NOTES. THE AMERICAN NOTE. SECRETARY LANSING TO AMBASSADOR ISHII, WASHINGTON, NOVEMBER 2, 1917[6]

EXCELLENCY:

I have the honor to communicate herein my understanding of the agreement reached by us in our recent conversations touching the questions of mutual interest to our Governments relating to the Republic of China.

In order to silence mischievous reports that have from time to time been circulated, it is believed by us that a public announcement once more of the desires and intentions shared by our two Governments with regard to China is advisable.

The Governments of the United States and Japan recognize that territorial propinquity creates special relations between countries, and, consequently, the Government of the United States recognizes that Japan has special interests in China, particularly in the part to which her possessions are contiguous.

The territorial sovereignty of China, nevertheless, remains unimpaired and the Government of the United States has every confidence in the repeated assurances of the Imperial Japanese Government that while geographical position gives Japan such special interests they have no desire to discriminate against the trade of other nations or to disregard the commercial rights heretofore granted by China in treaties with other powers.

The Governments of the United States and Japan deny that they have any purpose to infringe in any way the independence or territorial integrity of China and they declare, furthermore, that they always adhere to the principle of the so-called "open door" or equal opportunity for commerce and industry in China.

[6] *Ibid.*, pp. 264-265.

Moreover, they mutually declare that they are opposed to the acquisition by any Government of any special rights or privileges that would affect the independence or territorial integrity of China or that would deny to the subjects or citizens of any country the full enjoyment of equal opportunity in the commerce and industry of China.

I shall be glad to have Your Excellency confirm this understanding of the agreement reached by us.

THE JAPANESE NOTE. AMBASSADOR ISHII TO SECRETARY LANSING, WASHINGTON, NOVEMBER 2, 1917

SIR: I have the honor to acknowledge the receipt of your note of to-day, communicating to me your understanding of the agreement reached by us in our recent conversations touching the questions of mutual interest to our Governments relating to the Republic of China.

I am happy to be able to confirm to you, under authorization of my Government, the understanding in question set forth in the following terms:

In order to silence mischievous reports that have from time to time been circulated, it is believed by us that a public announcement once more of the desires and intentions shared by our two Governments with regard to China is advisable.

The Governments of Japan and the United States recognize that territorial propinquity creates special relations between countries, and, consequently, the Government of the United States recognizes that Japan has special interests in China, particularly in the part to which her possessions are contiguous.

The territorial sovereignty of China, nevertheless, remains unimpaired and the Government of the United States has every confidence in the repeated assurances of the Imperial Japanese Government that while geographical position gives Japan such special interests they have no desire to discriminate against the trade of other nations or to disregard the commercial rights heretofore granted by China in treaties with other Powers.

The Governments of Japan and the United States deny that they have any purpose to infringe in any way the independence or territorial integrity of China and they declare, furthermore, that they always adhere to the principle of the so-called "open door" or equal opportunity for commerce and industry in China.

Moreover, they mutually declare that they are opposed to the acquisition by any government of any special rights or privileges that would affect the independence or territorial integrity of China or that would deny to the subjects or citizens of any country the full enjoyment of equal opportunity in the commerce and industry of China.

SECRET PROTOCOL TO THE LANSING-ISHII NOTES. THE SECRETARY OF STATE TO THE JAPANESE CHARGÉ (SABURI), WASHINGTON, MAY 4, 1922[7]

AIDE MEMOIRE

The Japanese Chargé d'Affaires will recall that at the time of the exchange of notes between Mr. Lansing and Viscount Ishii, on November 2, 1917, there was recorded an understanding between them to the following effect.

[7] *Ibid.*, 1922, II, 595-596.

"Protocol

"In the course of the conversations between the Japanese Special Ambassador and the Secretary of State of the United States which have led to the exchange of notes between them dated this day, declaring the policy of the two Governments with regard to China, the question of embodying the following clause in such declaration came up for discussion: 'they (the Governments of Japan and the United States) will not take advantage of the present conditions to seek special rights or privileges in China which would abridge the rights of the subjects or citizens of other friendly states.'

"Upon careful examination of the question, it was agreed that the clause above quoted being superfluous in the relations of the two Governments and liable to create erroneous impression in the minds of the public, should be eliminated from the declaration.

"It was, however, well understood that the principle enunciated in the clause which was thus suppressed was in perfect accord with the declared policy of the two Governments in regard to China."

This understanding, although never made public, was of course intended by the two Governments to be an integral and inseparable part of the policy jointly declared by them in the notes exchanged between Mr. Lansing and Viscount Ishii.

In the Nine-Power Treaty which on February 6, 1922, the United States and Japan concluded jointly with the other Powers represented in the Conference on the Limitation of Armament, the principles and policies agreed to be observed in relation to China were explicitly formulated. In a message to the United States Senate under date of March 8, 1922 (of which a copy is attached for reference), transmitting, in response to a Senate Resolution, information as to the present status and binding effect of the Lansing-Ishii Agreement, the President had occasion to state that that agreement "has no binding effect whatever, either with respect to the past or to the future, which is in any sense inconsistent with the principles and policies explicitly declared in the Nine-Power Treaty" referred to above.

A resolution adopted by the Conference on the Limitation of Armament at its Fifth Plenary Session on February 1, 1922, contained the following provision:

"The Powers represented in this Conference, considering it desirable that there should hereafter be full publicity with respect to all matters affecting the political and other international obligations of China and of the several Powers in relation to China, are agreed as follows:

"1. The several Powers other than China will at their earliest convenience file with the Secretariat General of the Conference for transmission to the participating Powers, a list of all treaties, conventions, exchanges of notes, or other international agreements which they may have with China, or with any other Power or Powers in relation to China, which they deem to be still in force and upon which they may desire to rely. In each case citations will be given to any official or other publication in which an authoritative text of the documents may be found. In any case in which the document may not have been published, a copy of the text (in its original language or languages) will be filed with the Secretariat General of the Conference."

It would appear that under this resolution there rests upon the Governments of the United States and of Japan an obligation to communicate for the purpose of publicity not only the notes exchanged between Mr. Lansing and Viscount Ishii, but also the hitherto unpublished understanding recorded between them at the time of that exchange, if it be the intention of the two Governments to regard the Lansing-Ishii Agreement as still in force and to be relied on. The question thus arises whether it is the disposition of the Japanese Government to continue that agreement in force by filing it in accordance with the terms of the Resolution above quoted; or whether, in view of the making of the Nine-Power Treaty of February 6 last, the Japanese Government would be disposed to join with the Government of the United States in terminating by mutual consent the existence of the Lansing-Ishii Agreement as a separate understanding between the two Powers.

[The Lansing-Ishii correspondence was cancelled by a subsequent exchange of notes at Washington, April 14, 1923.]

The Chino-American Diplomatic Exchange Relative to the Lansing-Ishii Notes[8]

With the note of November 8, 1917, by which it communicated to the Wai Chiao Pu the text of this exchange of notes, the American Legation in Peking, conveyed to the Chinese Minister for Foreign Affairs the following communication:

"The visit of the Imperial Japanese Mission to the United States afforded an opportunity for free and friendly discussion of interests of the United States and Japan in the Orient by openly proclaiming that the policy of Japan as regards China is not one of aggression and by declaring that there is no intention to take advantage commercially or indirectly of the special relations to China created by geographical position. The representatives of Japan have cleared the diplomatic atmosphere of the suspicions which had been so carefully spread by German propaganda.

"The Governments of the United States and Japan again declare their adherence to the Open Door Policy and recommit themselves, as far as these two Governments are concerned, to the maintenance of equal opportunity for the full enjoyment by the subjects or citizens of any country in the commerce and industry of China. Japanese commercial and industrial enterprises in China manifestly have, on account of the geographical relation of the two countries, a certain advantage over similar enterprises on the part of the citizens or subjects of any other country.

"The Governments of the United States and Japan have taken advantage of a favorable opportunity to make an exchange of expressions with respect to their relations with China. This understanding is formally set forth in the Notes exchanged and now transmitted. The statements in the Notes require no explanation. They not only contain a reaffirmation of the Open Door Policy but introduce a principle of non-interference with the sovereignty and territorial integrity of China which, generally applied, is essential to perpetual international peace, as has been so clearly declared by President Wilson."

On November 9, 1917, the Wai Chiao Pu replied to the following effect:

---

[8] MacMurray, *Treaties and Agreements with and concerning China*, II, 1396-1397.

"The Government of the United States and the Government of Japan have recently, in order to silence mischievous reports, effected an exchange of notes at Washington concerning their desires and intentions with regard to China. A copy of the said notes have been communicated to the Chinese Government by the Japanese Minister at Peking, and the Chinese Government, in order to avoid misunderstanding, hastens to make the following declaration so as to make known the view of the Government:

"The principle adopted by the Chinese Government toward the friendly nations has always been one of justice and equality, and consequently the rights enjoyed by the friendly nations derived from the treaties have been consistently respected, and so even with the special relations between countries created by the fact of territorial contiguity but only in so far as they have already been provided for in her existing treaties. Hereafter the Chinese Government will still adhere to the principle hitherto adopted and hereby it is again declared that the Chinese Government will not allow herself to be bound by any agreement entered into by other nations."

FURTHER DEFINITION OF "SPECIAL INTERESTS." THE SECRETARY OF STATE
(LANSING) TO MINISTER REINSCH, WASHINGTON, APRIL 16, 1918[9]

SIR: The Department acknowledges the receipt of your despatch No. 1408 of March 6, 1917, requesting specific instructions in connection with the Department's telegram of January 27, 5 p.m., particularly with respect to the statement therein contained that "the Department recognizes that Japan has special interests in Manchuria."

In my conversation with the Japanese Ambassador I had in mind nothing more than to point out the difference between conditions in Shantung and those in Manchuria, and, in using the phrase "special interests," I had reference only to such specific concessions as the lease of the Kwantung Peninsula and the leases of the South Manchuria and other railways with the right to maintain railway guards, et cetera.

With respect to the notes exchanged in May, 1915, by Japan and China the Department has not altered its position as stated in its telegraphic instruction of May 11, 1915.

The assumption of the Legation, therefore, is correct, that the "special interests" of Japan, in the view of the Department, are to be understood as confined to those specific rights and privileges which were obtained by the Japanese Government from China and from Russia by way of international agreement.

The Department also approves of the Legation's reply to American citizens to the effect that they can fully engage in business in Manchuria.

[9] *Foreign Relations*, 1917, p. 187.

FORMATION OF THE FOUR-POWER BANKING CONSORTIUM, 1920

ALTHOUGH the Government of the United States withdrew in 1913 its support from the American Banking Group which was proposing to participate in the Six-Power Consortium (see p. 247), this policy was reversed when the United States entered the World War, the American government assuming the initiative in organization of a new consortium finally consummated in 1920.

HISTORY OF EFFORTS TO FORM A CONSORTIUM AND JAPAN'S FAILURE TO CO-OPERATE. THE ACTING SECRETARY OF STATE (POLK) TO THE AMBASSADOR IN JAPAN (MORRIS), WASHINGTON, FEBRUARY 28, 1920[1]

[Paraphrase]

The Department approached the Governments of France, Great Britain, and Japan more than eighteen months ago with the proposal that a new consortium be created with the view of extending financial aid to the Chinese Government. The terms of this proposal were communicated to you at the time and the aims and objects which this Government was hopeful would be gained by it were imparted to you. It was intended more than anything else that the Chinese should receive during this time of transition and when the economic needs were greatest the necessary financial aid in a way which would remove the tendency for the Chinese Government to gravitate politically toward any one power, and would prove to be a practical way of insuring the continued equal economic opportunities and chances for trade which are generally admitted to be necessary to prevent rivalries between nations which would endanger both the interests of the powers themselves and the natural progress of the country. The British and French Governments adopted the suggestions in principle as a substantial basis upon which a new consortium of banking groups in the several countries could be founded to supply needed loans to China. At a meeting held in Paris last May, the agents of the banking groups of France, Great Britain, Japan, and the United States accepted and confirmed these proposals, subject to the approval of their Governments. Both the banking groups and Governments in France and Great Britain and the bankers in Japan were actuated by a liberal and self-denying spirit, each taking an interest in removing as much as they possibly could disturbing and complicating motives from the negotiations which in their opinion should be conducted on the basis of well-founded economic policies.

To our disappointment Japan has shown herself disinclined to work in harmony, being alone in this attitude. Her Government did not inform its

[1] *Foreign Relations*, 1920, I, 497-499.

financial leaders at the time the proposals were first presented; it later neglected to suggest that they prepare to enter the proposed consortium by forming a financial group until after the lapse of eight months; for nearly a year it neglected to inform the other interested powers as to its feeling in regard to the entire scheme of such a financial combination. It then presented a proposal by which the special rights and interests which Japan claimed in South Manchuria and Eastern Inner Mongolia should not be included in the field of operations of the proposed financial combination, thereby bringing in entirely new issues not only alien to the intention of the proposed consortium but out of harmony with the spirit of liberality and unselfishness which had been a feature of all the exchanges of views regarding the proposal. By this procedure the success of the whole plan depended on whether the other powers interested would agree to grant to Japan a special position as regards rights, preferential and exclusive, which in fact admitted a new principle of spheres of influence in advance of and more extensive than had been recognized in China at any previous time. The other three interested powers made every endeavor to convince Japan that she should recede from her stand, but without success, even after this Government had made the concession that the interests of Japan would not be jeopardized in certain enterprises. You were advised through the Legation at Peking on October 15 that the Department, on October 11, replied to an inquiry from the Government of Great Britain fully explaining its attitude and no change has been made therein.

Considering all this our Government has decided that the time has arrived to go ahead and fully complete the proposed financial combination or to meet the new complication which Japan has created. This condition is fully realized by the American group who have sent Thomas W. Lamont as their agent to Japan. Lamont has no official capacity at all but is making the trip to confer with the bankers' group in Japan for the purpose of trying to obtain an agreement that will work satisfactorily. Aid him all you can with essential information and otherwise and work with him just as far as you are able to do so. Send complete reports. Instructions will be sent from time to time.

It is still our earnest desire that Japan should cooperate completely and heartily in a way that will give assured safety to her legitimate rights, surrendering nothing which justly is due her. In case, however, that desire can not be realized on account of the action of Japan, we will find it necessary, but with reluctance and the knowledge that we have vainly tried every means we had to secure harmonious action, to revert to the old form of national and individual action in spite of all its disadvantages of competition and conflict, giving our support to every proper financial concern in the United States which should wish to do business on an independent basis in China.

We would be keenly disappointed to find ourselves obliged to give up the hope of working with the Japanese Government in solving questions of basic concern to America and Japan on the basis of common motives and the acceptance by both countries of rules of action embodied in previous undertakings between the two nations and most recently reaffirmed in the notes exchanged between Secretary Lansing and Ambassador Ishii.

Repeat to the Minister in China for his information.

REJECTION OF JAPANESE FORMULA AS BEING UNNECESSARY TO PROTECT JAPANESE INTERESTS. THE DEPARTMENT OF STATE TO THE JAPANESE EMBASSY, WASHINGTON, MARCH 16, 1920[2]

The Government of the United States has received and carefully considered the memorandum under date of March 2, 1920, in which the Japanese Ambassador set forth the views of his Government as to the formation of the proposed international Consortium for loans to China; and it is happy to record the hearty gratification with which it has noted the disavowal by Japan of any claim to exclusive economic or political rights with respect to South Manchuria and Eastern Inner Mongolia.

The American Government cannot but acknowledge, however, its grave disappointment that the formula proffered by the Japanese Government is in terms so exceedingly ambiguous and in character so irrevocable that it might be held to indicate a continued desire on the part of the Japanese Government to exclude the American, British and French banking groups from participation in the development, for the benefit of China, of important parts of that Republic,—a construction which could not be reconciled with the principle of the independence and territorial integrity of China.

The Government of the United States is not unsympathetic with the professed objects of the principle embodied in the Japanese formula: it considers, on the other hand, first, that the right of national self preservation is one of universal acceptance in the relations between states, and therefore would not require specific formulation as its application in any particular instance; and, second, that the recognition of that principle is implicit in the terms of the notes exchanged between Secretary Lansing and Viscount Ishii on November 2, 1917. This Government therefore considers that by reason of the particular relationships of understanding thus existing between the United States and Japan, and those which, it is understood, similarly exist between Japan and other Powers proposed to be associated with it in the Consortium, there would appear to be no occasion to apprehend on the part of the Consortium any activities directed against the economic life or national defense of Japan. It is therefore felt that Japan could with entire assurance rely upon the good faith of the United States and of the other two Powers associated in the Consortium to refuse their countenance to any operation inimical to the vital interests of Japan: and that Japan's insistence that the other three Powers join with it in the proposed formula as a condition precedent would only create misapprehension. It is felt, moreover, that such a formula would not only be unnecessary, but would lend itself to misconstruction for the reason that it apparently differentiates between the status of South Manchuria and Eastern Inner Mongolia and that of other Chinese territory. The mere fact of differentiation would, it is apprehended, give rise to questions which would tend still further to unsettle the already complex situation in China. This Government is therefore hopeful that the Japanese Government may in view of its several existing relationships of understanding with the United States and the other two Powers be persuaded to rely upon their good faith in this matter and forego its proposal to require explicit guarantees, the mere statement of which opens the way for possible misconstruction and misapprehension in the future.

The Government of the United States has furthermore been happy to

[2] Ibid., I, 512-513.

note the readiness of the Japanese Government to enumerate the specific vested interests of its nationals, in Manchuria and Mongolia, which it would propose to exclude from the scope of operations of the proposed Consortium; although it finds it difficult to believe that in order to meet the necessities of Japanese economic or political security it is essential for Japan alone to construct and control a railway line of such a character as the one projected from Taonanfu to Jehol and thence to the seacoast.

It is hoped that the discussions now in progress in Tokyo between Mr. Lamont, on behalf of the American Group, and the representatives of the Japanese banking interests may result in such a complete understanding on the question of the specific enterprises in Manchuria and Mongolia, which it may be found mutually satisfactory to exclude from the operation of the Consortium, as would enable the Japanese Government to accord to that understanding its unqualified approval.

In conclusion, the Government of the United States takes pleasure in the fact that the frank interchanges of views which have thus far taken place appear to have resulted in a basis of mutual understanding which justifies the belief that a speedy completion of the organization of the Consortium is now possible.

The Lamont Plan with Instructions to Urge Co-operation of All Governments. The Secretary of State (Colby) to the Chargé in Great Britain (Wright), Washington, March 30, 1920[3]

The American Group is copying to the British and French Groups a message from Lamont dated March 26 from Tokyo indicating that' he has received from the Japanese Banking Group and from responsible members of the Government assurances warranting the hope that Japan is prepared to enter the Consortium without reservations if the other three groups authorize him to exchange with the Japanese Group letters recognizing that the South Manchuria Railway and its present branches and the mines subsidiary thereto are to be excluded from the Consortium; that the Taonanfu-Jehol Railway and branch to the Sea are to be included within the Consortium; and that the Kirin-Hueining, Chengchiatun-Taonanfu, Changchun-Taonanfu, Kirin-Changchun, Sinminfu-Mukden and Ssupingkai-Chengchiatun railways are to be outside the scope of operations of the Consortium; no mention being made of any general economic or political rights of Japan in Manchuria or Mongolia. Ambassador Morris also reports hopefully on the prospects of an early arrangement on this basis.

In view of the present favorable situation the Department concurs in the hope expressed by Lamont that the British and French Governments and Groups will give their approval to his proposal to waive any objection to the exclusion from the Consortium of the three railroads west of the South Manchuria line which were mentioned in section 3 of the list attached to the Japanese note of March 2nd. You will recall that the British reply of March 19th communicated in your No. 485 March 20th, 1 p.m. objected to the exclusion of these lines. This Government feels that nothing substantial would be lost by yielding on this point and that the agreement of the Japanese Government on more essential questions would be facilitated thereby.

You will please take this matter up as one of urgency with the British

³ *Ibid.,* I, 521-522.

Foreign Office and emphasize the fact that a satisfactory solution of the long pending question of the Consortium appears to be within reach if the British and French Governments and Groups give their assent to the interchange of communications proposed by Lamont.

Repeat this telegram as No. 641 to Embassy at Paris which it is desired should similarly inform the French Foreign Office of the tenor of this instruction and should request the cooperation of the French Government and Group in furtherance of the proposed arrangement. Although it would appear that the Japanese Government has not recently communicated with the French Government on this subject it may be that the latter will find the present juncture opportune for authorizing its Embassy at Tokyo to cooperate with the American and eventually with the British Embassies in such representations as may be found desirable to make to the Japanese Government in support of Lamont's plan.

WILLINGNESS OF JAPAN TO WITHDRAW PROPOSED FORMULA IF OTHER INTERESTED POWERS CONCUR IN UNITED STATES PROPOSAL. THE JAPANESE EMBASSY TO THE DEPARTMENT OF STATE, WASHINGTON, APRIL 3, 1920[4]

[A.] The Japanese Government have received the Memorandum of the United States Government dated March 16th, 1920, giving frank expression to its views again upon the proposal of Japan relative to the organization of a new Consortium for loans to China, and have taken it into their careful consideration.

[B.] The Japanese Government are happy to express the hearty gratification with which they have noted that the United States Government is fully appreciative of and even sympathetic with the principle embodied in the formula proposed by the Japanese Government. The United States Government however is inclined to think that the terms and character of the formula may be taken to indicate a continued desire on the part of Japan to exclude the other Powers from participation in the development of important parts of China, and that it is likely to create unnecessary misapprehension. The Memorandum adds that the United States Government is therefore hopeful that the Japanese Government will withdraw their proposal for the explicit guarantee embodied in the formula in question. The Japanese Government, while acknowledging that this suggestion of the United States is offered in the most friendly spirit, would like to state that they made the proposal now under review only because they felt it useful and important to do so in order to make clear the particular position which Japan occupies through the facts of territorial propinquity and of her special vested rights.

[C.] They never thought of any possibility of the formula giving rise to any such misapprehension or misconstruction as is pointed out by the United States Government. They are glad, however, to note that it is not so much to the principle of their proposal as to its form that the United States Government takes exception. Assurance is given in the Memorandum of the United States Government that the right of national self-preservation, which forms the basis of the guarantee required by Japan in order to assure the security of her national defence and the economic existence of her people, is not only one of universal acceptance but one of which the recognition is implied in the terms of the notes exchanged between Secretary Lansing and Viscount Ishii, so that the new Consortium would in no case embark upon

[4] *Ibid.*, I, 523-526.

any activities directed against the national defence and the economic existence of Japan and so that the Powers associated in the Consortium would refuse their countenance to any enterprise inimical to the vital interests of Japan. Accordingly, after deliberate consideration, the Japanese Government relying upon that assurance of the United States, have come to the decision to accept most willingly the suggestion of the United States Government and to forego their request for the acceptance of the proposed formula on the part of the other interested Powers, on condition that these Powers agree to the above understanding as formulated by the United States Government.

[D.] As to the railway and other enterprises which Japan naturally expects will be excluded from the scope of the common activities of the new Consortium, the United States Government expresses a doubt as to whether it is essential for Japan alone to construct and control such a railway as the Taonanfu-Jehol line. This railway, together with the line connecting a point thereon with a seaport, was projected with the strategic object of making it a means of common defence on the part of China and Japan against foreign invasion coming from the direction of Ourga, quite apart from the further object of facilitating development of the districts through which these lines run. It is, therefore, a matter of great regret and surprise to the Japanese Government that there exists the misunderstanding that these railways will eventually prove a menace to Peking. It is confidently hoped that Japan's position in this connection may be fully appreciated by the United States Government. The Japanese Government, mindful as they are of common interests of the Powers, have no objection to a scheme of making these two railways a joint enterprise of the new Consortium, but having regard to the particular relation in which Japan stands to these railways, it is hoped that the United States Government will lend their full support to the following propositions.

(1) In the event of the new Consortium projecting in future a scheme of extending the Taonanfu-Jehol railway to the north with a view to connection with the Eastern Chinese Railway, the assent of the Japanese Government thereto must be obtained beforehand through the Japanese group, inasmuch as such an extension being tantamount to a renewal of the so-called Chinchou-Aigun railway scheme against which a protest was lodged by Japan when the question was motioned [mooted?] some years ago, is calculated to have a serious effect upon the South Manchuria Railway.

(2) In consideration of the particular desire of Japan that these two lines should be built as speedily as possible, the Japanese group, after due consultation with the other groups, may be permitted to undertake their construction single-handed in the event of the other three Powers associated in the new Consortium being reluctant to finance it. In that case, having regard to the fact that these railways must cross the Peking-Mukden railway at a certain point, the American group will give their support to the overture which the Japanese financiers will make to their British colleagues with a view to perfecting the junction of these lines.

[E.] As regards concrete questions as to which of the options that Japan possesses at present in Manchuria and Mongolia in respect to railways, is to be excluded, in accordance with the understanding reached between the Governments of the United States and Japan, from the scope of the common activities of the new Consortium, the Japanese Government entirely share the view of the United States Government that a settlement satisfactory to both parties will be arrived at through the discussion now in progress in Tokio between Mr. Lamont and the representatives of the Japanese banking group. In this belief, the representatives of the Japanese banking group are authorized to proceed with the discussion with Mr. Lamont with the object of arriving at a settlement of questions of this nature.

REPLY TO JAPANESE NOTE OF APRIL 3 ASKING WITHDRAWAL OF PROPOSITIONS. THE DEPARTMENT OF STATE TO THE JAPANESE EMBASSY, WASHINGTON, APRIL 29, 1920[5]

The American Government has received the further memorandum of the Imperial Japanese Government of April 3d and after having given it careful consideration has the honor to reply as follows:

The American Government is much gratified to learn that the Japanese Government is prepared to accept most willingly the suggestion of the American Government to forego its request for the acceptance of the proposed formula which it had made in its note of March 2d.

As regards the two propositions mentioned in the Japanese Government's memorandum under acknowledgment the American Government much regrets that the Imperial Government should have raised these questions at a moment when it was hoped that the four Powers interested were about to reach an agreement on the basis of compromise which Mr. Lamont, the representative of the American banking group, appeared to have reached in Tokyo with representatives of the Japanese Group. The American Government fears that if the discussion of these propositions is insisted upon it will merely delay matters and in the interests of all parties concerned it sincerely trusts that the Imperial Japanese Government will be willing to withdraw them and to be satisfied with the general assurance to which the American Government has already offered to subscribe and which the Imperial Japanese Government has just expressed its readiness to accept.

In order to meet the wishes of Japan the American Government is prepared to agree to the terms of the compromise proposed by Mr. Lamont in Tokyo.

As regards proposition one, Japan practically asks for a right to veto the construction by the consortium of a line from Taonanfu to join the Chinese Eastern Railway on the grounds that such an extension would be tantamount to a renewal of the so-called Chinchou-Aigun Railway scheme against which Japan had lodged a protest some years ago. The Government of the United States has no wish to do anything which would conflict with the vital interests of Japan and the assurance to which it has declared its willingness to subscribe would appear fully to safeguard Japan's interests. It appears to the American Government that, with respect to the establishment of the consortium, a new era is about to dawn in which conditions have changed and it is now proposed that the Powers should work together in harmonious and friendly cooperation rather than in competition and the granting to any one party to the consortium of the power to veto the possible construction of a railway would appear to be contrary to the principles upon which the idea of the consortium is based.

[5] *Ibid.*, I, 536-538.

In the opinion of the American Government the contingency anticipated in proposition two would appear to be already provided for in Article IV of the Intergroup Agreement at Paris on May 12th, paragraph 19, of which the American Government has expressed its approval. The American Government sincerely trusts that the Imperial Japanese Government will recognize the friendly spirit in which these observations are made and that it will now agree to cooperate with the other three Powers along the lines of the proposed compromise. It notes with gratification that the Japanese Government is prepared to authorize the Japanese Group to proceed with the discussion with Mr. Lamont for the purpose of reaching a settlement. It expresses the hope that the Japanese Government will now see its way to give this authorization without the suggested reservations in order that the final arrangements between the groups may be concluded while Mr. Lamont is still in Peking and the necessary exchange of letters between the representatives of the Japanese and American Groups effected with the least possible delay.

EXPRESSIONS OF GRATIFICATION AT JAPAN'S CONCURRENCE IN AND SUPPORT OF CONSORTIUM. THE DEPARTMENT OF STATE TO THE JAPANESE EMBASSY, WASHINGTON, MAY 8, 1920[6]

The Government of the United States has been pleased to receive the Imperial Japanese Government's memorandum of May 8, 1920, in reply to that of the Government of the United States dated the 29th of the preceding month, and is deeply gratified to observe therefrom that the Imperial Japanese Government has no intention of insisting upon the explicit assurance or consent of the Government of the United States in regard to the two points raised by the Imperial Japanese Government with reference to the Taonanfu-Jehol Railway and the line connecting a point thereon with a seaport. The Government of the United States also takes note with sincere pleasure that the Imperial Japanese Government is prepared to lend its support to the conclusion of the arrangement between the banking groups concerned, and to give the arrangement the necessary confirmation upon the same terms as the Governments of the United States, Great Britain, and France have already done without conditions or provisos.

It is most gratifying to the Government of the United States that the underlying principles and policies of the new International Consortium are now so fully understood and agreed upon that the representatives of the banking groups may proceed to its formation and the consideration of the working details of its operation. The Government of the United States again can assure the Imperial Japanese Government that its sole aim in all the negotiations just completed has been to bring about an arrangement which would insure entire cooperation on the part of the interested Governments on a basis which would be to their mutual advantage and for the lasting benefit of China. The Government of the United States looks forward with keen anticipation to the friendly cooperation under the Consortium arrangement, with entire confidence that such practical joint endeavor is the beginning of a new era of good will and accomplishment for both Governments.

WASHINGTON, *May 8, 1920.*

[6] *Ibid.,* I, 541.

CHINA INFORMED CONCERNING THE NEW CONSORTIUM. THE AMERICAN, BRITISH, FRENCH, AND JAPANESE REPRESENTATIVES IN CHINA TO THE CHINESE MINISTER FOR FOREIGN AFFAIRS (W. W. YEN), PEKING, SEPTEMBER 28, 1920[7]

EXCELLENCY: The Governments of France, Japan, the United States of America and Great Britain considering that the time has now arrived to make a joint communication to the Chinese Government on the proposed scope and objects of the so-called New Consortium which has been under discussion between the four Governments for some time past, the undersigned representatives of France, Japan, the United States of America and Great Britain have the honour to state as follows:

In the course of 1918 the United States Government informed the other three Governments in question of the formation in the United States of America of an American group of Bankers for the purpose of rendering financial assistance to China. The principles underlying the formation of the American group were that all preferences and options for loans to China held by any members of this group should be shared by the American group as a whole and that future loans to China having a Governmental guarantee should be conducted in common as group business, whether these loans were for administrative or for industrial purposes.

In notifying the other three Governments of these proposals the United States Government recognised that the war had created such a mutuality of interest between certain Governments and peoples as to render this co-operation essential to any constructive programme of financial assistance to China. It was suggested therefore that the other Governments which were largely interested in China and in a position at the time to render such assistance— viz. France, Japan, and Great Britain—might be willing to join with the United States in its proposed plan and consent to the formation of similar national Groups organised on the same basis to act in cooperation with the American Group. In the proposal of the United States Government which in practice envisaged a reconstruction of the old Consortium it was specifically stated that there was no intention of interfering with any of the rights of that Consortium. The hope was expressed however that the new national Groups formed might be made so broad as to include the members of the former Consortium as well as others who had legitimate claims to such inclusion, so as to meet the larger needs and opportunities of China in a spirit of harmony and of helpfulness rather than of harmful competition and self-interest.

The proposal of the United States Government as here outlined received the most careful and friendly consideration on the part of the French, Japanese and British Governments which resulted in a meeting be[ing] held in Paris on May 11th and 12th, 1919, at which the chief Representatives of the four Groups were present to discuss the financial details of the proposed arrangement as well as the scope and limit of their activities.

A draft arrangement between the four Groups was then drawn up embodying *inter alia* the principles of the American proposals. While it is not the intention of the present Note to do more than outline the broad aspects of the question or to enter into financial details which await confirmation by the Groups at the forthcoming inter-group meeting to be held in New

[7] *Ibid.,* I, 572-574.

York in October next, we consider it advisable to make the position clear in regard to an essential point which might otherwise give rise to misapprehension, namely the amount of support to be given by the respective Governments to their national groups or to the Consortium as a whole.

It is to be understood that the Governments of each of the four participating Groups undertake to give their complete support to their respective national Group members of the Consortium in operations undertaken pursuant to the inter-group arrangement entered into by the bankers at Paris, which arrangement in turn relates to existing and future loan agreements involving the issue for subscription by the public of loans having a Chinese Government guarantee subject to the proviso that existing agreements for industrial undertakings upon which substantial progress has been made may be omitted from the scope of the arrangement.

A collection of documents which have passed between the Governments interested in the Consortium as well as certain letters exchanged between the American and Japanese Group representatives which are herewith enclosed will enable the Chinese Government to follow the course of the negotiations and understand the whole position.

In making this communication to Your Excellency the undersigned venture to reiterate the earnest hope of their respective Governments for the early consummation of a united Government in China so that the New Consortium may eventually be enabled to give practical expression to the desires of the four Governments concerned to assist in the future development of this country.

Y. OBATA

A. BOPPE

C. R. CRANE

B. H. CLIVE

XLI

THE WASHINGTON CONFERENCE AND AMERICAN POLICY IN CHINA, 1922

IN RELATION to American policy in China, the most significant achievement of the Washington Conference (1921-22) was the formulation of principles contained in the Nine-Power Open Door Treaty. This statement of principles should be compared with the more tangible stipulations contained in the Hay notes of 1899 (see p. 211). The Nine-Power Treaty gave the open door policy its first treaty definition. The Powers signatory to the treaty included the United States, Belgium, the British Empire, China, France, Italy, Japan, The Netherlands, and Portugal.

THE NINE-POWER TREATY ON PRINCIPLES AND POLICIES CONCERNING CHINA, WASHINGTON, FEBRUARY 6, 1922[1]

ARTICLE I.

The Contracting Powers, other than China, agree:

(1) To respect the sovereignty, the independence, and the territorial and administrative integrity of China;

(2) To provide the fullest and most unembarrassed opportunity to China to develop and maintain for herself an effective and stable government;

(3) To use their influence for the purpose of effectually establishing and maintaining the principle of equal opportunity for the commerce and industry of all nations throughout the territory of China;

(4) To refrain from taking advantage of conditions in China in order to seek special rights or privileges which would abridge the rights of subjects or citizens of friendly States, and from countenancing action inimical to the security of such States.

ARTICLE II.

The Contracting Powers agree not to enter into any treaty, agreement, arrangement, or understanding, either with one another, or, individually, or collectively, with any Power or Powers, which would infringe or impair the principles stated in Article 1.

ARTICLE III.

With a view to applying more effectually the principles of the Open Door or equality of opportunity in China for the trade and industry of all nations, the Contracting Powers, other than China, agree that they will not seek, nor support their respective nationals in seeking:

[1] S. Doc. 126: 67-2, pp. 893-897.

(a) any arrangement which might purport to establish in favour of their interests any general superiority of rights with respect to commercial or economic development in any designated region of China;

(b) any such monopoly or preference as would deprive the nationals of any other Power of the right of undertaking any legitimate trade or industry in China, or of participating with the Chinese Government, or with any local authority, in any category of public enterprise, or which by reason of its scope, duration or geographical extent is calculated to frustrate the practical application of the principle of equal opportunity.

It is understood that the foregoing stipulations of this Article are not to be so construed as to prohibit the acquisition of such properties or rights as may be necessary to the conduct of a particular commercial, industrial, or financial undertaking or to the encouragement of invention and research.

China undertakes to be guided by the principles stated in the foregoing stipulations of this Article in dealing with applications for economic rights and privileges from Governments and nationals of all foreign countries, whether parties to the present Treaty or not.

ARTICLE IV.

The Contracting Powers agree not to support any agreements by their respective nationals with each other designed to create Spheres of Influence or to provide for the enjoyment of mutually exclusive opportunities in designated parts of Chinese territory.

ARTICLE V.

China agrees that, throughout the whole of the railways in China, she will not exercise or permit unfair discrimination of any kind. In particular there shall be no discrimination whatever, direct or indirect, in respect of charges or of facilities on the ground of the nationality of passengers or the countries from which or to which they are proceeding, or the origin or ownership of goods or the country from which or to which they are consigned, or the nationality or ownership of the ship or other means of conveying such passengers or goods before or after their transport on the Chinese Railways.

The Contracting Powers, other than China, assume a corresponding obligation in respect of any of the aforesaid railways over which they or their nationals are in a position to exercise any control in virtue of any concession, special agreement or otherwise.

ARTICLE VI.

The Contracting Powers, other than China, agree fully to respect China's rights as a neutral in time of war to which China is not a party; and China declares that when she is a neutral she will observe the obligations of neutrality.

ARTICLE VII.

The Contracting Powers agree that, whenever a situation arises which in the opinion of any one of them involves the application of the stipulations of the present Treaty, and renders desirable discussion of such application, there shall be full and frank communication between the Contracting Powers concerned.

ARTICLE VIII.

Powers not signatory to the present Treaty, which have Governments recognized by the Signatory Powers and which have treaty relations with China, shall be invited to adhere to the present Treaty. To this end the Government of the United States will make the necessary communications to nonsignatory Powers and will inform the Contracting Powers of the replies received. Adherence by any Power shall become effective on receipt of notice thereof by the Government of the United States.

ARTICLE IX.

The present Treaty shall be ratified by the Contracting Powers in accordance with their respective constitutional methods and shall take effect on the date of the deposit of all the ratifications, which shall take place at Washington as soon as possible. The Government of the United States will transmit to the other Contracting Powers a certified copy of the procès-verbal of the deposit of ratifications.

The present Treaty, of which the French and English texts are both authentic, shall remain deposited in the archives of the Government of the United States, and duly certified copies thereof shall be transmitted by that Government to the other Contracting Powers.

XLII

CHINA'S FAILURE TO TAKE ADVANTAGE OF THE WASHINGTON CONFERENCE, 1923

CONDITIONS prevailing in China in the years immediately following the Washington Conference are discussed frankly by Secretary Hughes in the following memorandum. The memorandum is suggestive of the difficulties confronting the Powers in any effort to apply in China during these years the principles which had been enunciated by the Washington Conference.

CONDITIONS IN CHINA. SECRETARY HUGHES TO MINISTER SZE, WASHINGTON, JUNE 7, 1923[1]

Memorandum by the Secretary of State of a Conversation with the Chinese Minister (Sze), June 7, 1923.

The Minister called by instructions of his Government to say that he understood there was some proposal to delay the Conference on Extra-territoriality. He said that he understood that some of the members of the diplomatic corps in Peking were favoring this course. The Minister said that while it might probably seem to the Powers that there should be a postponement for a short time he hoped that there would not be an indefinite postponement; that such a postponement would have an unfortunate effect as the Government had looked forward with a good deal of expectation to this Conference and it was one of the matters decided upon at the Washington Conference. The Secretary said that the only reply that he could make at the moment was that the matter was receiving the most earnest consideration and that later the attitude of this Government would be stated to the Peking Government. The Secretary then said that the Minister must understand that conditions in China had given rise to a feeling of great discouragement; that instead of taking advantage of the opportunity afforded by the Washington Conference there had been disintegration; the Chinese Government had not been able to give protection to foreigners; that they had a very restricted area of authority and that they utterly failed to discharge their international obligations. This seemed to be a situation which was growing worse instead of better. The Secretary said there was no better friend of China than he was, but it must be understood that China must afford the basis for assistance and this they were not doing. The Secretary said, of course, it must be understood that he was not directing his statement to the Minister, individually, because he understood the difficulties of his personal position, but it was idle for China to declaim, as she had at the Washington Conference with respect to her sovereignty and her political integrity

[1] *Foreign Relations, 1923,* I, 624.

and her rights as a nation while, at the same time, she failed to provide a Government which could exercise a competent authority throughout her national territory, discharge her international obligations, and afford a basis for the development that all friends of China desired to see. The Secretary referred to recent events in China and to the banditry which existed, and the failure of the Chinese Government properly to cope with the situation.

The Secretary said that all these conditions must be taken into consideration in considering plans for the future and that he was studying the whole matter, including the question what should be done as to the Conference on Extra-territoriality.

The Minister referred to the disappointment in obtaining additional revenue, the delay in providing this revenue and the serious effect upon Chinese finances. . . . The Secretary said that, of course, it was to be regretted that there had been delay in the ratification of the Washington Conference Treaties, but there was no use of supplying money to China while it went through a sieve, and that the present difficulty was largely due to the fact that the Provincial Governors paid no attention to the demands of Peking and unless there was a stable government to assist, it was of little use to attempt to provide assistance; that all these matters would have to be carefully threshed out to see what could be done which would aid China, but that China must understand that she could not exhibit before the world inability to protect even the lives and safety of foreigners and at the same time demand foreign assistance.

XLIII

RECOMMENDATIONS ON EXTRATERRITORIALITY IN CHINA, 1926-1929

A COMMISSION to investigate and report on the exercise of extraterritorial jurisdiction in China, composed of representatives of the United States, Belgium, the British Empire, China, France, Denmark, Italy, Japan, The Netherlands, Norway, Portugal, Spain, and Sweden, was organized in accordance with a resolution adopted by the Washington Conference. The commission began its meetings in Peking, January 12, 1926, continuing its investigations until September, when a joint report was signed by the representatives. In view of the long history of extraterritoriality in China, and the frequent demands of China for its abolition, the recommendations of the commission are significant. With these recommendations is also printed the statement of Secretary Kellogg, January 27, 1927, concerning the policy of tariff autonomy and abolition of extraterritoriality, and the reply of the United States to China's request made in 1929 for immediate relinquishment of extraterritoriality.

RECOMMENDATIONS OF THE COMMISSION ON EXTRATERRITORIALITY. REPORT OF THE COMMISSION ON EXTRATERRITORIALITY, SEPTEMBER 16, 1926[1]

.   .   .   .

PART IV

The commissioners, having completed their investigations and having made their findings of fact as set forth in Parts I, II, and III of this report, now make the following recommendations.

The commissioners are of the opinion that, when these recommendations shall have been reasonably complied with, the several powers would be warranted in relinquishing their respective rights of extraterritoriality.

It is understood that, upon the relinquishment of extraterritoriality, the nationals of the powers concerned will enjoy freedom of residence and trade and civil rights in all parts of China in accordance and with the general practice in intercourse among nations and upon a fair and equitable basis.

RECOMMENDATIONS

I. The administration of justice with respect to the civilian population in China must be entrusted to a judiciary which shall be effectively protected

[1] U. S. Dept. of State, *Report of the Commission on Extraterritoriality in China* (Washington, 1926), pp. 105 ff.

against any unwarranted interference by the executive or other branches of the Government, whether civil or military.

II. The Chinese Government should adopt the following program for the improvement of the existing legal, judicial and prison systems of China:

1. It should consider Parts II and III of this report relating to the laws and to the judicial, police, and prison systems, with a view to making such amendments and taking such action as may be necessary to meet the observations there made.

2. It should complete and put into force the following laws:

   (1) Civil code.
   (2) Commercial code (including negotiable instruments law, maritime law, and insurance law).
   (3) Revised criminal code.
   (4) Banking law.
   (5) Bankruptcy law.
   (6) Patent law.
   (7) Land expropriation law.
   (8) Law concerning notaries public.

3. It should establish and maintain a uniform system for the regular enactment, promulgation, and rescission of laws, so that there may be no uncertainty as to the laws of China.

4. It should extend the system of modern courts, modern prisons and modern detention-houses with a view to the elimination of the magistrates' courts and of the old-style prisons and detention-houses.

5. It should make adequate financial provision for the maintenance of courts, detention-houses and prisons and their personnel.

III. It is suggested that, prior to the reasonable compliance with all the recommendations above mentioned but after the principal items thereof have been carried out, the powers concerned, if so desired by the Chinese Government, might consider the abolition of extraterritoriality according to such progressive scheme (whether geographical, partial, or otherwise) as may be agreed upon.

IV. Pending the abolition of extraterritoriality, the Governments of the powers concerned should consider Part I of this report with a view to meeting the observations there made and, with the cooperation of the Chinese Government wherever necessary, should make certain modifications in the existing systems and practice of extraterritoriality as follows.

1. Application of Chinese laws

The powers concerned should administer, so far as practicable, in their extraterritorial or consular courts such laws and regulations of China as they may deem it proper to adopt.

2. Mixed cases and mixed courts

As a general rule mixed cases between nationals of the powers concerned as plaintiffs and persons under Chinese jurisdiction as defendants should be tried before the modern Chinese courts (Shen P'an T'ing) without the presence of a foreign assessor to watch the proceedings or otherwise participate. With regard to the existing special mixed courts, their organization and procedure should, as far as the special conditions in the settlements and concessions warrant, be brought more into accord with the organization and procedure of the modern Chinese judicial system. Lawyers who are nationals of extraterritorial powers and who are qualified to appear before the extraterritorial or consular courts should be permitted, subject to the laws and regulations governing Chinese lawyers, to represent clients, foreign or Chinese, in all mixed cases. No examination should be required as a qualification for practice in such cases.

3. *Nationals of extraterritorial powers*

(a) The extraterritorial powers should correct certain abuses which have arisen through the extension of foreign protection to Chinese as well as to business and shipping interests the actual ownership of which is wholly or mainly Chinese.

(b) The extraterritorial powers which do not now require compulsory periodical registration of their nationals in China should make provision for such registration at definite intervals.

4. *Judicial assistance*

Necessary arrangements should be made in regard to judicial assistance (including *commissions rogatoires*) between the Chinese authorities and the authorities of the extraterritorial powers and between the authorities of the extraterritorial powers themselves, e.g.:

(a) All agreements between foreigners and persons under Chinese jurisdiction which provide for the settlement of civil matters by arbitration should be recognized, and the awards made in pursuance thereof should be enforced, by the extraterritorial or consular courts in the case of persons under their jurisdiction and by the Chinese courts in the case of persons under their jurisdiction, except when in the opinion of the competent court, the decision is contrary to public order or good morals.

(b) Satisfactory arrangements should be made between the Chinese Government and the powers concerned for the prompt execution of judgments, summonses and warrants of arrest or search, concerning persons under Chinese jurisdiction, duly issued by the Chinese courts and certified by the competent Chinese authorities and *vice versa*.

5. *Taxation*

Pending the abolition of extraterritoriality, the nationals of the powers concerned should be required to pay such taxes as may be prescribed in laws and regulations duly promulgated by the competent authorities of the Chinese Government and recognized by the powers concerned as applicable to their nationals.

Signed in the City of Peking, September 16, 1926.

STATEMENT CONCERNING UNITED STATES POLICY IN CHINA. BY SECRETARY OF STATE KELLOGG, WASHINGTON, JANUARY 27, 1927[2]

At this time, when there is so much discussion of the Chinese situation, I deem it my duty to state clearly the position of the Department of State on the questions of tariff autonomy and the relinquishment of extraterritorial rights.

[2] *Congressional Record*, 69-2, Feb. 21, 1927, p. 4387.

The United States has always desired the unity, the independence, and the prosperity of the Chinese Nation. It has desired that tariff control and extraterritoriality provided by our treaties with China should as early as possible be released. It was with that in view that the United States made the declaration in relation to the relinquishment of extraterritoriality in the treaty of 1903 and also entered into the treaty of Washington of February 6, 1922, providing for a tariff conference to be held within three months after the coming into force of the treaty.

The United States is now, and has been ever since the negotiation of the Washington treaty, prepared to enter into negotiations with any Government of China or delegates who can represent or speak for China not only for the putting into force of the surtaxes of the Washington treaty but entirely releasing tariff control and restoring complete tariff autonomy to China.

The United States would expect, however, that it be granted most favored nation treatment and that there should be no discrimination against the United States and its citizens in customs duties, or taxes, in favor of the citizens of other nations or discrimination by grants of special privileges and that the open door with equal opportunity for trade in China shall be maintained; and further, that China should afford every protection to American citizens, to their property, and rights.

The United States is prepared to put into force the recommendations of the extraterritoriality commission, which can be put into force without a treaty at once, and to negotiate the release of extraterritorial rights as soon as China is prepared to provide protection by law and through her courts to American citizens, their rights, and property.

The willingness of the United States to deal with China in the most liberal spirit will be borne out by a brief history of the events since making the Washington treaty. That treaty was ratified by the last one of the signatory powers on July 7, 1925, and the exchange of ratifications took place in Washington on August 6, 1925. Before the treaties finally went into effect and on June 24, 1925, the Chinese Government addressed identic notes to the signatory powers asking for the revision of existing treaties. On the first of July, 1925, I sent instructions to our minister in Peking, which instructions I also communicated to all the other Governments, urging that this should be made the occasion of evidencing to the Chinese our willingness to consider the question of treaty revision. I urged that the powers expedite preparations for the holding of the special conference regarding the Chinese customs tariff and stated that the United States believed that this special tariff conference should be requested, after accomplishing the work required by the treaty to make concrete recommendations upon which a program for granting complete tariff autonomy might be worked out. The delegates of the United States were given full powers to negotiate a new treaty recognizing China's tariff autonomy. At the same time, I urged the appointment of the commission to investigate extraterritoriality, with the understanding that the commission should be authorized to include in its report recommendations for the gradual relinquishment of extraterritorial rights. Prior to this, the Chinese Government urged the United States to use its influence with the interested powers to hasten the calling of the conference on tariff matters and the appointment of the extraterritorial commission and for each government to grant to its representatives the broad power to consider the whole subject of the revision of the treaties and to make recommendations upon the subject of the abolition of extraterritorial rights. This was in harmony with the views of the United States. Accordingly, on September 4, 1925, the United States and each of the other powers having tariff treaties with China evidenced their intention to appoint their delegates to the tariff conference. By a note which has been published, the powers informed China of their willingness to consider and discuss any reasonable proposal that might be made by the Chinese Government on the revision of the treaties on the subject of the tariff and also announced their intention of appointing their representatives to the extraterritorial commission for the purpose of considering the whole subject of extraterritorial rights and authorizing them to make recommendations for the purpose of enabling the governments concerned to consider what, if any, steps might be taken with a view to the relinquishment of extraterritorial rights. Delegates were promptly appointed and the Chinese tariff conference met on October 26, 1925.

Shortly after the opening of the conference and on November 3, 1925, the American delegation proposed that the conference at once authorize the levying of a surtax of 2½ per cent on necessaries, and, as soon as the requisite schedules could be prepared, authorize the levying of a surtax of up to 5 per cent on luxuries, as provided for by the Washington treaty. Our delegates furthermore announced that the Government of the United States was prepared to proceed at once with the negotiation of such an agreement or agreements as might be necessary for making effective other provisions of the Washington treaty of February 6, 1922. They affirmed the principle of respect for China's tariff autonomy and announced that they were prepared forthwith to negotiate a new treaty which would give effect to that principle and which should make provision for the abolition of likin, for the removal of tariff restrictions contained in existing treaties and for the putting into effect of the Chinese national tariff law. On November 19, 1925, the committee on provisional measures of the conference, Chinese delegates participating, unanimously adopted the following resolution:

The delegates of the powers assembled at this conference resolve to adopt the following proposed article relating to tariff autonomy with a view to incorporating it, together with other matters, to be hereafter agreed upon, in a treaty which is to be signed at this conference.

The contracting powers other than China hereby recognize China's right to enjoy tariff autonomy; agree to remove the tariff restrictions which are contained in existing treaties between themselves, respectively, and China; and consent to the going into effect of the Chinese national tariff law on January 1, 1929.

The Government of the Republic of China declares that likin shall be abolished simultaneously with the enforcement of the Chinese national tariff law; and further declares that the abolition of likin shall be effectively carried out by the first day of the first month of the eighteenth year of the Republic of China (January 1, 1929).

Continuously from the beginning of the conference, our delegates and technical advisers collaborated with the delegates and technical advisers of the other powers, including China, in an effort to carry out this plan—viz., to put into effect the surtaxes provided for in the Washington treaty, and to provide for additional tariff adequate for all of China's needs until tariff autonomy should go into effect. Until about the middle of April, 1926, there was every prospect for the successful termination of the conference to the satisfaction of the Chinese and the other powers. About that time the government which represented China at the conference was forced out of power. The delegates of the United States and the other powers, however, remained in China in the hope of continuing the negotiations, and on July 3, 1926, made a declaration as follows:

The delegates of the foreign powers to the Chinese customs tariff conference met at the Netherlands Legation this morning. They expressed the unanimous and earnest desire to proceed with the work of the conference at the earliest possible moment when the delegates of the Chinese Government are in a position to resume discussion with the foreign delegates of the problems before the conference.

The Government of the United States was ready then and is ready now to continue the negotiations on the entire subject of the tariff and extraterritoriality or to take up negotiations on behalf of the United States alone. The only question is with whom it shall negotiate. As I have said heretofore, if China can agree upon the appointment of delegates representing the authorities or the people of the country, we are prepared to negotiate such a treaty. However, existing treaties which were ratified by the Senate of the United States can not be abrogated by the President but must be superseded by new treaties negotiated with somebody representing China and subsequently ratified by the Senate of the United States.

The Government of the United States has watched with sympathetic interest the nationalistic awakening of China and welcomes every advance made by the Chinese people toward reorganizing their system of Government. During the difficult years since the establishment of the new regime in 1912, the Government of the United States has endeavored in every way to maintain an attitude of the most careful and strict neutrality as among the several factions that have disputed with one another for control in China. The Government of the United States expects, however, that the people of China and their leaders will recognize the right of American citizens in China to protection for life and property during the period of conflict for which they are not responsible. In the event that the Chinese authorities are unable to afford such protection, it is, of course, the fundamental duty of the United States to protect the lives and property of its citizens. It is with the possible necessity for this in view that American naval forces are now in Chinese waters. This Government wishes to deal with China in a most liberal spirit. It holds no concessions in China and has never manifested any imperialistic attitude toward that country. It desires, however, that its citizens be given equal opportunity with the citizens of the other powers to reside in China and to pursue their legitimate occupations without special privileges, monopolies, or spheres of special interest or influence.

XLIV

AMERICAN POLICY AND THE NANKING INCIDENT,
1927-1930

THE VICTORIOUS Kuomintang troops entered Nanking on March 24, 1927, where they instituted a systematic attack on the foreign community. American, British, French, Italian, and Japanese nationals were killed and wounded. The American, British, and Japanese consulates were raided. Much foreign property was looted or destroyed. To protect those foreigners who took refuge on the grounds of the Standard Oil Company, American and British gunboats shelled the area between this ground and the attacking Chinese. The United States united with the other injured Powers in protesting to the Kuomintang authorities in identical notes of April 11. The reply received by the United States was regarded as unsatisfactory (note of Eugene Chen, April 14). Here the co-operative policy of the Powers ended. The United States proceeded to conciliate the Nationalist Government of Chiang Kai-shek at Nanking, and on February 26, 1928, opened negotiations with it for a settlement of the Nanking incident. The Nanking Government by an exchange of notes of March 30 apologized offering full satisfaction for material damages. The United States deplored the necessity of the bombardment. There were also cautious references to revision of the unequal treaties. This was followed (July 25) by negotiation of a treaty recognizing China's tariff autonomy. Two years later a treaty of arbitration was concluded.

NOTE PRESENTED SIMULTANEOUSLY BY THE UNITED STATES, GREAT BRITAIN, JAPAN, FRANCE, AND ITALY TO THE CHINESE AUTHORITIES AT HANKOW AND SHANGHAI CONCERNING THE NANKING INCIDENT, APRIL 11, 1927[1]

Under [the instructions of] the American Government I am directed by the American Minister to present to you following terms (which are simultaneously being communicated to General Chiang Kai Shek, Commander-in-Chief of the Nationalist armies) for the prompt settlement of the situation created by the outrages against American nationals committed by Nationalist troops at Nanking on March 24 last:

One. Adequate punishment of the commanders of the troops responsible for the murders, personal injuries and indignities and material damage done, as also of all persons found to be implicated.

[1] *Treaties and Agreements with and concerning China, 1919-1929*, p. 216.

Two. Apology in writing by the Commander-in-Chief of the Nationalist army including an express written undertaking to refrain from all forms of violence and agitation against foreign lives and property.

Three. Complete reparation for personal injuries and material damage done.

Unless the Nationalist authorities demonstrate to the satisfaction of the interested governments their intention to comply promptly with these terms the said governments will find themselves compelled to take such measures as they consider appropriate.

UNITED STATES AND CHINA

EXCHANGE OF NOTES REGARDING THE SETTLEMENT OF THE NANKING INCIDENT, BETWEEN THE AMERICAN MINISTER TO CHINA AND THE MINISTER FOR FOREIGN AFFAIRS OF THE NANKING GOVERNMENT, SIGNED MARCH 30, 1928. —APRIL 2, 1928[2]

I. General Hwang Fu to Mr. MacMurray

With reference to the Nanking incident which took place on the 24th of March last year, the Minister for Foreign Affairs of the Nationalist Government has the honor to inform the American Minister that, animated by a desire to promote the most friendly feelings happily subsisting between the American and Chinese peoples, the Nationalist Government are prepared to bring about an immediate settlement of the case, along the lines already agreed upon as a result of the discussions between us beginning from the 26th February this year.

In the name of the Nationalist Government, the Minister for Foreign Affairs has the honor to convey in the sincerest manner to the Government of the United States of America their profound regret at the indignities to the American flag and to official representatives of that Government, the loss of property sustained by the American Consulate, and the personal injuries and material damages done to the American residents. Although it has been found, after investigation of the incident, that it was entirely instigated by the Communists prior to the establishment of the Nationalist Government at Nanking, the Nationalist Government nevertheless accepts the responsibility therefor.

The Nationalist Government have in pursuance of their established policy, repeatedly issued orders to the civil and military authorities for the continuous and effective protection of the lives and property of American residents in China.

With the extermination of the Communists and their evil influences which tended to impair the friendly relations between the Chinese and American peoples, the Nationalist Government feel confident that the task of protecting foreigners will henceforth be rendered easier; and the Nationalist Government undertake specifically that there will be no similar violence or agitation against American lives or legitimate interests.

In this connection, the Minister for Foreign Affairs has the pleasure to add that the troops of the particular division which took part in the unfortunate incident, at the instigation of the Communists, have been disbanded. The Nationalist Government has in addition taken effective steps for the punishment of the soldiers and other persons implicated.

[2] *Ibid.*, pp. 223-226.

In accordance with the well accepted principles of international law, the Nationalist Government undertake to make compensation in full for all personal injuries and material damages done to the American Consulate and to its officials and to American residents and their property at Nanking.

The Nationalist Government propose that for this purpose there be a Sino-American Joint Commission to verify the actual injuries and damages suffered by the American residents at the hands of the Chinese concerned, and to assess the amount of compensation due in each case.

Mr. MacMurray's Reply

The American Minister has the honor to acknowledge the receipt of the note of this day's date from the Minister for Foreign Affairs, which reads as follows:

[Here follows text of letter from General Hwang Fu.]

In the full realization of the inherent justice and honor of the Chinese people when not affected by the incitations of subversive influences, and with a deep appreciation of the sorrow and humiliation caused to all elements of that people by the Nanking incident, and believing that the earnest given as to the punishment of those guilty of the incident will be completely fulfilled at the earliest opportunity—particularly as regards Liu Tsu Han, who was personally responsible for the incident—the American Minister accepts in behalf of his Government the terms set forth in the note from the Minister for Foreign Affairs in definite settlement of the questions arising out of that incident.

Confident of the spirit of sincerity in which the present settlement has been made, the American Government looks to the loyal fulfillment of the said terms of settlement, as affording a measure of the good faith and goodwill with which it may anticipate being met, by the Nanking authorities in other phases of the relationships between the American and the Chinese peoples.

II. From General Hwang Fu to Mr. MacMurray

Referring to the notes exchanged this day on the subject of the settlement of the questions arising out of the Nanking incident of March 24th, 1927, the Minister for Foreign Affairs of the Nationalist Government has the honour to invite the attention of the American Minister to the fact that on that date fire was opened upon Socony Hill, at Nanking, by the American war vessels, *Noa* and *Preston,* then lying in port. In view of this fact, the Nationalist Government earnestly hope that the American Government will express regret at this action.

Mr. MacMurray's Reply

The American Minister has the honor to acknowledge the receipt of a note of to-day's date from the Minister for Foreign Affairs, in which reference was made to the fact that on March 24, 1927, the American war vessels, *Noa* and *Preston,* then lying in port, opened fire upon Standard Oil Company hill at Nanking, and in which the hope was expressed that the American Government would indicate their regret at this action. In reply, the American Minister has to point out that the firing referred to was in fact a protective barrage, strictly confined to the immediate neighborhood of the house in which the American Consul and his family and staff, together with many others, had been driven to seek refuge from the assaults of an unrestrained soldiery; and not only did it provide the only conceivable means by which the lives of this party were saved from the danger that immediately threatened them, but it also made possible the evacuation of the other Americans residing at Nanking, who were in actual peril of their lives. The American Government therefore feels that its naval vessels had no alternative to the action taken, however deeply it deplores that circumstances beyond its control should have necessitated the adoption of such measures for the protection of the lives of its citizens at Nanking.

III. From General Hwang Fu to Mr. MacMurray

Referring to the notes exchanged this day on the subject of the settlement of the questions arising out of the Nanking incident of March 24th, 1927, the Minister for Foreign Affairs of the Nationalist Government has the honor to express the hope that a new epoch will begin in the diplomatic relations between China and the United States; and to suggest that further steps may be taken for the revision of the existing treaties and the readjustment of outstanding questions on the basis of equality and mutual respect for territorial sovereignty.

Mr. MacMurray's Reply

The American Minister has the honor to acknowledge the receipt of a note of to-day's date in which the Minister for Foreign Affairs expressed the hope that a new epoch would begin in the diplomatic relations between the United States and China and that further steps might be taken for the revision of the existing treaties and the readjustment of outstanding questions on the basis of equality and mutual respect for territorial sovereignty.

Although the questions of treaty revision can scarcely be considered germane to that of amends to the American Government and its nationals for the Nanking incident, the American Minister is not averse to setting forth at this time what he has already made known in that regard to the Minister for Foreign Affairs in conversations with him last month.

It is unnecessary to recall the traditional friendship existing between the United States and China. As is manifest alike from the course of action consistently pursued by the American Government and from the statement of policy made by the Secretary of State on January 27th 1927, the Government and the people of the United States are in full sympathy with the desire of the Chinese people to develop a sound national life of their own and to realize their aspirations for a sovereignty so far as possible unrestricted by obligations of an exceptional character. With that in view, the American Government entertains the hope that the remedying of the conditions which necessitated the incorporation of such provisions in the earlier treaties may from time to time afford opportunities for the revision, in due form and by mutual consent, of such treaty stipulations as may have become unnecessary or inappropriate.

To that end, the American Government looks forward to the hope that there may be developed an administration so far representative of the Chinese people, and so far exercising real authority, as to be capable of assuring the actual fulfillment in good faith of any obligations such as China would of necessity have for its part to undertake incidentally to the desired readjustment of treaty relations.

THE UNITED STATES AND CHINA. TREATY GRANTING CHINA TARIFF AUTONOMY, PEIPING, JULY 25, 1928[3]

·   ·   ·   ·   ·   ·   ·   ·   ·   ·   ·   ·

ARTICLE I.

All provisions which appear in treaties hitherto concluded and in force between the United States of America and China relating to rates of duty on imports and exports of merchandise, drawbacks, transit dues and tonnage dues in China shall be annulled and become inoperative, and the principle of complete national tariff autonomy shall apply subject, however, to the condition that each of the High Contracting Parties shall enjoy in the territories of the other with respect to the above specified and any related matters treatment in no way discriminatory as compared with the treatment accorded to any other country.

The nationals of neither of the High Contracting Parties shall be compelled under any pretext whatever to pay within the territories of the other Party any duties, internal charges or taxes upon their importations and exportations other or higher than those paid by nationals of the country or by nationals of any other country.

The above provisions shall become effective on January 1, 1929, provided that the exchange of ratifications hereinafter provided shall have taken place by that date; otherwise, at a date four months subsequent to such exchange of ratifications.

ARTICLE II.

The English and Chinese texts of this Treaty have been carefully compared and verified; but, in the event of there being a difference of meaning between the two, the sense as expressed in the English text shall be held to prevail.

This treaty shall be ratified by the High Contracting Parties in accordance with their respective constitutional methods, and the ratifications shall be exchanged in Washington as soon as possible.

In testimony whereof, we, the undersigned, by virtue of our respective powers have signed this Treaty in duplicate in the English and Chinese languages and have affixed our respective seals.

Done at Peiping, the 25th day of July, 1928, corresponding to the 25th day of the 7th month of the 17th year of the Republic of China.

[SEAL]

[SEAL]

J. V. A. MACMURRAY

TSE VEN SOONG

THE UNITED STATES AND CHINA. TREATY OF ARBITRATION, WASHINGTON, JUNE 27, 1930[4]

Article I

All differences relating to international matters in which the High Contracting Parties are concerned by virtue of a claim of right made by one against the other under treaty or otherwise, which it has not been possible to adjust by diplomacy, which have not been adjusted as a result of reference to the Permanent International Commission constituted pursuant to the treaty

[3] U. S. *Treaty Series*, No. 773. Also S. Doc. 134: 75-3 (10239), pp. 4020-4021.
[4] U. S. *Treaty Series*, No. 857. Also S. Doc. 134: 75-3 (10239), pp. 4021-4022.

signed at Washington September 15, 1914, and which are justiciable in their nature by reason of being susceptible of decision by the application of the principles of law or equity, shall be submitted to the Permanent Court of Arbitration established at The Hague by the Convention of October 18, 1907, or to some other competent tribunal, as shall be decided in each case by special agreement, which special agreement shall provide, if necessary, for the organization of such tribunal, shall define its powers, shall state the question or questions at issue, and shall settle the terms of reference.

The special agreement in each case shall be made on the part of the United States of America by the President of the United States of America by and with the advice and consent of the Senate thereof, and on the part of China in accordance with its constitutional law.

Article II

The provisions of this treaty shall not be invoked in respect of any dispute the subject matter of which

a) is within the domestic jurisdiction of either of the High Contracting Parties;

b) involves the interests of third Parties;

c) depends upon or involves the maintenance of the traditional attitude of the United States concerning American questions, commonly described as the Monroe Doctrine;

d) depends upon or involves the observance of the obligations of China in accordance with the Covenant of the League of Nations.

Article III

The present treaty, in English, Chinese and French, shall be ratified by the President of the United States of America, by and with the advice and consent of the Senate thereof, and by the National Government of the Republic of China in accordance with Chinese constitutional law. The English and Chinese texts shall have equal force, but in case of divergence the French text shall prevail.

The ratifications shall be exchanged at Washington as soon as possible, and the treaty shall take effect on the date of the exchange of ratifications. It shall thereafter remain in force continuously unless and until terminated by one year's written notice given by either High Contracting Party to the other.

In faith whereof, the respective Plenipotentiaries have signed this treaty, in duplicate, in the English, Chinese and French languages, and hereunto affixed their seals.

Done at Washington this 27th day of June, one thousand nine hundred and thirty, corresponding to the 27th day of the sixth month of the nineteenth year of the Republic of China.

XLV

THE UNITED STATES AND THE MANCHURIAN INCIDENT, 1931-1934

THE FORMAL policy of the United States toward the conflict which developed between China and Japan in Manchuria in September, 1931, is illustrated by the following notes and the letter of Secretary Stimson to Senator Borah, February 23, 1932.

NOTE CONCERNING HOSTILITIES AT CHINCHOW. (RELEASED JANUARY 7, 1932.)[1]

The Secretary of State to-day instructed the American Ambassador to Japan and the American Minister to China to deliver the following identic note to the Japanese Government and the Chinese Government respectively:

With the recent military operations about Chinchow, the last remaining administrative authority of the Government of the Chinese Republic in South Manchuria, as it existed prior to September 18, 1931, has been destroyed. The American Government continues confident that the work of the neutral commission recently authorized by the Council of the League of Nations will facilitate an ultimate solution of the difficulties now existing between China and Japan. But in view of the present situation and of its own rights and obligations therein, the American Government deems it to be its duty to notify both the Imperial Japanese Government and the Government of the Chinese Republic that it can not admit the legality of any situation *de facto* nor does it intend to recognize any treaty or agreement entered into between those Governments, or agents thereof, which may impair the treaty rights of the United States or its citizens in China, including those which relate to the sovereignty, the independence, or the territorial and administrative integrity of the Republic of China, or to the international policy relative to China, commonly known as the open-door policy; and that it does not intend to recognize any situation, treaty, or agreement which may be brought about by means contrary to the covenants and obligations of the Pact of Paris of August 27, 1928, to which treaty both China and Japan, as well as the United States, are parties.

LETTER FROM SECRETARY STIMSON TO SENATOR BORAH. (RELEASED FEBRUARY 24, 1932.)[2]

February 23, 1932.

MY DEAR SENATOR BORAH:

You have asked my opinion whether, as has been sometimes recently suggested, present conditions in China have in any way indicated that the so-called Nine-Power Treaty has become inapplicable or ineffective or rightly

[1] U. S. Dept. of State, *Press Releases*, No. 271. See Secretary Bryan's note, p. 255.
[2] U. S. Dept. of State, *Press Releases*, No. 295. Cf. Hay's Open Door note to Great Britain, p. 211, and the Hay circular of July, 1900, p. 215.

in need of modification, and if so, what I considered should be the policy of this Government.

This treaty, as you of course know, forms the legal basis upon which now rests the "open door" policy towards China. That policy, enunciated by John Hay in 1899, brought to an end the struggle among various powers for so-called spheres of interest in China which was threatening the dismemberment of that empire. To accomplish this Mr. Hay invoked two principles: (1) equality of commercial opportunity among all nations in dealing with China, and (2) as necessary to that equality the preservation of China's territorial and administrative integrity. These principles were not new in the foreign policy of America. They had been the principles upon which it rested in its dealings with other nations for many years. In the case of China they were invoked to save a situation which not only threatened the future development and sovereignty of that great Asiatic people, but also threatened to create dangerous and constantly increasing rivalries between the other nations of the world. War had already taken place between Japan and China. At the close of that war three other nations intervened to prevent Japan from obtaining some of the results of that war claimed by her. Other nations sought and had obtained spheres of interests. Partly as a result of these actions a serious uprising had broken out in China which endangered the legations of all of the powers at Peking. While the attack on those legations was in progress, Mr. Hay made an announcement in respect to this policy as the principle upon which the powers should act in the settlement of the rebellion. He said:

> The policy of the Government of the United States is to seek a solution which may bring about permanent safety and peace to China, preserve Chinese territorial and administrative entity, protect all rights guaranteed to friendly powers by treaty and international law, and safeguard for the world the principle of equal and impartial trade with all parts of the Chinese Empire.

He was successful in obtaining the assent of the other powers to the policy thus announced.

In taking these steps Mr. Hay acted with the cordial support of the British Government. In responding to Mr. Hay's announcement, above set forth, Lord Salisbury, the British Prime Minister, expressed himself "most emphatically as concurring in the policy of the United States."

For 20 years thereafter the "open door" policy rested upon the informal commitments thus made by the various powers. But in the winter of 1921 to 1922, at a conference participated in by all of the principal powers which had interests in the Pacific, the policy was crystallized into the so-called Nine Power Treaty, which gave definition and precision to the principles upon which the policy rested. In the first article of that treaty, the contracting powers, other than China, agreed:

> 1. To respect the sovereignty, the independence and the territorial and administrative integrity of China.
>
> 2. To provide the fullest and most unembarrassed opportunity to China to develop and maintain for herself an effective and stable government.
>
> 3. To use their influence for the purpose of effectually establishing and maintaining the principle of equal opportunity for the commerce and industry of all nations throughout the territory of China.

4. To refrain from taking advantage of conditions in China in order to seek special rights or privileges which would abridge the rights of subjects or citizens of friendly states, and from countenancing action inimical to the security of such states.

This treaty thus represents a carefully developed and matured international policy intended, on the one hand, to assure to all of the contracting parties their rights and interests in and with regard to China, and on the other hand, to assure to the people of China the fullest opportunity to develop without molestation their sovereignty and independence according to the modern and enlightened standards believed to maintain among the peoples of this earth. At the time this treaty was signed, it was known that China was engaged in an attempt to develop the free institutions of a self-governing republic after her recent revolution from an autocratic form of government; that she would require many years of both economic and political effort to that end; and that her progress would necessarily be slow. The treaty was thus a covenant of self-denial among the signatory powers in deliberate renunciation of any policy of aggression which might tend to interfere with that development. It was believed—and the whole history of the development of the "open door" policy reveals that faith—that only by such a process, under the protection of such an agreement, could the fullest interests not only of China but of all nations which have intercourse with her best be served.

In its report to the President announcing this treaty, the American Delegation, headed by the then Secretary of State, Mr. Charles E. Hughes, said:

It is believed that through this treaty the "open door" in China has at last been made a fact.

During the course of the discussions which resulted in the treaty, the chairman of the British Delegation, Lord Balfour, had stated that

The British Empire Delegation understood that there was no representative of any power around the table who thought that the old practice of "spheres of interest" was either advocated by any government or would be tolerable to this conference. So far as the British Government were concerned, they had, in the most formal manner, publicly announced that they regarded this practice as utterly inappropriate to the existing situation.

At the same time the representative of Japan, Baron Shidehara, announced the position of his Government as follows:

No one denies to China her sacred right to govern herself. No one stands in the way of China to work out her own great national destiny.

The treaty was originally executed by the United States, Belgium, the British Empire, China, France, Italy, Japan, The Netherlands, and Portugal. Subsequently it was also executed by Norway, Bolivia, Sweden, Denmark, and Mexico. Germany has signed it but her parliament has not yet ratified it.

It must be remembered also that this treaty was one of several treaties and agreements entered into at the Washington Conference by the various powers concerned, all of which were interrelated and interdependent. No one of these treaties can be disregarded without disturbing the general understanding and equilibrium which were intended to be accomplished and effected by the group of agreements arrived at in their entirety. The Washington Conference was essentially a disarmament conference, aimed to promote the possibility of peace in the world not only through the cessation of competition in naval armament but also by the solution of various other disturbing problems which threatened the peace of the world, particularly in the Far East. These problems were all interrelated. The willingness of the American Government to surrender its then commanding lead in battleship construction and to leave its positions at Guam and in the Philippines without further fortification, was predicated upon, among other things, the self-denying covenants contained in the Nine Power Treaty, which assured the nations of the world not only of equal opportunity for their Eastern trade but also against the military aggrandizement of any other power at the expense of China. One can not discuss the possibility of modifying or abrogating those provisions of the Nine Power Treaty without considering at the same time the other promises upon which they were really dependent.

Six years later the policy of self-denial against aggression by a stronger against a weaker power, upon which the Nine Power Treaty had been based, received a powerful reinforcement by the execution by substantially all the nations of the world of the Pact of Paris, the so-called Kellogg-Briand Pact. These two treaties represent independent but harmonious steps taken for the purpose of aligning the conscience and public opinion of the world in favor of a system of orderly development by the law of nations including the settlement of all controversies by methods of justice and peace instead of by arbitrary force. The program for the protection of China from outside aggression is an essential part of any such development by the law of nations including the settlement of all controversies by methods of justice and peace instead of by arbitrary force. The program for the protection of China from outside aggression is an essential part of any such development. The signatories and adherents of the Nine Power Treaty rightly felt that the orderly and peaceful development of the 400,000,000 of people inhabiting China was necessary to the peaceful welfare of the entire world and that no program for the welfare of the world as a whole could afford to neglect the welfare and protection of China.

The recent events which have taken place in China, especially the hostilities which having been begun in Manchuria have latterly been extended to Shanghai, far from indicating the advisability of any modification of the treaties we have been discussing, have tended to bring home the vital importance of the faithful observance of the covenants therein to all of the nations interested in the Far East. It is not necessary in that connection to inquire into the causes of the controversy or attempt to apportion the blame between the two nations which are unhappily involved; for regardless of cause or responsibility, it is clear beyond peradventure that a situation has developed which can not, under any circumstances, be reconciled with the obligations of the covenants of these two treaties, and that if the treaties had been faithfully observed such a situation could not have arisen. The signatories of the Nine Power Treaty and of the Kellogg-Briand Pact who are not parties to that conflict are not likely to see any reason for modifying the terms of those treaties. To them the real value of the faithful performance of the treaties has been brought sharply home by the perils and losses to which their nationals have been subjected in Shanghai.

That is the view of this Government. We see no reason for abandoning the enlightened principles which are embodied in these treaties. We believe that this situation would have been avoided had these covenants been faithfully observed, and no evidence has come to us to indicate that a due compliance with them would have interfered with the adequate protection of the legitimate rights in China of the signatories of those treaties and their nationals.

On January 7th last, upon the instruction of the President, this Government formally notified Japan and China that it would not recognize any situation, treaty, or agreement entered into by those Governments in violation of the covenants of these treaties, which affected the rights of our Government or its citizens in China. If a similar decision should be reached and a similar position taken by the other governments of the world, a caveat will be placed upon such action which, we believe, will effectively bar the legality hereafter of any title or right sought to be obtained by pressure or treaty violation, and which, as has been shown by history in the past, will eventually lead to the restoration to China of rights and titles of which she may have been deprived.

In the past our Government, as one of the leading powers on the Pacific Ocean, has rested its policy upon an abiding faith in the future of the people of China and upon the ultimate success in dealing with them of the principles of fair play, patience, and mutual goodwill. We appreciate the immensity of the task which lies before her statesmen in the development of her country and its Government. The delays in her progress, the instability of her attempts to secure a responsible government, were foreseen by Messrs. Hay and Hughes and their contemporaries and were the very obstacles which the policy of the "open door" was designed to meet. We concur with those statesmen, representing all the nations, in the Washington Conference who decided that China was entitled to the time necessary to accomplish her development. We are prepared to make that our policy for the future.

AMERICAN POLICY, 1934. (RELEASED APRIL 30, 1934.)[3]

The American Ambassador to Japan, under instruction from the Department of State, called on the Japanese Minister for Foreign Affairs on April 29, and made a statement the substance of which is as follows:

Recent indications of attitude on the part of the Japanese Government with regard to the rights and interests of Japan and other countries in China and in connection with China have come from sources so authoritative as to preclude their being ignored and make it necessary that the American Government adhering to the tradition of frankness that has prevailed in relations between it and the Government of Japan, reaffirm the position of the United States with regard to questions of rights and interests involved.

The relations of the United States with China are governed, as are our relations with Japan and our relations with other countries, by the generally accepted principles of international law and the provisions of treaties to which the United States is a party. The United States has with regard to China certain rights and certain obligations. In addition, it is associated with China or with Japan or with both, together with certain other countries, in multilateral treaties relating to rights and obligations in the Far East, and in one great multilateral treaty to which practically all the countries of the world are parties.

Treaties can lawfully be modified or terminated only by processes prescribed or recognized or agreed upon by the parties to them.

In the international associations and relationships of the United States, the American Government seeks to be duly considerate of the rights, the

[3] U. S. Dept. of State, *Press Releases*, No. 587.

obligations, and the legitimate interests of other countries, and it expects on the part of other governments due consideration of the rights, the obligations, and the legitimate interests of the United States. In the opinion of the American people and the American Government, no nation can, without the assent of the other nations concerned, rightfully endeavor to make conclusive its will in situations where there are involved the rights, the obligations, and the legitimate interests of other sovereign states.

The American Government has dedicated the United States to the policy of the good neighbor, and to the practical application of that policy it will continue, on its own part and in association with other governments, to devote its best efforts.

XLVI

UNITED STATES POLICY SINCE THE OUTBREAK OF THE UNDECLARED WAR, 1937-1939

AMERICAN policy toward China since the outbreak of the undeclared war between Japan and China in July, 1937, has been expressed in a variety of notes, executive statements, and public addresses by officials of the Department of State. The United States continued its policy of "collaboration" with the League of Nations relative to Manchuria, and to the wider conflict in China proper.

The most important pronouncements of the American government, however, were contained in its notes to Japan (October 6, 1938, and December 31, 1938) touching the violation of American treaty rights in China.

UNITED STATES NOTE TO JAPAN REGARDING JAPANESE VIOLATION OF AMERICAN RIGHTS IN CHINA. (RELEASED OCTOBER 27, 1938.)[1]

Text of a note dated October 6, 1938, which the American Ambassador to Japan, Mr. Joseph C. Grew, addressed, under instruction, to the Japanese Minister for Foreign Affairs, His Excellency Prince Fumimaro Konoe:

The Government of the United States has had frequent occasion to make representations to Your Excellency's Government in regard to action taken and policies carried out in China under Japanese authority to which the Government of the United States takes exception as being, in its opinion, in contravention of the principle and the condition of equality of opportunity or the "Open Door" in China. In response to these representations, and in other connections, both public and private, the Japanese Government has given categorical assurances that equality of opportunity or the Open Door in China will be maintained. The Government of the United States is constrained to observe, however, that notwithstanding the assurances of the Japanese Government in this regard violations by Japanese agencies of American rights and interests have persisted.

As having, by way of illustration, a bearing upon the situation to which the Government of the United States desires to invite the attention of the Japanese Government, it is recalled that at the time of the Japanse occupation of Manchuria the Japanese Government gave assurances that the Open Door in Manchuria would be maintained. However, the principal economic activities in that area have been taken over by special companies which are controlled by Japanese nationals and which are established under special charters according them a preferred or exclusive position. A large part of American

[1] U. S. Dept. of State, *Press Releases*, No. 474.

enterprise which formerly operated in Manchuria has been forced to withdraw from that territory as a result of the preferences in force there. The arrangements between Japan and the régime now functioning in Manchuria allow the free movement of goods and funds between Manchuria and Japan while restricting rigidly the movement of goods and funds between Manchuria and countries other than Japan.

This channeling of the movement of goods is effected primarily by means of exchange control exercised under the authority of regulations issued under an enabling law which provide expressly that for the purposes of the law Japan shall not be considered a foreign country nor the Japanese yen a foreign currency. In the opinion of my Government equality of opportunity or the Open Door has virtually ceased to exist in Manchuria notwithstanding the assurances of the Japanese Government that it would be maintained in that area.

The Government of the United States is now apprehensive lest there develop in other areas of China which have been occupied by Japanese military forces since the beginning of the present hostilities a situation similar in its adverse effect upon the competitive position of American business to that which now exists in Manchuria.

On April 12, 1938, I had occasion to invite the attention of Your Excellency's predecessor to reports which had reached the Government of the United States indicating that discrimination in favor of Japanese trade with north China was likely to be effected by means of exchange control and to ask for assurances that the Japanese Government would not support or countenance financial measures discriminatory against American interests. Although the Minister for Foreign Affairs stated then that the Japanese Government would continue to support the principle of equal opportunity or the Open Door in China, no specific reply has yet been made by the Japanese Government on the subject of these representations.

The Government of the United States now learns that the Japanese authorities at Tsingtao have in effect established an exchange control, that they are exercising a discretionary authority to prohibit exports unless export bills are sold to the Yokohama Specie Bank, and that bank refuses to purchase export bills except at an arbitrary rate far lower than the open market rate prevailing at Tientsin and Shanghai. A somewhat similar situation apparently prevails at Chefoo. Furthermore, reports continue to reach the American Government that a comprehensive system of exchange control will soon be established throughout north China. Control of foreign exchange transactions gives control of trade and commercial enterprise, and the exercise, either directly or indirectly, by the Japanese authorities of control of exchange in north China would place those authorities in position to thwart equality of opportunity or free competition between Japan and the United States in that area. In such a situation, imports from and exports to the United States as well as the choice of dealers in north China, would be entirely subjected to the dispensation of the Japanese authorities. Notwithstanding the short time that exchange control has been enforced in Tsingtao, two cases of discrimination have already been brought to the attention of the Government of the United States. In one instance an American dealer in a staple commodity has been unable to export to the United States because Japanese authorities there have insisted that his export bills be sold to a Japanese bank at a rate so far below the current rate of exchange of the Chinese currency in the open market that such transactions would involve a loss rather than a profit; but a Japanese competitor recently completed a large shipment invoiced at a price in United States dollars which was equivalent to the local market price calculated at the current open market rate. In the other instance, an American firm was prevented from purchasing tobacco in Shantung unless it should purchase so-called Federal Reserve notes or yen currency with foreign exchange and at an arbitrary and low rate of exchange, conditions not imposed upon the company's Japanese or Chinese competitors.

The Government of the United States has already pointed out to the Japanese Government that alterations of the Chinese customs tariff by the régimes functioning in those portions of China occupied by Japanese armed forces and for which the Japanese Government has formally assured its support are arbitrary and illegal assumptions of authority for which the Japanese Government has an inescapable responsibility. It is hardly necessary to add that there can be no equality of opportunity or Open Door in China so long as the ultimate authority to regulate, tax, or prohibit trade is exercised, whether directly or indirectly, by the authorities of one "foreign" power in furtherance of the interests of that power.

It would appear to be self-evident that a fundamental prerequisite of a condition of equality of opportunity or Open Door in China is the absence in the economic life of that country of preferences or monopolistic rights operating directly or indirectly in favor of any foreign country or its nationals. On July 4, I spoke to General Ugaki of the desire of the American Government that there be avoided such restrictions and obstacles to American trade and other enterprises as might result from the setting up of special companies and monopolies in China. The Minister was so good as to state that the Open Door in China would be maintained and that the Government of the United States might rest assured that the Japanese Government would fully respect the principle of equal opportunity.

Notwithstanding these assurances, the provisional régime in Peiping announced on July 30th the inauguration as of the following day of the China Telephone and Telegraph Company, the reported purpose of this organization being to control and to have exclusive operation of telephone and telegraph communications in north China. There was organized in Shanghai on July 31st the Central China Telecommunications Company, and the Special Service Section of the Japanese Army has informed foreign cable and telegraph companies that the new company proposes to control all the tele-communications in central China. According to a semiofficial Japanese press report, there was organized at Shanghai on July 28 the Shanghai Inland Navigation Steamship Company, to be controlled by Japanese, the reported object of which is to control water transportation in the Shanghai delta area. According to information which has reached my Government, a Japanese company has been organized to take over and operate the wharves at Tsingtao which have hitherto been publicly owned and operated. Should such a development occur, all shipping of whatever nationality would become dependent upon a Japanese agency for allotments of space and stevedoring facilities. The wool trade in north China is now reported to be a Japanese monopoly and a tobacco monopoly in that area is reported to be in process of formation. Moreover, according to numerous reports which have been reaching my Government, the Japanese Government is proceeding with the organization of two special promotion companies which it has chartered and which it will control with the object of investing in, unifying, and regulating the administration of certain large sectors of economic enterprise in China.

The developments of which I have made mention are illustrative of the apparent trend of Japanese policy in China and indicate clearly that the Japanese authorities are seeking to establish in areas which have come under Japanese military occupation general preferences for, and superiority of, Japanese interests, an inevitable effect of which will be to frustrate the practical application of the principle of the Open Door and deprive American nationals of equal opportunity.

I desire also to call Your Excellency's attention to the fact that unwarranted restrictions placed by the Japanese military authorities upon American nationals in China—notwithstanding the existence of American treaty rights in China and the repeated assurances of the Japanese Government that steps had been taken which would insure that American nationals, interests, and properties would not be subject to unlawful interference by Japanese authorities—further subject American interests to continuing serious inconvenience and hardship. Reference is made especially to the restrictions placed by the Japanese military upon American nationals who desire to reenter and reoccupy properties from which they have been driven by the hostilities and of which the Japanese military have been or still are in occupation. Mention may also be made of the Japanese censorship of and interference with American mail and telegrams at Shanghai, and of restrictions upon freedom of trade, residence and travel by Americans, including the use of railways, shipping, and other facilities. While Japanese merchant vessels are carrying Japanese merchandise between Shanghai and Nanking, those vessels decline to carry merchandise of other countries, and American and other non-Japanese shipping is excluded from the lower Yangtze on the grounds of military necessity. Applications by American nationals for passes which would allow them to return to certain areas in the lower Yangtze Valley have been denied by the Japanese authorities on the ground that peace and order have not been sufficiently restored, although many Japanese merchants and their families are known to be in those areas.

American nationals and their interests have suffered serious losses in the Far East arising from causes directly attributable to the present conflict between Japan and China, and even under the most favorable conditions an early rehabilitation of American enterprise in China and of American trade with China cannot be expected. The American Government, therefore, finds it all the more difficult to reconcile itself to a situation in which American nationals must contend with continuing unwarranted interference with their rights at the hands of the Japanese authorities in China and with Japanese actions and policies which operate to deprive American trade and enterprise of equality of opportunity in China. It is also pertinent to mention that in Japan, too, American trade and other interests are undergoing severe hardships as a result of the industrial, trade, exchange and other controls which the Japanese Government has imposed incident to its military operations in China.

While American interests in the Far East have been thus treated at the hands of the Japanese authorities, the Government of the United States has not sought either in its own territory or in the territory of third countries to establish or influence the establishment of embargoes, import prohibitions, exchange controls, preferential restrictions, monopolies or special companies designed to eliminate or having the effect of eliminating Japanese trade and enterprise. In its treatment of Japanese nationals and their trade and enterprise, the American Government has been guided not only by the letter and spirit of the Japanese-American Commercial Treaty of 1911 but by those fundamental principles of international law and order which have formed the basis of its policy in regard to all peoples and their interests; and Japanese commerce and enterprise have continued to enjoy in the United States equality of opportunity.

Your Excellency cannot fail to recognize the existence of a great and growing disparity between the treatment accorded American nationals and their trade and enterprise by Japanese authorities in China and Japan and the treatment accorded Japanese nationals and their trade and enterprise by the Government of the United States in areas within its jurisdiction.

In the light of the situation herein reviewed, the Government of the United States asks that the Japanese Government implement its assurances already given with regard to the maintenance of the Open Door and to noninterference with American rights by taking prompt and effective measures to cause:

(1) The discontinuance of discriminatory exchange control and of other measures imposed in areas in China under Japanese control which operate either directly or indirectly to discriminate against American trade and enterprise;

(2) The discontinuance of any monopoly or of any preference which would deprive American nationals of the right of undertaking any legitimate trade or industry in China, or of any arrangement which might purport to establish in favor of Japanese interests any general superiority of rights with regard to commercial or economic development in any region of China; and

(3) The discontinuance of interference by Japanese authorities in China with American property and other rights including such forms of interference as censorship of American mail and telegrams, and restrictions upon residence and travel by Americans and upon American trade and shipping.

The Government of the United States believes that in the interest of relations between the United States and Japan, an early reply would be helpful.

UNITED STATES NOTE TO JAPAN REGARDING VIOLATION OF AMERICAN RIGHTS IN CHINA. (RELEASED DECEMBER 31, 1938.)[2]

Text of a note which the American Ambassador to Japan, Mr. Joseph C. Grew, communicated, under instruction, to the Japanese Minister for Foreign Affairs, His Excellency Mr. Hachiro Arita, on December 31, 1938:

The Government of the United States has received and has given full consideration to the reply of the Japanese Government of November 18 to this Government's note of October 6 on the subject of American rights and interests in China.

In the light of facts and experience the Government of the United States is impelled to reaffirm its previously expressed opinion that imposition of restrictions upon the movements and activities of American nationals who are engaged in philanthropic, educational and commercial endeavors in China has placed and will, if continued, increasingly place Japanese interests in a preferred position and is, therefore, unquestionably discriminatory, in its

[2] *Ibid.*, No. 483.

effect, against legitimate American interests. Further, with reference to such matters as exchange control, compulsory currency circulation, tariff revision, and monopolistic promotion in certain areas of China, the plans and practices of the Japanese authorities imply an assumption on the part of those authorities that the Japanese Government or the regimes established and maintained in China by Japanese armed forces are entitled to act in China in a capacity such as flows from rights of sovereignty and, further, in so acting to disregard and even to declare nonexistent or abrogated the established rights and interests of other countries, including the United States.

The Government of the United States expresses its conviction that the restrictions and measures under reference not only are unjust and unwarranted but are counter to the provisions of several binding international agreements, voluntarily entered into, to which both Japan and the United States, and in some cases other countries, are parties.

In the concluding portion of its note under reference, the Japanese Government states that it is firmly convinced that "in the face of the new situation, fast developing in East Asia, any attempt to apply to the conditions of today and tomorrow inapplicable ideas and principles of the past neither would contribute toward the establishment of a real peace in East Asia nor solve the immediate issues," and that "as long as these points are understood, Japan has not the slightest inclination to oppose the participation of the United States and other powers in the great work of reconstructing East Asia along all lines of industry and trade."

The Government of the United States in its note of October 6 requested, in view of the oft-reiterated assurances proffered by the Government of Japan of its intention to observe the principle of equality of opportunity in its relations with China, and in view of Japan's treaty obligations so to do, that the Government of Japan abide by these obligations and carry out these assurances in practice. The Japanese Government in its reply appears to affirm that it is its intention to make its observance of that principle conditional upon an understanding by the American Government and by other governments of a "new situation" and a "new order" in the Far East as envisaged and fostered by Japanese authorities.

Treaties which bear upon the situation in the Far East have within them provisions relating to a number of subjects. In the making of those treaties, there was a process among the parties to them of give and take. Toward making possible the carrying out of some of their provisions, others among their provisions were formulated and agreed upon: toward gaining for itself the advantage of security in regard to certain matters, each of the parties committed itself to pledges of self-denial in regard to certain other matters. The various provisions agreed upon may be said to have constituted collectively an arrangement for safeguarding, for the benefit of all, the correlated principles on the one hand of national integrity and on the other hand of equality of economic opportunity. Experience has shown that impairment of the former of these principles is followed almost invariably by disregard of the latter. Whenever any government begins to exercise political authority in areas beyond the limits of its lawful jurisdiction there develops inevitably a situation in which the nationals of that government demand and are accorded, at the hands of their government, preferred treatment, whereupon equality of opportunity ceases to exist and discriminatory practices, productive of friction, prevail.

The admonition that enjoyment by the nationals of the United States of nondiscriminatory treatment in China—a general and well-established right —is henceforth to be contingent upon an admission by the Government of the United States of the validity of the conception of Japanese authorities of a "new situation" and a "new order" in East Asia, is, in the opinion of this Government, highly paradoxical.

This country's adherence to and its advocacy of the principle of equality of opportunity do not flow solely from a desire to obtain the commercial benefits which naturally result from the carrying out of that principle. They flow from a firm conviction that observance of that principle leads to economic and political stability, which are conducive both to the internal well-being of nations and to mutually beneficial and peaceful relationships between and among nations; from a firm conviction that failure to observe that principle breeds international friction and ill-will, with consequences injurious to all countries, including in particular those countries which fail to observe it; and from an equally firm conviction that observance of that principle promotes the opening of trade channels thereby making available the markets, the raw materials and the manufactured products of the community of nations on a mutually and reciprocally beneficial basis.

The principle of equality of economic opportunity is, moreover, one to which over a long period and on many occasions the Japanese Government has given definite approval. It is one to the observance of which the Japanese Government has committed itself in various international agreements and understandings. It is one upon observance of which by other nations the Japanese Government has of its own accord and upon its own initiative frequently insisted. It is one to which the Japanese Government has repeatedly during recent months declared itself committed.

The people and the Government of the United States could not assent to the establishment, at the instance of and for the special purposes of any third country, of a regime which would arbitrarily deprive them of the long-established rights of equal opportunity and fair treatment which are legally and justly theirs along with those of other nations.

Fundamental principles, such as the principle of equality of opportunity, which have long been regarded as inherently wise and just, which have been widely adopted and adhered to, and which are general in their application, are not subject to nullification by a unilateral affirmation.

With regard to the implication in the Japanese Government's note that the "conditions of today and tomorrow" in the Far East call for a revision of the ideas and principles of the past, this Government desires to recall to the Japanese Government its position on the subject of revision of agreements.

This Government had occasion in the course of a communication delivered to the Japanese Government on April 29, 1934, to express its opinion that "treaties can lawfully be modified or be terminated, but only by processes prescribed or recognized or agreed upon by the parties to them."

In the same communication this Government also said, "In the opinion of the American people and the American Government no nation can, without the assent of the other nations concerned, rightfully endeavor to make conclusive its will in situations where there are involved the rights, the obligations and the legitimate interests of other sovereign states."

In an official and public statement on July 16, 1937, the Secretary of State of the United States declared that this Government advocates "adjustment of problems in international relations by processes of peaceful negotiation and agreement."

At various times during recent decades various powers, among which have been Japan and the United States, have had occasion to communicate and to confer with regard to situations and problems in the Far East. In the conducting of correspondence and of conferences relating to these matters, the parties involved have invariably taken into consideration past and present facts and they have not failed to perceive the possibility and the desirability of changes in the situation. In the making of treaties they have drawn up and have agreed upon provisions intended to facilitate advantageous developments and at the same time to obviate and avert the arising of friction between and among the various powers which, having interests in the region or regions under reference, were and would be concerned.

In the light of these facts, and with reference especially to the purpose and the character of the treaty provisions from time to time solemnly agreed upon for the very definite purposes indicated, the Government of the United States deprecates the fact that one of the parties to these agreements has chosen to embark—as indicated both by action of its agents and by official statements of its authorities—upon a course directed toward the arbitrary creation by that power by methods of its own selection, regardless of treaty pledges and the established rights of other powers concerned, of a "new order" in the Far East. Whatever may be the changes which have taken place in the situation in the Far East and whatever may be the situation now, these matters are of no less interest and concern to the American Government than have been the situations which have prevailed there in the past, and such changes as may henceforth take place there, changes which may enter into the producing of a "new situation" and a "new order," are and will be of like concern to this Government. This Government is well aware that the situation has changed. This Government is also well aware that many of the changes have been brought about by action of Japan. This Government does not admit, however, that there is need or warrant for any one power to take upon itself to prescribe what shall be the terms and conditions of a "new order" in areas not under its sovereignty and to constitute itself the repository of authority and the agent of destiny in regard thereto.

It is known to all the world that various of the parties to treaties concluded for the purpose of regulating contacts in the Far East and avoiding friction therein and therefrom—which treaties contained, for those purposes, various restrictive provisions—have from time to time and by processes of negotiation and agreement contributed, in the light of changed situations, toward the removal of restrictions and toward the bringing about of further developments which would warrant, in the light of further changes in the situation, further removals of restrictions. By such methods and processes, early restrictions upon the tariff autonomy of all countries in the Fast East were removed. By such methods and processes, the right of extraterritorial jurisdiction once enjoyed by occidental countries in relations with countries in the Far East have been given up in relations with all of those countries except China; and in the years immediately preceding and including the year 1931, countries which still possess those rights in China, including the United States, were actively engaged in negotiations—far advanced—looking toward surrender of those rights. All discerning and impartial observers have realized that the United States and other of the "treaty powers" have not during recent decades clung tenaciously to their so-called "special" rights and privileges in countries of the Far East but on the contrary have steadily encouraged the development in those countries of institutions and practices in the presence of which such rights and privileges may safely and readily be given up; and all observers have seen those rights and privileges gradually being surrendered voluntarily, through agreement, by the powers which have possessed them. On one point only has the Government of the United States, along with several other governments, insisted: namely, that new situations must have developed to a point warranting the removal of "special" safeguarding restrictions and that the removals be effected by orderly processes.

The Government of the United States has at all times regarded agreements as susceptible of alteration, but it has always insisted that alterations can rightfully be made only by orderly processes of negotiation and agreement among the parties thereto.

The Japanese Government has upon numerous occasions expressed itself as holding similar views.

The United States has in its international relations rights and obligations which derive from international law and rights and obligations which rest upon treaty provisions. Of those which rest on treaty provisions, its rights and obligations in and with regard to China rest in part upon provisions in treaties between the United States and China, and in part upon provisions in treaties between the United States and several other powers, including both China and Japan. These treaties were concluded in good faith for the purpose of safe-guarding and promoting the interests not of one only but of all of their signatories. The people and the Government of the United States cannot assent to the abrogation of any of this country's rights or obligations by the arbitrary action of agents or authorities of any other country.

The Government of the United States has, however, always been prepared, and is now, to give due and ample consideration to any proposals based on justice and reason which envisage the resolving of problems in a manner duly considerate of the rights and obligations of all parties directly concerned by processes of free negotiation and new commitment by and among all of the parties so concerned. There has been and there continues to be opportunity for the Japanese Government to put forward such proposals. This Government has been and it continues to be willing to discuss such proposals, if and when put forward, with representatives of the other powers, including Japan and China, whose rights and interests are involved, at whatever time and in whatever place may be commonly agreed upon.

Meanwhile, this Government reserves all rights of the United States as they exist and does not give assent to any impairment of any of those rights.

NOTICE OF TERMINATION OF TREATY OF 1911 WITH JAPAN. NOTE FROM THE SECRETARY OF STATE TO THE JAPANESE AMBASSADOR. (RELEASED JULY 26, 1939.)[3]

July 26, 1939

EXCELLENCY:

During recent years the Government of the United States has been examining the treaties of commerce and navigation in force between the United States and foreign countries with a view to determining what changes may need to be made toward better serving the purposes for which such treaties

[3] U. S. Dept. of State, *Bulletin*, Vol. I, No. 5.

are concluded.   In the course of this survey, the Government of the United States has come to the conclusion that the Treaty of Commerce and Navigation between the United States and Japan which was signed at Washington on February 21, 1911, contains provisions which need new consideration. Toward preparing the way for such consideration and with a view to better safeguarding and promoting American interests as new developments may require, the Government of the United States, acting in accordance with the procedure prescribed in Article XVII of the treaty under reference, gives notice hereby of its desire that this treaty be terminated, and, having thus given notice, will expect the treaty, together with its accompanying protocol, to expire six months from this date.

Accept [etc.]   CORDELL HULL

APPENDICES

PRESIDENTS OF THE UNITED STATES, SECRETARIES OF STATE, AND AMERICAN DIPLOMATIC
REPRESENTATIVES IN CHINA, 1839-1939

Presidents	*Secretaries of State*	*Diplomatic Representatives in China*
Martin Van Buren, of New York March 4, 1837– March 4, 1841.	John Forsyth, of Georgia, continued from preceding administration; retired March 3, 1841.	
William Henry Harrison, of Ohio March 4–April 4, 1841.	Jacob L. Martin, of North Carolina (Chief Clerk). *Ad interim* March 4-5, 1841.	
	Daniel Webster, of Massachusetts. Commissioned March 5, 1841; entered upon duties March 6, 1841.	
John Tyler, of Virginia April 6, 1841– March 4, 1845.	Daniel Webster continued from preceding administration; retired May 8, 1843.	Caleb Cushing, of Massachusetts, May 8, 1843. Commissioner and Envoy Extraordinary and Minister Plenipotentiary.
	Hugh S. Legaré, of South Carolina (Attorney General). *Ad interim* May 9–June 20, 1843 (died).	
	William S. Derrick, of Pennsylvania (Chief Clerk). *Ad interim* June 21-23, 1843.	
	Abel P. Upshur, of Virginia (Secretary of the Navy). *Ad interim* June 24–July 23, 1843; commissioned (recess of the Senate) and entered upon duties July 24, 1843; recommissioned January 2, 1844; died February 28, 1844.	
	John Nelson, of Maryland (Attorney General). *Ad interim* February 29–March 31, 1844.	
	John C. Calhoun, of South Carolina. Commissioned March 6, 1844; entered upon duties April 1, 1844.	
James K. Polk, of Tennessee March 4, 1845– March 4, 1849	John C. Calhoun continued from preceding administration; retired March 10, 1845.	

James Buchanan, of Pennsylvania. Commissioned March 6, 1845; entered upon duties March 10, 1845.

Alexander H. Everett, of Massachusetts, March 13, 1845. Commissioner. .

John W. Davis, of Indiana, January 3, 1848. Commissioner.

Zachary Taylor,
of Louisiana
March 5, 1849–
July 9, 1850.

James Buchanan continued from preceding administration; retired March 7, 1849.

John M. Clayton, of Delaware. Commissioned March 7, 1849; entered upon duties March 8, 1849.

Millard Fillmore,
of New York
July 10, 1850–
March 4, 1853.

John M. Clayton continued from preceding administration; retired July 22, 1850.

Daniel Webster, of Massachusetts. Commissioned July 22, 1850; entered upon duties July 23, 1850; died October 24, 1852.

Thomas A. R. Nelson, of Tennessee, March 6, 1851. Commissioner (resigned).

Humphrey Marshall, of Kentucky, August 4, 1852. Commissioner.

Charles W. Conrad, of Louisiana (Secretary of War). *Ad interim* October 25–November 5, 1852.

Edward Everett, of Massachusetts. Commissioned (recess of the Senate) and entered upon duties November 6, 1852; recommissioned December 9, 1852; retired March 3, 1853.

Franklin Pierce,
of New Hampshire
March 4, 1853–
March 4, 1857

William Hunter, Jr., of Rhode Island (Chief Clerk). *Ad interim* March 4-7, 1853.

William L. Marcy, of New York. Commissioned March 7, 1853; entered upon duties March 8, 1853.

Robert M. McLane, of Maryland, October 18, 1853. Commissioner.

Peter Parker, of Massachusetts, August 16, 1855. Commissioner.

James Buchanan,
of Pennsylvania
March 4, 1857–
March 4, 1861.

William L. Marcy continued from preceding administration; retired March 6, 1857.

Lewis Cass, of Michigan. Commissioned and entered upon

William B. Reed, of Pennsylvania, April 18, 1857.

duties March 6, 1857; retired
December 14, 1860.

Envoy Extraordinary and
Minister Plenipotentiary.

John E. Ward, of Georgia,
December 15, 1858. Envoy
Extraordinary and Minister
Plenipotentiary.

William Hunter, Jr., of Rhode
Island (Chief Clerk). *Ad interim* December 15-16, 1860.

Jeremiah S. Black, of Pennsylvania. Commissioned and entered upon duties December
17, 1860.

Abraham Lincoln,
of Illinois
March 4, 1861–
April 15, 1865.

Jeremiah S. Black continued
from preceding administration;
retired March 5, 1861.

William H. Seward, of New
York. Commissioned March 5,
1861; entered upon duties
March 6, 1861.

Anson Burlingame, of Mas-
sachusetts, June 14, 1861.
Envoy Extraordinary and
Minister Plenipotentiary.

Andrew Johnson,
of Tennessee
April 15, 1865–
March 4, 1869.

William H. Seward continued
from preceding administration;
retired March 4, 1869.

J. Ross Browne, of Cal-
ifornia, March 11, 1868.
Envoy Extraordinary and
Minister Plenipotentiary.

Ulysses S. Grant,
of Illinois
March 4, 1869–
March 4, 1877.

Elihu B. Washburne, of Illinois.
Commissioned and entered upon
duties March 5, 1869; retired
March 16, 1869.

Hamilton Fish, of New York.
Commissioned March 11, 1869;
entered upon duties March 17,
1869; recommissioned March 17,
1873.

Frederick F. Low, of Cal-
ifornia, September 28, 1869.
Envoy Extraordinary and
Minister Plenipotentiary.

Benjamin P. Avery, of Cal-
ifornia, April 10, 1874.
Envoy Extraordinary and
Minister Plenipotentiary.

George F. Seward, of Cal-
ifornia, January 7, 1876.
Envoy Extraordinary and
Minister Plenipotentiary.

Rutherford B. Hayes,
of Ohio
March 5, 1877–
March 4, 1881.

Hamilton Fish continued from
preceding administration; retired March 12, 1877.

William M. Evarts, of New
York. Commissioned and entered upon duties March 12,
1877.

James B. Angell, of Mich-
igan, April 9, 1880. Envoy
Extraordinary and Minister
Plenipotentiary.

James A. Garfield,
of Ohio
March 4–
September 19, 1881.

William M. Evarts continued
from preceding administration;
retired March 7, 1881.

James G. Blaine, of Maine. Commissioned March 5, 1881; entered upon duties March 7, 1881.

Chester A. Arthur, of New York September 20, 1881– March 4, 1885.

James G. Blaine continued from preceding administration; retired December 19, 1881.

Frederick T. Frelinghuysen, of New Jersey. Commissioned December 12, 1881; entered upon duties December 19, 1881.

John Russell Young, of New York, March 15, 1882. Envoy Extraordinary and Minister Plenipotentiary.

Grover Cleveland, of New York March 4, 1885– March 4, 1889.

Frederick T. Frelinghuysen continued from preceding administration; retired March 6, 1885.

Thomas F. Bayard, of Delaware. Commissioned March 6, 1885; entered upon duties March 7, 1885.

Charles Denby, of Indiana, May 29, 1885. Envoy Extraordinary and Minister Plenipotentiary.

Benjamin Harrison, of Indiana March 4, 1889– March 4, 1893.

Thomas F. Bayard continued from preceding administration; retired March 6, 1889.

James G. Blaine, of Maine. Commissioned March 5, 1889; entered upon duties March 7, 1889; retired June 4, 1892.

William F. Wharton, of Massachusetts (Assistant Secretary). *Ad interim* June 4-29, 1892.

John W. Foster, of Indiana. Commissioned and entered upon duties June 29, 1892; retired February 23, 1893.

William F. Wharton, of Massachusetts (Assistant Secretary). *Ad interim* February 24, 1893, to close of administration.

Grover Cleveland, of New York March 4, 1893– March 4, 1897.

William F. Wharton continued, *ad interim,* from preceding administration to March 6, 1893.

Walter Q. Gresham, of Illinois. Commissioned March 6, 1893; entered upon duties March 7, 1893; died May 28, 1895.

Edwin F. Uhl, of Michigan (Assistant Secretary). *Ad interim* May 28–June 9, 1895.

Richard Olney, of Massachusetts. Commissioned (recess of the Senate) June 8, 1895; entered upon duties June 10, 1895; recommissioned December 3, 1895.

William McKinley,
of Ohio
March 4, 1897–
September 14, 1901.

Richard Olney continued from
preceding administration; retired March 5, 1897.

John Sherman, of Ohio. Commissioned March 5, 1897; entered upon duties March 6,
1897; retired April 27, 1898.

Charles Page Bryan, of Illi-
nois, November 10, 1897.
Envoy Extraordinary and
Minister Plenipotentiary.

Edwin H. Conger, of Iowa,
January 19, 1898. Envoy
Extraordinary and Minister
Plenipotentiary.

William R. Day, of Ohio.
Commissioned April 26, 1898;
entered upon duties April 28,
1898; retired September 16,
1898.

Alvey A. Adee, of the District
of Columbia (Second Assistant
Secretary). *Ad interim* September 17-29, 1898.

John Hay, of the District of
Columbia. Commissioned (recess of the Senate) September
20, 1898; entered upon duties
September 30, 1898; recommissioned December 7, 1898,
and March 5, 1901.

William Woodville Rock-
hill, of the District of
Columbia, July 19, 1900.
Commissioner.

Theodore Roosevelt,
of New York
September 14, 1901–
March 4, 1909.

John Hay continued from preceding administration; recommissioned March 6, 1905; died
July 1, 1905.

William Woodville Rock-
hill, of the District of
Columbia, March 8, 1905.
Envoy Extraordinary and
Minister Plenipotentiary.

Francis B. Loomis, of Ohio.
(Assistant Secretary.) *Ad interim* July 1-18, 1905.

Elihu Root, of New York.
Commissioned (recess of the
Senate) July 7, 1905; entered
upon duties July 19, 1905;
recommissioned December 6,
1905; retired January 27, 1909.

Robert Bacon, of New York.
Commissioned and entered upon
duties January 27, 1909.

William Howard Taft,
of Ohio
March 4, 1909–
March 4, 1913.

Robert Bacon continued from
preceding administration; retired March 5, 1909.

Philander C. Knox, of Pennsylvania. Commissioned March
5, 1909; entered up duties
March 6, 1909.

Charles R. Crane, of Illinois,
July 23, 1909. Envoy Ex-
traordinary and Minister
Plenipotentiary.

William James Calhoun, of Illinois, December 21, 1909. Envoy Extraordinary and Minister Plenipotentiary.

Woodrow Wilson, of New Jersey March 4, 1913– March 4, 1921.

Philander C. Knox continued from preceding administration; retired March 5, 1913.

William Jennings Bryan, of Nebraska. Commissioned and entered upon duties March 5, 1913; retired June 9, 1915.

Paul S. Reinsch, of Wisconsin, August 15, 1913. Envoy Extraordinary and Minister Plenipotentiary.

Robert Lansing, of New York (Counselor). *Ad interim* June 9-23, 1915; commissioned (recess of the Senate) June 23, 1915; entered upon duties June 24, 1915; recommissioned December 13, 1915; retired February 13, 1920.

Frank Lyon Polk, of New York (Under Secretary) *Ad interim,* February 14–March 14, 1920. [No Secretary of State or Acting Secretary of State, March 15-21, 1920.]

Bainbridge Colby, of New York. Commissioned March 22, 1920; entered upon duties March 23, 1920; retired March 4, 1921.

Charles R. Crane, of Massachusetts, March 22, 1920. Envoy Extraordinary and Minister Plenipotentiary.

Warren Gamaliel Harding, of Ohio March 4, 1921– August 2, 1923.

Charles Evans Hughes, of New York. Commissioned March 4, 1921; entered upon duties March 5, 1921.

Jacob Gould Schurman, of New York, June 2, 1921. Envoy Extraordinary and Minister Plenipotentiary.

Calvin Coolidge, of Massachusetts August 3, 1923– March 4, 1929.

Charles Evans Hughes continued from preceding administration; retired March 4, 1925. Frank Billings Kellogg, of Minnesota. Commissioned February 16, 1925; entered upon duties March 5, 1925.

John Van A. MacMurray, of New Jersey, April 9, 1925. Envoy Extraordinary and Minister Plenipotentiary.

Herbert Clark Hoover, of California March 4, 1929– March 4, 1933.

Frank Billings Kellogg continued from preceding administration; retired March 28, 1929.

Henry Lewis Stimson, of New York. Commissioned March 5, 1929; entered upon duties March 28, 1929; retired March 4, 1933.

Nelson T. Johnson, of Oklahoma, December 16, 1929. Envoy Extraordinary and Minister Plenipotentiary. September 17, 1935, Ambassador Extraordinary and Plenipotentiary.

Franklin Delano Roosevelt, of New York March 4, 1933–

Cordell Hull, of Tennessee. Commissioned March 4, 1933; entered upon duties March 4, 1933.

The Church and American Policy in China*

RELIGIOUS ORGANIZATIONS AND TREATY REVISION—Your Legal Advisor hesitates to communicate certain work he is now doing on behalf of the new proposed treaties for China, since he is doing this work voluntarily as an American citizen rather than as a Chinese official following out Government instructions. It is essential, however, that your Excellencies be entirely informed of this work.

In my last report I called attention to the slow but sure development of American public sentiment in the matter of negotiating a new and equitable tariff and trade reciprocity agreement.

. . . .

There is only one obstacle to this New Deal in Sino-American relations, and it is this point—referred to above—which I find it so difficult to mention much more so to describe: I refer to the unfortunate influence of certain religious groups in the United States.

As the son of a Methodist minister, my reverence for the memory of my father, my real affection for Christian endeavor, and the esteem in which I hold many splendid friends of mine who are missionaries, all hold me back from making such serious charges. But my years of experience under the United States Government, with Dr. Sun, and with your excellencies, have conclusively proven to me that the greatest obstacle to China's freedom is the sinister political influence which hangers-on of the missionary movements exert in the political centres of the West.

THE PROFITEERING AND POLITICAL POWER INVOLVED IN MISSIONARY ENTERPRISE—The political strength of the churches in America is one of the most vivid characteristics of American life. The churches exert enormous power in all public matters which they construe as affecting morality or righteousness.

. . . .

In foreign policy the churches are equally powerful. Soviet-American relations for the last sixteen years have been determined largely by the influence of the Church lobbies.

It must be explained that the church organizations—by the very reason of their tremendous extent—attract an undesirable sort of pulpit politician to their committees. And in the vast non-religious ramifications of such organizations we find lawyers, financiers, publicists and promoters who—by mixing religion with the ordinary practice of their professions—earn very substantial livings. Some of the categories of these persons are: 1. Lawyers, members of churches, who derive fees from the estates of deceased persons who have left money or other property to the foreign missionary societies;

---

* *Report* by the Legal Adviser (Judge Paul Linebarger) to the National Government of China, Washington, Feb. 15, 1934. These extracts from this previously unpublished report of the late Judge Linebarger are here printed by special permission of his son, Dr. Paul M. A. Linebarger. They reveal aspects of policy which frequently do not appear in published diplomatic correspondence. The late Judge Linebarger enjoyed exceptional opportunities to view the fundamentals of American policy. He was a judge of the United States Courts in the Philippines, a member of the bar of the French Mixed Court and the International Mixed Court of China, the author of *Sun Yat Sen and the Chinese Republic,* and finally Legal Adviser to the National Government of China.

2. executors and other officers of such estates; 3. business agents and managers of the missionary societies (who negotiate contracts for printing, real estate, non-clerical personnel etc.) and are generally highly salaried as well; 4. banking representatives who handle the missionary funds, and derive profit from them; and loan investment agents. These types of missionary officials, among whom there are a large number—of course—of perfectly sincere and honest men, are present in China as well as America. In China, however, they are entrusted with smaller sums of money and are generally less competent and influential.

It is obvious, that with the enormous power of the churches—which in domestic American affairs is generally for the betterment of the community—and the large sums of money concerned, together with the general ignorance of the broader aspects of missionary enterprise, the profiteers and exploiters of the missionary movements find it easy to profit extensively. And these exploiters fight every movement for liberation of the Chinese nation because it might affect their privileged position in Chinese politics, through the conceded cities of the Coast and other points of vantage.

Land values might change. The Chinese Christian movement, and the sinicization of the churches in China—advocated by all liberal missionaries—might gain way and prevent the full exercise of their privileges gained from intra-church politics, job-swapping, and nepotism. In the case of the exploiters of the missionaries who are in China, personal investments of their own might decline.

This type of missionary will not move out of the way of Nationalist armies. Imagine a Buddhist priest telling the Allies to detour at Verdun! They provoke incidents and call upon gunboats to avenge them with bombardments. They encourage a pessimistic outlook on China, defame the Chinese government, over-emphasize the communist and Japanese dangers, and picture China as a ridiculous, poverty-stricken, godless, anarchist area— to stir the American public to sympathy and contributions!

The majority of the foreign missionaries in China, hard-working, devoted men, are embarrassed by this over-generous political assistance. The action of these homeland religio-political profiteers handicaps the cause of Chinese Christianity, by making it impossible for a patriotic Chinese to join with any of the scores of varieties of conflicting Christian sects, in a hysterical slander of his native land.

The freedom of China, by the abolition of the Unequal Treaties, will give Christianity its greatest impetus in the Far East. But the hostile self-interested groups hiding in the churches will fight Chinese liberation every inch of the way.